HOLLYWOOD SPEAKS!

An Oral History

Also by Mike Steen

A LOOK AT TENNESSEE WILLIAMS

THE BIOGRAPHY OF PANDRO S. BERMAN

MIKE STEEN

HOLLYWOOD SPEAKS!

An Oral History

G. P. Putnam's Sons, New York

TO MY SISTER, DOROTHY, who would weep tears of joy and sadness whenever Jeanette MacDonald and Nelson Eddy sang "Ah, sweet mystery of life at last I've found thee! Ah, at last I know the secret of it all! . . . For 'tis love and love alone that rules forever!" This romantic ideal still lingers among the countless memories in her alert mind, giving comfort, while her body lies stonelike in the grip of multiple sclerosis. . . .

Grateful acknowledgments to

DORIS KEIBEL

MARGE STROMNES PRICE

MARK FABIAN

DeWitt Bodeen and other staff members of the Margaret Herrick Library at the Academy of Motion Picture Arts and Sciences

James Powers, administrator of the Louis B. Mayer oral history program at the American Film Institute

Dr. Martha Lou Adams, of the Department of English at Northeast Louisiana University

Contents

INTRODUCTION

What Is Oral History?

IN the past few years, the widespread availability of the portable
tape recorder has made possible a method of interviewing which has
come to be known as oral history. The aim of an oral historian is to
gather and preserve spontaneous conversations with persons who
have made significant contributions in various fields of our society.
The major part of these conversations must come from the inter-
viewees as they retell the events of their lives which have influenced
the history of art, government, science, education, and so on. The
interviewer should speak the minimum necessary to keep the conversation going, to interject certain clarifying dates and facts, and to
make statements which will stimulate the memory and opinions of the
interviewee. The most authentic oral histories are those in which the
recorded conversations have been transcribed to the written page
verbatim. Little or no editing is done. This is the technique employed
by the pioneering oral history programs at Columbia University, the
University of California at Los Angeles, and The American Film
Institute. Such manuscripts can become quite lengthy and are
valuable in their entirety only to students and researchers. In a book
prepared for the general public, such as this book, a great deal more
editing is required in order to have clearer reading material. However,
it is still important to retain the particular conversational quality of
each interview so that the personality of the interviewee is easily
recognized. That is to say, when an oral historian edits his material, he
must not tamper with the speech patterns, the choice of words, or the
sentence structure that represents the humor, intelligence, character,

and emotion of his interviewee. To do that would be to tamper with history.

On the other hand, can oral history really be called history? Is it truth? Can it be authenticated? The fact that it is coming from the mouths of people who made that history is not a guarantee that they "tell it like it is" or "was." Usually they do, but there are a few exceptions. Truth or the whole truth is sometimes missing. There are valid reasons. A person rarely tells everything he knows or expresses his innermost opinions because he is afraid of offending some one or some group and thus jeopardizing his position, job, or career or of exposing himself to libel. Also, ulterior motives can affect an interview so that it becomes a tool for expounding special points of view or for furthering self-esteem and self-promotion. Age, too, enters into it. It is understandable that a person in the prime of a career with much at stake may not talk as straightforwardly as a retired person. Then there is always the possibility of one's memory being dimmed, erroneous, or even exaggerated.

Regardless of these and other drawbacks that may come to mind, oral history has immense value as long as one remembers that any history book, written or spoken, is usually the work of one man. To get at all the facts, one must go to many other sources before reaching any deep understanding or possible conclusion.

Not only should history be informative, but it should be entertaining. Since our subject matter, motion pictures, is a segment of the entertainment industry itself, I hope we are a few steps ahead. The format of this book is to have each chapter deal with one of the credits you see on the screen as a movie begins. Each chapter is a taped interview with one person who has had an outstanding career in that particular category whether it be leading player, makeup artist, screenwriter, set decorator, or special effects expert. Nearly all categories of credits are included in this book, but it would be prohibitive to have each and all of the fine artists and crew members who compose a film production company in one volume. The value of the whole team is indisputable.

Each interview follows, more or less, the same pattern: The person gives an autobiographical sketch, tells how he trained for and got into the motion-picture business, explains what his job entails, reminisces about films he has worked on and people he has worked with, and sometimes expresses his opinions on various aspects of the industry.

The following tape-recorded conversations are meant to help one understand, appreciate, and enjoy the history of motion pictures.

MIKE STEEN

Silverlake,
Los Angeles, California
April 6, 1973

HOLLYWOOD SPEAKS!

An Oral History

The Leading Man

HENRY FONDA

Mike: I'm especially honored, Mr. Fonda, to have you as the first chapter of this book. I think your long career represents more than any other actor's in America a well-rounded one. You have continually performed on the stage, where you began, and in motion pictures and television. It's a record career I don't think anybody can equal right now in American theater!

Fonda: I love to hear your words, but I'm not trying to set any records or anything. I'm doing it just because this is what I want to do and it's the way to have the fullest life for me. To do it all, theater and films.

Mike: Well, I believe that natural approach to things is what comes across in your acting and makes it so believable. That has helped you sustain your career for around forty-five years! Let's see, you were born in Grand Island, Nebraska, May 16, 1905.

Fonda: Yes. My father's business at the time took him to Grand Island. That's where he and my mother happened to be when I was born. I think within six months they went back to Omaha, and I was brought up there. I call Omaha home.

Mike: As a youngster, you never had an ambition to go into theater, did you?

Fonda: No. On the contrary. When I was at the University of Minnesota, a guy who was involved with the undergraduate dramatic club, the Masquers, came up and introduced himself. When I understood finally what he was trying to say to me or suggest to me, I just turned and ran. The whole idea scared me so!

Mike: You were actually studying journalism, weren't you?

Fonda: Well, journalism was what I was hoping would be my major. You don't start your major until your third year. My first two years I took all the English and writing courses I could. I didn't ever get to journalism. I realized I wasn't getting anything out of college I had dreamed about. If you were going to major in journalism, you would strike your freshman year for one of the school publications. At Minnesota there were two: the university daily paper and the monthly humor magazine. You would go out for one or the other and hope your senior year you'd be the editor, managing editor, or editor in chief or something. This is the way you would progress if you were good at what you were choosing to do. I wasn't able to do that because I was working my way through. I lived at a settlement house where I was a resident worker. I had to be back there within minutes after my last class to take a group to a playground or the gym or some place. So I wasn't able to do any of the extracurricular things. I wasn't athletic, but I would like to have gone out for the swimming team, maybe the basketball team. I couldn't do any of those things. So I was discouraged, and after two years I didn't go back, that's all. It was when I went home to Omaha that Dorothy Brando, Marlon's mother, called my mother and I became involved with the Omaha Community Playhouse.

Mike: Could you tell about your first experience being in a play there?

Fonda: The beginning of it I remember because it was so different from anything I had ever known. I didn't want to do it. I only did it because I was too bashful to say strongly, "Don't do this to me. Leave me alone." I found myself cast in this play because Dorothy Brando was a friend of my family's. I remember the first readings and rehearsals only with a remembrance of how self-conscious I was. I thought everybody was looking at me. I kept my head down in the playbook, a Samuel French version of Philip Barry's *You and I*. I had never even read out loud! When I finally did sort of look up, and I don't know how many days it took, they weren't looking at me. They all had their own problems. So very slowly I relaxed enough to look around me. I don't remember what it was like to play a part. What I remember is being onstage, before the curtain went up, in a living room like this except that that long wall over there is a curtain that's down. And you can look through doors into wings, and there is an electrician over there. And you can look overhead, and there's a lot of rigging up there. I remember when the curtain was down and we were getting ready, they put the stage lights on—that is, the room lights in the set and the overhead borders and so forth. You could hear the hum of an audience on the other side of the curtain. I remember sitting there and hearing this and then hearing that hum die down as the houselights dimmed. The audience knew something was going to happen, so they stopped making their hum. I remember the curtain going up because of the spotlights in balconies and the footlights and so on. Those physical things I remember. The act of being an actor, playing a part, not one memory! We played for a week, and in the meantime what I was enjoying was the people, the backstage, the whole other thing. I still never thought about being an actor. That was the first play of the season. It was September. For the rest of that year, through May, I was at the playhouse all the time. I didn't act; but I painted scenery, and I did all the things that a voluntary worker does around a little theater like that. There are hundreds and hundreds of jobs. The director, Greg Foley, was from Iowa State. He was the only salaried man. As far as my family was concerned . . . I don't know. They didn't say, "Hey, you're a bum." But they must have wondered. Here's their young man out of two years of college, but he's not doing a damn thing. He's hanging around this playhouse group. Because Doe Brando was involved with it, they weren't vagabonds, but it was something different.

Anyway, there was no objection on the family's part, but when the season was over, Dad said, "Well, it's been a fine year. You've had a lot of fun. Now I think you better sit down and find out what you're going to do with yourself. Get a job." I looked in the want ads and saw this ad for a file clerk for a retail credit company. I wrote a letter, and eventually I was the one who was hired. I don't know why, but I was. I had nothing special to offer. I was a young twenty-year-old boy just out of two years of college. Not prepared to do anything special at all, but they didn't need anybody to do anything really special. I had to learn filing. It was very complicated, and I spent most of that summer at the office every day, including Saturday, learning this cross-index file system at the Retail Credit Company. You know what the Retail Credit Company is? They may do other things, but as far as I was concerned, they investigate insurance applications. If you apply for insurance of any kind, the insurance company sends your name and what they know about you to the Retail Credit Company. And it's like detectives they send out. There were three or four of them at the office in Omaha, which was a home office. They'd go out and ask neighbors and other people about a guy's credit ratings and whether he's a good risk. Their report gives the insurance company an idea whether or not they're going to write the insurance. That's what the Retail Credit Company does. It's a national company with offices in all the cities. Anyway . . . I'm there.

So now in September Greg Foley comes back, the director, and he called me and said he had decided to open the coming season with a play called *Merton of the Movies*. I'd never heard of it, but just the fact that Greg Foley was back and wanted me to be involved on it again, I said yes! When I told the family, Dad didn't think it was such a good idea for very valid reasons. I had a new job that looked like it had some potential for advancement. And he didn't think I could do justice to two things like that. Well, I decided that I wanted to, and I felt that I could. And it got really to the point of an argument. It was a question of whether I was going to obey my father or not. I was old enough now that I could move out, and I thought, "I'll move to the YMCA, which isn't expensive, and I'll do both." Well, Mother was a pacifist, and she came in and calmed things over so that I didn't leave home, and I did keep my job, and I did start rehearsing *Merton of the Movies*. I got up before everybody else did to go to my company office. From the office I'd go to a drugstore and have a sandwich and a malted milk, then go to the playhouse to rehearse. I'd come home after everybody was in bed. So I rarely saw anybody in my own family. And when I did see my father, it was a tense situation between us, and we didn't speak! He had been overruled, and I was living in his home and not doing what he wanted me to do. This routine went on for five or six weeks. In little theater most of your actors are holding a regular job. They could be bank presidents, house painters, or shoe salesmen. Whatever it is, they've got something else to do. So you can only rehearse nights and weekends. But eventually we opened, and my two sisters, my mother, and my father came to the theater. Afterward Harriet, one of my sisters, came back and said, "We won't come backstage. It's crowded. We'll wait for you back home." So eventually I got home, and my family were waiting for me in the main room. Harriet, my mother, and Jayne were in one grouping, and Dad was sitting apart in his chair behind a paper. Since he and I hadn't spoken for weeks, I didn't start it with him. I went to them. They were very enthusiastic. Everything was superlatives, and it went on and on and on. Then Harriet said something that sounded like it was going to be a criticism. She didn't even get to it. She said, "Well, there was one place I thought if only—" And Dad said, "Shut up! He was perfect!" I've told that story many times, and it always grabs me because my father was something special. When he approved, that was putting on the badge! From then on I couldn't make a mistake as far as my father was concerned.

I kept my file clerk job. Meanwhile, a friend of the family had a son at Princeton who decided he didn't want to go to Princeton anymore. He was a spoiled son, so his mother was agreeable. She had sent him a car, and he wanted to drive home by way of down the coast to Florida, then through New Orleans and up to Omaha. His mother didn't want him to drive alone and asked if I would go to drive with him. She knew it meant my having to quit my job, so she would pay for my going a week ahead and seeing plays in New York. I had never been there and thought it was an exciting offer. No objection from my father at all. I went down to the office the day I was going to leave. No notice because I had to do it right now. I went to the manager, who's my boss. I don't remember . . . Brewer! I do remember his name! I went into Mr. Brewer's office and I told him I was quitting because I had a chance to go to New York. He was stricken. I'm making this a point because it's an actor's story. He said, "Fonda! Jesus, Fonda! Do you realize I was planning to send you to Atlanta to the home office!" In other words, if I had stayed, I might be the branch manager in Milwaukee or someplace today! It's an actor's story because you never know when you come to those crossroads. I've had many in my life, and that was one of the first.

I went to New York, and I saw nine plays in six days by going to three matinees. Then I went down to Princeton and made the long homecoming drive with Hunter. By the time we got home it was around Easter. Shortly afterward an Omaha reporter called me. A man named George Billings was touring around in a solo portraying Abraham Lincoln doing the Gettysburg Address or something. And he was staying at the hotel in Omaha. The reporter had interviewed him and found out he had been getting an awful lot of mail from Lincoln buffs. He had been sent enough material to write a little sketch, but he couldn't write. George Billings was once, I think, a studio carpenter in Hollywood. He looked like Lincoln, so they had used him in this picture. He had his own beard. He wore the top hat and the shawl and the frock coat on the street; he didn't just do it on the stage. Anyway the reporter told me, "I think you can get yourself a job if you go down to see this man." I went down there, and I wound up taking this material home and writing a sketch. It was just a matter of putting letters together. There was a little scene where Lincoln is near the front during the Civil War. I played his private secretary, in uniform. They are going through the day's mail, and each letter would give Billings a chance to give a little Lincoln anecdote. And the scene wound up with the order for the execution of a young soldier because he had fallen asleep on sentry duty. This is all absolutely in history. Lincoln has the execution order and the feathered quill to sign it, and then there's a letter from the boy's mother, which I read, pleading for her son's life. I finish the letter, and the pit orchestra starts playing "Hearts and Flowers." Scout's honor. Exactly "Hearts and Flowers," and Billings, as Lincoln, would cry, and a tear would roll down and drip off his beard. I would look at him and think, "How does he do that?" Anyway, we did that on one-night stands all over Iowa and Illinois for three months, and I got a hundred dollars a week! I thought, *"Wow!"* That's when I saw acting as a profession for me. I could get paid for it!

The third season for me at the playhouse began, and they decided to put me under contract as an assistant director. I was given five hundred dollars. Not for a week or a month, but for the *season*. I lived at home, of course, with no expenses. That same season I played opposite Doe Brando in the Eugene O'Neill play *Beyond the Horizon*. At the end of that season I was ready to make the break! I was going to go to New York. I was as naïve as is possible. I had no idea what I was getting into: that it was a rat race. A rassle. That you could starve to death. And I did. Not to death, but I starved a lot. But everybody did. We all starved together, and it wasn't tragedy.

I drove East with some friends. I got the ride because their home was on Cape Cod, Massachusetts, and I wound up on Cape Cod. By that time I had learned there was a summer theater in Provincetown and another one in Dennis called the Cape Playhouse. I was driven up to Provincetown and let out, and then my friends drove back to the south of the Cape. I went out to the wharf, and I went to the box office, and I said I was looking for a job. They said, "We don't give jobs here. We cast in New York, and we're all cast." I said, "Oh, thank you," and I turned around. I had to wait for the train to go out. I walked down the beach and saw Eugene O'Neill's home from a distance, and then I took the train to Dennis, which is halfway down the Cape. I got off, walked from the station, asked for directions, and finally found the Cape Playhouse. There wasn't anybody at the box office, but I went through a door and I saw that they were rehearsing on the stage. There was a director and his crew of assistants. One of them looked around and saw me and came back and asked me what it was I wanted. I told him and he said, "Well, we're all cast. We cast in New York." I said, "Fine," and left. I couldn't get out of Dennis till the next day 'cause the train only came through once a day at noon or a little after noon. So I had to find a place to stay.

I walked around and came upon a sign, ROOMS AND BOARD. I got a room, walked around some more, had a hamburger someplace, and finally went home to bed. I didn't know until I got up in the morning and went downstairs that this boardinghouse was where most of the cast and the director were living. It was a community breakfast at a big oval table. I recognized some of their faces, not right away, just from having looked at the photographs in Samuel French versions of different plays: Laura Hope Crewes, Romney Brent, Minor Watson, Peggy Wood, and lots of others whose names I don't remember right now. They couldn't have been nicer when they introduced themselves to me. I had breakfast with them, and at the end of the conversation they understood why I was there, but there wasn't any work for me. They had a cigarette on the lawn before they walked across the fields to the theater for the rehearsal. My train didn't leave for several hours. So they said, "Why don't you come over with us and watch?" There was nothing else to do, so I did. During the time I was sitting in the back row watching, one of the assistants whispered to some other stage manager or something. They were all queer, and I didn't know what the word meant. He came back and said, "We can't give you a job, but we can keep you busy as a second or third assistant stage manager if you can keep yourself." I said, "Sure!" I had a hundred dollars. So I went back and got a permanent room, and I was a third assistant stage manager. I put props on the tables and things like that.

About the third week they were going to do *The Barker*. I had never heard of the play, but the director looked at me and figured, "This guy is the right character, but whether he can act or not, I don't know." So he sent for me. He explained it to me and said, "Do you think you can play it?" I just said yes, and he said, "Well, read some of this." I read some of it, and he said, "Well, I don't know. It's taking a big chance. There are two other juveniles who are permanent juveniles here in the company. They both want to play it. I think if you can act, you're right for it. I don't know." Well, in stock you open on a Monday night, and you start rehearsals on the next play the next morning, Tuesday. So they finally opened the play they had been rehearsing on Monday night, and Tuesday morning everybody went over to start rehearsal on *The Barker*, and he still hadn't said. But he handed me the sides and said, "I want you to read it this morning. I don't mean you're going to get it, but in this first rehearsal I want you to read it for me." Minor Watson played the barker, a carnival barker. He has a son who he has left on the farm. He doesn't want his son to have anything to do with this carnival life, but his son runs away from the farm to be with his father and arrives at the carnival halfway through the first act. In this first rehearsal everybody is reading from their script and the director is saying, "Why don't you try going over there and sitting on the barrel?" So you write on your script, "Cross to barrel." And you go over there and sit. It's all very slow, you know, mapping out where you're going to be on the stage. So nobody is looking or acting or anything like that. In the meantime, because it took about an hour to get up to my entrance, I'm off in the sidelines, and I learn the lines for my first scene. This is very unprofessional, but I don't know that. So when I came on, I didn't have my script in my hands. I *am* the guy, right off the farm, and I'm saying, "Hello, Dad." And he says, "What the hell are you doing here? I left you on the farm." And then the script indicates the father strikes the son. So he gives a weak gesture denoting that he knows he's supposed to hit me, and he misses me very far. But I react as if I've been struck hard and I drop to the floor. This is how naïve and unprofessional I was, but I got the part! It was a part that Norman Foster played originally in the theater with Claudette Colbert. Claudette was the snake charmer, and they had the affair. Anyway, I got the part. Well, a lot of people saw it, and a lot of people were excited and came around and said nice things. I thought, "Here I go!"

The next week, however, a friend of mine, Bernie Handigan, caused me to become involved with an organization called the University Players. They were Harvard and Princeton boys and some Vassar and Radcliffe and Smith girls who wanted to be professionals eventually. They wanted to get as much experience as possible before they were graduates. So they got together and organized this summer theater. My friend, who was an Omaha boy going to summer school at Harvard, knew a lot of them. We went down there, and the play they were doing was *The Torchbearers*, a comedy about little theater. Josh Logan was playing a character in the play. Kent Smith was in it, and Myron McCormack, and some others whose names you may or may not remember. John Swope, who wasn't even an actor and didn't expect to be, was down there because he was friends with everybody in it. But he was playing one of the characters, too. It was funny, and I laughed. I laughed hysterically. And I wasn't putting it on. When I went backstage with Bernie to meet them all, they somehow knew I was the one that had laughed that much, and that turned them on. They asked me to join them! I went right back to Dennis and packed up my little suitcase and came down and joined the University Players!

I was with them for the rest of the life of the University Players, which was about three more summers and a winter season in Baltimore after they were all graduated. And it was great! It was experience for all of us that you couldn't buy today. We were creating our own experience. We did ten plays every summer! And you could do whatever you wanted to do. I would direct one week. I would play the principal part, the star part, another week. I'd play a butler the next week, maybe. Design the scenery another week. 1928, '29, '30, and '31 . . . four great summers! At the end of those summers the rest of them went back to college, but I went back to New York. Starved a lot, but I also got jobs.

That first winter I went down to Washington, D.C., where I was a professional member of a semiprofessional group that was doing plays for children at the Wardman Park Theater. Actually they brought me and Kent Smith down to strengthen their company because they weren't professional till they brought us down. We did *A Midsummer-Night's Dream, The Prince and the Pauper, Tom Sawyer, A Kiss for Cinderella, The Wizard of Oz,* and, you know, classics for children. And, again, a fantastic experience that you can't get today! For the youngsters coming up in the theater today, it just isn't available to them. I'm saying this 'cause I'm just hitting some of the hundreds and hundreds of parts I was allowed to play in the University Players, in this repertory company in Washington, and later in a stock company in East Orange, New Jersey, and elsewhere.

After four summers on Cape Cod, the University Players were all graduated by now. They were faced with the same problem I had had about "What do you do after the summer season is over?" So we booked ourselves into a theater in Baltimore as the University Players. We opened in repertory, meaning a different play every performance. You would play one play on a Monday night, again on a Wednesday matinee, and maybe on Thursday night. Another play would be Tuesday night and Wednesday night. We were getting good reviews and good responses, but Baltimore didn't understand repertory. That may not be the fair way to say it. It wasn't working because people would come to see a play on a Thursday night, let's say, and tell their friends it was a wonderful play. And somebody else would come and it was a different play. It got confusing. We changed from repertory to straight stock after two weeks. Very successful, though. That company included Margaret Sullavan, Kent Smith, Josh Logan, and all the names you've seen related to the University Players. At the end of that season everybody was going back to the Cape for the summer-stock season. I was older than everybody else, and I was concerned that I wasn't really getting ahead as fast as I thought I should. New York managers, directors, agents, and producers had not been seeing us up at the Cape because we were very early in the summer theater idea. We were about the second year there was such a thing as a summer theater. Now, after four years, they were all over the East. A lot of them were much closer to New York than we were. I thought, "Well, I'm just gonna have to split and get a job somewhere closer to New York where they're trying out new plays and New York managers see them."

I thought in early June I had the job I was looking for: the tryout of a new play on Long Island. If it was any good, the chances of my coming with it when it came to New York were good. We had never done that on the Cape. We had never tried out new plays. We did established Broadway successes. While I thought I had this job, at the last minute I discovered I didn't have it. The author decided he wanted somebody else, and the director who had chosen me apologized. But now it's toward the end of June and summer theaters are already cast! So I was high and dry! An agent friend of mine apologetically said, "I don't know what I can do. I'm looking through our card file. I can send you to Surry, Maine, as a handyman. You drive a station wagon and take care of the other actors' trunks from the station to the theater. You work backstage. Rustle props and so forth." It paid my board and room and thirty-five dollars a week. I took it because I couldn't not.

I went to Surry, Maine, and I was that handyman. There was a scenic designer. There was an electrician. Usually in the small summer theaters that's the crew backstage. Between the two of them it's designed, constructed, painted, set up, and lighted. I'd been involved with that kind of thing before, so I was sort of a third handyman. Toward the end of the summer, the scenic designer had a fight with the producer and quit. I told the producer that I could do the job, that he didn't have to go to New York and sweat it out. So I became the scenic designer for the last three or four shows.

The last show was *Michael and Mary*. It's a British play. Edith Barrett had done it in New York, and she was now touring it in a kind of package deal of summer theaters. That meant she would arrive in time for the dress rehearsal. You would have been rehearsing all week with your local cast, and she would pick it up at the dress rehearsal. The scenery was three sets. Fairly complicated for a little summer theater which didn't have a loft. It didn't even have wings. I had a problem with what to do with three sets. It just wasn't that big a theater. I solved it by painting the flats on both sides so that one side would be the fireplace for one scene, and just turning it around, it became the fireplace for a different scene. A window would turn around and be a window in another scene. I juggled the sets so it worked. Edith Barrett was very impressed with the scenery, and she said nice things to me. But what I didn't realize is she told a lot of other people. Now, after that, I sweated out the winter. I don't remember what it was, but nothing exciting. It would have been stock in East Orange, New Jersey, maybe. The next summer I discovered I couldn't get arrested as an actor, but I had my pick of all the summer theaters as a scenic designer because Edith Barrett had told the people who ran them, "There's a young guy up there at Surry, Maine, that's something!" So a lot of friends said to me, "Fonda, face it. For Christ's sake you're a scenic designer. Why don't you just settle for it? You're not going to be an actor." I wouldn't accept that.

But I had to work, and I did accept a scenic designing job at the Westchester Playhouse, Mount Kisco. This is forty-five minutes from New York, and that's the reason I chose it. About the middle of the summer they had an open week suddenly, and they came to me—*they* meaning there were two producers, partners. Did I know of a one-set comedy with five characters? Now this is what producers are always looking for in little theaters 'cause it doesn't cost them anything. The royalties aren't very big. The cast isn't too big. You know, three or four or five characters in one set. Well, I didn't have to think too long because I remembered that in Baltimore we had played *It's a Wise Child*, which is a one-set five-character play. One of the characters is the iceman who has a small scene in the first act and a short scene in the third act. He's not the principal character, but he's the one you talk about when you go home because it is such a funny part. I said, "I can save you the salary of an actor because I've played the iceman." I didn't tell them it was *the* part. I said I could do the scenery and play the part, too. Great. And I came back the next season to the Westchester Playhouse as an actor playing all the leads because of the iceman! Now, I'm telling that story because it's a career story, a typical actor's story. You never know, as I said earlier about the Retail Credit Company, when you come to that fork, which road you take. Because I'd accepted the job to go to Surry, Maine, to drive a station wagon, which was a real comedown for me after the years I'd been playing all the leading parts all over, two years later I'm at the Westchester Playhouse playing all the good parts!

Now I've skipped something, and I will have to go back because the winter before this—this is the winter in New York after I had been the scenic designer at Westchester—Jimmy Stewart's in town, and we're roommates. We're looking for work, and we hear that Leonard Sillman is doing a revue called *New Faces*. We found out he was rehearsing in some cold barn some place, and we went over there. It was no skin off his butt to take us because he was rehearsing outside of Equity and not having to guarantee salaries to anybody. So we joined him. Stewart was there only a week because he got cast in *Yellow Jack* by the director Guthrie McClintic. But I stayed and eventually I opened in *New Faces*. I did some pantomimes with Imogene Coca, and I was in some sketches and so forth.

It was on the strength of my work in *New Faces* that Leland Heyward, whom I had known for several years, but he had not been my agent, signed me on an exclusive agent contract. Then, during the next summer when I'm up at Westchester playing all the leading parts, he called me and asked me to come to California. He was on a business trip to Hollywood, but his office was usually in New York. I wasn't interested in movies at all, and I just let him know. I told him I wasn't going to come. He sent me a long, long wire trying to tell me why it was important. He said I didn't have to stay. I sent him a

one-word wire, no, thinking I was being funny. Then he called me on
the telephone. He's a very persuasive man. Eventually he persuaded
me. Without committing myself, when I had a week off at Westchester, I flew to Hollywood at his expense. He met me at the airport and
drove me back to the Beverly Wilshire Hotel, where he had a suite
ready for me. It was hot. In the middle of summer. I remember that. I
took a shower. When I came out of the shower, Walter Wanger, a
name that meant nothing to me, was in the living room of the suite
with Leland waiting for me. About a half hour later I found myself
shaking hands with this man on a contract. A deal to make two films
for him each summer for a thousand dollars a week, and I could go
back to New York for my winter seasons. I remember later walking
up Wilshire Boulevard with Leland and saying, "There's something
fishy." It just didn't make any sense 'cause this guy didn't have a clue
who I was. He'd never seen me. It was Leland Heyward, the
supersalesman. Leland till his dying day reminded me that I said,
"How can I get out of it?"

Anyway, now I had a contract with Walter Wanger, but I went
back to Westchester because I had two plays left to do that summer.
One of them was *The Swan* in which I played the tutor. Geoffrey Kerr
played the prince. Francesca Bruning was the princess. June Walker,
who was married to Geoffrey Kerr, came up to see it. Geoff and I
were dressing together, and I remember June said something to Geoff,
"Wouldn't he be wonderful as the farmer!" I didn't know what she
was talking about. The next week I got a call from Marc Connelly,
who had written and was going to direct a play called *The Farmer
Takes a Wife* on Broadway. June Walker was signed to do the play. So
I drove into New York and had a meeting with Marc Connelly at his
hotel. I wound up having a short reading for him. He said, "What's
your salary?" I said, "Mr. Connelly, you know, my salary—I've been
getting thirty-five dollars a week at Westchester." He told me to go
over to the office of Max Gordon, who was the producer. He said,
"Tell them two hundred dollars a week. I'll call up ahead of you, so
they'll expect you." I said, "That's fine!" I signed a contract with Max
Gordon to do *The Farmer Takes a Wife*.

The story I'm going to tell you now is another actor's story.
There're two basic kinds of actors' contracts. A run-of-the-play
contract and a regular two-week-minimum standard contract. The
latter means they can let you go, but they have to give you two weeks'

notice before they can fire you, and you have to give them two weeks' notice before you can quit. That's the contract I had. We opened in Washington to glowing notices. The next day when I went to the theater, 'cause it was an out-of-town tryout and we were still rehearsing, Max Gordon's business manager was waiting for me at the stage door with a run-of-the-play contract! I thought to myself: "If he wants a run-of-the-play contract, I can get more money!" So I stalled a little. I had no agent over my shoulder working for me. The manager realized I wanted something more, so he said, "What did you have in mind?" I said, "Well, two and a quarter." So I got two hundred and twenty-five dollars. I could have probably got five hundred or seven hundred and fifty. I don't know. But that's how naïve I was. We opened in New York eventually and got the same glowing reviews. It was a big hit, and Fox bought it for a film. Fox was not Twentieth Century-Fox in those days, it was just Fox. They variously talked about Gary Cooper and Joel McCrea, but eventually they decided they wanted me. They found out I was already under contract to Walter Wanger, and they borrowed me from Walter and paid him five thousand dollars a week. Walter paid me half the overage, which was four thousand, so I got half of that. I got that two thousand, plus the one thousand I was contracted to do. So I got a total of three thousand a week, and Walter got two.

Mike: Since your first film was *The Farmer Takes a Wife* and you had just played it on Broadway, what adjustments did you have to make from stage to film?

Fonda: To begin with, Marc Connelly is a very good stage director. He's a good actors' director. Up to that time my experience had been stock where you rehearse a week, and you're lucky if you've got any kind of a slant on the character or have had any kind of direction more than somebody to help you get from a chair to a table. *Farmer* was really my first experience where I had four weeks of rehearsal before opening to an audience. Then another three to four weeks of tryout performances where you're performing to an audience and rehearsing during the daytime. So this is an extensive preparation for your performance before you open in New York. Now I'm saying all that because Marc and I, in working on the character, would find, especially after we were working with audiences, how to get a particular laugh. As an example, my character, Dan, had a line when Molly asks him something about horses. Do I like horses or something like that? And he says, "Yes, ma'am. Mostly I admire cows." Marc knew there was a laugh there, and we discovered the only way we could get it was with a pause between "Yes, ma'am" and "Mostly I admire cows." With a pause there was a laugh, without, there wasn't. All right. Now I'm making the movie. Victor Fleming was directing. We got to that particular line when she asked the question and I'd say, "Yes, ma'am [pause]. Mostly I admire cows." After the rehearsal and just before we were going to shoot it, Vic said, "Hank, cut that pause after the 'yes, ma'am.' Just cut it to shorten it." I said, "Hey, Vic, it took us about eight weeks, Marc Connelly and I, to discover that's a laugh line. The only way we could get that laugh was with that pause." And Vic listened and said, "Ah! Okay." So I read it with the pause. In the cutting room they cut the pause out! So you're at the mercy of a lot of other people in the film medium!

Mike: Do you recall any other adjustments you had to make as a newcomer to the film medium?

Fonda: I remember when the movie script was given to me. I didn't quite understand it because it was written in a different way. A play script is written so that in the middle of the page there's the character's name and his dialogue is right under it. Stage business is in parentheses between the name and the dialogue. But movie scripts in those days had two columns. The left side of the page had the character name and the dialogue. The right side had camera movements and business. The character names would be in capital letters. Molly, let's say, would be in capital letters. And if it says, "MOLLY crosses to bar and walks through the door," it says that on the right-side column. And if there's a camera movement, it would also indicate that there—"DOLLY with her," for instance. I didn't understand it. As an example, in one of the first scenes in the hotel lobby Molly is there, and my character, Dan, comes in, and we have some dialogue. And we go into the dining room, "DOLLY with them," and we leave the dining room "DOLLY with them." There was no character in the Broadway play named Dolly, but I thought, "Well, they always change it in films." I had to ask Victor Fleming. I said, "I like this script. It's very good, but who's Dolly? She's always there, but she never says anything." Well, he laughed of course, but that's again how naïve I was.

All right, now we get to the first day and we're shooting. Not on a stage, not on a theatrical stage, not even a movie stage. We're shooting outdoors. Now I played this for almost a season in New York where it's on a proscenium stage and there are no real horses, there's no water, there are only stage trees, a stage blacksmith and forge, not real fire. Now we're really outdoors. It's real water, a real boat, and real horses are dragging the boats in the canal. There's a blacksmith with a real forge, etc. Anyway, that's pretty exciting! It helps the make-believe, you see. And I'm having a hell of a time! We're rehearsing one of the early scenes, and just before we're going to shoot it, Victor took me aside with his arm around my shoulder and said, "Hank, you're mugging a little." Now that's a dirty word to me! Always has been. That's overacting. I'm in shock, but not for very long because I realize I'm playing it exactly the way I played it in the theater, which ain't necessary. He explained that to me. He said, "You don't have to project to the balcony or the back row. That camera that's looking at you, that eye, that does it. And there's a microphone right there, just off camera. You talk the way you would be talking to the person if he's next to you in real life. In a conversational tone." I said, "Sure."

And that's the last time I was ever accused of mugging. I discovered in that one fast lesson that it's simply bringing it back to total naturalness, which is not difficult for me because what I had been striving for the years I had been in the theater was to make the audience believe that it's absolutely real and they're not watching an actor. I achieved that over the years, and I'm not aware of playing. Sometimes, as a member of the audience myself, I would often see a performance that was good and exciting, but I wouldn't forget for one minute that it was an actor up there because it was an actor's performance. Other times I would see a performance where I was not aware of that, and I would think, "There! That's what I want to do!"

Anyway, over those years I was making my rules. Not in a hidebound way of writing them down, but in an instinctive way, back in my mind, "Dear God, don't let me ever be caught acting." And when somebody says to me, as Victor Fleming did, "You don't have to project." Man! That's where I live! Actually, I have to work to get projection, especially on the stage 'cause it's easier for me to do what I like to do with a character: play him for absolutely real, don't let them see the wheels go around. When I begin rehearsals for a play, it's very false for me to start with projection, because it sounds wrong. I will baby-up on it. That's an expression boys use playing marbles. Instead of shooting from a distance in trying to knock the other guy's marble out, babying up is to shoot your marble in closer, and then you've got a closer shot at it the next time. The expression, to me, means gradually. So in early rehearsals of a stage play I don't try to project anything. At the point where I'm beginning to work without the script, which is still two to three weeks before performance time, and I'm looking at the other actors on the stage and at that big expanse out there, that's when I make myself realize that eventually it's got to be at a bigger level.

Mike: What effect does that have on other actors? Are they going through that same process to project?

Fonda: Well, I've found most actors have to be goosed to do it as strong as it has to be. I will either make the director insist, or I will talk to the other actors myself, if I'm that friendly with them, and say, "Look, you son of a bitch, they're not going to hear you. You better start getting used to it now or it's going to be difficult if you have to suddenly start doing it." In other words, I'm using my experience to help an actor who maybe hasn't had that much experience to realize the time is going to come when an audience is going to be hollering at him from the back row, "We can't hear you!" And that is something you don't want to hear, I'll tell you! It's shattering. And I've had it happen in bad theaters. The Shubert Theater in New Haven is an example. Latecomers come in, and there's rustle and noise. The people in the back rows can sit there and shout, "Louder!" You cringe, I'll tell you! So you have to learn to enunciate without sounding like you're enunciating and get some pressure in back of it so that there's volume, so it can be heard and not make it sound like it's shouting.

Anyway, the studio was very happy with *Farmer Takes a Wife* and thought they had a new team with Janet Gaynor and Henry Fonda. Walter Wanger loaned me to them again, and they put Janet and me together in a remake of *Way Down East*. Janet started the picture but fell off a pony and got a slight concussion and was replaced with Rochelle Hudson. Then Walter Wanger loaned me out to RKO for the Lily Pons film *I Dream Too Much*. So my first three films were all loan-outs and all made in 1935. Wanger just didn't have anything to shoot. I guess he was beginning to prepare *The Trail of the Lonesome Pine*.

Mike: *The Trail of the Lonesome Pine* [Paramount, 1936] which Henry

Hathaway directed was a pioneer film in the fact it was the first outdoor color film. Also, I read that Al Capp got his idea of how his comic strip character Li'l Abner should look from your character in that film.

Fonda: He's never told me, but I was told he has said that.

Mike: Well, by this time, did you feel you wanted to remain in movies?

Fonda: I still was in love with the theater and looking for something to take me back to the theater. But I didn't read any play scripts I liked until *Blow Ye Winds*, which was in 1937. In the meantime, I can say I was not unhappy working in films. It was a new experience. I didn't know that it was going to be like that. I really hadn't had any ambition to be in the movies. I had resisted offers several times when I was struggling in New York. All the studios had talent agencies back there. They would go to plays and see the young aspiring actors. They would test them on sound stages in New York and very often send them to Hollywood on stock contracts, seventy-five dollars a week or a hundred dollars a week. Jim Stewart was sent out on a stock contract. I had turned down those opportunities because I wasn't interested. I did a test with a girl as a favor to her. She was being tested by Fox, but they asked *me* to sign, and I wouldn't do it.

Mike: After your first few films were you happy with the way your film career was going? Did you feel you had some control over the parts you would take?

Fonda: To a certain extent. I did a couple I wasn't happy about when I was under contract to Wanger. I think he got disillusioned as an independent producer. He did two or three that were good pictures, but he also did some programmers, as they can be called. He put me in a couple of them. I don't know that I could even remember the names of them, but—

Mike: Well, you had *The Moon's Our Home* in 1936.

Fonda: Well, that was a good one! That was with Margaret Sullavan.

Mike: Then you made *Spendthrift*, also in 1936.

Fonda: *Spendthrift* was a bad one.

Mike: Next was *You Only Live Once* with Sylvia Sidney and directed by Fritz Lang in 1937.

Fonda: That was a good one. I didn't get along with Fritz Lang, but it was a good film. A good script.

Mike: I should think your background of Middle America was quite a contrast to Fritz Lang's Middle Europe background.

Fonda: Well, it wasn't that because I've worked with foreign directors either here or abroad and I get along fine. No. I don't mean to put Lang down. That's not fair 'cause he's considered one of the giants in the business. He's had some classics. But he started in the silent days, and I think he resented sound because he wasn't able to talk to actors during the performance. He was a conductor. He was a master puppeteer. He literally liked to manipulate an actor. If he could, and the camera didn't pick it up, he would literally move your hand into a shot with his hand on you. He couldn't talk since it was in sound, but he would be waving his hands frantically at you, and it was very disconcerting. I've got dozens of Fritz Lang stories and I was telling my stories one night at a party. Charles Boyer was in the group, and when I finished, he said, "I've got one." He did *Liliom* [France. Fox, 1935] with Fritz Lang, and in the death scene Charles was laying out in the bed and his feet were bare. The camera was on a close-up of him. Lang was standing beside the camera and he said, "Charles, now, when I pinch your toe, you close your eyes. And when I pinch your toe again, you open your eyes. And when I pinch your toe again, you roll your eyes." He was literally giving Charles his cues by pinching his toes! This is the way Lang worked. Well, it's not the way I work, but Sylvia loved Lang. She got along just fine with him. I didn't. I fought all the way.

Mike: While we're on the subject of directors, you worked two or three films with Otto Preminger, another Middle Europe type director. Did you find a similarity between him and Lang?

Fonda: No. I get along with Otto famously. When you like Otto as I do, and I'm very fond of him, it's embarrassing to have him lose his temper and do the thing that he's famous for: chew somebody out, the cameraman, or the assistant director, or an extra or a bit player, or somebody like that. It's always unnecessary. I've done three pictures with him. And he directed the play *Critic's Choice* in 1960. He chewed out the electrician one day at a rehearsal, and the electrician walked off the set and quit. It wasn't necessary. These are embarrassing things, but it's never happened with me or with any good actor. He's a very sensitive director with actors. I know from the way he's worked with me, and I've seen him with other actors. I've seen him with

Franchot Tone, for example, in a picture we were in together, *Advise and Consent* [Columbia, 1961]. I was on the set, and Franchot, as the President, was having to speak to a group of journalists. It was a long speech, and he did a take of it. Then Otto took Franchot aside and just talked to him quietly for two or three minutes. Franchot came back for a second take, and what happened was incredible. It happened because Otto knew just the right words to use. That's the rare thing in directors, to be able to communicate with actors. Sidney Lumet is one of the best at it. Strangely enough, Henry Hathaway, who's had no theater background, instinctively knows the right words to use. The clue word. The one word maybe that will make you say, "Oh, yeah, why didn't I think of that? Of course!" And your short hairs stand up and you say, "Let me show you!" Otto's like that. He's also a son of a bitch and can be a bastard, but not with me. And I'm fond of him.

Mike: I worked as the dialogue director on *Hurry Sundown* in 1966 with Preminger. I remember he was always gentlemanly with your daughter Jane, but other stars of the film like Faye Dunaway, John Phillip Law, and Diahann Carroll he certainly jumped on!

Fonda: Well, if he jumps on you, you don't like Otto. There's no reason you should.

Mike: The director you have worked with the most is John Ford. Seven films!

Fonda: Who is unlike any of them! Insofar as communication is concerned, there's practically no communication! That's in the sense of communication between actor and director for performance. He doesn't like to talk about it. If you try to pin him down about your character, he will put you down in such a scathing way that you will want to bleed! You bleed internally! But he's got something else. I don't know if I could ever explain it or articulate it. He's an instinctive director like there are instinctive actors. He instinctively knows, for instance, when an actor is ready to perform. He doesn't say, "How do you feel? Are you ready? Are you up to it?" or anything like that.

An example would be the scene that people always remember of mine in *Grapes of Wrath* [Fox, 1940] when my character, Tom, says good-bye to his mother. It was a very emotional scene. Now Jane Darwell, playing Ma Joad, certainly knew all the things that were inherent in the scene. We both knew the potentials in the scene, but we didn't talk about the scene to each other. We had only gone over our lines a couple of times sitting in chairs side by side while Ford wasn't there. The camera had to follow me out of a tent, then move down a track until I sat on a bench with Ma Joad. And once we're sitting the camera moves in to us for a two shot, then we do the dialogue. It took a lot of rehearsal for the camera to maneuver the various positions and for the cameraman to know that the lights were all right. But in every rehearsal when we would sit on the bench, at which point the camera holds steady, Ford would cut the rehearsal. So Jane Darwell and I never got to play the scene in a rehearsal! As a result, after an hour and a half or so, Jane and I were both like racehorses, chomping at the bit. You know, "Hey, fellows, let us go! We got a scene to play here!" Ford knew we were like that. Not one word was said about it, but I knew Ford well enough, and I know him today well enough, to know that that son of a bitch—I say son of a bitch full of love—knew instinctively that he was leading us right up to it, then holding us back. And when he was ready, we went! And we really played that scene 'cause we *were* ready, and he got up and walked away from it. He liked to be able to do scenes, particularly that kind of scene, in one take. He wanted the spontaneity of whatever would happen the first time. If somebody dropped a hammer, unless it was on a word, he'd say, "Fuck it. I don't care. Take it out of the sound track." He would hate to do it more than once, unless there were technical things that were difficult for the cameraman.

Anyway, that's Ford. He was an incredible man but wouldn't talk about your problems as an actor. I know on the picture I did in Mexico with Dolores del Rio, *The Fugitive* [RKO, 1947], by this time I knew Ford pretty damn well, and I knew better than to talk about my character to him. J. Carrol Naish played a great character role in *The Fugitive*, but before the rest of us left to go to Mexico, Naish went into Ford's office to talk about his part. Ford just changed the subject. As a result, Naish stayed up here for two weeks by himself and worked out an accent and characterization. When he got down there, the first time he was working in a scene he used this accent, and Ford just chewed him out so! I'll never forget it as long as I live. The most embarrassing language! I can't remember all the dirty words! Just shameful, rude, everything. Well, it just destroys an actor to be talked to like that. And whenever Naish would want to talk about a scene, Ford would say, "I'm not gonna do it." He'd just tear the page out of the script and throw it away! This is Ford. He's an Irish son of a bitch, but he was certainly one of our giants. When he was cooking on all burners, there was nobody like him! You can talk about Ford forever and not repeat yourself.

Mike: Some people have felt that he did have a sadistic streak.

Fonda: Yes. He did. He does still. Like Otto, though, he never used it on me. He would have a whipping boy. Duke Wayne was very often his whipping boy. I only did one Ford film with Duke, *Fort Apache* [RKO, 1948], but I knew "the family" well enough to know that Duke was very often Ford's whipping boy. Ward Bond was a Ford whipping boy, too. But both of them knew Ford well enough to know they were being used, and they didn't let it get to them. Walter Brennan couldn't take it. He did *My Darling Clementine* [Fox, 1946]. He said he'd never work for Ford again, and never did. And there were other actors who wouldn't.

Mike: I remember in another John Ford film, *Drums Along the Mohawk* [Fox, 1939], there's a scene where you are being chased by some Indian braves, and it just goes on and on and on like a marathon race. I often wondered, having worked with Ford myself on *Horse Soldiers* [UA, 1959] and witnessed his sadism, if maybe in that chase scene he was giving you that treatment.

Fonda: No. That run was done over a period of about twenty-seven days that we were on location in Utah. We were up pretty high, between nine to eleven thousand feet at various times. While shooting some other scene, Ford would see a possible site for me to be running through as part of that chase sequence. So he would holler at the wardrobe man to change my wardrobe to the wardrobe I wore for the run. I would suddenly drop whatever I was doing that was being filmed. Probably I was raking the corn or whatever, and suddenly Ford would put a camera on a tripod. I'd go over there and do a running shot. A run-through might be a hundred yards, jumping over a log and ducking under something. Then I'd change back into my wardrobe for the scene we had been filming. This would be going on all the time we were on location! The last time—well, it wasn't the last time I did it, but the last part of the sequence as you see it on the film—he knew that eventually I was to be running into what was to be dawn, 'cause I'd been running all night. He couldn't shoot at dawn, but he had picked a spot where a sunset would look like dawn. He would send a man by car to that spot every afternoon to find out if there were certain kinds of clouds. When he finally got the report that the clouds looked like they were going to be the kind of formation he wanted for a dawn effect, he would leave the set we were working on and drive to the sunset location, which was on the edge of one of those buttes in the Utah mountains where the scenery just falls away and you only see sky and clouds. So we get there, and they set the camera up on a tripod that's going to see me coming out of the woods and run by and disappear into the sunrise with the Indians gradually falling off. The reason for telling this story is that this may be Ford being a sadistic son of a bitch, but I don't really think so. When the shot was over, everybody is right there still in a group around the camera, except me. I am out of sight because I've disappeared over the edge of the butte. When you run like that at ten thousand feet, you are really out of breath. So I'm walking back slowly, still panting. By the time I got back everybody was gone. One of the standby cars was waiting for me. Now these were dirt roads, and I drove all the way back to the camp, a thirty- or forty-minute drive, taking their dust! And I'm trying to get a lot of oxygen because I was out of wind. I bawled the shit out of Ford, you know, with humor, when I got there.

Mike: Working on a John Ford film is like being a member of a stock company since he uses many of the same people over and over. You were used to that because of your summer stock experience. When working with the same actors, you know what to expect of them and how you can rely on them, don't you think?

Fonda: Yes, I do! A good repertory company is the ideal thing in the theater to get a good performance. The most recent play I did was *The Time of Your Life* just a year ago. We rehearsed it here for four weeks. Then we played it at the Kennedy Center in Washington and in Philadelphia and Chicago and wound up out here on the Coast. There was just something about the play, about the company itself, the actors that were chosen to play the parts, and the director! We became a family. And we weren't a repertory theater that had played together in eight other productions. This was the first time most of us had been together. But we got what critics were calling some of the best ensemble acting they had seen! That's what ensemble acting is! Being familiar with each other and knowing how to work together well. In the Plumstead Playhouse that I'm associated with we have had the same actors on various plays, but it's really not an ensemble group. We've done three shows. We did *Our Town* four times with at least three different companies. I played the same part, but it's not a repertory company. The closest we came to repertory was when we did *The Front Page* and *Our Town* at the same time, and most of the cast were in both plays.

Mike: You directed the version of *Our Town* that was done out here?

Fonda: Yes. We had been on Broadway. We hadn't expected to come out here, but when James Doolittle of the Huntington Hartford Theater asked us to come out and made it possible, we decided we would. We couldn't get all the actors who were in the company in New York. So half of them we had to recast. And I directed that Hollywood production.

Mike: You also directed *The Caine Mutiny Court-Martial* out here. Is directing as creative an outlet as your acting?

Fonda: Well, it never occurred to me to say to myself that one is more than the other. I enjoy directing. I haven't done a lot. Actually I guess *Our Town* and *Mutiny* are the first that I've done since the old stock days, although I have been involved with the direction of the things I've acted in more than the average actor, I'd say. Because when you get to be forty-five years in the business, I think directors listen to you or ask you. I haven't ever tried to take over in any way, but you can't *not* be involved in any medium, in films, or television, or in the theater if you've been at it as long as I have, or as long as Jim Stewart or Lucille Ball. You just can't *not* be involved because you know things by experience that a younger director not only doesn't know but is happy to have you show him.

Mike: Have you ever been very involved in the writing of scripts?

Fonda: The closest I've ever come to writing anything I've acted in was a picture I did in England with Annabella, *Wings of the Morning* [Fox] in 1937. The director, Harold Schuster, was a friend of mine who had been the editor of my first two films. He had always been promised he would be given a job as a director. He had been sent to London as the editor on *Wings of the Morning*. There was a prologue in the picture that involved Annabella, but not me. By the time I got there the original director had been fired and Harold had taken over. We took a cottage together in Jarrod's Cross, Bucks, fifteen minutes from the studio. He wasn't that happy with the script and we would work together on scenes or rewrite dialogue. I can't think offhand of any other time I've done that, other than the kind of thing you do on a TV set when you're doing a series like the two I did, *The Deputy*

[NBC, 1960] and *The Smith Family* [ABC-TV, 1970]. You haven't time to go back to the author, so you just rewrite the dialogue a little bit, not on a big scale. But I wouldn't say that I've been a writer. I don't think I could be.

Mike: You've played a lot of actual, historical characters. For instance, you played Abe Lincoln as a young man in the film *Young Mr. Lincoln* [Fox, 1939] and again as President in the play *The Trial of Abe Lincoln*. You also played Frank James in two films and Wyatt Earp in *My Darling Clementine* [Fox, 1946] and then General Theodore Roosevelt in *The Longest Day* [Fox, 1963]. As an actor preparing for that type role, how do you go about finding the character?

Fonda: I don't know that I can be of much help on that. I'll talk, and maybe you'll find out from the words I use. I don't know. I think the work is done by the playwright or screenwriter. I think when it's written out, if the actor is right for the part, he doesn't have to do anything except play the scene that's been written by a writer. Now, that isn't to say he doesn't have to go to the makeup department to have his nose fixed to look like Lincoln, but I didn't do any research particularly. Maybe I didn't have to. I'd been a Lincoln fan, if that's the way to say it, most of my life. Long before I knew I was going to become an actor, I had read Carl Sandburg's three books on Lincoln. And in my library I've got a lot of books on Lincoln that I've enjoyed reading. So I've known a lot about Lincoln. I suppose that was my homework. I didn't do anything special when I was given the part.

Actually when they asked me to play *Young Mr. Lincoln*, I said no, because I didn't think I could play Lincoln. Lincoln to me was a god. It was just like asking me to play Jesus, or something, you know! They finally talked me into doing a test. Without being committed to it, I went to Twentieth Century-Fox. I played a scene with a girl. I went to makeup first, and they took two or three hours to put the nose and the wart on and fix my hair. I did the scene. The next day I went in to see it, and I'm sitting in the projection room, and it starts on the screen. I see this guy and I thought, "Well, I'm a son of a bitch! It looks like Lincoln!" Then he started to talk, and *my* voice came out, and it destroyed it for me. I said, "I'm sorry, fellows, it won't work." I went home. Months later Ford, who hadn't been assigned to the picture at the time I tested, was assigned. I guess somebody said to him, "We think Fonda's the guy, but he somehow doesn't want to do it." And

Ford must have said, "Well, send him in. Tell him I want to see him." And I got a call to come in and see John Ford! Now I'd never met Ford. I knew his work. I'm a fan of Ford's, too. I remember going into his office the way a recruit would go in to the admiral. That's the way I felt. I was a movie star. But I felt like a recruit, you know, with a white hat in my hand. He was typical Ford that first time. I've known him ever since, intimately, and I'll never forget: He looked up at me from under the hat he had on, and the patch on the eye, and either the handkerchief in his mouth or the pipe or whatever he was chewing on, and said, "What the fuck is all this shit about you not wanting to play this part?" He can only talk by using all the bad words! What he was doing was shaming me. He said, "You think you'd be playing the goddamn great emancipator, huh? He's a goddamn fucking jake-legged lawyer in Springfield, for Christ's sake!" He went on at more length, but what he did was to shame me into playing *Young Mr. Lincoln*, and that started the whole romance. What do I do to prepare myself to play a historical character? I don't feel that I did anything special. I let them make me up. Then I played the guy that the screenwriter, Lamar Trotti, wrote. He had written a beautiful script. They came to my home and read me the script in my living room. I said, "Fellows, I think it's wonderful!" I cried and everything. "But I can't play Lincoln." And they went away. So when I did do it, I just played the guy that was written. I can't really help anybody on "How do you do it?" I learned the lines. That's the way Spencer Tracy answered: "You learn the goddamn lines and try not to fall down or bump into chairs!"

Mike: Although you worked at Fox very often during the late 1930's, you weren't a contract player there, were you?

Fonda: No. A few years after I started with Walter, he dissolved his corporation, and I became a free-lance actor. I remember one of the first things I did at Fox as a free lance was *Jesse James* [Fox, 1939], with Tyrone Power playing Jesse. Frank James was the second part. I liked it, but I wasn't sure. I was a very good friend of Henry Hathaway's. I asked Henry to read the script. I said, "Should I play Frank?" He said, "Shit, yes! Grab it!" And I did. Of course it turned out that Frank James was the part most moviegoers remembered 'cause he was more of a character. Eventually I played him again in *The Return of Frank James* [Fox, 1940].

Mike: Another of your first films as a free-lance actor was *Jezebel* [Warner's, 1938].

Fonda: Yes. Bette Davis got an Academy Award for her performance as Jezebel. I had been sent the script, but it was Willie Wyler. I knew him by reputation as being a director that took sixteen weeks' minimum to do a film. I also knew that my first child was going to be born on the twenty-first of December. My wife had to have a Caesarean, so you could just call your shots. It was to be December 21, in New York, and I was damned sure I ought to be there. I couldn't be there if I was going to do *Jezebel* for sixteen weeks, so I turned it down. Through my agent, Leland Heyward, Wyler came back and said to him, "If I guarantee Fonda will be in New York on the twenty-first of December, will he take it?" On that basis, and it was in the contract, I took it. From the time I started until the twenty-first was eight weeks, which is a fair time to shoot a picture. He got me back to New York on the twenty-first, and he was eight more weeks on the picture. It wasn't easy to do. It wasn't easy for Bette, because Wyler had to stop shooting scenes after my presence in a scene ceased and go pick up something else I was in. Then, after I was gone, he had to go back with Bette to pick up scenes that would immediately follow my exit or something like that. I guess it's rather well known that there are actors who didn't like Wyler, just like there are actors who didn't like Ford or Fritz Lang, etc., because Wyler was known to want to shoot a lot of takes. You know, fifty takes and that kind of thing. Humphrey Bogart said he'd had a bad experience with Wyler. Bogie warned me. He said, "Jesus, don't touch it. Don't go in there." Anyway, I did and had a very good experience. Wyler and I got along famously. We're still friends. He never took fifty takes, though he might have taken thirty! But it was never without a reason. I've worked with John Stahl who was a director who would take it over and over again without telling you why. It was as though he was saying, "If they're going to give me actors like this, what are you going to do?" You know? But with Wyler, every time he did it again he gave you something to think about. He'd say, "This time in the middle of the scene react to a mosquito bite." These inventions would just come to him. He was rehearsing with film really! And that wasn't bad because I like rehearsals. So it was a good experience with Wyler, and I liked it very much.

Mike: You were not interested those days in a contract at a studio. Naturally being a free-lance actor you could pick better parts.

Fonda: Yes.

Mike: But when the film *The Grapes of Wrath* came along at Twentieth Century-Fox, I believe because John Ford wanted you for the part so much and you wanted the part so much, it became a—

Fonda: Well, it was bait! Zanuck had tried to get me under contract even before *Jesse James*, and I had resisted it. I was very happy doing free lance. I was working a lot at Twentieth Century, but it was my choice of pictures I wanted to do. *Young Mr. Lincoln* was as a free-lance actor. *Drums Along the Mohawk* was as a free-lance actor. And *Grapes of Wrath*, as you have already suggested, was bait. I did want the part. It was a choice part! It was another picture with Ford, and Ford wanted me. I had a long meeting with Zanuck. Obviously I fell for what he said because I signed his contract. He had a lot of reasons. You know: This was the plum part, and it was going to be the big feature of the year for Fox, and if he put me in that, he didn't want to jeopardize the product by having me go to MGM to do a film with Joan Crawford. I remember he used that. Jesus Christ! One of the first pictures I did for him when I came back from the war was with Joan Crawford! Now I don't mean to say it's bad to work with Joan Crawford. But that was his expression. It was fate.

I did sign the contract, and I regretted it from the day we finished *Grapes of Wrath*. Oh, I had some good films during my contract period at Fox, but they were almost all on loan-out. I would fight Zanuck and win some of them, but lose others. When I would win, I would be lucky to be loaned out for films like *The Lady Eve* at Paramount [1940] and *The Male Animal* at Warner's [1942]. One loan-out was to RKO for *The Big Street* [1942], which was a good one with Lucille Ball. So, except for *The Ox-Bow Incident* [1943], which Zanuck didn't want to do, I was unhappy at Fox. Zanuck allowed Bill Wellman to do *Ox-Bow Incident* because Bill made a deal with him—I think Bill didn't want to do *Thunder Birds*, a picture about training pilots or something like that. But they made a deal that Bill would do *Thunder Birds* for Zanuck if Zanuck would let Bill do *Ox-Bow* first. During shooting Zanuck didn't pay any attention to Bill and let him do the film. Bill delivered the film to Zanuck. They released it without any kind of fanfare, and to Zanuck's surprise it began to get the attention of the critics and became a prestige picture, which today

Zanuck is proud of and takes bows for it! But he didn't want to have anything to do with it! And except for that, I can't remember another film that I was happy with at Fox, you know.

Mike: Weren't you happy making *The Return of Frank James*?

Fonda: No. Because, again, it was Lang. Oh, shit, he came to me with tears in his eyes and said he'd learned his lesson and so forth. Why Zanuck ever thought he would be the right kind of director for a Western I don't know, 'cause he wasn't at all. He was the same man he'd been on the other one I did with him, *You Only Live Once*, in the sense he was preoccupied with his camera. He painted with his camera. For example, in *You Only Live Once* there is a scene between Sylvia Sidney and me at supper after our marriage. The camera started on an insert of the marriage certificate that was leaning against the vase, and it backed away until it showed our two plates and that we had finished dinner, our dessert of ice cream and cake. Then it backed away until it could see the two of us looking at each other with dialogue. We were all day long! One whole day shooting just that thing there! He would do it one time; then he would come in and take the spoon and change the way the ice cream was in the dish and do it. Then he'd change the spoon prop. Then he'd stand and blow cigarette smoke into the shot. He was doing this kind of thing all day long!

This is the way he worked. In *The Return of Frank James* I had a scene where I come into a barn hunting down John Carradine, who has killed Jesse. I had to come in to a point, look around, hear something, and exit. That's all there was to the scene. We were about five hours doing it because Lang decides he wants cobwebs from the overhead beam down to the post that stood where I had to stop for a moment. So they send to the special effects department, and a guy comes down and blows cobwebs around. It's easy to do. But then Lang would come in and break holes in them to make them look like old cobwebs. Pretty soon he was breaking so many holes that the entire thing collapsed, and the effects guy would end up having to do it over. I sat there watching. By this time I knew Lang so well I would make bets with guys that we would be three hours, fucking with the cobwebs in a scene where I come in and stand for two seconds, then walk out! Also, during the *Return of Frank James*, we were on location up by Lone Pine. This is God's place! God put the lake there and the mountains and the trees. And God had stricken a tree by lightning, and it had fallen down a hundred years ago, you know. It's just a long

dead trunk with those spurs from where the branches had been
sticking up. There it was. And it was a natural. Only by the time Lang
got his camera set up, the log wasn't in the right position. They had to
move that mother that's four feet in diameter at the base and eighty
feet long. Then they had to build a platform and put the camera at
another angle. It just became difficult. Ford would have come in there,
looked at that natural beauty, and said, "Oh, shit!" and put a tripod
down and shot it. But not Lang. He killed three horses up there,
because of the altitude. Running horses uphill at a flat-out gallop so
many times that their hearts just burst that night. That's the kind of
man he was. So it was not a good experience, but it was not a bad
picture. Somebody saw it the other night on television and told me
they enjoyed it. Anyway, I didn't enjoy working with Fritz Lang.

Mike: That old-fashioned way of making films where economy didn't
interfere as much as it does now did have advantages, though, if a
director didn't go as way out as Lang did.

Fonda: Well, Ford was the master at it. He used whatever happened.
An example is when we were on location for *Fort Apache* at
Monument Valley. There are about four hundred Mormons that Ford
has got from someplace near there to be extras. He's put them in
cavalry uniforms, and they're all on horseback. They're out of sight
beyond a sand slope waiting to start the scene. And there's an
assistant with a walkie-talkie who, when he gets the sign from the
camera that we're ready, will give them the cue. They are supposed to
appear, then come at a slow pace, in two long columns right by the
camera. Monument Valley! The most photogenic place in the world!
You can see the cameraman licking his chops and dreaming about
that Academy Award that's going to be on his mantel when he's all
through. Beautiful clouds. The sun. They're just about ready, and it
starts to rain! Ford says, "Roll 'em!" And the cameraman looked at
Ford and was just stricken. Ford says, "Roll 'em, for Christ's sake!
Am I gonna have to get up and roll those goddamn cameras? ROLL
'EM!" And they rolled them, and the cameraman cried, probably, but
Ford knew what he was doing. He got those guys riding down, and
you could just barely see the rain a little bit. It wasn't even back-lit.
But the leather on the saddles and bridles was wet and glistening. It
was different! You can always shoot sun, but by God, something like
that! And he shot it while it was there. It lasted just long enough for
the take.

I was on location with Sidney Lumet in Central Park on a film in 1958, *Stage Struck* it was. We had started filming in the morning, then broke for lunch. I lived only four blocks away, so I'd gone home for lunch. When I came back—this was winter—it was snowing. Great big lazy snowflakes just coming right down, steady. It didn't look like it was ever going to stop. Sidney Lumet and the camera crew and the assistants stood there looking at each other, saying, "Jesus Christ!" Sidney didn't mind the snow, but he couldn't be sure. You see, you can't control it. It's not your snow with cornflakes and the wind machine. It's real snow. He had a scene with me on a bench with a guy, Christopher Plummer. We had dialogue. Sidney had anticipated about four camera setups. He was going to bring Christopher walking in with a dolly shot, then bring me in. This would have taken the rest of the afternoon, and maybe the snow wouldn't last. If he got committed to snow, and then he's not finished shooting and there's no snow, he's dead. I said, "Fellows, can I give you a little lesson from John Ford? Forget your dollies, forget your trucking shots, and everything else. Put the camera on a tripod, and shoot it as fast as you can and get this, 'cause this is something else!" When that snow comes down and hits your eyelash and melts on camera, that's real! You don't get that very often. Usually it's the cornflakes that stay there all through the shot. They looked at me, then looked at each other, and they did it. He had to just change his concept. Instead of dollies, a couple of tripod setups. Anyway, what I'm saying is the old way still works, and there are still a few people around who appreciate it and know what it means to put the camera on a tripod fast, like John Ford, and get a shot.

Mike: We've already talked about much of your career that took place after World War II. Before we go farther into those years, would you tell about your time in the Navy?

Fonda: Well, I joined the Navy the day I finished *The Ox-Bow Incident*. I went downtown for my induction, but before I got on the bus to San Diego, I learned Zanuck had pulled some strings in Washington and got me deferred. I was never so mad in my life. He had a picture he wanted me to do called *The Immortal Sergeant* [Fox, 1943]. The whole idea made me mad that a movie producer would have the strength to go through Washington and have a man who had joined one of the services deferred. Anyway, I came back and did *Immortal Sergeant*. I didn't enjoy it because John Stahl was the director. Other than that there was a group of good actors, Tom Mitchell and Maureen O'Hara. But Stahl was a real son of a bitch. He was the kind of director who would do it over and over again without any reason, just as to say, "Well, I have to do it over again because they gave me lousy actors." We were all downbeat, and everybody hated him. I finally chewed his ass out on the set, and my coworkers gave me a silver cigarette box with all their initials engraved on it. I still have it around somewhere.

Mike: On completion of *The Immortal Sergeant* you went into the Navy as an enlisted man. Were there serious private reasons why you joined when you could have stayed civilian?

Fonda: Well, I guess they weren't private in the sense that I don't want to talk about it. But they were my personal reasons. Partly my self-consciousness. I don't like to name names, but I don't know how some actors who didn't go could work with an open face. Now I didn't have to because I had three children, and I was over the age of draft, although everybody had to sign up for the draft. I know Jim Stewart was one of the first movie actors drafted. But I wouldn't have been drafted with a family to support. Three children. And I was over the age. In 1940 I was thirty-five. Since my character the audience always saw on the screen was a young man, much younger than I really was, my self-consciousness made me feel that parents and loved ones of other boys who had gone would look at this young, supposedly healthy stalwart on the screen and say, "Why doesn't that son of a bitch go? My boy goes, but he doesn't go." It's not valid, but that's the way I am and I joined. Not without my wife's understanding and permission, of course. I mean I didn't run away and join.

Mike: I have a friend who was in training at the San Diego Naval Training Center the same time you were. He said you were quite often put on because of being a well-known film star to attend social functions high-ranking officers might have, functions that would not ordinarily include an enlisted man.

Fonda: Anybody in my position had to put up with the same thing. You just accept it. You can't fight against it. I tried hard to. They tried to divert me into other things in the Navy. To photographic things or to entertain at the Navy Radio Hour. I went in as an enlisted man, went through boot camp and quartermaster school, and was assigned to a destroyer in Seattle. While out on the destroyer, I got orders to report to Ninety Church Street in New York to be decommissioned for a moment, then sworn in as lieutenant, j.g. Now, this wasn't my idea. I didn't want to be an officer. John Ford had wanted me to join his group, and I didn't do that. That was earlier than I thought I needed to go. But anyway, somebody in Washington had seen I was in the Navy and said, "What the hell is he doing on a destroyer as a quartermaster? Get him back here, and we'll have him direct training films." And that's where they sent me. That was not my idea of going to war. I don't like to sound like an eager beaver. I was, but I don't like to sound it. I wanted to shoot the guns. I didn't want to make training films. I was fortunate I got out of it. I mean, I got diverted. I met a commander who was sympathetic, and he had my orders changed. I went to Quonset Point, Rhode Island, and went through the ACI (Air Combat Intelligence) school, which was a new thing the Navy had to train officers to brief and interrogate pilots before and after their missions. It was a job the Navy had never had to have before, and they were handpicking men to do that. I went through that and went to the Pacific in the forward area. Didn't have any fun. I hate war, you know, but I felt I had to be in it, and what I had to do was pretty dull. A lot of paper work. Work on an admiral's staff. That was it.

Mike: I know you received a Bronze Star and a Presidential Citation during your tour of duty. When you were discharged, did coming back into your profession present any problem after having been gone from it a few years?

Fonda: No. There was no problem. None of us were much in a hurry to get back to work. Jim Stewart got back about the same time I did. He'd been in the European theater. His house had been rented while he was away. He couldn't get the tenants out, so he moved in with us, in our guesthouse, and stayed with us almost five months. It was a merry-go-round! Everybody was giving parties! There was a party every night, and we'd come back and sit and play records and drink beer and shoot the bull, you know, late at night. Both of us got back in September and I think it was June before I did my first film. I think it was about the same time for Jim. I did *My Darling Clementine* as my first film after the war. John Ford directed it at Fox.

Mike: Were you obligated to go back under contract to Fox?

Fonda: Yes. But while we were away, Olivia de Havilland had a suit with Warner Brothers, and she won the suit. She had a seven-year contract with Warner Brothers, and they were trying to tack on to that seven years all the months she was on suspension for refusing to work. She sued them and won. You couldn't add on anything to that original contract. And as a result, when we all came back from the war, Stewart's contract was expired at MGM. Jim is such a sentimental guy he was ready to re-sign because Mayer wanted him to. But Leland Heyward, who was still our agent, wouldn't allow him to. I remember Jim's story about how he went to MGM and sat in Mayer's office while L. B. Mayer cried tears trying to reemploy him! But he kept his back up and he didn't re-sign, so he became a free-lance artist. My contract at Fox had one year to go. That meant I owed Zanuck three movies. He wanted to renegotiate, and I wouldn't. So the best he got was for me to give him the three movies over a period of three years. I did two. I did *My Darling Clementine* and I did *Daisy Kenyon* [Fox, 1947]. Outside of Fox during that period, I did *The Long Night* [1947], *Fort Apache*, and *The Fugitive* at RKO and one with Jim Stewart called *Miracles Can Happen* at United Artists [1948]. I'd only done two of the three I owed Fox when *Mister Roberts*, the play, came along, and I went to New York to do that. I was gone from Hollywood for seven years doing three plays, *Mister Roberts*, *Point of No Return*, and *The Caine Mutiny Court-Martial*.

Mike: When you went to New York to do *Mister Roberts* in 1948, it was just about the time that television was becoming a serious threat to the movie industry. . . .

Fonda: If it was so, I wasn't aware of it. I may have read it, but I wasn't that conscious of television. I didn't have a set, I don't think. I don't remember watching television. I think my first awareness really of television was when we had opened in *Mister Roberts* and Ed Sullivan had *The Toast of the Town* program. He did one of his shows from the Alvin Theater, where we were playing, featuring scenes from the play and interviews with me, the director, Josh Logan, and the producer, Leland Heyward. Then later I did a thing for Ed Sullivan on the same show on which I was a kind of host. I'm just remembering! It was all such a new thing. The cameras would go on, and the red light would be on at the top of the camera to indicate which camera was pointing to you and was the camera on the air.

Mike: In the late forties fewer films were being made, and a lot of top stars were doing fewer pictures. Most of them didn't have the alternative you did to go on the stage because they weren't trained on the stage.

Fonda: Maybe so. I wasn't aware of it. I went back because you just could not miss doing *Mister Roberts*. When it was offered to me, I leaped at it. As I've already indicated to you and you understand, the theater is my first love, and when you've got a play like that, you don't miss it. And after having that joy, Leland produced another play, *Point of No Return*, and I went right into that after I'd finished the national tour of *Mister Roberts*; I did that for two years. Also an international tour. And then came *The Caine Mutiny Court-Martial* which I played in for little over a year. So I didn't do a film for about seven years. Not because they weren't offered, but because I was where I was having fun. I was getting my kicks! And actually it turns out, as I have been persuaded now to believe by my managers and agents, that is a mistake! If you're in show business, you've got to play all sides of the street. You can't leave one medium for the other too long. Audiences forget, and producers forget. So since then, I have tried to go back to the theater every other year. And in the past ten years I've been lucky that that's the way it's been. I've had a Broadway play every other year between *Two for the Seesaw*; *Critic's Choice*; *Silent Night, Lonely Night*; *A Gift of Time*; and *Generation*.

Mike: Other actors who have played with you onstage say one of the best traits you have is the habit of *listening* to whomever you are playing a scene with.

Fonda: I think, again, I probably learned that from being in the audience and watching other performers. I would read reviews of a play or hear about a play and think, "Boy, I want to see that!" It might be the third or sixth month before I could get a chance to see it, and it wouldn't be what I'd read about or what I'd expected! Because the actors weren't listening anymore. It's the easiest pit to fall in. You can automatically hear your cue and come to the proper life when you're having your line. It's so easy when the other guy's talking for you to be looking at him but thinking: "Am I going to go to Sardi's tonight? Where am I going to eat afterwards?" Or whatever. You can see, at least I can, the difference between an actor that's listening and one that's not listening. Maybe the average audience doesn't notice it, but for reasons they're not able to put their finger on, it's better to them when the actors are listening. Only a professional would probably be aware of it. I'm very aware of it, and sometimes in my life, as a member of an audience, I've said, "By God, don't let that ever happen to me." Listening is just as important as talking because you're hearing it for the first time. "The first time" are the operative words to me. It must be to the audience "the first time." It was written as a play, but it's supposed to be something that's just happening. Although they are lines written for me by a playwright, I'm supposed to be saying them off my head. It's coming out of me. That's what I am, as an actor, doing: taking these words a man has written for me but making them sound as though it's a thought that I have just had. Likewise, if somebody is talking to me, it's the first time I am hearing those words. Now they may not be earth-shattering so that you indicate you're listening very hard and you react too big, but whatever they are, it's the first time you've heard anybody say that, and they're saying it to *you*.

Mike: It keeps a performance from becoming mechanical.

Fonda: That's the discipline you have to give yourself. And if an actor isn't prepared to discipline himself that much, he ought to get out of the business or say, "Okay, I will only play it for three weeks because I can't stay excited any longer than that."

Mike: So, ultimately, it depends a lot on the material, doesn't it? If it's material you really enjoy playing, you can keep it fresh longer.

Fonda: Well, I'll tell you that if it's material you enjoy playing, it's a lot easier! I've had to play material that I didn't enjoy very much for as long as two years! *Point of No Return*, as successful as it was, was a difficult play to do. It was not rewarding for me as an actor, but I didn't let down. I didn't let anybody not feel that it was the first time. *Two for the Seesaw* was even more difficult for me because I was a one-dimensional character playing against a fully three-dimensional character. That took more concentration for me, and discipline for me, to keep it going against a vaudeville act on the other side. Audiences couldn't understand what the hell was eating this guy because he wasn't drawn in more than one dimension by the playwright. Now, I'm saying that, but critics and other people said it, too. So, it's not as though I'm copping out because it's well known.

Mike: In *Mister Roberts* you played over sixteen hundred performances.

Fonda: *Mister Roberts* was something special. I did it for almost seventeen hundred times over a period of four years. And the last performance was as much fun as the first performance and was better than the first performance! Josh Logan, who directed it, will say it was better. I don't have to say so. Anybody else who saw it—and many people saw it many, many times—said, "It just gets better!" Now I don't remember whether I used the expression to you about "take out the improvements." Did I tell you that story?

Mike: No.

Fonda: How do you get better if you're as good as you can be? If the performance of the cast of *Mister Roberts'* opening night was as good as it must have been to get the acclaim that it did and the cheers that it got, what do you do to make it even better the second night, the second month, the second year, and the fourth year, and so on? Because there *is* such a thing as the "wrong improvements."

The best way to describe that is to tell the example, and it's a true story: George M. Cohan, playwright, star, director, everything, wrote a play that he produced and directed and starred in. It opened on Broadway and was a big hit. It ran on and on and on. And about the second or third month the actors arrived backstage a half hour before curtaintime, and there was a notice on the bulletin board saying, "There'll be a rehearsal tomorrow at two thirty to take out the improvements," signed by George M. Cohan. That means there is such a thing as the "wrong improvements"! For example, when you try too hard to get a bigger laugh than it was the night before, or you hear a little laugh one night and you try to make that a bigger laugh and you get things out of proportion. Or you overplay because you like the sound of the laughs. So, in a long-run show, there are ways to overuse something good that you had opening night that the director brought out of you. Getting it back to the level it should be on is "taking out the improvements."

At the same time, there are fine subtleties which are the "right" improvements that are only obvious to the director or writer. To Josh Logan, as an example, on *Mister Roberts*. Bob Keith, who played Doc with me the first year, and who is an actor like I am who only wants to get better, would come to my dressing room all the time, and we would sit and talk about the scenes. Now we've got two great parts and some great scenes going for us. We talked about the scenes and found out little subtleties in character and thoughts that we hadn't thought of before in spite of the intensity of rehearsals and tryouts with Josh. The second year you're still finding them! That's what makes it fun for me to continue to do a part I really like night after night in a long run because you can keep it fresh.

Mike: Joshua Logan would return to have rehearsals periodically, wouldn't he?

Fonda: He did. Often he would have to because he would have to put in replacements. When Bob Keith came to Hollywood, we had to put in another Doc. Over the four-year run, I played with four different Docs. Four different Lieutenant Pulvers. The young actors who were playing Ensign Mannion, new young actors, would get better parts, and we'd have to get a new Ensign Mannion. So every time there was a replacement the stage manager would get them ready, but then Josh would come in for the final two rehearsals, let's say, with the principals. He was also always coming to a performance every several weeks unless he was out of town or something. He would frequently come backstage with notes that might make it necessary for us to have a rehearsal. But I must say, over the years Josh would just sort of shake his head about me, and Bob Keith particularly, and say, "Bastards, I don't know what you do, but you just get better!" That's the best thing I can be told by a director or anybody. How could it be better is what Josh meant, because it was as good as it could have been opening night.

Mike: Do you mind talking about the experience filming *Mister Roberts* [Warner's, 1955] for which John Ford began the directing but—

Fonda: Well, I do mind because—

Mike: All I know is that he began it, and then someone else finished it.

Fonda: Well, when we got back from location, Ford had a kidney attack and had to have an operation. He would have been off five to eight weeks, and Leland Heyward, the producer, couldn't afford to close down the picture. So, without losing a beat, Leland got Mervyn LeRoy to come in overnight. There aren't many directors you can get to come in and take over like that. As Josh Logan put it once, "It's like a cook taking over a soufflé in the middle from another cook!" It's pretty delicate. But Mervyn did, and that was the real reason Ford was off the picture. But there had been problems before that which are probably what you allude to. They were unpleasant and shouldn't be talked about too much. It has to do with the fact that Ford, for all his greatness, is an Irish egomaniac, as anyone who knows him will say. And when you got right down to it, he didn't know what to do with

Mister Roberts that wasn't repeating what was successful in New York. He was trying to do things to the play that would be his in the film. Those of us who had been close to the play, Leland, Josh and I and others, felt Ford was tampering with something that was pretty good to begin with, and we weren't happy with it. There was one nurse in the play. And it was as though Ford figured if one nurse was funny, four nurses or five nurses are funnier, but they weren't. He didn't want to shoot the scotch-making scene at all! I guess he just didn't know what he could do to that scene that wasn't a copy of what Josh did on Broadway. And we hadn't shot it while he was on the picture. But after he was off the picture, we put it back in. He had left it out of the script.

Mike: Was Josh Logan at one time mentioned to direct the film?

Fonda: Well, we took it for granted that Josh was going to direct the film after the play was a big hit! The play went on and on and on. Josh, because of the success of the play, was also going on to other jobs. *South Pacific*, and I'm not sure what films, but he did several things. Eventually, when Leland was ready to make the movie, Josh was on to something else and said, "Go ahead without me." But during the run of the play, we used to sit and drink together after the theater. We used to go to 21 or someplace and talk about where we would go to shoot the film. We talked about going to the Caribbean, maybe, and get a Navy boat and just live on the boat and make the movie! Well, it didn't happen that way.

Mike: Was your stage experience in *The Caine Mutiny Court-Martial* a rewarding one?

Fonda: Oh, you bet! It sure was! In a special way, more than anything else has been. I had a special problem as an actor in it that I'd never had before. I played Greenwald, who in the first act sits and doodles as he listens to the proceedings of the trial. But the second act is his act when he takes over the cross-examination of Queeg, the officer on trial. And then there's the epilogue. We opened in Santa Barbara, and we played it for fourteen weeks across the country, mostly one-night stands on the way to New York. Charles Laughton had postponed a tour of his own to direct this. Now he had to leave, once we had opened, to resume his own tour, a one-man show. He sort of put me in charge, meaning we didn't have a chance to rehearse anymore. We traveled by bus a great deal of the time, and what I did was to sit next to one cast member on the bus for a while, then move over next to somebody else and just talk about scenes. We played in any number of cities, and without fail every single reviewer commented about this brilliant play, *but* said the epilogue was gratuitous, embarrassing, unnecessary.

I collected all those reviews because I knew, when we got to Boston, Charles was going to be available again and Herman Wouk, the author, would join us. I had my meeting with them, and I showed them the reviews. I said, "Not only the critics, but our friends, who have come backstage to talk to us, agree we don't need the epilogue." Well, Laughton got the message right away. Wouk understood what I was saying, but he insisted on keeping it. To him that was the reason he wrote the play. That's what he had to say. Well, listening to Wouk, Laughton realized we had to go with the epilogue, but if we were going to go with it—and this is where Laughton's genius came in—then the audience had to be made to want to hear it. So he explained to Wouk that it would be necessary to add short sentences and short scenes through the body of the play which would make the audience not totally satisfied, still unresolved, so that at the end there's still the question "What's eating Greenwald? There's something the matter with Greenwald." Then the audience would want something more and welcome the epilogue that was going to explain. P.S. Herman Wouk wrote those scenes. We put them in. We opened in New York. In those days there were twelve critics in New York. There were twelve papers. Not one critic said the epilogue was unnecessary. On the contrary they said: "Son of a bitch! He hits you with one climax, then hits you with another one on top of it!"

Now my problem as an actor stemmed from the fact the audience was made to want to see that epilogue and were spellbound through it. My friends who would come backstage after that weren't able to talk. They'd just say, "You son of a bitch!" Maybe the next day or the next week they would be able to say, "Goddamn, that was a great night, but you know I don't think I buy that epilogue." So, as an actor, my problem was that I couldn't allow the audience to intellectualize at the moment. I had to grab them emotionally, and the only way to do that was to grab them as Greenwald got so emotionally involved himself that he couldn't stand that son of a bitch Queeg and threw it in his face. If you could hold the audience like that, they weren't going to stop and say, "Oh, I don't know if I understand what he's trying to say. I don't believe that." When Jane was beginning to think seriously about being an actress I used my experience solving that scene as an example. I used the simile of an amphibian plane that has a particular design of the hull. There's a step, and it's called a step, underneath that keel. The plane is very sluggish when it's down in the water. But when the pilot gets up to a certain speed, he's able to pick it up onto the step. Then it's just riding on the step. It's on the water still, but ready to soar! That's the way I would feel if I really got it going when I started that scene. I was up on the step! Then all I had to do was just keep it controlled, just stay there 'cause I could go now. Go, go, go! But you had to feel you had the reins in control all the time. I've seen actors let their emotion go till they just slobber, slobber. Then you don't want to watch anymore, and it becomes embarrassing. But if you can control it, you can hold an audience in the well-known palm of your hand so that they can't stop to think about the words and think as I've already said, "Now, why would he have to give us that shit about his mother being melted down into soap? That's not necessary." The next day or two is when you think about it. And the whole philosophy Wouk had in that scene most people did take exception to.

Mike: One thing you've occasionally done as an actor, which is more a British approach than American, is that, if a choice part comes along which you really like, you will take it and not be so concerned that it may not be the leading part. That is the mark of a true professional, I believe, and it is difficult in this country to have that attitude toward roles you will play.

Fonda: Well, I don't think it's difficult. Maybe other people feel differently, and they can't do what they think would be lowering their standards to take less than the star part. I don't do it in any sort of conscious thinking about it. I do what appeals to me. However, I have done a lot of things that didn't appeal to me that have been starring parts. Agents and managers to whom I pay a lot of money for advice will tell me if I want to indulge myself in the theater and films, I have to do a certain number of what are called box-office pictures, or I would be out of the business. You can't make a career out of a *Twelve Angry Men* [UA, 1957] or an *Ox-Bow Incident*. I understand it, believe it, and agree, because they don't make enough money. Not that those two films lost money. They were both profitable pictures, but it took a year longer to go to profit, which is not an exciting thing for backers and producers who are looking for *The Godfather* [Paramount, 1972], of course. So I have done my share of pictures geared to please the box office, like *Sex and the Single Girl* [Warner's, 1964], *Battle of the Bulge* [Warner's, 1965], and some others when I am a free-lance actor and don't have to do them. But my advisers were right. I am still considered a box-office actor because of some of those pictures that I hated.

Mike: I think there have only been two or three pictures in which you played parts that weren't American characters. One was when you did *The Fugitive* in Mexico, and then, in Rome, the epic film of *War and Peace* [Paramount, 1956]. *The Fugitive* was a fine film, but *War and Peace* had a certain amount of criticism. I know you wanted to play the role of Pierre with more characterization than the director or producer wanted you to.

Fonda: It was only the producer. Dino de Laurentiis. I had my fights with him. If he wasn't on the set, the director was with me. King Vidor was for anything I wanted to do. If I wanted to wear glasses, for instance, I'd put them on in a scene. But if Dino de Laurentiis came on the set and I was wearing glasses, he'd go to King Vidor and say, "What is this with Fonda? Take those glasses off." So, having already shot some of the scene, we'd have to have a shot within the scene where I am seen taking the glasses off so it didn't look like suddenly I have glasses on, suddenly I don't. So, if Dino de Laurentiis was there, I'd have to play it his way, like a leading man. If he wasn't there, I would try, as best I could, to play the Pierre I had in mind. When they offered me the part, I thought they were insane, you know! To offer Pierre to me, from Omaha, Nebraska! But it was such a good part, and the script that was sent to me, Irwin Shaw's script, was such a good script, that I thought, "I'm not going to tell them I think they're crazy. If they offer this to me, I'm going to take it because I think it's a challenge and a good part!" What I didn't realize until I got to Rome was that Dino de Laurentiis had signed Audrey Hepburn for Natasha, and his idea was to have two handsome leading men. In place of Mel Ferrer and Henry Fonda, he might as well have had a Rock Hudson because that's what he wanted: attractive leading men. The character I wanted to have Pierre be was not what De Laurentiis had in mind. So it didn't come out as much of a character as I would like it to have been. Pierre's got two left feet. Also, I would like to have worn padding under my wardrobe, but I couldn't get away with that.

I played the priest in *The Fugitive* because John Ford beckoned me.

I didn't think I was right for that either. Actually, when he first talked about it, I kept arguing with him about it. José Ferrer hadn't made a film yet. He was becoming a real hot actor in New York and was getting ready to do *Cyrano de Bergerac* on Broadway. He came out here to cast a Roxanne. He's an old friend of mine, and I thought, "There's the guy for this!" So I told Ford, "I got a man who's a hell of an actor that I think would be right for this part!" I brought Ferrer over to Ford's office. They got along famously, and it was set. Ferrer was going to play the priest. But he was committed to go back and do *Cyrano* first. He didn't think it was going to run longer than about seven weeks, but it did, and he was obligated to keep it going as long as it would run because of the people who had put up the money. So, suddenly Ford's ready to go with *The Fugitive* and Ferrer's not available. Well, Ford beckoned to me again, and in those days when Ford beckoned, I went. I still don't think I was the ideal casting for the part, but it was a good experience, and you know, I love Ford.

Mike: Do you enjoy location filming?

Fonda: Yes, I do. I enjoy any kind of location more than studio shooting only because of the reality to it. My film with Alfred Hitchcock, for instance, *The Wrong Man* [Warner's, 1957], we shot mostly in real live sets back in New York in the areas and situations where the story really happened. He finally came back here and finished the film at the studio with studio sets because he was having so many union problems in New York. But it was great to have been working *in* the subway, *in* the Stork Club, *in* the courtroom where he was arraigned, *in* the real jail. I mean with real prisoners who would walk down the corridor. Those weren't extras behind the bars. They were for real!

Mike: *Twelve Angry Men* in 1957 was your first and only venture as the producer of a film. Was that because that particular story interested you?

Fonda: Not really. United Artists in those days was making deals with stars like Burt Lancaster and Kirk Douglas, etc. Stars were given an opportunity to produce at United Artists who would finance and release the film. The attractive thing was if the picture made money, you made it on a corporate tax basis rather than a personal income tax basis. When you got two hundred thousand dollars as an actor, you paid seventy-five or eighty percent of it back in personal income tax. If you made that kind of money or more as a producer, it was corporate tax, which was a hell of a lot less. I'm sure you're aware of that. So that's the reason this was an attractive deal from United Artists for any of us. They made it available to me, and I took it without any idea what I was going to do. Actually Bob Blumofe, who was with United Artists in those days, called me and said, "I think I've got an idea you might like. Come on down to the studio." I went down and we went to a screening room. He screened the television show of *Twelve Angry Men.* I was very impressed by it, and we decided that would be the picture I would do. I met with the writer, Reginald Rose, and he said there was no problem at all to get a screenplay. He said, "I had to cut my script down to fit the hour on television. There's another twenty minutes easy that I took out of the original script." So we got under way. I had known Sidney Lumet as an actor and as a young director in an actors' workshop. I remember when we were doing *Mister Roberts* in New York a lot of the actors would go down and work at his workshop during the day. I went down to watch a couple of times. This was Sidney's project, the workshop in a loft downtown someplace. Anyway, I knew that he'd come up and become a stage manager, then a director in television. And I knew from a lot of actors who had worked with him they adored him because he was an actor's director. He had communication. He knew how to talk to an actor. So I chose Sidney to direct *Twelve Angry Men* because I knew we would have two weeks to rehearse and he could get performances out of actors. What I got was a bonus I didn't count on: his incredible use of the camera which he had learned in television.

Mike: He uses two or three cameras at a time and therefore does a lot of his cutting or editing when shooting.

Fonda: I don't know what he did on television because I never worked with him on television. But what he had learned was a movement of the camera. And what he was smart enough to realize was that *Twelve Angry Men* filmed all in one room could become static. He kept that from happening with the movement of his camera. After two weeks of rehearsal we went onto a sound stage and started to film it. Our first day we filmed the entrance only of these twelve men into the jury room. They've been in the courtroom for many weeks of a trial which you're not an audience to, and now they're filing into this room to decide their verdict. Sidney, in a *continuous action shot* with his camera that took all day—and this is going to be only about two minutes on the screen—introduced to the film audience every one of those twelve men in some little casual way. It was an incredible technical feat for everybody because the camera moved in a full circle around the room. The twelve characters were all established, as well as the four walls of the room. He showed us everything about that room: the windows, the fan, the drinking fountain. This was Sidney. I was terribly impressed with him, and so were all the other actors. We had a shooting schedule of twenty-one days. Rather than shoot in sequence, which you would have thought we would have done in that kind of picture, when he had a certain camera setup, he would do every scene in the script that required the camera to be in that position. Say, the camera would be on two actors for a scene. After that scene was gotten, Sidney would say, "Now take their coats off, loosen the ties and put some sweat on them, and we'll shoot scene ninety-two," which is forty pages further, but requiring the same setup or camera and light position.

Mike: All the actors in that film were New York stage actors. Was that planned?

Fonda: No, except that we knew the best actors were from the theater whether they'd ever been in films or not. Some of them live out here now, but at that time they all lived in New York, and I did, too. That's why we shot the film there, in a set that was built on a sound stage there.

Mike: Do you recall anything particular about the filming of *Advise and Consent*?

Fonda: Well, I remember it was like live sets. We filmed in Washington, D.C., except for the Senate and the White House, which they wouldn't let us use. They were going to, but they changed their minds at the last minute. We shot in the real room where the Senate subcommittee had its hearings and the journalists had their tables. They were real journalists, too! That was one of Otto's ploys. I'm sure you're familiar enough with Otto to know how hep he is about publicity. So he had the real journalists, people who would write columns and stories about the making of this film, sitting at the journalists' tables and being photographed for this scene! We were in that room for a lot of days. We also shot a lot on the streets in Washington. And I remember one apartment scene between me and another actor. Otto had found an apartment that wasn't air-conditioned, and after they put the lights in there it was a hundred and forty degrees! The problem was to keep the two actors mopped down so that we didn't in a long take just start dripping right out of our hairline right down into our faces! We finally got the scene so you never see how hot we really were, but all of us were wringing wet!

Mike: You did a couple of films after that which were also concerned about government at a high level. *Fail Safe* in 1964 and *The Best Man* in 1964.

Fonda: *Best Man* was a good experience. That's one of the few pictures I've done that the director—and this was Franklin Schaffner —rehearsed. He had a producer that was understanding enough to agree it was all right, and we had two weeks of rehearsal, which made a lot of difference.

Mike: Your character could be identified with Adlai Stevenson, couldn't it?

Fonda: Well, he was when it was done in New York. The characters were variously identified as Adlai, as Richard Nixon, and as Harry Truman. I think the author, Gore Vidal, intended they would be. They weren't carbon copies. They weren't biographical, but they were closely patterned after those men. The man of integrity, the man with no integrity, and the old politician.

Mike: How did you like being directed by a fellow actor in *Sometimes a Great Notion* [Universal, 1971]? Paul Newman.

Fonda: Paul wound up directing it. It started with another young director. We rehearsed two weeks in Oregon. That kind of rehearsal was a little bit different than the rehearsals with Sidney Lumet and Frank Schaffner. We rehearsed in a high school auditorium just some of the dialogue scenes. We would rehearse in the mornings, and then we'd break for lunch, and then we'd go to one of the locations to learn how to handle a power saw or how to cut a giant tree down and handle the heavy equipment. Richard Jaeckel learned how to operate the crane. So that was not rehearsal in the sense of rehearsing a part, but we were getting a lot of background and color. Then we started shooting, and it turned out from the beginning that the director was so preoccupied with his camera that it was like "Screw the actors!" I mean that's an exaggeration, because I don't think he would ever think that. He was incredible with his camera. It was always something with the camera. He was zoom happy and crane happy. This is all right, but there's such a thing as characters and performance, too. If he had you doing something because the camera was better if you did it, rather than if it should come out of character, then that's when all actors would rebel. Paul rebelled and I rebelled. Paul, as the producer, would very often walk off in the woods with the director and talk for two or three hours, and everybody would just sit down. Eventually after about five weeks it got to be too much. I think Paul resisted the idea of firing the director because he felt in his bones he would then have to do it himself. Paul didn't want to have to wear the two hats of actor and director on the same film. He is a good director, but he's smart enough to know he shouldn't direct himself. He tried to get one of his friends like Paul Bogart or George Roy Hill to take over. But they, like any good director, said, "No, no. I'm not going to come up and take over in the middle." So Paul had to himself.

Paul is a good actor's director, being a good actor himself. He also knows how to handle a camera. But he learned—not that he had to learn—how tough it is to wear the two hats! I remember in one scene we were around the big long table in the kitchen where the family ate. Pa's at the head of the table, that's me, and Paul's next to me on one side, and the whole family is there. It's a long dialogue scene, and we rehearsed it for a long time because it was a good scene. Finally we were ready to shoot it. The scene starts, the dialogue is going, then suddenly it stops, and it's not the end of the scene! It was Paul's cue. He was wearing his director's hat, you see. He was watching the other performers, even though he was in the scene. And he's thinking in back of his head something like, "If I do another take, I'm going to ask her to sit over there, etc." Then, suddenly it's his cue, and there's silence, and he says, "Oh, shit!" Anyway, it's tough! He was directing the picture in spite of it. I don't think it was as good a film as it might have been. Not because of Paul. I felt they tampered with it in the cutting. They took scenes out of their original sequence and moved them into other sequences. Juggled scenes. I don't think they improved the film by playing with it. But they might have had a problem I wasn't aware of when they were putting the picture together. It was a fun old part to play for me, and I enjoyed it!

Mike: In sustaining your career so successfully have you paid special attention to working with the right people such as costars, cameramen, directors, and writers?

Fonda: No. Not consciously thinking that careerwise it would do me well to star with certain other stars. I'm about to turn down Elizabeth

Taylor as a wife in a picture. I suppose if you're career-minded, to play opposite her would be a good thing to do. But I don't like the part. Now this very afternoon they're going to deliver to me a new version of the script. Some rewrites. Maybe I'll change my mind! Anyway, no, I've never thought about my own cameraman. That's Marlene Dietrich. I don't mean to put her down, but if you're involved with camera angles, then you should have your own man. Especially if your career is "married" to one cameraman who has been very good for you. I wouldn't blame Marlene or Claudette or anybody else to work with the same cameraman. I'm not career-minded even in the sense of how long will it last. I guess my agents are. They're sure trying to persuade me to do this picture with Elizabeth!

Mike: Your first consideration, then, is wanting to play the part?

Fonda: Wanting to play it! Being excited! I said to my agent on the phone I didn't like it. He said, "Don't say no. Come in and talk about it." So the next day I went in, and we had a talk for about an hour. He said, "I feel strongly you should do this. There are a lot of reasons you should do it." He was giving it to me! Then I had to say, "Well, let me try to explain me to you. I just finished three weeks on a film for television at Universal." I don't do many of those. Not because they are just for television but because I don't like them, the scripts. But this one I liked. I said, "David, for three weeks I've had fun. I was home every night studying my scenes for the next day, and it's been exciting for me because the scenes were good. I knew that when I went to the set the next day and played a scene, the director was going to say, 'Son of a bitch!' And he did. You know it ahead of time. If it's a good scene, you can read it and right away know what you can do with it. In this picture with Elizabeth Taylor there's not one moment that I can think of myself as an actor who says to himself, 'Oh, boy! I see what I can do!' Or that anybody would say, 'Shit! Did you see Fonda in that? Goddamn, he was good!' " I said, "The most they would say is, 'He looks pretty good for sixty-five or however old he is.' 'Cause that's all the part is. He's described early in the script as the most handsome and distinguished man of his age, and he's been married to her for twenty-five years."

Mike: In cases like that do you suggest changes that would make the part more attractive to your accepting it?

Fonda: Only when I think a script *should* be changed. I said, "Look, I don't think this script needs to be changed. This guy shouldn't be any more than that. It's the story of Elizabeth's character who's going to Switzerland to have her face lifted because she figures she's lost her husband's love." She has her face lifted, and it's such a fantastic job that they don't know her in Switzerland where she convalesces and stays to live even after she's well. She looks like a young thirties. And there are young Italian sex boys who are flipping out for her. One of them seduces her. She's not unwilling. But when the husband comes, he's not in love with her anymore. He's got his chick back home! The husband character is nothing but a straight leading man. I said, "I paid my dues. I played those parts in stock years ago, and there's nothing to them. There's no challenge to the character at all. There's not a *scene*." I told them it wasn't necessary to change the script. Your sympathy and the story should be with her. Well, they are not buying that. They think there should be more to this man's character. I told them if they wanted to rewrite and go to that effort, I'd read it, but not to do it just for me.* On the other hand, there have been things I've wanted to do that I didn't think were polished enough writing and asked them to work on the script. There were two short scenes in *The Red Pony,* the television movie I just finished, which I felt could be improved. I had a meeting with the director and the producer, and they agreed absolutely. The scenes were rewritten and put right. I do that when I can. Yes.

Mike: Being an actor is certainly a creative outlet for you, but you are also considered one of the best, if not the best, painters in the film colony.

Fonda: Well, painting certainly is creative and that does fulfill something in me. I didn't even start till I was in my late forties. My first painting was when I started to sketch in pastel chalks when I was doing *Mister Roberts* on Broadway. So it was about 1949. I discovered very quickly what a great therapy it is. In the theater you have to live your life to be at your physical and emotional peak from eight thirty P.M. till eleven P.M. Those are not normal hours. A businessman is at his peak during the daylight hours. So you live a different life when you're in the theater. It's even different from an actor in films. You come off the stage at eleven o'clock, let's say, and you are very

---

* Mr. Fonda liked the rewrites of the script, *Ash Wednesday,* and will make the film. Following, he will make a film in Italy titled *My Name Is Nobody.*

charged up! It's usually one or two o'clock before you can go to sleep. So you sleep till ten or eleven in the morning. You have your breakfast. Then you have your second meal at five o'clock, so it's not too close to your performance time. Then you rest. At least I do. Sometimes I nap from about five thirty till seven. Then go to the theater. And after the theater you have your third meal, either at home or at a restaurant. Now I'm saying all that to say I've discovered I could come right home from the theater being charged up and have a light supper, and I could paint, and that charged-up feeling would shed off me like blankets falling off me. I would be onto a painting, and I couldn't wait to get home to work on it some more! I discovered the precise way I paint takes such concentration that it becomes therapy. It's creative and a joy to me to be able to do something that somebody admires, that somebody wants to buy, or that I can give to my friends and they are proud to own. That's a great joy.

Recently my friend Andrew Wyeth, who has seen some of my paintings, told this man from the Franklin Mint, "You ought to go see Fonda." This man was looking for what he calls celebrity painters, but they have to really be able to paint, not just be celebrities. The Franklin Mint wanted to reproduce and sell them to their exclusive mail-order list for a good deal of money. Anyway, this man came out here and bought a painting of mine for a hell of a lot of money and wants me to do one or two a year for them. This is a kick that somebody like that wants to pay a lot, lot, lot of money. I'm not quoting figures, but I've had paintings auctioned off at charities for fifteen hundred and two thousand dollars. It's a lot more than that! I'm still in shock.

Mike: Any other creative pastimes?

Fonda: I'm also an organic farmer. This isn't creative, but it is something inside me. I don't come from a farm. None of my background has prepared me to be a farmer. And I'm not a farmer in Bel Air in the strict sense! But I am a gardener. And I don't mean flowers. I mean vegetables. I'm an organic gardener and I have been for a long time. In my Brentwood house I had nine acres, and I did it on a much bigger scale than I'm able to do here. I make my own compost. That's why I have the chickens. And if I don't get enough from the chickens I go to a friend out in Malibu and bring back a big plastic garbage bag of good rotted horse's shit. I use it all over the place, and my vegetables are delicious and succulent. They're just great. I also have a workshop where I do not craftsmanship sort of things, but repair work. I even do my own plumbing and electricity when it's not so complicated that I have to call a plumber or electrician.

Mike: I read that as a boy you were a Boy Scout and were awarded about eighteen merit badges. I think that something like that does develop and prepare a person to carry a variety of interests through life.

Fonda: I'm sure. I think I got a lot of my interests from my father, too. Watching him. He had a workshop in the basement and was always tinkering.

Mike: Your offspring Jane and Peter are also talented people. Do you think that talent or creativity can be inherited?

Fonda: No. But I'm sure it "rubs off" some way. I don't know anything about creativity. When I say that, I'm probably trying to shuck any credit for anything. But I don't think it's inherited. There are too many sons and daughters of fine performers who wanted to follow in a parent's footsteps and fell on their asses. Didn't have it. As a father, when my kids decided that's what they wanted to do, I didn't try to discourage them or encourage them either. I'm aware of what pitfalls and heartbreaks there can be in the business. I didn't become a stage father. But I didn't have to hold my breath very long because they both showed they had talent and ability very early.

Mike: Being the elder by two years, Jane went into the profession before Peter did, I believe.

Fonda: No. Peter committed himself to an acting career first. When he was twelve, thirteen, and fourteen years old, he was in a boarding school, Fay School in Southborough, Massachusetts. They didn't have any drama group, but Peter organized one. He wrote, produced, built the sets, made the costumes, and played five parts! That's my boy! And from then on he was involved. When he got to the University of Omaha, he was in the drama group there. He did several roles. I went back to see him in *Harvey*. He played Jimmy Stewart's part. I was involved in something out here with Josh Logan and Leland Heyward. It might have been the film of *Mister Roberts*. Josh was like a godfather to both Peter and Jane, and Leland had been married to Margaret Sullavan, living a block from us, and his three children grew up with my three children. So, when I'm going off to see Peter in the play, they were curious. When I came back, they wanted to know what it was like. I said, "Well, I'll tell you! The Josephine Hull character—that's the sister role that Helen Hayes at one time played, too—that character would be about forty-eight years old, I suppose, not over fifty. I think the character of the family attorney would be fifty, maybe. In the prime of life, both of them, let's say. And the character Peter was playing should be that same age bracket. Now, they're being played by eighteen-, nineteen-, and twenty-year-old undergraduates at school! So the cast overcompensates for this difference in age. The girl who played the Josephine Hull part bent way over, and she only took tiny little steps. And if somebody was talking to her, she didn't just turn her head, she turned her whole body like she was arthritic. This is playing eighty-eight years old! This isn't forty-eight! The man that played the lawyer had a cane, and that cane was shaking in his hand all the time. And when he sat down, he carefully lowered himself into the chair. An old, old man." I said, "Peter didn't do anything like that." Now I don't know, 'cause I didn't ask him, if he didn't do it because he knew better or whether he didn't know what to do. Peter was just Peter, his own age. He got all his laughs. He was very funny. And I like to think he didn't play the older age because he knew better.

Now, in the meantime, Jane went through Emma Willard. Her last year at Emma Willard, I was asked to come back to Omaha, along with Dorothy McGuire, who had also started there, to do a play for the benefit of the playhouse for their building fund for their new theater. In February of 1955, Dorothy and I decided we would go back in July and do *The Country Girl.* Along about June, my sister Harriet, who was involved with the playhouse, called me and said, "We've got everybody cast except for the little ingenue. I've got a great idea. Why doesn't Jane play it?" I said, "Oh, Harriet, Jane isn't interested. And I'd be so worried whether Jane fell on her face, and I'm going to have all my worries to get up in this part in the nine days of rehearsal." She said, "Oh, relax, for Christ's sake. I'll worry about Jane. You worry about yourself." I said, "Well, you can ask her." So Harriet called Jane, and Jane said, "Sure, it sounds like fun!" So we went up to her graduation, after which she and I flew to Omaha to start rehearsals. I can only tell you she was absolutely delightful in a very small part. She was very real. Nothing self-conscious or amateur in any way. It was just like she was born to it. It was natural. She was on television to be interviewed for publicity . . . I don't do those things, so I sat home watching this girl. She was totally at ease, articulate, a good conversationalist, but when it was all over, that was it. She'd had fun, but she had no ambition to be an actress. Another year or so, when Jane was at Vassar and after I had just done *Twelve Angry Men,* we took a house for the summer on Cape Cod. Jane, it turns out, was excited about going there. I didn't know why, but it was because she had met a young man from Yale who was to be stage manager for the summer at the Cape Playhouse at Dennis. Now this playhouse is where I started, when I first went East, the apple-cheeked boy from Nebraska. That was in 1928, and now we're in 1958, thirty years later! Jane said, "I think I'd like to join the apprentice group at the theater!" She meant she would be closer to her boyfriend more than she meant she would be interested in learning to act. Anyway, she did join the apprentice group, and some character actress from New York coached these people, who paid three hundred dollars each to go to the school. It's a big racket! They did one performance just one afternoon. A Restoration comedy. Imagine amateurs doing Restoration comedy! Jane played a small part of a maid. We went, and when she made her entrance, nobody knew who she was; but you could feel the audience reaction, through just an intake of breath or a little movement, to the presence this girl had. As the maid with a little apron and saying madam this or madam that, that's all. But that girl walked on with a presence! Now that's something you don't inherit, but you are *born* with it. You don't learn it. You don't learn charisma, presence, the electricity, the chemistry, or whatever the words are to describe what some people have that other people don't have. She had it. There was no question about that!

Now, later in the season, the producers of the theater persuaded me to come do *The Male Animal.* I said, "Shit, fellows, I'm on vacation." But they were persuasive, and I finally said okay. Actually, I thought it would be fun because I had done the movie but I had never done the play. Then they said, "Why doesn't Jane play the little ingenue part?" I said, "I don't think that's very fair because she's not really that ambitious to be an actress. At least she doesn't sound to me like it. And I know there are some professional actresses in this company who would like to play that part." They said, "Don't you worry. The best girl will get the part. We'll have an audition." Jane got the part. Well, again, she was absolutely charming, absolutely natural and wonderful. And I remember thinking, but I never said it to her, "God, if she ever does decide she wants to be an actress, she's gonna do all right 'cause she's got it! She's got the looks, the presence, the charm, and everything else!" But when that play was over, again, no interest to take up acting professionally. She and the young man were engaged by this time, and he didn't want her to be an actress. He was going to be a writer. This was "Goey" Franciscus, James Franciscus, who later became an actor that we know who he is. Anyway, that's who she got engaged to, but it didn't last very long. She decided she didn't want to finish Vassar and told me she'd like to go to the Sorbonne. You don't go to the Sorbonne just because you want to. You have to be a graduate or an exchange student or something. So she couldn't get in the Sorbonne. But she was hot to go to school in Paris, anyway. By this time she wanted to study art. I thought, "How wonderful! God, imagine if my father had been able to send me to Paris, if I'd wanted to go to Paris, when I was that age! I can afford to. I think that's wonderful." So I made it possible, and she went to Paris to the Beaux Arts for one semester, but it didn't work out. It wasn't what she was looking for. She came home Christmastime and didn't go back. She became a kind of butterfly in New York, going to parties. And she was on the cover of magazines because she was Jane *Fonda*. I mean *Vogue* and *Harper's Bazaar* and that kind of thing. From that she began to get modeling jobs. But as Jane *Fonda*. She wasn't an unknown model. She was Jane *Fonda* modeling for a photographer and getting paid for it. Then we were out here one summer because I was doing some picture, and we rented a house in Malibu. Down the beach were Lee Strasberg, his wife and his kids, Susan and John. John was about Peter's age, and Susan was Jane's age. And we used to go down there for barbecues, and they'd come up to our house for barbecues. We were seeing a lot of each other during the summer. I didn't know that Jane was lying on the beach with Susan and some other young actor listening to them talk about acting, but she was. And at the end of the summer she said, "Dad, I think I'd like to study with Mr. Strasberg." That was the first indication, and she was already out of college.

So Peter started working toward a career first, and he did *Blood, Sweat and Stanley Poole* on Broadway in 1961. Jane's start was a tentative one. My guess is she didn't want to commit herself totally. She wanted to be able to turn away from it if she found she wasn't any good or didn't like it. She started studying with Strasberg in his private classes. Eventually she did get excited. Words were said that made sense to her, and she auditioned and was accepted at the Actors Studio. Then Josh Logan was going to do the movie *Tall Story* [Warner's, 1960]. Of course he already knew Jane and that she was a young girl thinking seriously about acting. That was the first large-scale professional thing she did.

Mike: After all these successful years in films and in the theater do you still call the theater your first love?

Fonda: I love them both, but one of the great advantages I love about the theater is that it gives you the chance to rehearse and know what you're going to do. You don't get that in the film medium. We saw the film version of *Sleuth* [Fox, 1972] the other day and Laurence Olivier's performance is really something incredible! It may be out of proportion to what the play deserves, but that's beside the point. Even Olivier, as great as he is, couldn't have given that performance in the way films are usually produced. The usual procedure for a film is that you are given a script and you say, "Yes, I will do that." You make your deal, and eventually the assistant director telephones you and says, "We're going to start tomorrow morning on stage nine with scenes forty-four and forty-five." You go to the set and rehearse scenes forty-four and forty-five with the director for an hour. Maybe fifteen minutes. Maybe two hours. But whatever, that scene is shot that morning, usually that morning, and goes to the laboratory, and that's your performance! Locked in! Before filming *Sleuth* they rehearsed six or seven weeks, and it shows! I saw Michael Caine, Olivier's costar, the other night, and we were talking about it. It's such a joy to be able to do that. It makes such a difference! In my eighty-odd films I've had only five where I had a chance to rehearse. Three with Sidney Lumet, who always rehearses at least three weeks. And *The Best Man,* which we rehearsed for two weeks. And *Sometimes a Great Notion* with Paul Newman, which we rehearsed for two weeks. It always pays off in performance, in production, in every way. You can go faster. The director knows. The cameraman knows. Everybody knows.

Mike: What is your opinion of the new technique they have developed to shoot on video tape and then transfer it to film?

Fonda: Well, I'm only aware of video tape as it's been used in some television specials that I've done. I'm not aware of any difference. It's a mechanical thing that doesn't affect an actor. The only thing that's a little different is you play longer scenes. You're not limited to the footage of film in a camera, a thousand-foot roll of film. With television you can play a half hour scene if you want to.

Mike: That's an advantage for the actor, don't you think?

Fonda: It is! Oh, yes. Just the advantage of playing longer scenes. Of course it is. It's not broken up. The disadvantage of television is the small amount of rehearsal. Well, I've had one television experience that wasn't bad. I did *The Petrified Forest* with Betty [Lauren] Bacall and Humphrey Bogart. It was in the old days when it was live. It wasn't on tape. We rehearsed for three weeks, which is a fair amount of rehearsal. We could have gone onto a stage and performed it on a stage. Instead, we performed it for cameras, and it was put out live on the air. It was like a good play, and it got good reaction. I remember Bogart had not worked in television before. He said, "God, this is fun going through rehearsals! Is it always like this?" And I said, "No, it ain't always like this, Bogey!"

Mike: Now that they can transfer tape to thirty-five mm film electronically—

Fonda: I've heard this is so.

Mike: It seems it's the coming thing.

Fonda: They're beginning to think about doing it for feature films, you mean?

Mike: Yes.

Fonda: Well, if it's going to cost less, that would be the thing that would make producers decide to use it. It would necessitate rehearsals because you couldn't do half hour scenes or full acts on tape without a lot of rehearsal. One of the reasons you do films and TV now with such little rehearsal is that you only do thirty-second or one-minute scenes. If it's longer than a minute, it's so long that they write it up in a column! You know, "They did a two-minute scene over at Warner Brothers yesterday! The crew all applauded!"

February 1–6, 1973

The Leading Lady

ROSALIND RUSSELL

Mike: I understand you are from a professional family, that your father was a lawyer and your mother was also a professional.

Russell: It's true my father was a lawyer, but my mother was a professional only to the extent that she was a schoolteacher. Like my sisters and I she was graduated from the Notre Dame Academy, the convent, in my hometown of Waterbury, Connecticut, and taught two or three years in a private school for young women before marrying my father at the age of twenty-two.

Mike: So she probably had a love for the arts, being a teacher.

Russell: Yes. I am one of seven children, Mike. There were three younger than I and three older than I. I always call myself the ham in the sandwich. Although my parents loved the theater, they were rather shocked at the idea of my entering it because in those days it was still thought that women of the theater were rather on the shady side. My reason for entering the theater is that my father drew a quite unusual will. He became a heart case when he was in his late fifties and knew he was leaving these seven children in the care of my mother, who was thirteen years younger than he. Father died at age sixty-three. His will read that all of us would be supported while getting our education, but once we were out of school, we had to go to work for three years without income from his estate. We were not rich people, but we were very comfortable people. He was afraid we might stop being educated, and like most people of that era, education to him was a very important thing. So after his demise in my last year at Marymount College, I had to go to work or go on being educated. I always tell the story that I have one sister who went to school until she was thirty-five. She took crewel, and she learned sewing. She did anything. Finally, I said, "What on earth are you taking now?" She said, "I'm taking smiling lessons!" and roared with laughter.

I was graduated in the Depression, so what on earth could I do? I was equipped to teach school only. This paid very, very little in those days, and I didn't care for the idea anyway. It didn't have enough glamor for me. I said, "Oh, the theater! That's it! Actresses make a great deal of money." So I went to my mother and said I wanted to go to the American Academy of Dramatic Arts in New York. She said, "What are you going to do there?" I said, "I'm going to learn to teach dramatic art," which she liked very much because I had been in lots of plays in school. I was always in the plays because you could cut classes. From the time I was a freshman I found out that was a great racket. Once I was in *La Bohème.* Now, if you know anything about my voice, you know that was pretty horrendous. I think I emptied the hall when I was doing that. Anyway, I went to the American Academy, and the day I was graduated my mother and aunt were there. The graduation was held on the stage of the Lyceum Theater. Eddie Robinson made the address. Then, while getting our wraps backstage, a man came up and said, "Miss Russell, I am from a stock company in Greenwich, Connecticut, and I would like you to join our company this summer." I was so stunned I didn't know what to do. I hesitated and thought, "What do you say in business?" So, I said, "Well, how much do you pay?" That's the way you go about this. He said they paid one hundred and fifty a week. It was more money than I had ever hoped to make, and remember, this is the Depression. I was so staggered by the amount that, again, I didn't know what to do. I thought, "In business you always bargain." So I said, "I don't think that's enough." At that, this gentleman, whom I have never seen since, backed out of the room staring at me. That taught me a great lesson. My mother gave a little tea for me after graduation, and she went around the room telling all her friends, "Rosalind was offered a job! A man was there who offered her a hundred and fifty dollars a week to act in the professional theater!" From that I knew she wouldn't be too upset if I went to work in the theater. Then we went on a little trip to Bermuda. When we came back, I remained in New York to get a job. I was there five days when my mother called me up and said, "Now, Rosalind, it should be obvious to you by now that you are not wanted in the theater. I think you had better come home." Funny thing, I got a job the next day!

Mike: Your first professional work did turn out to be in stock, didn't it?

Russell: Yes, in Saranac Lake, New York, where we did two plays a week and I played the leads. How I ever learned all those lines I'll never know, but it taught me to be a quick study.

Mike: Then you soon got to Broadway itself.

Russell: Yes. My first play, I believe, was either *Talent* or *Company's Coming,* both of which were disastrous. *Company's Coming,* I think, ran two weeks. Frieda Inescort starred in that. *Talent,* starring Mady Christians, never did open, but we had some dress rehearsals with audiences, previews we call them, at the John Golden Theater. So, actually, my first real Broadway appearance was in 1931 in *Company's Coming.* Then I did *The Garrick Gaieties* for the Theatre Guild, the last one they did, and the only one they did uptown because it was a potpourri of all *The Garrick Gaieties* that had ever been done. I went in it to do sketches, not to sing or dance, but I wound up doing both, if you will pardon the expression. Particularly with the singing! We played ten performances, and then we went on the road. In those days, the Theatre Guild had difficulties in fulfilling their commitments on the road for their subscribers. Their subscription was very important to them. They had shows touring like *A Month in the Country* and *Green Grow the Lilacs,* which later became the musical *Oklahoma!*

Then I went to work for a producing outfit called Wee-Leventhal which, as all actors know, paid the least money of any organization that ever existed. Wee was a Scotsman, a very tall, skinny man, and Mr. Leventhal was of the Jewish faith, small, but very nice. I refused to work for minimum. I had gotten quite a fancy sum of money from the Theatre Guild and was very impressed by that. So I said, "No. I just can't do it." They gave me five dollars more, and I said all right! I just wasn't going to work for scale which was nothing at all in those days. Wee-Leventhal sent out plays on what they called the subway circuit, but when they said subway circuit, it really wasn't too accurate because you also played places like Newark, and Philadelphia, and Baltimore, and as far as Washington. I did two plays for them. One was a mystery, and while I was in it, I was seen by a movie talent scout. This man from Universal came across the river to Newark and looked at the talent.

Mike: I read two conflicting biographies on you, Roz. One said you were brought to Hollywood by Metro-Goldwyn-Mayer, but the other said you were first under contract to Universal, so let's clear that up.

Russell: Well, what happened was I made a rule when I first went into the theater that I would answer all calls from the agencies whether I was working or not. So, after the talent scout had seen me in Newark, I got a call from the Chamberlain Agency to go to the Universal offices, which were in Radio City. I thought, "Oh, I won't go there." But I was walking with another actor, talking as much as I'm talking now, and I talked so much that I got in the elevator with him. Up we went. Just as the elevator door opened, I heard, "Miss Russell, please. Miss Rosalind Russell, please." I wasn't going in there, but when I heard my name, I said, "Pardon me," and stepped out into a sea of actors that were waiting to be interviewed, and I went in. They offered me a contract, but again, they didn't offer me very much money. By this time I was making a bit of a name. I said, "No, no, no, no. I won't go to Hollywood for that little, but I'll tell you what I'll do. You can send me to Hollywood. I will test for two weeks, and you will pay my expenses at the hotel and my fare out and one hundred dollars a test, and you will have an option on me, and then you will pay me the sum that I want." So that is how I came out here, but I never did appear in front of a camera for Universal. In the meantime, I went to live with a dear friend of mine, a girl I had known in stock. I had played stock in Worcester, Massachusetts, and lovely places like that in between other engagements. So I was staying in a hotel in Hollywood and my girlfriend said, "You can't live at the hotel. Come up and live with us." She and her husband lived up on the La Brea Terrace. I moved in. She was still an actress, and she came home one evening and said, "Roz, there is a part at Metro they tested me for, and I told them I was all wrong for it but that I had a friend who was perfect for it. Her name is Roz Russell, and she is out here. So they said to send you over, and they will test you!"

Mike: You were out of your Universal contract?

Russell: No. I was still very much in it! I said to my friend, "I've heard at Universal that they are going to take up my option for seven years. I can't do that. I can't bear to stay there." I didn't know what to do. Metro made the test and said they wanted to sign me! How was I to get out of this seven years that were going to come up? At that time Mr. Carl Laemmle, Jr., was running Universal, not his father. We called around about him, and all we heard was that he liked attractive women. So we sat up all night planning, and I got inspired. I went over the next day to meet Mr. Laemmle, who had never seen me. He had been in Europe. I wore a red print dress. I can see it now. It was a good dress, but it was not the most becoming on me. It had a boatline neck. I was very skinny, and I let my collarbones show. I wore some white shoes that were not clean, I had a white linen hat that was wrinkled, and I had lipstick that was caking in the corners of my mouth. And I had nice gloves. The outfit wasn't comical, but it was really pretty sexless. And I wore a very tight bra which I didn't need, being sunken-chested. Mr. Laemmle was very polite, but I couldn't look at him. He said, "You're the young actress from New York." I said in a nasal voice, "I'm very unhappy here." He said, "Pardon me?" I said, "I'm just very unhappy here." He said, "I hope no one has mistreated you." I said, "No. No. I'm just very unhappy here, and I want to go back to New York." This went on for about ten minutes, and he said, "Well, I think we can arrange for you to go back." I said, "I want to go back, and I need a piece of paper to tell me I can go." There was an agent named Al Melnick sitting outside who knew me from New York. He couldn't get over the way I looked and was acting. He kept saying, "How are you, Roz?" I would only reply a quick, "I'm fine." It was a riot. So within about ten minutes I got a release and went to Metro. Oh, dear! The part I had tested for at MGM was actually in a film starring Helen Hayes, and they didn't put me in it in the long run.

Mike: But you did sign with them?

Russell: Yes, in 1934 and they put me right away into *Evelyn Prentice*.

Mike: With William Powell and Myrna Loy.

Russell: Yes. That was my first film. The second one was *The President Vanishes*. It was a loan-out to Paramount. I was loaned out a great deal. I played featured roles and was able to do three pictures at one time. I asked not to play leads yet because I wanted to learn the technique of filmmaking and of my work. I played the second woman from about nine months to a year. I played the love competition to Myrna Loy or Jean Harlow, which was always a laugh. Clark Gable would go for me for ten minutes, then run right back to Jean Harlow. I wasn't very convincing in those parts because I was always very lofty, very "Lady Mary." I had lines like: "What can you see in that girl? Dear me. She seems so vulgar."

Mike: One of the films you made with Jean Harlow and Clark Gable was *China Seas*, in 1935.

Russell: Yes, it's a classic. Again, I was very British. I came from jolly old London and went out to the wilds of China. In the picture Clark asks Jean, "Why don't you like her?" whatever my name was, and Jean says, "I don't know. She's just so 'refeened.' " It's a pronunciation I've used ever since. I'll say, "She's one of the 'refeened' types." I don't even know anymore that I'm saying it.

Jean and I became very good friends. I made three pictures with her. No one would believe that she would rather have not been a picture star. She wanted to get married and have the "chillens," but she had a mother and stepfather who had other ideas. They wanted her to have a career, and, of course, she was having a great glamorous one at the time. She was always a sweet person, childlike almost, but I think she was rather unhappy under it all.

Mike: What was the first film in which you had the lead?

Russell: *Craig's Wife*, another loan-out to Columbia in 1936, with John Boles and Billie Burke. It was from a George Kelly play. In 1950 Joan Crawford did it as *Harriet Craig*.

Mike: What film do you think made you a star?

Russell: That's easy. *The Women*, made from the Clare Boothe Luce play in 1939.

Mike: That did it for quite a few, didn't it?

Russell: I think I really won the brass ring there! *The Women* had thirty-five speaking parts. The two lead parts were played by established stars, Norma Shearer and Joan Crawford. I had the third part, but really the best part, of Sylvia Fowler. And then all the others, Paulette Goddard, Joan Fontaine, Mary Boland, from whom we bought this house, Phyllis Povah, Hedda Hopper. It's endless! Later *Rebecca* was the picture that made Joan Fontaine, did for her what *The Women* did for me.

Mike: George Cukor directed *The Women*. Had you worked with him before?

Russell: Indeed not.

Mike: It was probably an ambition to work with him, though.

Russell: He didn't want me in the part. He didn't know me. But he was marvelous. George I'm very fond of, an old and dear and very precious friend. But they had engaged Miss Chase, Ilka Chase, who had played it in New York. I couldn't understand why I wasn't tested. I had never played comedy for Metro or for anyone. I had just finished a drama, *Night Must Fall*, with Robert Montgomery. Hunt Stromberg produced that, and he was going to produce *The Women*. So I went to Elizabeth Arden one day and I came out in a rather red hat. Dolled up, you know. I drove to the studio. It was about five in the afternoon. I knew Hunt, and I went up to his office and said, "Hunt, tell me. Why haven't you tested me for the part of Sylvia? Why haven't you considered me at all for it?" Well, I don't want you to drop dead at what he said, but I am going to tell you. He said, "We considered you, but you are too beautiful." I said, "Well, now, Hunt, just a minute. Oh, darn it. I don't have any witnesses and, darn it, no recording equipment, but would you say that again?" He said, "Yes. You are too beautiful." I said, "Now, Hunt, that is ridiculous. Just ridiculous." He said, "What we want is somebody to look funny." So I crossed my eyes and said, "Will this do? If not, I'll go down to the makeup people and come back with a wart!" He said, "We would like to get a laugh every time she pokes her head around a door. You are a very fine dramatic actress, but you are not a comedienne." I said, "Ah, ah, ah, ah, ah, you cannot say that. No decisions can be made like that until I've played comedy. Then you might say 'you don't make me laugh.' That is your privilege. And the same about the sex appeal. Until I've played a love scene, don't say whether or not I have sex appeal. I might play a love scene that will send you. You don't know. But after I do one, you can say, 'I'm sorry, Roz, you leave me cold. Nice girl, but you just leave me cold.' " We laughed and had a friendly chat, and I went home. As I came into my house, the phone was ringing. It was Hunt and he said, "Roz, I want you to come and make the test." I must say, my first words were, "What about Miss Chase?" He sharply replied, "You haven't got the part yet." But he said, "Her contract isn't exclusive for this part alone. She'll get something else, if and when, but. . . ." So they sent a Red Arrow delivery boy with the script.

The next day I went to the studio to see the director, George Cukor. He was very honest. He said, "I don't want you. I don't see you in this part, although I appreciate your work. They have asked me to test you, however, so we are going down on the set and work." We went to the set, and he was an entirely different person. He gave his all to directing me. I asked how much film was in the camera, and whatever they answered, I said, "Would you mind putting in a full load, a full one thousand feet? I would like to try to do this in two or three different ways." I had to do the scene alone. I got something from wardrobe with fringe on it and a crazy hat and came in doing the scene. I did it first in high comedy, what we call drawing room comedy, and finally I did it in a very exaggerated way. The next day they called me. I could hear them laughing in the projection room. Hunt said, "Roz, you have this part." I said, "Oh! That's great!"

We had to start quite soon. Adrian made the clothes, and on we went! The first day I started to play it in a certain way, and Cukor took me aside and said, "No, no, no. You're not doing it right. I want you to play it like you tested. Right out. Way out." I said, "George, oh, what will the critics say?" He said a thing to me I never forgot. He said, "You know, you have a very big audience at the Plaza Theater in New York," which was considered a tiny little theater, "but in Waukegan they've never heard of you. Now you do as I tell you and play it that way." Then he explained why. He said, "Don't be the heavy in this piece. You must be a woman who makes trouble, but you must do it with humor. Otherwise, when you break up the marriage with a child involved, you are a real villainess. Don't do that. You'll throw this thing off-balance. I want you to do it that exaggerated way you did in the test." George was an enormous help. He changed my career. No question that I owe it to George. He has wonderful insight into women. He had me doing things that frightened me at times. For instance, there was a powder room scene, sort of an El Morocco powder room. There were many women in the powder room. George said to me. "Now, when all those other women leave, I want you to examine your teeth." I said, "What?" He said, "Yeah. I want you to look at your teeth in the mirror, then put your lipstick on and take your finger and spread it all over your mouth." I said, "George! You have been peeping!" He said, "I know when women make up in front of other women, they do it rather daintily, but when you are alone, you do do those things." He gave you wonderful pieces of business.

Mike: George has the distinction of being known as just about the best woman's director there is.

Russell: Oh, many men have been very successful under his direction, too. He worked with one fine male actor many times, and he made him look great, and his name was Spencer Tracy!

Mike: Right away, when *The Women* was successful, you became a light comedy star.

Russell: Yes, I was immediately loaned out to Columbia for another comedy, *His Girl Friday*, with Cary Grant, based on the hit play *Front Page*. During that picture, Cary introduced me to an agent named

Frederick Brisson, a charming Danish-English friend of his who was to become my husband. My one and only! Meantime, I was given such good parts with very good people, and I was happy doing comedy because I personally love to laugh. There is a great feeling to make others laugh. You sort of get paid per line, as it were, if you get the laughs.

Mike: About this time you got into your career women era.

Russell: Yes. Those parts went on and on! I played twenty-three different career women. If you need an operation, I am capable, you know! I have played a doctor, a psychologist, a newspaperwoman, a nurse, a head of an advertising firm, an actress, a professional pilot, a lady judge, and so on. I always say those pictures were remade with Doris Day where they could get a little more sex into them than we were allowed. And a song or two.

Mike: Most of your career woman pictures were made at Columbia, right?

Russell: Right. I had the same office set in I don't know how many pictures! Ten or fifteen! The same cameraman, Joe Walker, and the same propman named Blackie. The opening shot was always an air shot over New York. Then it would bleed into my suite of offices on the fortieth floor of Radio City. I would have the same desk and the same side chairs and bookcase. Out the window behind me was always a view of the Empire State Building, in order to identify the setting. I used to say to Joe Walker, "Joe, where was the Empire State Building in the last picture?" which had only been a couple of months before. He would say, "I had it a little to the left." I'd say, "Well, this time throw it over on the right." Then I would say, "Blackie, how many telephones did we have last time?" He'd say, "You had about nine." So I'd say, "Well, throw in thirteen. This will be a big double *A* picture!" I would always open with about the same dialogue, give a lot of cheap orders.

During this era, I was invited to give a speech in San Francisco at the Business Women of America convention. They had about six million members. It was held at the Cow Palace. The night before there was a small banquet at which I was very impressed by the deans of colleges, women judges, and a remarkable group of executives to whom I had to make my talk. I was as nervous as I could be. I thought, "Well, for heaven's sake, say something you know a little about instead of trying to get into an area about which you know nothing." Believe me, there is a plethora of those! So I thought, "Well, I'll talk about the career women I've played since these *are* career women." I said, "You go to nice offices, but I have one that's on the fortieth floor of the Radio City Music Hall Building! How many phones do you have? Two, three, four? I have twelve! And, I have an all-male staff who sit there as I give my orders. Fred MacMurray has been sitting there all that time with his hat down over his eyes. I spot him and say, 'Have you been listening to this meeting? Who are you?' He says, 'I'm from the press.' Then I go out to have lunch with him. Then we go to my penthouse. I never do get back to the office. He says to me, 'You're really a wonderful woman underneath all this brashness, this executive ability of yours.' I sort of push him aside, and then I go to Europe. Get on the boat. That's the next place I go. I also go, later on, to my resort home, which is in the Adirondacks or Southampton. Finally, I settle down in a mosquito-ridden cottage with Fred MacMurray or Ray Milland in New Jersey. I don't know why you women work the way you do because. . . ." I gave them plenty of laughs because I had played the Hollywood version of many of those present.

Mike: When you married Frederick Brisson in 1941, your own career was not interrupted?

Russell: Well, it made a great difference in my planning of my life. Although Metro wanted me to sign another long-term contract, I said no. I wanted to free-lance because I wanted to have a family. I sure failed there with only one son, but a larger family was our intention. When a professional woman such as myself marries, you have to make the decision whether your marriage and family is first or second. My decision was that my family would come first regardless.

Mike: In your case doesn't being married to someone in the industry, a stage and film producer, make it easier to understand each other's careers?

Russell: I think so. I never understood people saying they were incompatible because their careers clashed. I would think two people in the theater would understand each other's moods and the demands made on one. For instance, an actor and an actress. Why should she be jealous of her husband? She certainly can't play the part he is offered. But they say a certain amount of friction or jealousy enters show business marriages because one becomes more popular than the other or something like that. Well, that might happen if your career comes first. Doesn't matter if it isn't first.

Mike: Did you have some special design in building your career, like the type parts you wanted to play?

Russell: The only design I ever had was to do a variety of work in order to become better at what I was doing. There is a tremendous amount of dissatisfaction with your work when you see yourself on the screen. In doing stage work it is probably a blessing that you are unable to see and hear yourself, but film is another story. I would see myself and be horror-stricken that I would make so many faces and gestures. My eyes would flash around in my head, and I used my hands constantly. I think anybody with whom I've worked—and there have been hundreds of people—would admit I worked very, very hard. I am totally devoted to my work and, I hope, extremely professional. I never did say I wanted to be this or that kind of actress or that I wanted to play Mary, Queen of Scots, the Queen of the Nile, a Shakespearean character, or anything else. My career, before and during World War II, kind of went along on its own. Of course, there is the transition of going from a leading woman in your twenties into your thirties and forties. This, luckily for me, was not too difficult because I have always felt that I am a character actress.

Mike: Shortly after World War II, there was a decline in studio production, and television started becoming a threat. This brought about the first real venture into the independent production companies. You were one of the first stars to form your own company with your husband and Dudley Nichols, the director.

Russell: That's true. We had a company for a short while called Independent Artists, Inc. The most famous of these companies, however, was Liberty Films made up of three or four excellent directors. It was not very successful either. I was always heartsick about that. I was a great believer in the independent companies because my theory on what has happened to the industry is that it didn't reinvest itself with its talent. We didn't train others. Most industries make certain that they broaden, that they do more research and learn more. They gamble now and then. This did not happen in the movie industry, and we are paying for it now. Rather than take television, for instance, to our bosoms, they did everything to ignore television. Every contract was drawn so that you couldn't go on television. "Don't go near it. It's demeaning." Instead of saying, "Let's investigate this and make it worthwhile. Let's see if we can get it on film." These are our mistakes. And often, yes, putting relatives in jobs you knew they didn't belong in. Jobs they were not capable of handling. Putting them in a job without their learning the business. The men who were good at filmmaking usually came up from the bottom, from the prop department, cutting rooms and so forth. You can't take some young man because he is related to the head of the studio and have him producing pictures. It doesn't necessarily make him a filmmaker to give him a cast, a script, and a bundle of money.

Mike: So, as has been said, "The industry today is permeated by people who are deal makers, but are not filmmakers."

Russell: Yes. We should have been training our successors all along. You see them now coming out of colleges and universities.

Mike: Perhaps the industry didn't want to train new people because they would then have a threat to their jobs. Too much competition, and a danger of being replaced. Remember the Bette Davis film *All About Eve* which dealt, in part, with that subject?

Russell: I personally think competition is healthy and that there is room for everyone with talent. I never worried about Jean Harlow, we'll say. You only might worry about someone who could get a part you were right for and could play it better than you could. Carole Lombard could make me pretty nervous! She was a brilliant comedienne and far more beautiful than I. Other big stars, say Mae West, I didn't need to worry about. There's room. Especially when they were making fifty-two pictures a year to fill the theaters.

Mike: Most of your early career you were identified with comedy, but in 1947 you made the highly dramatic film *Mourning Becomes Electra*. That was quite a switch for you and a challenge.

Russell: Well, that happened at RKO after I made *Sister Kenny* there. That is, it was, in a way, a result of my doing *Sister Kenny,* which took me four or five years to get made. I had met Sister Kenny and wanted very much to help this woman. I had been to Minneapolis and stayed with her, and she had stayed in my guesthouse here in Beverly Hills when she came out to work in the various children's wards of local hospitals. I became enamored of her and admired all she was doing. She did enough, believe me, to bring about the Salk vaccine. She took this disease, poliomyelitis, and rattled it around until something was done about it. Every good doctor, orthopedic doctor, admits that. I finally got Dudley Nichols to direct me in a film on her life. Dudley and I became very great friends. This was a man I so admired. He had a wonderful mind and great humor and style in his writing and directing. After we finished the picture, he, too, fell in love with Sister Kenny. He went to Minneapolis, saw the treatments. She had been through two ghastly epidemics there which included over four thousand sick children each time!

Then Dudley called me one day and said, "Now that I've done that for you, I want you to do something for me." I said, "What is it?" He said, "It's *Mourning Becomes Electra*." I said, "Ohhhh, Dudley, I don't know." I wanted to do a comedy but of course, I said I would do it. I actually thought I should be playing the mother, but he wouldn't hear of it. He said I wasn't quite old enough at that time, but still and all I had never had trouble looking older in other parts. However, I played the daughter, Lavinia. When the picture was released, audiences were not ready for this drama, this Greek-like tragedy really. Dudley was absolutely devoted to Eugene O'Neill and refused to cut or change anything that would mar this great writer's great work. So the picture became very lengthy. Now I do believe it is a classic. I was sorry Dudley didn't live to see its acceptance, but he knew. He felt it in his heart. He had said, "Someday they will appreciate this picture." Michael Redgrave, now Sir Michael, was a joy to work with in that.

Mike: In the early fifties, the fact that still fewer films were being made began affecting everyone's careers quite seriously. Even Marilyn Monroe left Hollywood and went to New York to study at the Actors Studio, try to become a better actress, and try to get into a Broadway play. She became close friends with theatrical giants like Elia Kazan, Tennessee Williams, and Arther Miller, later her husband, but no play materialized. You yourself also made the wise choice of again associating with the Broadway theater.

Russell: Well, that all came about through the very reason you mentioned. I was not in demand as a movie actress. *Mourning Becomes Electra* had not been successful, nor was *Sister Kenny* the most popular picture ever made. I was walking around the block with my husband. We were talking, and I said, "You know, I can't have the heads of the five or six studios out here making decisions for my life. I must remain in charge of my career." Freddie said, "What are you talking about?" I said, "I am going to leave Hollywood and go back into the theater. I have to find out if I have an audience and if I can act. It is the only way I can do it." He said, "When are you going to do this?" I said, "What's today?" He said, "Saturday." I said, "I'll go Monday!" I packed my bags and went! Some play manuscripts were sent to me right away. *Bell, Book and Candle* was sent to me for the possibility of a road tour. I said, "I'll do it." My agent and everybody called and said, "You're not going to be a road actress!" And they quoted names of slipping stars, which I won't do now. "You won't do like so-and-so and so-and-so!" I said, "I *will* do like so-and-so. I am going to find out." I stayed exactly sixteen weeks on the tour. It was a smash. I learned a great deal from it, learned the feel of a live audience again, and reworked my timing, my listening, my concentration, and so on. Then I was ready to do the musical *Wonderful Town* on Broadway.

Mike: Which was based on the play *My Sister Eileen,* which you had done as a movie at Columbia in 1942 with Janet Blair and Brian Aherne.

Russell: Yes. I was scared to death at the thought of getting up on the stage and singing and dancing, but I am so happy I did it. Freddie thought I was quite mad. He said, "What are you doing?" I said, "If I am ever going to do a musical, I am going to do it now." He was a little worried about the appeal of the story line, but I would hate to think of the television series, short stories, and even some longer stories which have been based on the idea of two girlfriends, one of whom can't get a man and the other one can. You really have the edge if you are playing the one who can't, as I was. Everybody pulls for you.

Mike: Just after you wound up your very successful run in *Wonderful Town,* Carol Channing having gone into the part for you, you made another quite unusual decision: In 1955 you took a supporting role in a movie—the part of the schoolteacher, Rosemary, in *Picnic,* based on the award-winning play by William Inge. Incidentally, Marilyn Monroe also made her return to movies in another William Inge hit play, *Bus Stop,* around that time!

Russell: Yes. Both films were directed by Joshua Logan. I loved doing *Picnic.*

Mike: Since it was not a leading part, I remember people in our business were impressed and surprised you would accept it. You wanted to do it because it was such a marvelous acting part in a very important movie.

Russell: Oh, yes. It was done right in this room. Josh Logan came to see me and he didn't get . . . *nic* out. He said, "Roz, would you like to play Rosemary in *Pic—*" I said, "Yessss!" He said, "Wait a minute. Maybe you wouldn't. You know it isn't the lead." I said, "I'm going to do it!" I was very flattered that he would see me as an old maid schoolteacher in Kansas. I had been playing those Park Avenue dames for so many years. Bill Inge had sisters who were schoolteachers. That helped him in writing about Rosemary so perceptively.

Mike: Bill Inge told me he liked your performance very much.

Russell: How nice! But a great deal of it was cut. That's the other little thing one regrets. I had two or three scenes in my room, none of which were in it. One of these scenes I particularly regretted being cut. She was waiting for her boyfriend, Howard, played by Arthur O'Connell, and she went to the mirror. She looked at herself and took her hands and tried to pull her face up. Then she picked up the mascara and spit into it and put it on her eyes. You knew by the way she pulled her face up that she wished she were younger, and she did the typical thing of somebody who tries to cover it with makeup. It didn't run seven seconds, but it said so much. When you lose a scene like that, it hurts.

Mike: Josh Logan had also directed the Broadway production of *Picnic.*

Russell: Yes. It was material he was very familiar with.

Mike: I guess you would prefer to work in a movie for a director who had done the play, too.

Russell: Well, yes, if the play was successful. Then you know the director has been very close to the characters and knows the pitfalls. "No, no, no. We tried that in Boston. It didn't work, so don't do it that way. Get out of that." It becomes second nature to them.

There's something I want to say about my experience with *Picnic* that is very important: It is the saddest thing to me that in this country you can't play what is known as the second or third or fourth important part without people thinking you have dropped down in stature. This is not the case in England or in other countries. The attitude here is ludicrous. The next thing I played I had difficulty over my contract and billing. "What do you mean you want such-and-such? You just played a third-rate part." This is unanswerable. You become inarticulate with rage. This still goes on. I'm sure it keeps a lot of people from taking certain parts. I couldn't get my salary back up to where it had been before I did *Picnic*. So then I had to go do *Auntie Mame* on Broadway.

Mike: *Had* to do *Auntie Mame*?

Russell: I had to go back to a vehicle in order to say, "I can still play a starring vehicle even though I played that there third-rate part." *Mame* was like falling off a log for me. That's so easy for me to play, whereas it is not easy for me to have to play *Picnic*. They don't understand that.

Mike: You opened on Broadway in *Auntie Mame* in 1958, played it for two years, then did it as a movie. Would you say Mame was your favorite part?

Russell: Well, Mame became an institution, and frankly I had a sister very like her. A sophisticated woman, yet a naïve woman. A rare combination. To tell you the truth, Mike, I have played Mame all my life. It became more concentrated and better focused, but all the career women I played were Mame type characters. You know, giving a lot of silly orders and wearing quite mad clothes. I even did a picture in 1955 called *Never Wave at a WAC* in which I played a Washington hostess who came down the stairs, the same way Mame does, into a crowded party with all the Senators there and so on. "No, no. They will never pass that bill." "Hello, Charlie." "Oh, that hat is a dream on you, Martha." "Oh, doesn't she look awful!" I mean, I did all that forever and a day. So Mame was just a very good repeat, as it were. Even my part in *The Women* was Mame. Mame was just as good without money as she was with money. She was a woman who loathed bigots. Everybody would like to have an Auntie Mame or a pal like Mame who comes in and gives a lift all the time. "Never mind about that. Everybody over to my house." Many people have said to me, "Roz, you should have played Mame all your life. You were wrong to try to do various other parts." Well! I could have just kept playing *The Women* from the time that happened back in 1939. Honestly, in my opinion, my career would have gone to an even higher level. Bob Hope plays Bob Hope. Jack Benny plays Jack Benny. There's nothing wrong with this. You find a character, and it works for you. Mame certainly worked for me. Even truck drivers and taxi drivers in New York still yell at me, "Hi, Auntie Mame!" And little children in a shop or store speak to me. I always say, "You can't know who I am." They say, "Oh, yes, I saw you on television. You're Auntie Mame. My

mommy let me sit up and watch *Auntie Mame.*" Because it's clean.
Mike: When it was done later as a musical on Broadway and called just *Mame* with Angela Lansbury, did you see it?
Russell: No, I never did see it, and not for that reason. I didn't go to New York in the year and a half, or whatever it was, she was in it. But I am very happy she played it. She is a fine actress, excellent. Angela Lansbury has always been a great actress. People said, "Nobody could play this but you." I said, "That is absolutely nonsense."
Mike: How do you compare the role of Auntie Mame to the role of Mama Rose in the film you made of *Gypsy*?
Russell: Well, I tried to do *Gypsy* in more or less the opposite way. I tried to make her a real bitch. A stage mother to end all stage mothers. As a result, she did not get the sympathy Mame gets. She is just not as likable. The rapport with the audience is not as acute. Then there's that thing about playing an actress which has always existed in the theater as far as audiences are concerned. The so-called private people consider theatrical people slightly mad! Which I suppose they have to be to be in the business. They're in another orbit. The atmosphere surrounding them is not quite the atmosphere that surrounds the earth.
Mike: Is it true you turned down starring in *Hello, Dolly!* on Broadway?
Russell: Yes. I wasn't excited over it when I read it. I thought it just another musical, and frankly, I didn't think the script very good. It only has one good number, the title song, and that wasn't even in it at that time. It is hard to visualize all Gower Champion added in directing *Hello, Dolly!* There's no question that his inventiveness had a great deal to do with its success. What can be layered onto a show like that is the difference between a hit and a semihit or a failure. It also needs a popular star.
Mike: You were quoted once in a Hedda Hopper column as saying, "A star is a person with an enormous audience acceptance who is aware of weaknesses and has genuine humility. A great star is rare."
Russell: I'm not going to change that! Actually Judy Garland said that to me. I was doing *Wonderful Town* while she was appearing at the Palace. She came over to see me backstage one night. I said, "Oh, how about you down the street there! I've seen you at the Palace. That's something down there!" She said, "Well, I've found out that I

have an audience, and when you have that, no one can take it away from you. You earn that, and it belongs to you." Judy always had it. That's what a star really is.

Mike: In the last ten or twelve years, in my opinion, Hollywood has not produced many big stars. There are people who take starring parts and are forced on the public, but just because they have a lead in a picture doesn't make them a star. I can't think of a real movie star having been made since the whole factorylike system of the major studios collapsed. Perhaps Robert Redford has been the last big star created who has sustained public appeal year after year.

Russell: I suppose there are those who could argue that point. Of course, I agreed with the star system having finally been accepted in it. I think it is sad the young actors and actresses don't have any big organization behind them that keeps presenting them to the public so that the public is educated to their qualifications, their charisma, their charms, their abilities, and so on. Without that it is a hit or a miss. Then the parts that are being played! I am so anti all of that. It's very painful for me to see a movie in which people are going out with a gun, machine gunning down fifty people, and committing all sorts of other violence. And all these skin pictures! I'm so against them. I hear people defend these pictures. They say, "Well, there are many four-letter words in them, but they are so artistically done you just have to go see them!" Well, I ain't got to go see them. Then they say it is a phase and it will pass. The pendulum will swing back and come to a neutral point. That's nonsense because they seem to be more and more popular by each week's grosses, plus the fact there is a constant younger generation that grows up with a definite curiosity about these things. I don't say a film should lack reference to and a display of sex when it thrusts the plot forward and has an emotional content with meaning. It's just all the filth I dislike. Your friend Tennessee Williams has used four-letter words in some of his writing, but always it's indigenous to what he is writing about, always it is a statement that is describing the emotions at the moment. Never was Tennessee's work reviewed as filth for the sake of filth. It's way beyond that. There's a big difference.

Mike: Do you think films teach behavioral patterns?

Russell: They certainly do! They're very influential. There is no question about that. I think when you have to take the blessed sacrament, which is the host, the mass, the transfiguration of the body and blood of Christ, and make a commercial film of it, there is something wrong. To reach that far for a laugh, and that's what it's intended for, is wrong. That would refer in my opinion to any religion. If you do that to any part of the Bible, any part of Christianity or the Jewish faith, it is totally callous, tasteless, graceless, and really crude. I think it is pathetic.

Mike: Do you think there are people or organizations that come up with the money to back films like this because they want to undermine religious beliefs, especially Christian beliefs?

Russell: Do I think there is a conspiracy of that sort?

Mike: Well, not a conspiracy, but an unwritten attitude of many filmmakers and their backers.

Russell: I think probably the number one sin of the world is that of an ingrate. The second one is greed, which brings out the worst in us. The kind of movie being made is governed by the almighty dollar. They wouldn't be being made if they weren't being supported so that they make money. But when people start kidding me that they are artistic and that's the reason for them, I say that's ridiculous. They are embarrassing. I don't consider myself a cube. For one thing, I'm just too old to be a cube. I feel I have been reasonably in touch with life.

Mike: I don't think all these films are being supported that much. Many people I have come into contact with don't go to the movies very much because of these type films.

Russell: Well, we've driven away some of the audience; however, if I showed you the newspaper now, I could point out the three or four pictures that are making money, huge sums of money, and every one of them is filthy. On the other hand, there was a comedy made about not smoking which opened as a big success, but was never pushed far enough to have people really grasp this thing. Full of laughs, but not supported. This is a very sad commentary on us, on our nation. I've heard people say, "They've finally made a picture I can take my children to see!" These people, believe me, are the first ones down to the X-rated pictures! The family doesn't do much together anymore. That's the car, the bus, the pogo stick, I don't know what it is, but the family doesn't go any place anymore. Kids hitchhike rides to the beach, and the picnic is sure out of style. So this business of, "If I could only take my children . . ." is just so much talk. Why, they dump the children out to see the Western and they go down to the X film. "I'll pick you up in two hours. If it goes on the second time, you sit through it. I'll be back." And off they go with Mabel. Tillie and Mabel are off to the skin flick. I also have friends who say, "I feel I have to see it to keep up with what's going on." There are millions of those "just to know what's going on" people. That's what is making the money.

Mike: Do you think films should carry messages in them? I know of some producers and directors who won't consider a script unless it carries a social comment.

Russell: Films can carry marvelous messages of great love, of things that count, of things that have meaning. They don't have to be revolutionary, and they don't need the message of the radical to overthrow the government. No.

Mike: But it certainly has become a primary purpose in filmmaking to carry a social or political message that will influence the audience's point of view, rather than just entertain them.

Russell: That very word "entertainment" is what we have lost. The primary purpose of films, until recently, was always to entertain. There is a very nostalgic thing going on now in that many movie theaters are reviving films of the thirties and forties, so that television isn't the only place you can see these wonderful old movies. I'm beginning to be an addict! Oh, boy! They are so marvelous!

Mike: I can't think right off of any star who has stuck by Hollywood to the degree you have. *The Citadel,* made in England in 1938 because it is set there, was the only film you ever made abroad in its entirety.

Russell: I've made my films in Hollywood all along and enjoyed it. There's a long list of people here who contributed to what I know, what I have, what I have enjoyed, and what success I have known. 'Tis ever thus, and I am eternally grateful.

Mike: You have never appeared in a so-called runaway movie. One that runs away from Hollywood to be made in a low-economy country.

Russell: I must face the fact that many people do go to foreign countries because of cost. Maybe, I, too, will find it necessary. I am very pro labor. I am a member of three unions myself, but I'm afraid things have gotten to the point that labor costs are suffocating what little film production is still left in Hollywood. Our technicians are the finest in the world, the best trained and with the best experience, but the "below the line" part of a film budget which they represent has become too heavy. The individual has a right to as much money as he can earn, but I think the whole thing needs explaining and revamping on everybody's part. That would be a very big help in keeping production here. It has gotten to the point that they don't write stories that fit here. And if there is a story that is indigenous to this place, they will make the change. They will say, "How about making this take place in South Wales or Spain? We can get a couple of people with accents." Now this is wrong! So I think we'll have still more changes made in the way films are made here.

Mike: Your personal relationship with crews has always been happy?

Russell: Just delicious. I am such an admirer of them. I have seen some individual men who do the work of four men literally. They lug that iron, and they watch everything. Great gaffers who climb up a ladder fifty times to fix a spotlight and make it just precisely right. You've got to get the crew on your side. They have to have a rooting interest in the picture. I've seen too many films where a crew doesn't respect the director or the star and it becomes a disaster. It is very sad to see a picture come apart at the seams. In such cases the crew doesn't cheat, but they work without that extra enthusiasm you have to have.

Mike: Have you usually had good working relationships with your directors?

Russell: Yes. I think films are definitely a director's medium. They have a canvas to paint, as it were. The success or failure of the picture truly depends on them. A writer can have done a superb job, and a brilliant cast can be assembled; but the director can butcher it. He can take that film and absolutely wreck it. A good director can also do the reverse. He can take second-rate material and not greatly talented people and make that script and those people look better than they are. In my opinion there are not many great directors. No more than there are greats in anything. My own films are perfect examples of whether a director is really good or inferior. We are the victims of them. They are like conductors. I play the fiddle, but he has the ability to make me play it far better than I ever knew I could. He can give you great confidence and sweep and color because most actors are frightened. You are always self-conscious enough not to want to make a damned fool of yourself. I remember Howard Hawks did not want me in *His Girl Friday*. He did not select me by any manner or means. Of course, it had been a great man's part, but Howard got the idea of changing it to a woman. I believe they had tried to cajole Ginger

Rogers and any number of other actresses into doing it, but they all said no. Well, I didn't have any choice. I was just sent from MGM to Columbia with my little cigar boxes of makeup. Mr. Hawks was not happy about it, but Harry Cohn said, "You go up on Sunset Boulevard and see this girl in *The Women* and you will want her." Whether or not Mr. Hawks went, I don't know, but there he was stuck with me. For two or three days on the set he didn't say a word to me, but I kept working away in there with Cary Grant. Finally, I went to Cary in private and said, "Cary, what about this man? I don't know if he likes what I'm doing or not." Cary said, "Don't worry about it, Roz, that is the way he is." I said, "But I do worry about it. I need all the help I can get." So I walked over to Mr. Hawks who is a great big tall man with Icelandic blue eyes. He sat slumped in his director's chair, which is what he does, but he sees everything. I said, "Mr. Hawks, how am I doing?" He stood up—and he looked about eight feet tall to me—and said, "Keep doing what you're doing." I said, "What is that?" He said, "Keep pushing that Cary Grant around all you can." He had been closely observing me those two or three days. He saw what I could do, and he encouraged me to go further and further, to do all that sort of overlapping Cary and I did.

Mike: One of the advantages of being a star is that very often you can pick your director, can't you?

Russell: Yes. I admit that, but one has to have the ability to choose the right director. Sometimes one doesn't make the proper choice, because one isn't willing to take the criticism you need from a director. You should be able to take a verbal beating from him now and again. He has to keep you in line. I know one's best work is always done under a tough director. Rather, the word is *demanding* director. He is totally the boss of the production. Unfortunately, a director who has done his homework, knows his camera setups, knows his film, and knows the temperament of all the people with whom he is working is hard to find. The perfect director is one that does not inflict his own touch, his own stamp, his own personality into the work. That is, he gets that in there, then withdraws it and makes you the figure in the forefront. He makes you the person that is real. He gets all the phoniness out of you. If he doesn't get it one way out of performers, he gets it another way. He knows how to go in the back door, the side door, and everything else. He will go up to you and say, "What you are doing I want you to mean a hundred times more." If you can't do it, he will explain to you how you can. How you can become more real. There are very few that are that brilliant, and they are the ones you want to work for! I'll have to admit I have to settle many times for second- and third-rate directors, and it has always showed. The trouble is that many times they leave stars on their own when they really need a director's help. We all need as much help as we can get in every phase of filmmaking, in lighting, in writing, in direction, in coaching, in—

Mike: Speaking of writing, aren't parts written sometimes so they are tailored for certain stars? Say, a writer knows your acting ability and style so well that he writes a part to fit you.

Russell: I think that was done more in the old days than it is today. Now the material is the number one requirement, and so it should be. Although many is the writer who screams at his material being destroyed. In the studio heyday some executive would say, "Oh, this is a Carole Lombard type of part" or "This is a Myrna Loy type part" or "This should go to a dramatic actress" or "This is for Crawford" or "Write a script for Joan Crawford" or "Try to team Gable and Crawford together again" and so on. That was the place you tried to get to, where they would start writing scripts for you, so that you would get a Roz Russell script. I finally got into that when I was doing the career women roles. If one went well, they would say, "Write another career woman for Roz." A very lovely compliment was paid to me some years ago by another actress. I might as well say who it was. It was Irene Dunne. She said, "You know, Roz, you have never had an enormous picture to help you the way I had *Cimarron*. You have struggled through some very poor material and have always been better than that material." It was very nice at the time. It was before I got great vehicles like *Auntie Mame* which sustain you.

Mike: When you read the script of a film you are about to do, do you make suggestions as to how scenes might be rewritten or worked over?

Russell: No, I really don't go quite that far. You learn from experience, and I hope I have learned something in my thirty-seven years of work in films. What I look for in the writing are scenes one will remember years after seeing the picture. If I said to you, "What do you remember, Mike, about *Going My Way*?" you would tell me you remember the "Too-Ra-Lo-Too-Roo-La" singing scene. In *Gone with the Wind* you would right away say you remember the burning of Atlanta or where Clark Gable says, "I don't give a damn." You would pick out scenes that were big scenes, not necessarily big with masses of people but potent scenes. If the script doesn't have those memorable scenes, and I have played many a script that hasn't, the film will be a disaster. Now, believe me, if you have six memorable scenes, it's pretty safe you are going to have a hit. If you have four, you're still in business, but if you have only two, you are not in business.

Mike: How do you feel about producers?

Russell: I'm quainty dainty about that. By that, I mean I am old-fashioned because I think producers should still be functioning as they did when they were at the height of their importance. Now they have been relegated into a position where they are supposedly just money raisers—the man who puts the package together, who goes out and gets the original money and makes the deals. Then, when the enterprise is in full bloom, the current system chops off all the buds and lets it die. This is wrong. The history of motion pictures proves the value of the producer in his former capacity. I'm a great believer in history. We should read more of it and learn more about the past experiences of other people. How much closer we would all be if we did that. Including the generations. I'm off what we were talking about, but I'm coming right back. If the generation right below me, the children, knew our history better, we would be closer. The youngsters simply have not made a study of our generation or any other. I'm all for them, but in that they are lacking. Sooner or later they will catch up. The sooner, the better. But it is the same with the producer. He was very essential, even if you limit his capacity to just a sounding board. He was the man who would keep track of everything going on in the industry. That is, seeing every picture, watching the progress of every director, actor, writer, set dresser, designer, and so on. He was the man who gave an overall aura of taste and feeling. It was certainly the producers who were great, say, for the Marx Brothers, who had to have a kind of producer who understood their abilities and the way they could best work. You rely on so many things in a producer, and working without one is wrong. I have never believed the same person can perform the combined duties of a director, writer, actor, and producer on a film. If you name one, I would say, "Where is the second?" Probably the nearest one to it, and I don't know how much he wrote, would be Orson Welles.

Mike: To remain a star, one must keep in front of the public by being seen in films frequently enough and by being read about and talked about. Is having a public relations representative a requirement to sustain one's image?

Russell: I've never had one, but plenty of people do think it necessary. What certainly is necessary is the selling of a picture. There's a lack of that. They don't sell film anymore. They throw it on the market without much care or thought, and if it isn't a total smash in the first two theaters, they abandon it and sell it to television. I know of several very worthwhile pictures that have simply disappeared because there was no care given. That is going to be changed, Mike. This will never do. The distribution end of this business is going to be changed radically. Very soon. Think of all the time and effort and blood, sweat, and tears that go into a film, and then it is handed over like you do the body to a surgeon, and that's it! That is not going to be tolerated, and I am far from alone in this! There are so many ways of testing a film. If you have a film there may be doubts about, you put it in a couple of four-hundred- to six-hundred-seat theaters and you leave it there until you see whether or not anybody comes. It must be given time to come to life and have its break.

Mike: And you don't think a star needs a publicity agent to sell them to the public?

Russell: No. I have just learned it is far more important to go on a television show now and then. I had not been on television since years ago when I did *Wonderful Town* as a special or since I opened the NBC studio out here in another special with several other stars. And I have been on several Academy Awards telecasts. Recently, however, I have gone on talk shows for the first time to do some work for the fight against arthritis. I never in my life have had so much mail! You are seen by millions and millions of people, and I think that is as good an ad as you can get. I wasn't used to that. I am still staggered, can't get up from under the mail, and I did only three shows, Mike Douglas, David Frost, and Johnny Carson.

Mike: Arthritis is the latest of many charity works for you, isn't it?

Russell: Yes, it is. I had a very severe case myself, and I have been quite lucky to overcome it. A famous doctor who lectures all over the world on arthritis was examining me. He said, "Many people in your industry have this disease." I didn't pay much attention until he added, "None of them will admit it." I wondered why. "There are many things I can understand not admitting, but why this?" He said,

"They think it is a disease that goes with age." I laughed. He continued, "Many children get arthritis, and some infants are even born with it." I didn't know that. I said, "I'll tell you something. If and when I beat this here rap, I'll do something about it." So, when I did get well, I kept my promise and I am still doing it and enjoying it and finding it very interesting. It is something people kick under the rug too much and try to hide. One should never be ashamed of anything like that but should encourage others. We have seventeen million victims in this country alone! I went to London and did a big charity there for the Kennedy Institute of Rheumatology which does research. It was very successful in raising money.

Mike: You have always involved yourself in charitable organizations.

Russell: I was brought up that way, Mike. My brothers and sisters and I were brought up to be part of the community in which we lived. We had to be of service to it. I really don't deserve any credit. It is something my father thought we should do and educated us to do. When the aunts and uncles came around and gave you a dollar or five dollars, part of it had to go to charity. We each had to pick a charity. Some picked tuberculosis, some the blind, and I picked crippled children. The ones in the braces, as it were. That is why I became interested in Sister Kenny. I have worked mostly in hospitals. I am on three or four hospital boards. I have known wonderful women who have worked very long and hard, and I think it is far better than sitting around playing bridge all day long. I helped form an organization when I first came out here called the League of Crippled Children, and one of our rules was that every woman had to do some work, not just donate money.

Our charities within the industry are very fine also. What we do for the Motion Picture Relief Fund is marvelous. We are very privileged people, and for the adulation we receive, one should make a return. I'm a great believer that you have to put something back in for all you take out.

Mike: You also find time for church activities.

Russell: I belong to our congregation here in Beverly Hills, the one I call "Our Lady of the Cadillacs."

Mike: And you are quite active socially, aren't you?

Russell: Over the years I have had lots of friends, not only in the movie industry, but in the musical world, in the professional world, lawyers and doctors and their wives. Freddie and I go with many groups of people, which I find interesting. It isn't just a theatrical crowd, although, when you are with your own kind, you are able to talk shop. One thing about our business: The people in it are fascinating and terribly alive. They come into a group, and they take off. They don't sit like dead wood. They have the quality of being able to have fun and to contribute fun. I always laugh when people say, "Hollywood is crazy and everybody in it. Everybody is a fake and a phony," or, "Oh, they have gone Hollywood!" This is nonsense. Hollywood couldn't be a more average place to live. It's up to you. If you are going to go off the deep end, you can do it anywhere. To sustain in any profession or job, the number one thing you have to have is self-discipline. A lot of young people come to me and say, "I would like to be a star and I know I can be. I have talent. My mother says so. And I am taking dancing and singing." I say, "That's fine, but talent is the last thing you need." They say, "What?" I say, "You can buy talent. If you can afford to buy a fiddle, you can buy fiddle lessons and learn to play that instrument. But first you must have discipline and good health." Sometimes I work with actors who are far better performers than I, but you can't hear them three feet away. They have no projection, and that is because they don't have good health. In order to have good health you have to have discipline. Then you have to be able to fail, fail miserably, and come up from it. Some people can never take failure. And failure loves failure, by the way. Once you are down, they say, "Join the party and try to bring everyone else with you." Failure is rough to go through, but you can go through it and learn from it and try not to do it again. You have to have the capacity for working hard, for listening, and for having a certain humility so you can learn. Then, if you have a little talent, it's nice.

Mike: In building and sustaining a career, isn't it important to have contacts with influential people in the industry on a social as well as a business level?

Russell: I have never found that necessary. Freddie and I have never had a soul in this house we didn't like personally. This is our island, and we have never entertained for that reason at all. I have never tried to entertain *the right people* in order to get a job.

Mike: One thing I have noticed through the years, Roz, is that you have kept up a style of living that the moviegoing public would expect a movie star to have. You still uphold the tradition of the glamorous

Hollywood movie queen, and you seem to have an organized pattern that you follow in your life.

Russell: Oh, I suppose so. The only thing I can say about a life-style is that I keep myself busy. This morning I was saying to my Kirkie, my chambermaid, as I looked out my bedroom window, "You know, I've never sat down in that garden." Maybe five or six times for five minutes, but I leap up because I like to garden. I would rather work in it than sit down in it! We have lived here so long, since a little after we were married, and we don't change a thing. We just keep it up, keep it clean and painted. It is comfortable, and we spend most of our time here, although we travel a lot. Freddie has business in New York and London. We go to London often and see all the theater. I think Freddie has an option on a play there now. I have always wanted to travel to China and never thought I'd make it. There seems a flicker of hope in that direction.

Mike: In the current phase of your career you often play star vehicle roles which don't require a well-known leading man, if any; however, in the past you have been costarred with the most famous male actors. What was it like to play with some of them?

Russell: Well, you know about Clark Gable being called the great lover. He got that reputation because he was never awkward in filming a love scene. He was a very graceful man. He knew where to put the feet! You see, when you kiss someone, you never stand toe to toe. It won't work that way. You have to put the feet in between each other's. You often have to figure love scenes out before photographing them. You know, the way they bend you back on the couch and all that. The director may say, "You're pulling your neck all out," or "You've messed her hair up," or "There's too much of your shadow covering her face." Gable never had the slightest problem. He just grabbed you, and not violently. That's another trick. It can never be harsh. It may have to look that way, but it can't actually be performed that way or it will come over awkward on the screen. Gable had a lot of class, that boy, lots of style and humor.

I've been very lucky with all the leading men I've worked with. Cary Grant was a lot of fun on the set. Once we were shooting a scene for *His Girl Friday*. I was typing, and he came in and stood behind my back. He played the whole scene standing there next to my desk, telling me what to do, "Hildy, you've got to do this," and "You come with me," and "Tear up that page," and I was saying, "You keep quiet while I'm typing," and all of a sudden he walked away. He had nothing on below the waist but underwear shorts. He had a shirt, tie, vest and coat, but there he was in his undies, which was just a gag. We had to cut and start all over. Cary was full of crazy jokes, and I loved working with him.

One of the nicest men I ever worked with was Errol Flynn. Isn't that funny? You don't think of Roz Russell and Errol Flynn, that swashbuckling sort of character, but I made *Four's a Crowd* with him in 1938 at Warner Brothers. Errol had meticulous manners and was such a handsome man!

Another Englishman I liked working with was Ronald Colman. *Under Two Flags,* that was Ronnie. He was charming, but he never would kiss you on the mouth. He always got over on the corner of your mouth because of the better camera angle. He knew the camera better than any actor I have known. He also played a little bit to your ear, never looking you in the eyes, so that his face would be more turned toward the camera. That was always a little disconcerting. After I couldn't find his eyes, those beautiful orbs of his, I asked, "What is he doing?" And I learned something. It was only my third or fourth film.

Mike: Do you think he was just being aware of how he should be photographed, or was that his way of trying to steal the scene?

Russell: No, that was the way he worked with everyone. He couldn't have been more polite. He was the essence of good manners.

Mike: But I suppose you have had experiences when somebody tried to steal the scene.

Russell: Oh, that's useless with me, kid! No, no. Those people are easy to put down. Anybody starts to upstage you, you simply turn your back to the camera, then the director has to come around to take a close-up of you. It's a technical thing. The director *must* do it. But if the director catches it before it's too late, he will say, "Hold it. Wait a minute. Mike, you are upstaging Roz." And if you keep doing it, he looks at his watch and says, "OK, reverse the camera and get a close-up of Roz." Then I say to Mike Steen, "Aha, now guess who's going to be in, you or me?" It is a waste of time to do those things. It is a sign of somebody who is terribly insecure and undisciplined. All that counts is to get a good scene, in which case you will both look good.

Mike: Have fellow actors and actresses in your films often become your close personal friends?

Russell: Not as a rule because everyone is so busy while on the set. Occasionally friendships develop, but unless you do become pals and go to each other's houses to dine, you never see much of one another. During my contract days at MGM, I think I knew Myrna Loy as well as any of them. When she was married to Arthur Hornblow, I went often to dinner at their home in Hidden Valley. Myrna and I still have a lot of laughs about the fact that I was her "threat." The studio had me in reserve if Myrna balked at a part. That is the way the studio was run. The first line of defense, and the second line, and practically the third line. Myrna was often trying to change her contract and get a little more bread. Louis Mayer or someone would say, "That's all right. Roz Russell will play the part." On one such occasion, I was in the wardrobe department getting a fitting for the part and Myrna came in and said, "They gave me the raise, Roz." I simply took the dress off and handed it to her and said, "Good luck, old girl!" I don't think I was too disappointed about that one, but I was often disappointed over other work she would get that I thought I could do.

However, the studio was like a big family for the most part. I suppose there was feuding here and there, but no person worried you who wasn't directly competing with you. You'd say, "Oh, there goes Judy! Hi, Judy! Good luck on your picture." There was no way you were going to play her part, or she yours. So there never was that feeling of jealousy or envy.

Mike: Weren't you at MGM when Greta Garbo was still there?

Russell: Yes. We all used to go and peek at Garbo and watch her work when we could sneak on the set.

Mike: She didn't want you watching?

Russell: No, no! She had a maid named Hazel Washington who later became my maid for years. I guess Garbo didn't keep her on between films because she traveled so much. She used to go back to Sweden a lot to see her brother. Hazel transferred to me and always spoke very warmly and lovingly of Garbo. I would see Garbo on the lot, but I have met her more often in New York.

Mike: Most of your career you have been connected with three studios, MGM, Columbia and RKO. Are you partial to any one of them?

Russell: I guess I'm most nostalgic about Metro, having started there.

At Christmastime it was happy hours! Champagne would flow! During the year there were golf tournaments, bowling, etc. Every morning while you got your makeup and your hair done, you heard all the gossip of the lot: "What did you do last night?" or "Where did they go?" or "Who's got that picture?" or "See if you can get me one of the scripts. Is there anything in it for me?" Then there was much carrying on about the war bond tours, service to the country, being able to do Red Cross work, and so on.

Mike: During World War II you did entertain troops, sell war bonds, and work for the Red Cross.

Russell: Oh, yes. All during it and even after. While I was pregnant in 1943, I gave a Christmas party down in the desert outside Indio for the Fourth and Sixth Armored divisions. Crazy. It was a wonderful party, though. This was Patton's group. I asked myself what do these boys want? First they want girls; then they want alcohol; then they would like some money. So I had all three! I didn't have alcohol. I had beer. I went to the general down there, General Woods, and he gave me permission to have beer. I took down four or five hundred women in buses, put up a dance floor out on the sand with all the tanks surrounding it. It was a sight to behold. Oh, boy, those boys had the time of their lives! I had the men come through a bullpen with tickets to dance. Those girls were exhausted, I can tell you.

Mike: The girls were volunteers?

Russell: All of them. Lots of actresses and secretaries. We met in Hollywood at the Palladium parking lot. I had to have coffee and doughnuts on the buses, and I had to stop twice between here and Palm Springs for nose powdering. I tell you the logistics were something! I fed the girls in Palm Springs; then we went on another hundred miles into the desert to where the party was held. It had everything: food, a Christmas tree, and a big show. I had Red Skelton be Santa Claus. We gave away prizes and money. And the crazy thing, I didn't know how many men were in a division. I asked an officer, "What's that other group over there?" He said, "That's another division." I said, "Invite them too!" I raised all the money to give that party in about three days up here on the telephone.

Speaking of Christmas parties, every year from the time I came to Hollywood I have given a Christmas Eve party. I have it for all the strays. I was alone, very lonesome and homesick for my family, so I had people in that were in the same situation. When I married

Freddie, he had his strays and the party has gone on traditionally every year. Of course, there were dropouts because many of the strays would marry and have children. This party became quite famous. I have games of all kinds which I preside over at a microphone. We have music and carol singing and a buffet in the dining room all night long. Terribly, terribly big. Among the things we do is trim hats. Everybody gets a paper bag with a row of pins on top of it, and inside the bag is a feather, a veil, and a flower—several items like that which are simply ghastly-looking. All the lights are put out in the whole house. You are given about five minutes to do it, and the paper bag becomes the basic hat. Then the lights go on, and I tell you, you have never seen sights like it! You can't believe how fantastic and funny they are. I give prizes, and this particular game Gary Cooper always won. I don't know if it was because he had been an artist and was able to draw, but he always made the most original hat! I went to visit him just before we lost him and he asked me to go to the closet and open the door. I did, and up on the shelf were the hats he won by. He had kept those paper hats! He said, "Roz, those were some of the best times I have ever had in my life, coming to you on Christmas Eve." He was a lovely man.

Mike: Tyrone Power was one of your dear friends, too, wasn't he?

Russell: Yes. He came here often to dine, and Freddie and I went to his home often to parties. I knew him before the war and after he came back. Of course, he was a breathtakingly good-looking man. There isn't a great deal one can say except that he was one of the kindest and most concerned people I have known. Always inquiring about our son, Lance, always interested in you personally and how you were feeling, full of laughter, full of warmth. When he came in, the whole room lit up. His condition to me—well, I think he should still be with us, but we can't get into that.

Mike: What about Frank Sinatra?

Russell: What about him?

Mike: You have been very close to him. And on the 1973 Academy Awards he presented the Jean Hersholt Humanitarian Award to you!

Russell: Ohhhh, he is quite a guy! Frank is a remarkable human being. Very colorful. He is several people, all interesting. He is a man with concern for people—not only his friends, but people he doesn't know. I guess there is just reams that could be written about the things he has done for people which no one knows other than the recipients.

He likes it that way. I was told once by Dean Martin that both of them on their way from their dressing rooms to the stage of a nightclub would go through the kitchen and look after anybody with problems, actually with or without problems. But they never wanted it known and said if anyone told what they were doing for them, they wouldn't help them anymore.

Mike: When Frank Sinatra made his farewell appearance at the fund-raising gala for the Motion Picture Relief Fund in June, 1971, for which you were the women's chairman, he said to you, "Someday, Roz, you will feel like retiring, too!" How about that?

Russell: Well, retirement to me wouldn't mean retiring from life because I'm just as interested in doing other things as I am in acting. But retirement from acting? No! I would never say so, anyway. I think those things just happen. Things change, as they should, but I'm not planning on retirement. I am planning to do a play about Aimee Semple McPherson, and it's quite an undertaking. Freddie and I have been working on this for years and years and years, the way he did with *Coco.*

Mike: *Aimee* is to be for Broadway?

Russell: Yes. We bought Lately Thomas' books, which are *The Vanishing Evangelist* and *Storming Heaven.* He is a delicious man, this Lately Thomas, which is not his real name, but the material is so gigantic that it has been taking forever to edit. We have it now in fairly good form. So that is a huge project. Freddie is always so busy. He produced *Twigs* with Sada Thompson. That's on a national tour now. Soon he plans to produce *Aimee*, which is next on my agenda! Retirement is not right now in my book!

August 4–6, 1971

The Character Player

AGNES MOOREHEAD

Moorehead: My father was a Presbyterian minister in Clinton, Massachusetts, where I was born. Later we moved to St. Louis,

Missouri. I began acting in musical stock with the St. Louis Municipal Opera when I was ten years old. My ambition to have a career as an actress was very strong. To train for that profession I attended the University of Wisconsin, Columbia University, and the American Academy of Dramatic Arts. After any actor or actress finishes school, there come those very difficult years of pounding the pavements looking for jobs and trying to establish a reputation within your profession. One thing you can't train for, but that you have to have plenty of, is good luck!

Mike: Luck, combined with training, talent, and endurance, enabled you to become one of the finer and better-known character actresses in America. What is your personal definition of character acting?

Moorehead: To begin with, each and every role an author writes is called a character. For convenience, however, the term "character acting" is generally used to distinguish supporting roles from leading roles. The leading man or leading lady type role is more confining to the performer and is thought of as being a straight part. Of course, there are exceptions. On the other hand, character acting gives the performer a much greater variety of roles in which he can be cast. And in each individual role the character actor is rarely limited in the amount of characterization he can invent. He is like a painter with a very large palette of colors from which to paint an interesting picture with dimension. It can be a subtle performance or an eccentric one.

Mike: Would you say it takes more talent or training to play character parts than to play straight leading roles?

Moorehead: I think anybody who is a good actor certainly has to have a tremendous amount of background and experience. Just because one may have an interesting personality so that he or she can walk around a stage and say the lines doesn't make one a good actor. It is presentation and experience that really make a good actor. Serious actors are constantly studying to expand or enlarge what talent they have or what personality they have. If an actor doesn't work, he goes backward. It's like any good sport really. If a swimmer doesn't swim a great deal, his breathing isn't correct, and he can't go as far. It's the same way with the stage. You have to be constantly in it, and you learn by being with good people. That is, if an inexperienced lead who has an interesting personality is surrounded with an outstanding cast, his personality can expand and become fascinating and brilliant.

Mike: Which, I suppose, makes some star personalities ticket sellers, although they can't act too well.

Moorehead: There are a lot of people who some producers think are box office who can't bring a nickel into the theaters today. These people are thought of as box office because they have been in the public eye a great deal, yet audiences don't particularly accept them. I think American audiences are very discerning. I find them very warm and eager to sit there and be entertained by someone who knows how to entertain them. You cannot look down on an audience. One presents his talent as humbly and modestly as possible and hopes the audience will be entertained by it. But there are many actors who think they are geniuses and that all they have to do is get up and say one line and people faint! Well, they are wrong.

Mike: Do you think the best training ground for talent is still the stage?

Moorehead: I think anything you do for any audience is training ground. Radio was a tremendous training ground for many people, including me. It was extremely difficult because the characterizations you made, whether you were a lead or a supporting player, had to be in your voice and your thoughts. That's all you had to work with! In television you not only have a situation where the audience sees you, but a situation where the actor doesn't have to think as much. All the cards are put on the table, which I'm not particularly keen about doing. I don't believe in playing a whole game in front of an audience. I believe in playing part of it and in letting the audience play the rest of it. For instance, my attitude is: "All right, I'll start the tears, but you do the crying." That's because I myself have to keep composed and know what I'm doing up on that stage. I can't constrict my voice, nor can I have my nose run, nor the tears go out and my mascara get messed up. But I can give an effect through which you become so involved that *you* cry, and you think that I'm doing it. That is the magic of the theater! How it happens, I cannot explain. But the exciting thing is to be able to characterize and get people to believe what you are characterizing.

Mike: You have played character parts in every entertainment medium, haven't you?

Moorehead: Yes. When you are a serious actor, you can't limit yourself to one medium. Nor should you limit a single performance. Imagination should never be limited. It should be free and open, so it can soar. It might not be right, but at least it is unlimited. One has physical limitations or voice limitations, but the creativity in a person should not ever be limited. I think one can recognize a creative limitation because you feel you'd like to go beyond what you are doing. A great director can usually stimulate an actor into those margins of creativity that go beyond what he thinks he is capable of. I know there were a lot of times when Orson Welles would be directing me that I would get to a certain point, then wonder what I could do next. I would know there was something more I should do. Then Orson would come up with a suggestion, and I would begin to create more. I would do a better job than I ever thought of doing! This is one of the most exciting things about acting, but not many directors can be so inspiring. Nevertheless, you should always try to go way beyond what you think you can do, or it becomes mediocre. It goes halfway and stops. And there are a lot of halfway actors in this business who are perfectly satisfied with what they do. An actor should never be satisfied with anything he does.

Mike: With fewer shows in New York and fewer films being made, there is not much work for actors nowadays. So, do you think it is advisable for young people to spend four or more years in college training for an acting career?

Moorehead: Yes, I do if they have the ambition and show enough talent.

Mike: You don't think the odds are more against a person's making a career of acting than they used to be?

Moorehead: I know the odds are greater, and that's why the more preparation one has, the better off he will be. I had a college education with a number of degrees. I worked in the theater in the summertime and went to school in the winter. I took everything that I possibly could in drama. After I got out of the university, I went to New York and auditioned for the American Academy of Dramatic Arts. At that time the head of the school was a Mr. [Charles] Jehlinger, who was a marvelous teacher. He said to me, "You don't need to come to this school. You've had a lot of training. Go out and get a job." I thought he didn't want me! I thought, "Oh, I can't stand it. I'm not very good." Tears began rolling down my cheeks, and he said, "Well, if that's the way you feel, we'd love to have you, but you don't have to have us."

Actually, I learned a great deal at the academy. I learned a tremendous amount of technique which I hadn't known before, although I had sought it by being with good people previously. When I entered the academy, I was more mature and I had the valid experiences of the university to help me. I was able to cope better with whatever I had to learn. For instance, I could understand my scripts better. I knew what to expect. I understood the purposes and intents of writers and so on. I wasn't just pulling things out of the air which a lot of actors and actresses do when their minds haven't been trained. Everything I worked with in college I've used in the theater.

Mike: Today when a student finishes college and tries to start an acting career, he finds few places to prove his talent and show what he can do. The gap between college and full-time professional work is frustrating.

Moorehead: Yes. But I must say that between coasts there are some marvelous circles of culture, dramatic circles that have done some very good work and are very serious about theater. That seems to be the only proving ground, but when those people come out here, they can't get anywhere without an agent. They have to buck up against agents who say, "What have you done?" They may reply, "I played the lead in such and such a thing in Dallas." And the agent will say, "But what film do you have on yourself?" They have to say, "I don't have any film." That more or less ends the conversation. So what do you do? It's very difficult. Very seldom does an agent, director, or producer look at a person and say, "By golly, that person has something! We'll take a chance!" There are few breathtaking personalities. It's very, very difficult for newcomers now. You either go to New York and pound the pavements or come to Hollywood directly.

It was easier when I started out, and even then, I thought it was hard. I came in during the Great Depression. We had no agents, but once in a while agencies like the Chamberlain Brown or William Morris offices might send out a call for three hundred people to go to some audition. These people would be gone through like they were cattle! You were nearly always on your own. If you found a production going on, you had to get to that producer by continual pounding on his door. That's what I had to do, and fortunately I came in contact with radio. I did radio and theater back and forth. And then I was most fortunate that Orson Welles crossed my path and liked me very much. We played together as actor and actress. He liked the way I played, and he believed in me, you see. I was lucky. I was with him seventeen years! It was he who brought me out here to Hollywood. I have him to thank for it. He thought I could play anything. It didn't make any difference what part. If it was a strange part, he said, "Give it to Agnes. She can play it." It was his confidence in the fact I could play it, with his direction, that helped me very much in my career. I'm not saying it was all easy. I've had hard times, too. I've had starvation times so that I know what it means to be hungry and not be able to pay the rent. Spencer Tracy, or any of the people who came up in a difficult way, would have told you the same thing. But at least in that time we had good stock companies in which you could learn your trade better. We had the repertoire companies of Stuart Walker and Jessie Bonstelle and other fine people. But they don't exist anymore because people don't attend the theater the way they used to.

Mike: Do you, as a leader in your profession, feel an obligation toward guiding and training young actors?

Moorehead: Yes. I try. I am deeply involved with an acting school that has five faculty members and teaches classes in technique. We offer similar instruction in the important things I had at the academy: voice, speech, fencing, ballet, interpretive reading, pantomime, and performed scenes. Unfortunately, in a lot of acting workshops they just study a play and put it on, and their technical work is bad because they have not studied technique.

Mike: Actors at that type of school seem mostly to want to have a showcase and be discovered.

Moorehead: That's right. But it takes a long time to be discovered or get a break, and that is disappointing to the actor. He expects fame overnight, and you can't get fame that way. Sometimes it takes your whole lifetime. And sometimes you don't get it at all. But you do it anyway! Why? Because you love it, because you think you have something people will like, because you believe you can deliver something that will touch the hearts of the audience, and also because there is a certain amount of exhibitionism in acting, a certain amount of vanity that the actor has. But first of all, you do it because you love it. However, I'm sorry to say that the way theater and pictures are nowadays you can't often love the play, nor can you like the role because it is most likely an ugly role, but sometimes you have to take it to keep the wolf from the door.

Mike: One creative outlet that you have had through the years, Miss Moorehead, is in touring colleges and universities and giving readings and lectures. That must be very gratifying.

Moorehead: It is, and I think anyone in the profession should do this. Of course, I realize there are a great number of professional actors who are not equipped to do this because they don't have the background. Also, they are incapable of appealing to young people and simplifying what young people should know. They haven't the ability to teach, really, because like any profession, teachers are born to be teachers. Still, I think if an accomplished actor feels he can guide a young person and inspire him to do something that is qualified, he should do it.

Mike: Do you express your creative nature any way outside the theater?

Moorehead: I fool around with colors and decorating, which I thoroughly enjoy. Also, I scribble a bit for my own particular pleasure. This scribbling might be something I want to do in a future show.

Mike: What are some of the roles you have enjoyed playing the most in motion pictures?

Moorehead: The Chinese woman I played in *Dragon Seed* with Katharine Hepburn was a good character part. In *Mrs. Parkington* with Greer Garson I played a character lead who was a chic and attractive society woman. Of course, the old maid sister I played in *The Magnificent Ambersons* for Orson was a beautiful, beautiful part. And in a film with Susan Hayward called *The Lost Moment* I played the strange part of a hundred-and-four-year-old woman which was fun. Bud Westmore created my makeup for that. I've enjoyed each of the many characters I've played. I have no favorites really. I have enjoyed, and still enjoy, the fact that many character parts are a challenge, and I try to make them effective and meaningful.

Mike: Many people have a tendency to think of character roles as dramatic or tragic parts, but comic character roles have been plentiful, haven't they?

Moorehead: Many actors have created comic characters on which they have built their careers. Look at them: Laurel and Hardy were characters, weren't they? And Arthur Treacher and Eric Blore. Frank Morgan was a great comic actor. We all recognize Charlie Chaplin's comic tramp character as a classic. There are so many of them. Look at Walter Huston, who not only played leads, but played marvelous characters, comic and tragic. I think the best example of a star who plays character roles is Laurence Olivier. He's a leading man who plays character leads that are unequaled.

Mike: In the weekly television series called *Bewitched* you played the witch who is the mother of the younger witch, Elizabeth Montgomery. By your being so well known as this sustaining character, do you feel audiences identify you with it so much that they are reluctant to accept you in some other role you might play in a motion picture?

Moorehead: Naturally people remember my witch character because they see it all the time, but I never have tried to establish an image. I don't want an image of any one type character or personality. When people say to me, "Oh, we just love you as the witch!" I say, "Yes, on Thursday nights." The witch is a character I have built up and expanded and enjoyed playing. It's fun playing with Elizabeth, and we are very fond of each other. The show itself isn't anything that gives the audience a kind of breathtaking hour, but it has a smile and an emotional release. Children love it, and it is clean. The character I play brings order out of chaos. I don't know anybody who hasn't said at some time, "Oh, I wish I didn't have to sweep the floor. I wish I didn't have to clean this or that. I wish I could snap my fingers and everything would be done!"

Mike: Do you think films should be presenting messages as much as they do, that we have gotten away from entertainment for the sake of entertainment?

Moorehead: I don't believe in bringing in messages. People don't want to be preached to; they want to be entertained. If a film brings in a moral or social lesson in an incidental way or if a character gets his comeuppance, I think that is right.

Mike: Who have been some of your favorite directors to work with?

Moorehead: Henry Hathaway, Edward Dmytryk, and many other good solid directors who make very good pictures.

Mike: Do you get along well with directors and vice versa?

Moorehead: Oh, I think so. I think they know they can trust me and that I'm cooperative and they don't have to worry about me, and that I will follow their line of thinking so that our thoughts merge pretty well. If there is any problem, it can be ironed out very quickly without any fuss or fury. I think temperament is all right in its right place, which is within the work. I don't think temperament should be outside the work because that is a form of weakness that will deteriorate you. It's usually false anyway! Everyone has a certain temperament, the feel of the way you attack things, and I think that can be put into your work, put to work in a channel that will do you some good.

Mike: Have you ever had parts written especially for you?

Moorehead: Oh, I suppose there have been. I think when Orson Welles wrote the screenplay of *The Magnificent Ambersons*, he wrote the character I played with me in mind.

Mike: Do you enjoy going on location to make films?

Moorehead: Very much. I love location work. I love seeing the freedom it gives to the camera. The scope of the camera is so wonderful, especially in Cinerama. I was on location in Kentucky and southern Illinois during the Cinerama production of *How the West Was Won*, and it was tremendously interesting. Another interesting location was when we made *Hush, Hush, Sweet Charlotte* in Baton Rouge, Louisiana. I was surrounded with the best, most seasoned professionals such as Bette Davis, Olivia de Havilland, and Joseph Cotten and the director Robert Aldrich.

Mike: Have you made many films on location outside the United States?

Moorehead: Oh, yes. Sicily, Italy, Yugoslavia, France, Spain. And I enjoy them thoroughly. Love working in Europe!

Mike: Do you prefer certain actors and actresses to work with?

Moorehead: You like the best. The better the cast, the better you are. I've worked with the tops, and I think they are marvelous. I'm always excited at doing scenes with people who are very experienced and know what they are doing. It's the people who don't know what they're about and are self-indulgent who are very difficult to play with.

Mike: Do you think there is much truth in the statement that actors are more self-centered than the average person?

Moorehead: They are a breed unto themselves. I must say that! They are highly sensitive, easily hurt, and they are amusing, creative, interesting, and, many times, exciting people. They have a patois conversation that is all their own, so that an outsider really feels like an outsider because he just doesn't know that particular kind of theater talk or the various things that happen that theater folks know about and feel comfortable speaking about. I don't think actors are particularly self-centered. Maybe you find it sometimes, but you might find it in any business.

Mike: But it takes a lot of self-centeredness, or at least self-confidence, to lose one's inhibitions and perform before an audience or a camera, doesn't it?

Moorehead: I don't know about inhibitions because I never had any trouble with creating something. I never thought I was inhibited. I don't think my life has been inhibited in any way. I'm disciplined, and when one is disciplined in or out of the theater, he's free. My life has been very free. I know right and wrong, and I abide by the rules and regulations of my life. In my work I don't feel I am prevented from doing something because I couldn't do that particular thing in my own life. There are many people in the theater who are dull outside their work, but when performing come to life. Maybe that has to do with inhibitions. They seem to expand with an audience, when given something to do, and they hide behind the character. I never thought of hiding behind the character, but a lot of people, I suppose, do. They use beards and different kinds of clothes to hide behind. Then they can shoot out another type of personality rather than their own.

Mike: Do you find it necessary to mix your professional life with your private social life? Is it all part of your career?

Moorehead: It's seldom that you make real close friends in the theater. You have a lot of acquaintances and people whom you can say hello to and sit down and talk to, but no really close friends. You go into a picture, and you like everybody, and you have a good time; but when the picture is finished, it is seldom that you find you are invited out to dinner, or that you invite them over to dinner, or that you get closer to them. I find, too, that when you are starring in a play, you have a certain responsibility to the cast. You have to keep that cast together; therefore, you can be friendly, but you can't be overly so because then you don't have the respect and you don't have the authority. I did some pictures at MGM with Greer Garson, and she and I are very good friends. We evidently had very good chemistry together, so we visit back and forth. I'll go over to her place and have tea or visit her down in Dallas, and it's fun. It's a warm and close relationship. Debbie Reynolds and I have another extremely close relationship. It developed during *How the West Was Won*, and we seemed to carry on from there. Carroll Baker played one of my other daughters in that same picture, and we got along fine, but we don't now have any contact as friends. So I can say I have an awful lot of acquaintances in the business, but very, very few close friends.

Mike: It is often said that whom you know is extremely important in building a career and holding on to it.

Moorehead: Well, I think so. It's the contacts that you make. Certainly, if it hadn't been for my knowing Orson Welles as well as I did, I might not have been out here. Sure, it's a series of contacts. The contacts I made in radio and the contacts I made out here while under contract to MGM. And my knowing Charles Laughton so well that all of a sudden I was in a play with him that lasted for four years in the early 1950's! *Don Juan in Hell* was one of the great successes of our era and toured all over the country. It was one of the most exciting pieces you could possibly have in the theater.* Well, what was it? Paths crossed, and evidently the chemistry was right!

Mike: Earlier you said one has to expand and grow in his profession. How do you apply that to your friend Orson Welles, who reached a pinnacle of attainment in his early career but has not been very prominent for many years now?

Moorehead: You always find great points of brilliance in things Orson does today, and there isn't anything he does that does not fascinate you. You find things that surprise and interest you. But you must realize that Orson is hampered by a great number of obstacles, by production, and by money. If he has a picture he wants to make in Europe, he has to put certain people in it, in order to get the production, whom he might not want to put in it. There are a lot of things that enter into it. However, a person of Orson's caliber always keeps busy. He's always doing things. He's either narrating, or he's doing television, or he's on BBC, or he's doing a picture, or he's directing something. He never stops! Good, bad or indifferent, and he's right! You can't have successes all the time. Acting is a gamble, and the most insecure art you can be in, I think. Other artistic endeavors afford more security. For instance, if a writer's book is successful, he has it right in his hand and can say, "This is my book! Read it." It's the same way with a painting; it is there. And a great piece of music can go on and on and on. But an actor cannot point to

* Miss Moorehead again toured in this play in 1972–73.

his performance continually and say, "This is what I did." Not even if it's on film, because film becomes dated. An actor can only point to himself and say, "Here is my manufacturing plant. It's all I have to rely on."

Mike: What do you think of the present state of the motion-picture industry?

Moorehead: All mixed up. They better get with it! Believe me! You cannot nourish anything that is fine, and could take on greater fineness, in the gutter. I think the major trouble with the entertainment world today is that it has become so permissive that it gets ugly, corrupt, and dirty. That will destroy it. Gutter life never is successful. It might shock to a point and be a curiosity, but it will destroy the mind. It appeals to the lowest, most unattractive facets of human nature. And to think how saturated the industry is with producers who desire to make money from that type of appeal! I saw a picture the other night with children in it who used some very permissive words. Now, I'm sorry, but the children in the audience get those ugly words in their subconscious minds. So do grown-ups. If a dirty word is said over and over again, pretty soon you will say it and think, "Well, there's nothing to that." That's where the destructive part of it comes in because it causes one to lose perception of what is right or wrong or what is good or bad taste, and one's mind functions on a lower level than what it is capable. The use of the brain is lessened. Animallike behavior is based on instinct and habit; it doesn't require an alert, aware, and trained mind. So I say refinement, manners, and morals indicate a greater use of one's mental powers. These things make us distinguishable from lower animals. I don't care what anybody says about movies containing vulgar language and actions—they are corrupt and destructive!

Mike: Would you turn down a job if you had to speak foul language?

Moorehead: I won't say dirty four-letter words. Believe me, I just won't do it. It disgusts me, and I don't want to be around it. I don't want to hear it. I don't want to get into that kind of muck. I'm not interested in that kind of thing. I don't care if the whole world likes it. There are people who say to me, "Oh, well, that's life, Agnes." Well, it isn't my kind of life! I don't say or read things that will stultify my particular creativity, and that's what will do it. Every time it will do it. It will destroy you. It's just like a drug, you know: "Let me see some more. Let me read some more, because it feels so good." Just like a drug, it destroys!

Mike: So you would reject a role you thought was morally wrong?

Moorehead: Sure, if I didn't think it was in good taste. I'm not a prude by any manner of means because I've been in the theater a long, long time and I've heard everything. But I think it is possible to do things with taste, so that the imagination of an audience is stimulated better than it would be by vulgarity. There have always been beautiful plays and films to which no one takes offense because they have been done tastefully and with good judgment. And it is strong film and theater. I hope that's what will again dominate. I think it will because the larger audience has had its stomachful of dirty films. They just don't go anymore. People don't want to see that kind of life. They can see it in the papers and hear it on the news. They're sick and tired of it and don't want to pay three dollars to go into a movie theater and see it. They can't be bothered with it.

Mike: Do you think the entertainment industry is too full of people who are mainly interested in the commercial aspects of it?

Moorehead: In the money, yes. And the love of money is the root of all evil.

Mike: The desire to make money has always overshadowed the desire to make artistic films in Hollywood, but now it has increased to a very damaging degree.

Moorehead: Well, I remember when Mr. Mayer, Louis B. Mayer, was alive and I was under contract to him at MGM. He was interested, naturally, in making a profit for MGM, but he was very careful about the stories in which he presented his stars. There was never a picture in which I performed that he didn't come onto the set before we started the picture and congratulate everybody by saying he was so glad they were in the picture and that he knew it was going to be a fine picture. That was an exciting thing. Well, this was the head of MGM. You try to find them now who will come down and give you a pat on the back! They couldn't care less!

Mike: Of course, nowadays, one successful movie can make a fortune and the producer can retire; he doesn't have to be concerned with having a good reputation in order to continue. If he has a good reputation for making money, that seems to be all he needs.

Moorehead: But that doesn't make for good work. People will work better when someone in authority comes on the set and says, "It's marvelous! Enjoy it because you're going to be wonderful working together!" It's that kind of thing that keeps that dough together; otherwise, it becomes flaky and will not adhere.

Mike: So a lot of the people who function in films are the people who will compromise with and be a part of the commercial setup?

Moorehead: You can't help a certain amount of it. On the other hand, there's someone like Aaron Spelling who produces movies for television. He said, "I use the old people. They're the ones I can rely on. I know I'm going to have good performances."

Mike: But there are many creative people who have chosen to bow out of the business because they can't cope with the commercialism of it any longer.

Moorehead: It's the stories. If it was a good story, they could cope with it.

Mike: I'm referring to the overall commercial approach to the making of a film today, the story included.

Moorehead: You have to adjust yourself the best you can and still keep your standards. I feel that way because I'm in the commercial end of it. I've been doing television for seven years, and I don't think of it as my particular standard; regardless, I have had to adjust to that commercial medium. And it is commercial. There's no theater about it. Television *is* a commercial. It sells a product. I don't care how good you are, if you can't sell the product you're out! In the theater you're not selling detergents or anything. You're doing it because you want to be in a good entertaining play. Also, in television you have different minds controlling things. You have that Madison Avenue mind, which is only interested in the product to be advertised.

Mike: Do you believe there is a lack of good creative writing?

Moorehead: Believe me, I don't know how these writers stand it! Any good writer can become a hack in a short time. Do you realize how they have to grind those things out for television?

Mike: Some writers are writing below themselves.

Moorehead: There are good writers around, but many of them write themselves out with all that pressure on them day after day. Writing for television is difficult because it's so fast and demanding. They have to grind them out like sausages!

Mike: Do you think they find any artistic gratification in it at all?

Moorehead: Oh, to a point. There are a few rare shows like *Hallmark* and some of the programs on the educational channel, Channel 28, which have high quality.

Mike: Do you think motion pictures will ever regain the importance they used to have, in spite of television?

Moorehead: They could, but it will take people who love the business and have taste and judgment.

January 7, 1971

A Struggling Young Actor

DAVID CANNON

Mike: What made you want to be an actor, David?

Cannon: To explain that, I would have to fall back on the cliché of an unhappy childhood. My parents were divorced when I was eleven, and I was sent off to military school before my twelfth birthday. I stayed there through age seventeen. As a kid, I guess you would describe me as an outsider. A kid who never quite fit in, who never felt he was part of what was going on. This subsequently led me into what you would refer to as an acting-out phase of juvenile delinquency. Getting into and out of trouble as a teen-ager. Being thrown out of one military school and going to another. Drinking. Raising hell. Being slung in jail. This sort of thing.

I remember when I was in the seventh grade there was a girl about eleven or twelve who was a grade ahead of me. She was a queen as far as I was concerned. When I met her, she looked at me and her eyes got wide and she said, "Gee! You look like a movie star!" That always stuck in my mind. Later, in military school when I was going through all the unhappy experiences and maladjustments, I kept going back to the idea of being an actor.

Mike: Do you feel these experiences gave you more sensitivity?

Cannon: Definitely. I didn't grow up in a family environment. I never knew what it was like to live in a home with a family. So I grew up hard and quick. This naturally made me more sensitive to everything around me. There was a lot of pain, a lot of bitterness, a lot of resentment. I entered college with this same renegade feeling.

Mike: A feeling that if you gained public attention through a mass medium it would be a type of love given you that you have missed?

Cannon: Yes, that's very valid. One of the greatest thrills I know is to be onstage after a performance and hear the applause of the audience. It's overwhelming! I'm sure that subconsciously I interpret this as a form of acceptance. I remember one night in London when I was in my middle twenties studying at the Royal Academy of Dramatic Arts. I was playing the part of Willy Loman in *Death of a Salesman* in the West End of London. It was a prodigious effort because Willy of course is a sixty-two-year-old man. We had been in constant rehearsals for six weeks. Hour after hour I had fought and struggled to get this man, to get his age, the whole range of emotions that Willy feels. We opened on a Monday. It was very successful. The next afternoon I received a telegram from one of the biggest agents in London congratulating me on my performance. When I walked onstage *that* night in the opening scene, the feeling of elation I had was incredible. I heard Laurence Olivier once say that before his first entrance for *Richard III* he knew as he opened the door that he could do no wrong. That was the feeling I had that night. At the curtain call a large part of the audience rose and gave us a standing ovation. I literally felt like throwing myself out into the audience because the feeling of acceptance was so great.

Mike: Did you go to England with the idea of an acting career in mind?

Cannon: Yes, I went there to prepare as an actor. My life up until my third year in college had lacked any direction. I had engaged in a lot of self-destruction, studying just enough to get by. I had found no channel for these very strong feelings. I was in an English class once at Emory University in Atlanta, and someone asked me if I would be interested in reading for a play the school was doing. I went along and read and was cast in a small part in a play called *Tiger at the Gate.* I did several other parts at Emory. From that point on my one aim became to somehow get to California and become involved in the acting profession. So I did come to California and enrolled at San Diego State College. I took a major in psychology and a minor in theater arts. I took every acting class they had going, every voice class, every fencing class, and I was in every play I could get into. I was totally committed by the time I graduated from college, and within a week I was on a ship on the way to London to audition for the Royal Academy of Dramatic Arts. I arrived in London with about thirty dollars. There were nine hundred people to audition. We had to wait outside in the hallway. When it was your turn to audition, they rang a little bell. You had to go onstage and give your name and what scenes you were going to do. You had to do one piece from Shakespeare and one piece from a modern play. I can tell you it was one of the most frightening moments of my life. Fortunately, I managed to be in the twenty-eight they accepted.

Mike: You could perform for the public while you were there?

Cannon: For the first year you do nothing but work on basic skills. You do productions within the academy which are reviewed by the staff, but you don't go before the public until your fifth term. Then you are in a classic Greek play. The last three terms you are in what amounts to a repertory company formed of RADA players, students at the Royal Academy. Of course, this means that we can perform in the RADA Theatre in the West End of London without being subject to the English Equity laws which ordinarily make it next to impossible for a foreign actor to work in England. We perform in a regular theater before a London audience and London agents and so on. That is where I did *Death of a Salesman.*

After that play I was approached by Al Parker and his wife, Maggie Parker, who had one of the largest agencies in London. They became my representatives. I had received a letter from the Royal Shakespeare Company in London expressing an interest in me and asking me if as an American I would be able to get a work permit from the British Home Office and English Equity. Through the Parker Agency we investigated every avenue and found out it was virtually impossible. They are very strict on all foreigners who desire to work in Britain. As a matter of fact, I graduated from the Royal Academy on the twenty-third of July, 1968, and I had to be out of the country by the twenty-eighth! My allotted time in the country expired and I could not get an extension. So I had to leave.

I had heard there was a lot of film activity in Rome. My agent said there was a part open in the film called *The Adventurers* which was being made in Rome from the Harold Robbins novel. Mrs. Parker wired the director that I was leaving immediately for Rome. She wasn't aware that I had only about fifteen dollars to my name! My last week at the academy I had sold most of my clothes and belongings to raise a few dollars to be able to get out of town. The director in Rome took the telegram to mean I was flying by jet to Rome and would be there the next day. No one was aware that I was going to have to cross the English Channel on the ferry and start hitchhiking from Calais, France. This took me nearly four days to do. I slept in fields and carried a rucksack on my back. While this was going on, the director in Rome wondered where the hell I was. He thought I had arrived but was enjoying myself, boozing it up and taking my sweet time in getting in touch with him. I arrived in Rome totally exhausted and immediately found a cheap hotel, the Salvation Army Hotel, down in the working-class section. I went right to sleep for about fifteen hours. The next day I called the director. He said, "Where the hell have you been?" I said, "Didn't Mrs. Parker tell you I was hitchhiking?" He said, "No. We expected you the next day. Your part's been filled." So I went out to see him in person. He said, "We do have a small part. We don't know how small it is because it's being rewritten. But you would be playing John Ireland's secretary. John Ireland is playing a Texas Senator who is a millionaire, so you might have a couple of scenes, and it will be a little bit of money and a few days' work." So I said fine.

In the meantime Mrs. Parker had written to a Mr. Guidi of the Dino de Laurentiis Studio about a film called *The Five S.O.B.'s*. I went to see him, and we hit it off fine, and he offered me the part of a young pilot in the movie. It was to star George C. Scott and to be directed by Arthur Hiller. Mr. Hiller was coming to Rome in a week or ten days. I said fine, because it was a good little dramatic part. A good thing to start off with. So Arthur Hiller came to town, and I met him. Suddenly there was some talk of my playing one of the leads, one of the five SOB's. This was fantastic to me! I had only been out of drama school two weeks! Then unfortunate things began happening. First off, George C. Scott dropped out of the film to go into a movie called *Patton*. Then we found out Arthur Hiller, the director, was no longer interested. Mr. Guidi was flying back and forth to California and New York trying to get a director. They had five versions of the script from which they couldn't decide on one. So we waited, and we waited. Meantime, a friend from the academy and I were both cast as British cavalry officers in a film called *The Adventures of Girard*. We were waiting for that to begin. What we came to realize is a schedule in Italy means very little. In fact, it doesn't mean a damn thing! If they say they will begin shooting in September, that may well mean January! As it turned out I did this small part in *The Adventurers* on location south of Rome. I still waited for *The Five S.O.B.'s* to begin, but more and more time passed. My money ran out, and I did day-work in some terrible Italian films just to stay alive. Finally, I had a call from Mr. Guidi to come out to his office, at which time he very sheepishly informed me *The Five S.O.B.'s* had been indefinitely postponed. I couldn't really blame *him*. This is just the way things happen. I think this experience points up the thing that is so important in this business: being in the right place at the right time. If things had just turned the other way, I'm sure I would have come into Hollywood in a very different position. Anyway I left Rome and went back to London, where I made further inquiries about a work permit and about going to work for the Royal Shakespeare Company. It was to no avail. I arrived back in the United States, sadder but wiser, and came to Hollywood. The Al Parker Agency had written to the Marvin Josephson Agency here in Hollywood, and I was signed by them. They later became affiliated with the Ashley-Famous Agency, which in turn became the International-Famous Agency, by whom I am presently represented.

Mike: Do you think the atmosphere in Hollywood right now is good for a struggling actor to get ahead, to fulfill his ambitions?

Cannon: Well, I came to Hollywood with a headful of idealism, with some starry-eyed ideas. I had been one of the six out of my class to graduate with honors from the Royal Academy. I don't know what exactly I anticipated when I came to Hollywood, but at least I anticipated an opportunity—an opportunity not only to succeed, but an opportunity to fail as well. I think if someone gives you an opportunity and you fail, the responsibility is yours. But I think the biggest disappointment for me here has been the lack of a chance to display or to utilize the abilities that I know I have. The abilities that I have taken the time, the money, and the effort to train. I have very real idealism and strong feelings about the profession and the industry. I am not here for the fast buck. This is my life. I am really interested in film. I am devoted to it. I do not mean to criticize my agency because they are in a very difficult position. The people in my agency are genuine people, and I think are genuinely interested in me as a human being. And I communicate with them as a human being.

This isn't true with a lot of agents around town, and it is a tragic situation. I know full well that a lot of people on the other side of the desk are not aware of the agonizing pressures and frustrations that a trained and sincere actor who is a craftsman can meet with. Too often the actor is a commodity. Too often a phone call from an actor is a bothersome, tiresome thing. It's too easy to say, "He's in a meeting," or, "He's on another phone, can we return the call?" Fortunately I don't have that experience with my agency, and this is to their credit. However, I am with a very large agency with many clients. I am an unknown with a conspicuous lack of film on myself, and I have found in Hollywood that film is the name of the game. Film is the magic word. I sometimes feel that people in this town believe the established actors were born already having film. I mean, I've been around town and given good auditions doing scenes from plays. I've stood up in front of casting directors and done speeches from Shakespeare. I've done soliloquies from Tennessee Williams. I've gone through the whole Hollywood interview bit.

The Hollywood interview is a thing that interests me. I think, perhaps, if I were a casting director or a producer, I might fall into the same thing. I might be guilty of the same thing. But I think that many times the qualities that people in the producing and casting side of the industry look for in an office interview are the qualities that are best displayed not by an actor but by a standup comedian, a nightclub personality. The sort of facile, scintillating personality type of thing. The only example I can give is the guy who goes to a reading for a play and gives a beautiful reading. The producer and director are absolutely bowled over, and they cast the guy. Then four weeks later they realize he can't act. That he hasn't developed one inch above the original reading. I believe oftentimes the most sensitive and capable actors, the actors with the most depth, are those who are the least adept at this sort of office business. The light, meaningless repartee one is expected to engage in during a typical Hollywood interview. Maybe I am saying this defensively because I am by nature a reticent, introspective person. I try to speak when I have something meaningful to say. I don't find a hell of a lot of things funny. Sometimes I think casting people are not looking for actors, but nightclub entertainer type personalities. This is one explanation as to why so often they go wrong in their casting and why one sees, quite frankly, so much bad work being done on television and in movies. That's not to say there's not a hell of a lot of good work going on.

But I think it is extremely difficult for a young, unknown actor, however highly trained he might be, to go in cold, without film, then come out of an office with a job. If you don't have a decent piece of film on yourself, you are at a tremendous disadvantage. At least twenty actors with film have been seen before you, and if none of those twenty fit the bill, then possibly you are given an interview. You may go in and give a damn good reading, and in the time between your leaving the office and the time when your agent gets in touch with the casting agent you might have lost a part, because these people are so set with the idea that if it's not on film it's not real. The casting people succumb to the doubts, fears, and sort of suspicion that accompany an actor who is starting out and doesn't have film to show. They are afraid to take a chance and jeopardize their own security. Why should they when they can call someone with whose work they are familiar? This is the thing the new actor goes up against every time he walks into an office and must overcome, if possible.

Mike: Also, since there are fewer films being made nowadays, well-established actors are in bad need of work and will take smaller parts which used to be given to lesser known or unknown people.

Cannon: Yes. You have name actors that will take the so-called cameo role that in other days the young actor starting out might have been given. There just isn't that much work around, and there is a certain amount of nepotism. Also, directors have a small group they like to work with again and again. It's a matter of cracking that group. That is almost impossible.

Mike: What are some of the things you do to try to get a job?

Cannon: You can occasionally call people you think you have favorably impressed. But there again, I have no desire to bug anyone, to pester anyone. You can make suggestions to your agent as to parts you have heard about that you think are right for you. But in a big agency, if you are an unknown actor, you've got to realize that you are a certain way down the list. This means you are not sent on interviews as much as you should be because there are some established people in front of you who will be sent first. So you are fighting it on two fronts. I know for the first few months I was here I paced the floor. I beat the hell out of the punching bag at the gym. I did everything waiting for that phone to ring. Now I have managed to channel some of this energy, this frustration, into writing. I've completed one screenplay, and I'm working on another. So, when the phone doesn't ring, I keep busy at the desk and typewriter. I'm not at a coffeehouse with other actors talking about this and that and what they have coming up. I think that is pathetic. I mean, if you don't have anything coming up, say so. One of the cruelest things about Hollywood is delusion. I see so many people with no training and very little talent who seem to be deluding themselves. It is a question I constantly ask myself. It's this thing of having to stay in touch with reality.

Mike: Nevertheless, those people who appear to have no training or talent many times get ahead!

Cannon: No doubt about that. I know people who have done it. There is a certain amount of casting that goes on at parties and that kind of stuff. OK. That's fine. But I wonder how far these people get ahead. I try to look beyond the odd TV job now and then or the bit in the movie here and there to a substantial career. I've tried to build this career gradually, steadily on a solid basis ever since I got interested in acting. OK, some guys come to Hollywood with no training, but with a quirk of personality, hit it lucky. But I find it difficult to believe that they will have any lasting success. I think there have been some rather tragic examples of this regarding certain people here in Hollywood just recently. Guys who were fair-haired boys discovered in bars or here and there who now put ads in the trade papers or go on late-night talk shows looking for work. They've come to the end of the road. As far as I'm concerned, that sort of thing is built on a house of sand anyway. It's bound to be of limited duration. I want to be the best. I want to do good work, really good work. And I want to go on studying and improving. I think I've gone about it the right way.

Mike: I've observed through the years that a person who joins forces with another who has the same aim often makes it to the top. Two can make it easier than one, by complementing each other and putting their drive and contacts and efforts together. An ambitious actor marrying an actress who is just as intensely ambitious as himself. Two can fight the struggle better than one. Also, I know of alliances being made between an actor or actress and his or her agent on a romantic basis. The actor will make the agent actually fall in love with him so that the agent works harder to promote that actor who is the love object. There are any variety of situations taking place which form an alliance so that a person isn't struggling alone.

Cannon: I think that is very important. In my own personal case, my wife works as an assistant to a literary agent here. She's working on her master's thesis at present because her ambition is to teach in college. But we both have certain common goals and ideals that we share and support each other in. I also have some friends, very decent people, who share a lot of the ideas I have. Right now I am working on a project with a friend of mine who is a wonderful actor who studied at the Bristol Old Vic in England. He's experienced a lot of the difficulty and frustration that I have. I'm working very hard on a script that we hope to do on a very low budget. We have certain people who are interested in helping us raise the money. We want to involve a lot of creative people in a participation type effort and get this picture made.

Mike: Since you haven't been given an opportunity to show what you can do, you are creating your own opportunity.

Cannon: Exactly. I'll still go out on interviews, but I don't intend to sit and wait for opportunity to come along. I don't like to stand by. Nelson Rockefeller once said, "I'm not made up of standby material," and this really impressed me because I like to feel that I'm not either. Well, by the common measuring sticks that are used in Hollywood today, I'm nothing. I'm unknown, and to some people I would be nobody. But I don't accept that. And to sit back and moan and cry and feel sorry for oneself is the worst possible thing an actor can do. I think, at the same time, that a certain amount of pain, frustration, and anguish is not a bad thing for an actor. To be at the depths of these feelings awakens things in an actor that can be used in his art. I read somewhere that English actors act with their voices, Russian actors act with their whole lives. I think that's the secret. You've got to act or write with your whole life. Any artistic endeavor has got to involve all that is inside you.

Mike: Writing is a creative outlet that you yourself can control without having to depend on someone else to hire you to be creative.

Cannon: But a writer must have a lot of discipline. You and I don't operate a drill press at Lockheed. We don't pump gas. We don't punch a time clock at any factory. We do not do the eight to five work. We're self-employed; therefore, a large part of our lives is nonstructured as opposed to most guys. So it is contingent upon our personal discipline to structure our lives in a creative fashion. I have to realize I have a job. A job that is imposed on me by myself. Part of that job is getting to a gymnasium and working out so that I am fit and in shape. This is part of an actor's job. Part of his job is doing a certain amount of work on his voice, and a large part of my job is going to the desk and the typewriter and sitting down and working on scripts. There's no one to tell me I've got to do it. I've got to tell myself. I have to prevent events from controlling me and must maintain a grip on time and events.

Mike: Do you spend time in acting class continuing your training?

Cannon: Frankly, I tell you, I would like to study with a particular teacher here in town, but it's a matter of finances at present. I find to be able to study with the right teacher is expensive. I just can't manage it at present. I don't think talent leaves you. I think if you are alive and aware and thinking, you can pretty much stay up with your talent. If you've had training, you do things instinctively when you are acting. I went to England as an amateur with ability, and I returned as a professional. But still, I definitely would like to be studying with Estelle Harman here, and I intend to when things are better. I want to continue to explore and expand and never, never be satisfied with a performance.

Mike: When you finished school in England, why did you choose film work instead of trying for the legitimate theater?

Cannon: There were several reasons, Mike. Some psychological and some very practical. I had done quite a bit of stage work in college and at the Old Globe Theater in San Diego. In England I was involved around the clock for almost three years in stage productions. I had the choice when I returned to the States of going to New York instead of Hollywood. Quite frankly, New York at that point of my life, and now also, was a physical environment containing particular circumstances and situations that I couldn't face up to. I felt for physical and psychic reasons I just couldn't go to New York and try to make a start. It's an environmental thing. I just don't dig the city. I've been there about four times, and it is something I didn't want to expose myself to. I didn't want to live in New York. I didn't want my wife to live there. Also, I think the stage training and experience I have had is a very good background for cinema.

Mike: Once you gain a position as an actor through films, will you want to do occasional stage work?

Cannon: Definitely. In fact, if something came up right here in town, I would do it. I would love to get into a Shakespeare production, or a

Shaw, or Ibsen or Tennessee Williams. There is another very practical reason I came to Hollywood. That is that I am very much interested in cinema. I think it is a fascinating medium, and the highest-paying jobs are in films and television. To get my schooling at the Royal Academy in England, I had to go quite a bit into debt by borrowing money. Several thousand dollars which has to be repaid. Because of that obligation, it is more practical to work in Hollywood.

Mike: At present do you earn enough in acting to live on?

Cannon: No, I don't. My wife works. Recently, I've gone out on some interviews for television commercials. Always, I keep in mind that these things are not important. What is important is what I am doing at the typewriter, and of course the fact that the right part just might come up.

December 12, 1969

The Screenwriter

STEWART STERN

Mike: Since you, as a writer, contribute the first and perhaps most important ingredient to the making of a motion picture, the screenplay, it would be interesting to know and understand the events and experiences of your life which developed that talent. Therefore, Stewart, I'm going to ask you to go more into the details of your background, if you don't mind.

Stewart: All right. New York was my home for the first twenty-four years of my life. My father is a physician who had his office in our house, so I was born at home on the dining-room table! My mother is self-taught, a very well-read woman who is up on everything in literature, theater, music, and the other arts. She was the youngest child of my grandmother, an Orthodox Jewish lady from Hungary who had been a pioneer. Grandma and Grandpa Kaufman staked out a claim in the Dakota Territory and built a sod house. They had a very tough life as farm people and withstood about six winters there before they gave up. Grandma always observed the Jewish Sabbath on Friday nights and Saturdays. The Sioux Indians loved the smell of her baking and would come by and eat her egg bread. Sometimes they were there when she would bless the wine in Hebrew, and they'd sit in their blankets and listen very respectfully. She was good at midwifery and got such a reputation among the Indians that they would bring their squaws to the sod house when they were ready to have their babies, and Grandma helped deliver them. In return, the Indians used to hunt meat for her, but she would only eat kosher, so her husband and brothers always told her they went to Devils Lake to buy it when actually they made a deal with the Indians to leave the meat on the other side of the hill so Grandma never knew what she was eating! My mother was born after Grandma went back to Chicago. About that time Grandma's second oldest daughter married Adolph Zukor. By the time Mom was in her teens, Zukor was well established as a pioneer in the motion picture business. Through him my mother met a lot of theater people and caught the acting bug. She studied at the American Academy of Dramatic Arts and had small parts in several Broadway musicals. Grandma thought it was sinful for a girl to be on the stage. It broke her heart that Mom was exhibiting herself publicly. She let her unhappiness be known to Uncle Adolph, who did everything he could to make my mother give up the stage. She did but never got it out of her system, even after she married my father.

Mike: Was your mother's love of theater a strong influence on your youth?

Stern: Very much so. As a child I was extremely imaginative. I lived in fantasy a lot and was somewhat solitary. Another strong influence was the fact I had a younger sister who was very sickly and extremely protected. They used to have a screen around her bed. I was told not to make any noise or let her see me because Marjorie was not supposed to get excited. If she did, she would turn blue and have convulsions, and they would have to hold her under cold water. It was as if I were still an only child, but that someone else had come into the house whose existence was mysterious to me. She was such a tender, vulnerable baby. Another deep influence was my love for animals. I loved cows! Uncle Adolph had a thousand-acre estate across the

Hudson River called Mountain View Farm with a purebred Guernsey herd on it. We used to go out there every summer. I remember when the Lindbergh baby was kidnapped, they put bars on all the windows of the house I lived in with my cousins. The farm had everything a kid could possibly want. I loved to swim in the enormous pool, but mainly I wanted to be with the cows! I identified with them in some curious way, or rather with their calves. Whenever I could get away from my governess, I wandered with the cows as if I were one of them, and I found great peace. One of the sweetest things I know, even today, is a dairy barn when the cows come in. There's something deeply satisfying to me in the sound of their eating, chomping that dry mash before they're milked, and the clank of the pails, the clash of the stanchions. I used to model cows in clay when I was three years old.

Mike: Were your parents aware of an artistic bent developing in you?

Stern: Yes. And my father is an artist as well as a physician. They started me at the Ethical Culture School in New York where a child's talent was stimulated to grow. Individuality was respected and nurtured. We had cooking and sewing classes, as well as shop. We cooked meat on hot stones. Our experience as first graders was akin to the life of early man on earth. The theory was that an individual grew and developed and learned just as the human race had done, or tried to do. That helped the imagination.

Mike: Did you attend much of the New York theater as a child?

Stern: Often. Probably the most decisive moment in my life was the first Saturday matinee of *Peter Pan* my mother took me to see, at the Civic Repertory Theater, with Eva Le Gallienne playing Peter in a production she had directed. It was the most incredible moment I've ever had! She was an astonishing Peter Pan because she understood what Sir James Barrie meant in his writing. It was a stealthy theft when Peter flew off with those kids! It was a crime, a kidnapping on the part of a jealous delinquent who couldn't stand to see children happy with a mother. The flying was incredible! You really couldn't see the wires. Le Gallienne didn't smile much as Peter Pan. She was furtive and watchful and dangerous and devious and thrilling! At the end she came out for a solo curtain call and for the first time openly smiled. As the applause got bigger, the smile got broader until she spread her arms and flew over the audience and touched the hands of the kids in the balcony and flew back! That moment clinched it for me. From that point on I *was* Peter Pan. My mother had to make me a Peter Pan suit, and my room was turned into the Never-Never Land. I had animal skins on top of my bookcase. The minute I got home from school, I'd put on my Peter Pan suit and lie on top of the bookcase wrapped in skins, with a rubber knife in my teeth. My father didn't take to that too well, so on my tenth birthday, in 1932, he arranged to show the first Johnny Weissmuller Tarzan picture at my party. I stopped being Peter Pan and changed my room to a jungle with vines my sister knitted on her "Knitting Nancy." I was always organizing the kids at school into bands of apes and elephants. I was pretty big, so I was always Tarzan. My special friend was Hallee Morris, and she played Jane, until I hit her with a hammer for a reason I've now forgotten. So my hunger for theater was a combination of being excessively imaginative as a child, having an artistic father and a mother who had been frustrated in her own ambitions and who recognized similar ones in me and was absolutely determined to let those be fulfilled.

Mike: What was your first conscious attempt as a creative artist?

Stern: I suppose it was drawing and painting. I drew cows and other animals when I was very, very young. It helped me remember the summers I spent in the country. But there was some extraordinary thunderhead of rage building up in me already. Even the most bucolic scenes I painted, when you look at them through the eyes of somebody my age who is psychoanalytically oriented, have a tremendous hidden fury. I suppose that's why I began to write, to set straight that enormous conflict that I can only see the shadow of. It's still there. I think an awful lot of my writing is an attempt to organize that chaos into some kind of harmony so that just for a second it comes to rest and I can catch my breath. Even though it is not solved, it *appears* to be solved in some idealized way. Then another storm starts!

Mike: You began writing when you were in college?

Stern: Yes. But at first I was an art major. When the time came for me to go to college, people kept recommending Iowa for its wonderful art department. Since it was in farming country, it held a certain fascination for me. Also, I had always been very protected. I had been with the same kids since the time I was six, mostly the children of upper-class Jewish professional people. I felt it would be a good thing for me to get away from New York and everything that made me feel safe and see what would happen if I got lost in a huge Midwestern university. When I got off the train at Iowa City, I heard one baggage handler say to another, "There's another one of them from Jew York." I thought, "Oh, my God! What am I going to run into here?" There was no room for me at the dorm, so they gave me a list of approved boardinghouses. I wandered around town with my suitcase all day long knocking on screen doors. Those doors would open off old Victorian porches with gliders and potted ferns. A wave of sauerkraut would come out and hit you in the face. But they never opened the door all the way. They'd look you over and say, "Jew boy?" and shut the door again. Finally this lady took me in and gave me a room. I hated that first year, but the next year I was able to move into the dorm, where I began to make friends. It was a much happier experience. I changed my major to theater arts and drama and was graduated in 1943, *magna cum laude,* Phi Beta Kappa, all the honors I was supposed to have. My dad said I was finally "an accomplished fact." They activated my ROTC class during the final school semester. Wherever we walked on campus, we had to go in twos, marching at attention. It was all pretty silly to me. I flunked out of Officers' Candidate School at Fort Benning, Georgia, because they said I didn't understand the "spirit of the bayonet." I'm delighted to admit that. They sent me to the 106th Infantry Division and eventually made me a rifle squad leader. I trained two squads of guys who were sent off to combat as replacements; then the whole division moved to England aboard the old *Aquitania.* We were spread in a thin line from St.-Vith, Belgium, to the Luxembourg border when Von Rundstedt attacked on December 16, 1944. He pulverized our division, but certain elements held. Our company was one of those. My buddy, Jimmy Sramek, and I somehow held our squad together. We fought as we fell back toward Malmédy, formed little circles of defense at village crossroads, got surrounded and sneaked out through German lines in the middle of the night. Over and over. It was incredibly cold. My pants were torn off on a barbed-wire fence, so I was pretty much bare-ass during the Battle of the Bulge. While Jimmy and I had the squad, nobody died; I don't know how that happened. On Christmas Eve I could no longer load my rifle or walk. My hands were stiff as wood, and the fingers were so frostbitten that if you bit the ends of them, your teeth didn't leave an impression. And my feet were no good anymore. We all had trenchfoot. The circulation had stopped, and they'd turned black. I made it back to the States after talking them out of a four-way amputation of my limbs. By the time I went to meet Jim Sramek when his troopship arrived after the war, I was a Broadway actor and really impressed with myself. A blessed man, Joe Fields, had given me my first job in a play he had written with Jerry Chodorov, *The French Touch*, which René Clair directed. My family said I was great. I had two lines, but they were deathless. The play lasted about seven minutes on Broadway. It had fine moments, but it never found its style.

Mike: When did you move to Hollywood?

Stern: In 1945. I came to California really to start life on my own. Uncle Adolph, chairman of the board of Paramount Pictures then, was convinced Hollywood was the place for me to be, but it seems he was alone in his opinion. I moved in with a paraplegic veteran and his wife who had an extra room and tried to find work. Nothing. My war savings soon gave out, and none of my relatives were inundating me with work. Somebody living at my rooming house had just promised me a job in the packing department at Schenley's, when I ran into Joe Fields again. He said, "Which relatives are you working for?" I said, "Are you kidding?" and told him I might go to work at Schenley's. He said, "That's ridiculous. You should be writing or directing or acting." He had a contract at Eagle-Lion Studios to write screenplays and to direct. He promised that if I came out there the next day, I was going to be a dialogue director. I didn't know what that was, and neither did he. He said, "I'm going to take you in to meet the executives and anything they ask you, you say *yes!*" We met with Brynie Foy, who was head of the studio. Joe Fields said, "This is Stewart Stern. Would you believe it if I told you he directed the Chicago company of *Doughgirls* and the national companies of *Junior Miss* and *My Sister Eileen*? He's a triple-threat man. You ought to put him to work." I nearly died. None of it had happened, but Joe said later it would have if he had known me that early. Foy looked at me and said, "Aren't you a little young to have done all that?" and I said *yes!* They took me to see Irving Lazar, who was head of the story department. He put me to work at seventy-five dollars a week.

Mike: What did you do as a dialogue director?

Stern: I rehearsed the actors, rewrote scenes, and even directed Turhan Bey! And I got in the way a lot. Howard Koch, who was later head of production at Paramount, was an assistant director on the first film I worked on, *Philo Vance's Gamble* in 1947. I sat right in front of the camera because I wanted to keep my eyes on the actors. He called my attention to the fact that I was the only thing on the screen and asked me to get out of the way. So I climbed way up to the grid and lay down on the catwalk. When one of the actors blew his lines, the director yelled, "Line!" and my voice came wafting down from the top of the stage! The job was a terrific experience. I really developed my voice!

Mike: Were you still trying to channel your career into acting and writing?

Stern: Yes. I would write stories in the seclusion of my rooming house. And I went to the Actors' Lab at night to continue my acting studies. They had fabulous teachers, among them David Alexander and Danny Mann. And Joe Papp was a fellow student. About that time a weird thing happened which dated back to when I was twelve years old and had gone to visit my cousin Jane Loew, granddaughter of Marcus Loew and daughter of Arthur Loew, Sr., at their villa at Glenn Cove, Long Island. Arthur Loew, Jr., was there, too. He and I shared a room. He had to go to bed early because he was only nine years old, but I was allowed downstairs to eat with the grown-ups and see the movie because I was twelve. When I came up to go to bed, Arthur sat up and turned on the light and said, "Stewart, we're going to be best friends, and we're both going to work in the movies, and we're going to have an apartment together in Hollywood." Then he went to sleep. So fade out—fade in: Hollywood, 1948. I'm twenty-six years old. The phone rings. Arthur Loew, Jr., twenty-three, whom I hadn't seen since we were boys. He said, "Well, have you found a place?" I said, "What do you mean?" He said, "Don't you remember? We're best friends, and we're going to have an apartment together and work in the movies!" We found a place south of Pico Boulevard. And we are best of friends. And we did work in the movies. He went to work at MGM. I remained at Eagle-Lion.

It was through Arthur that I really became a writer. He read and liked the short stories I had written. His father had secured MGM financing and release for a pet project of his called *The Search* which Fred Zinnemann had directed with Montgomery Clift. I thought it was the best film I had ever seen, and I wanted to meet Zinnemann in the worst way just to tell him what I thought of that movie. Arthur knew him and showed him my short stories. The outcome was that Zinnemann hired me to go to Israel with him to do research and write a screenplay for a project he had in mind. From that point on I was a writer, and Fred was my teacher. We went to Israel in the first year of its existence. The war was still going on, through the so-called truce. I learned through Zinnemann where drama lay, that you have to go to the source. And he taught me to write "in grunts": use images and behavior when you can, words as a last resort, *few* words—grunts. It was a searing experience to be in a Broadway theater one night and two nights later on a battlefield stepping over bodies, watching mass burials, standing guard at night talking to people, digging out their stories. People talk better in the dark. A lot of my research has been done at night. They forget you are there and are able to reach themselves. Out of the Israel visit I was able to write a story which never got anywhere, but at least Fred was aware of my existence as a writer.

When Arthur's father was going to produce another film, he put me to work rewriting a screenplay that Alfred Hayes had done called *Teresa*. I broke the story down psychologically. It was about a GI returning to New York with his Italian war bride. I went to the Veterans Administration, where they let me hear hours and hours of tape on the case histories of real GI's similar to the character in our story. Then I went to every location in New York that I wanted to use in the new script. There was one sequence where Teresa, the war bride, came past the Statue of Liberty. I wondered how that would really feel to people coming over for the first time. I arranged through some of the immigration groups to be put aboard a refugee ship while it was still beyond Ambrose Light. The ship was loaded with survivors from concentration camps. I stood in the dawn and mingled with them. Suddenly, Liberty's torch came out of the fog! Someone shouted. It was a most dramatic moment. They all crowded over to that side of the ship, and you could feel it listing as everybody hung over the rail weeping. I was really moved, because I had always taken it so much for granted. To see what freedom meant in that year and what this country still stood for was overpowering! To see them meet their relatives whom perhaps they had never seen! As each one came down the gangplank, someone called the name to relatives over a loudspeaker, and they'd rush to each other across that enormous empty space! Couple by couple, family by family. A whole new screenplay was born that loosely used what Alfred Hayes had done, but also used what Fred Zinnemann taught me about going to the source. And Zinnemann agreed to direct it.

Mike: Wasn't much of *Teresa* filmed in Italy?

Stern: Yes. I did research there, too. Zinnemann was busy editing his latest film, *The Men,* and had not had a chance to get over to Italy to find locations or the girl to play the lead, so he sent me. As someone who had tried so hard to be an actor and had met with so many frustrations, mostly owing to agents not having seen my work and not knowing who I was, I knew how difficult it was to get to the people you had to get to. Therefore, I put ads in the Rome papers. I said we were casting for the lead, an Italian girl of a certain age who needn't ever have acted and who didn't need to speak English. I sat there every day and saw hundreds of girls with their grandmothers! I took pictures of everyone who came. As I went north doing my research, following the route of the Fifth Army, I put ads in the papers of all of the cities I came to. Every night when I'd get to a new town there would be all those girls waiting to be interviewed. That's how Pier Angeli got the part. We did the same stunt when we were looking for a young actor to play the American soldier boy. I suggested we put ads in the New York *Times,* hire a theater, and see every actor who had not been shown to us by an agent. Hundreds came. That's how we found John Ericson.

Mike: You and Zinnemann certainly had a close working relationship.

Stern: He had me stay with him on the set throughout the making of the film, let me prepare the screen tests, help with the looping, even coach the actors. He is a director who is not so arrogant as to consider himself the *auteur,* a generous, practical man, and a film genius too. Alfred Hayes and I were nominated for Academy Awards for the story of *Teresa.* Soon afterward I did another film with Fred. We both volunteered our services for it since it was for the Los Angeles Orthopedic Hospital. It was a short documentary called *Benjy,* and it won an Academy Award.

Mike: Did MGM release that also?

Stern: No. Paramount contributed its facilities. I had been under contract to MGM since *Teresa.* Just after the Academy Awards, Nick Schenck came out and fired me and almost everyone else! I went back to New York and wrote three *Philco Playhouse* dramas for Fred Coe, the producer. One of them was the story of my grandmother and her Dakota sod house. Another was called *Thunder of Silence* and starred Paul Newman. It was my first meeting with Paul. Our friendship grew out of that. The show was telecast for Thanksgiving, 1954. Afterward I came back to California for a visit and stayed with my cousin, Arthur, Jr.

I arrived at his house to find somebody in the living room whom I had never seen before—an odd young man with no front teeth. He had lost them in a fall out of a barn when he was a kid in Indiana. Now he had broken his upper plate, and it was away being fixed. He said he was James Dean, but I didn't know who that was; I hadn't seen his plays or heard anything about *East of Eden* being filmed. He was sitting on a revolving chair and said a very curt hello. Arthur had to go upstairs for some reason. I sat in the other revolving chair. Jim turned his back on me, so I turned mine on him. We sat there like two bookends for about ten minutes. Then, for some reason, he mooed like a cow! And I mooed like a cow. Then he mooed better like a cow, and I mooed better than he did. Then we did sheep, chickens, horses, pigs. Somewhere in the middle of the pigs we turned and looked at each other and laughed. He asked me if I wanted to go to the movies. He seemed very anxious to get me there. He took me to a theater in Encino which said, "Major Studio Preview!" and sort of sneaked in. He unbuckled the velvet rope and pushed me into the VIP section. I said, "We're going to get caught." He said not to worry, and we sat down. Pretty soon on came the credits: *East of Eden* starring James Dean! I really could hardly believe it. I said, "Is that you?" He kind of giggled and nodded and gave me his toothless smile. We left before the lights came up at the end. He wanted to know what I thought of it. I told him it was probably the most exciting performance I had ever seen, except for Brando in *Streetcar,* Ethel Waters in *Mamba's Daughters,* Laurence Olivier in *Oedipus,* and Beatrice Lillie in anything. A couple of nights after the preview, I went to a party at Gene Kelly's home, and Nick Ray was there. Nick seemed interested in me. He kept talking about *Teresa* and how much he liked that.

A couple of days later my agent took me on an interview to Warners. We ran into a friend who said Nick Ray wanted to see me in his office. I went over there. He asked me if I wanted to write a story about young people in trouble called *Rebel Without a Cause,* which he was going to direct. Gradually it appeared that Jimmy and composer

Lenny Rosenman had talked to Nick about me. That's how I began a second career in Hollywood. Nick was in agony, a kind of private hell, at that time. A creative hell. He had a concept and a vision of what he wanted to say, but he had not found a way to say it through the writers he had had. He was almost inarticulate about what he wanted and why he was not satisfied. Through all-night sessions, talking mainly about ourselves, I began to get a picture of what that agony consisted of. Nick, like most artists, is part child. His child-part talked to my own. His bewildered adult talked to my bewildered adult, and out of the horns of our own private dilemmas, I began to get a picture of what we both wanted to say through a story about children. I think that every story ends up being about ourselves. Every character is another aspect of who we are. The outside story is only visible and attractive to us if it corresponds to something in ourselves. That's what you are drawn to, and that's where the empathy is in what you write. It comes in many disguises. Sometimes you don't even know it. You only know the feeling of recognition when you finally come to a comfortable road, and you have to follow. If you try to do it before you've found that, truth is unavailable and you are writing in spite of yourself. Once having found the impulse from Nick, I began to try to objectify it in the way Zinnemann had taught me. Since we were dealing with young people in trouble, I went to where they were, which was Juvenile Hall. I spent ten days and nights posing as a social worker while the kids were brought in and interviewed, and the parents confronted the kids. I was allowed to sit in solitary with some of them. One was thirteen years old and had spent six of those years in institutions!

Mike: Did you also have long discussions with James Dean about the character?

Stern: No.

Mike: Was he anything like his character in *Rebel*?

Stern: He was just as funny. As to the rest of his nature, Jimmy never talked about his personal anguish directly. He would talk about it cryptically, or ironically, or mockingly but never confidingly. He didn't show you very much. He'd challenge you to find him. Then when you'd found him, he'd still make you guess. It was an endless game with him. The thing people missed about Jimmy was his mischievousness. He was the most constantly mischievous person I think I've ever met. Full of tricks, full of magic, full of outrageousness.

A lot of it not done out of anguish. A lot of it done out of a desire simply to amuse or entertain himself. One of Jimmy's main sources of entertainment, as it still is for Marlon, was to watch people's reactions to unexpected provocation. He loved to force people alive! To catch them off guard. It embarrassed them, but it also gave them the experience of being themselves, and showed them to him. Sometimes its effect seemed cruel. I remember one day we were walking toward the commissary at Warner Brothers and an executive, Steve Trilling, a very nice man, came walking down the studio street with somebody from New York who apparently was a big stockholder and who had seen Jimmy in *East of Eden* and was very anxious to meet him. Steve called Jimmy over and said, "I'd like you to meet the man with the money." Jimmy reached in his pocket and took out all his change and flung it at the man's feet and walked away! We got to the commissary and ordered coffee. He sat for a long time without saying anything, but brooding and hurt and full of regret. Then he turned to me and asked, "Why do I do that?" It was a curious reaction. When he would do things that hurt people, it was as if they had done them to him.

Mike: Did you use any of that rebellious personality of his in the writing of *Rebel*?

Stern: I'm sure I did, but not consciously. We all absorb each other. People who struggle toward art are brothers. It goes back to something Marlon Brando said to me once. Marlon and producer George Englund had hired me to go with them to Southeast Asia to see if we could find a story about the United Nations. I felt very estranged and frightened of being with Marlon. I had never known him except as somebody whose work I was in awe of. I avoided being alone with him because I thought I would seem dull. He was aware of it. One night in New York at the Plaza Hotel I had come back from a date and was standing in my room. It was snowing out, and I had the window wide open. The lights were off. I was thinking, "Here I am with Marlon Brando to whom I cannot even speak, about to go off with him for four months in Asia. What in hell am I going to do, how will I survive it?" Suddenly, I felt a hand on my shoulder. It was Marlon. He said, "Don't you understand who your family is?" I said, "What do you mean?" He said, "All of us who have been through a crucible of pain can sniff each other out like dogs. *We are our family.*" I think that James Dean was part of our family, and so is Nick Ray. Certain aspects in Nick in his crucible, Jimmy in his crucible, me in my crucible, and Peter Pan in *his* crucible all met in *Rebel Without a Cause*. Without needing to use specific aspects of Jimmy's personality I became infected by it, was already infected because I was in the same family. Nothing he did could surprise me since it was already inside me.

I realized I was, in a funny way, writing *Peter Pan* when I wrote *Rebel,* because *Peter Pan* is basically a story of juvenile delinquency told in Victorian terms, the story of an envious, jealous boy, as Le Gallienne was right in playing him, locked out by his mother. In order to bear that, he acts out a life in which there is no pain and in which he can vanquish anything. It is a magic life that involves great speed, where you can fly in defiance of gravity any distance, where you can overpower people larger than you are simply by wishing it, where no blood is ever drawn that is yours, where you can create a mother who is all good and all love so that you don't have to experience the rage and envy that are inflamed by an initial rejection, and where you forget everything. Not only everything painful, but everything good, so that Peter Pan has no memory. Barrie makes it very clear that the tragedy of *Peter Pan* is not that Wendy can no longer fly, but that Peter still can. Very similar things were at work in Jimmy, and are still at work in me, and are very much at work in many young people. I've always wanted to do a production of *Peter Pan* in which the boys wear blue jeans with "Lost Boys" printed on the bottoms! In a sense Woodstock was as much a Never-Never Land as exists in Act Two of *Peter Pan*. It's the ritual coming-together-without-pain of people who feel estranged from an original loving experience in their lives and who are unable to withstand the angry emotions that go with that. In *Rebel Without a Cause* the three young people make up their own world as they go along. Two of them adopt a child, the character Sal Mineo played. Jimmy becomes the Pretend Father, the brave man who can stand off the pirates (the police and the rival gang). All nobleness. He doesn't want any trouble. Natalie Wood's character was the Pretend Mother. They were the parental ideal for this misbegotten child. But of course, it couldn't survive, because nothing can survive in its pure state, or without pain, or without memory.

Mike: Were you on the set most of the time during shooting?

Stern: Not on that one. When they were about to start, Jimmy disappeared, and no one could find him. He had been given a script, but there was no sign that he would ever appear again. One morning at four o'clock my phone rang. At the other end of it a cow mooed, and I mooed back, and said, "Where the hell are you?" He said, "In New York." I said, "They're looking for you. They're liable to cancel the picture and put you on suspension!" He said, "Do you want me to do the picture?" I said, "What has that got to do with anything?" He said, "If you want me to do the picture, I'll come back." I said, "If that's the way you put it, I can't tell you I want you to do the picture. I don't want that responsibility." First of all, I can never tell if what I have written is any good. Some days I can read it, and it just seems like the most feeble, inept work, and I have all I can do not to destroy it. Other days I might see its merit. Secondly, I could not understand why Jimmy said that if he did the picture, he would be doing it for me, because we did not have that kind of friendship. I wanted to be Jimmy's friend, but I never felt I was. Whether in fact he came back to Hollywood and did the picture because he thought I wanted him to, I will never know.

Mike: One reservation I have about the film is that I thought the parents of James Dean's character came across too theatrical.

Stern: I know what you mean. The major failing of *Rebel* is that Nick Ray was much too hard on himself as a father, and I was much too hard on my parents as a son. I was still in that stage of my own growth where I was blaming them and demanding they change and conform to my idea of what I thought parents should be. The result was that much of the writing and the direction of the parents was exaggerated and heavily biased, and brought a cartoon aspect to the film, so it never seemed to be all of a piece. The poetic truth of the relationships among the young people was constantly being undermined by the way the parents were made to behave. Of course, I'm a perfectionist, and most people I talk to don't agree with me at all.

Mike: Another reservation I have is that I firmly believe violent behavior on the screen teaches young people to copy that same type of behavior. Also, when a film is that commercially successful, it starts a flock of cheaper films which capitalize on the sensational action without making some saving moral statement to justify the violence shown.

Stern: From the beginning Nick, Jimmy, and I were aware *Rebel* was a unique opportunity in our lives to say something about the nature of loneliness and love. Although our elements were "real," the thing we strove for had a kind of mythic scope. Even the conception of the story told in a single day, from dawn to dawn, was mythic rather than real. The love was bigger than life; so was the ferocity. We were disappointed on the one hand that certain events of ours were emulated in later films and even, to some extent, in life itself, regrettably. But something else, which was much more important, came out of that film, and that became the saving part of the James Dean legend. It was the recognition of an attempt to control the violence we all contain, not to let it rule us. The character James Dean played depicted a kind of manhood that did not need violence to assert its power. A manhood that announced itself in the willingness to be against the pack, therefore brave, and also unpopular. It was an attempt to define masculinity in a different way at a time when it seemed all to be leather and boots. The kids caught that. They caught the undercurrent of sweetness in Jim Stark and in the actor who portrayed him and the longing for a lost, loving world, where people could drop their bravado and treat each other gently. I think that is what communicated and thus created the best of the James Dean legend and inspired the generation we are astounded by now.

Mike: After James Dean was killed in the auto wreck in 1955, what compelled you to write a documentary film about his life called *The James Dean Story*?

Stern: Two things. One was that it was already being made and I couldn't stop it. The other was that it afforded the opportunity to help the worst of the legend die. Even though I understood a great deal about the James Dean legend, I saw no healthy purpose in pretending Jimmy was still alive or pretending he was more than he was. I understood the reluctance of young people to let go. No one wants to let go of a hope, and Jimmy represented to them a sense of the best in themselves. He seemed to promise recognition to them of what they were and what they hoped to be, so that they wouldn't be left feeling so alone and misunderstood as a generation. The suddenness of his death and its cataclysmic nature made it really unbelievable. Jimmy was unique. He wasn't just young, and he wasn't just a rebel. His personality spoke to a unique part of young people: It spoke to their sweetness. Ruth St. Denis once said, "The mission of the artist is to give to people in the audience a glimpse of themselves at their most exalted," and I think Jimmy did that for the kids. I think John Kennedy did that. I don't mean to be disrespectful in making the comparison, but I don't know anybody else besides the President and later, his brother, whose deaths caused the kind of despair that Jimmy's did. The Kennedys appealed to our sweetness, too, and for a time we felt capable of anything. There was a letter Jimmy wrote to his young cousin, Markie. I have a copy of it. Markie had sent Jimmy some drawings, and Jimmy had thanked the boy but said he felt the need to warn him about something. He said that anyone could draw soldiers and guns and prisons with barred gates and locks on them, but that they were not good things to draw. He told Markie he lived on a land greatly blessed by God, and it was better to draw pictures of trees, clouds, the earth, hills and mountains, and all the animals at home. Jimmy begged him to draw places of shelter and people who were free. A violent legend did not suit such a man.

Mike: Didn't James Dean have his own hero to look up to in the person of Marlon Brando?

Stern: Of course. He adored Marlon. One hears all sorts of stories about how Jimmy stalked him all over New York, but he never discussed Marlon with me. I know Marlon well, but there was so little time to know Jimmy. His whole career was only those three films which spanned about a year and a half from *East of Eden* to *Giant*. I think as Marlon influenced Jimmy, Jimmy influenced Dennis Hopper. There seems to be a chain of inherited curiosity, an eagerness to experiment and break down old walls, that passed between those men. Marlon really broke with almost everything we were used to and came upon us hotly, bringing a new life-style. Marlon and the Beatles had probably greater influence on the shape of the performing arts and the concept of masculinity than anyone in this century! They stamped themselves on two generations. Jimmy certainly felt he was brother to Marlon, both creatively and personally, and Dennis felt he was brother to Jimmy in the same way. We don't have in this country the opportunity to apprentice ourselves to people we admire in order to learn from them what they know. It's not customary to teach what we know to someone who admires us. So fanship becomes an unofficial apprenticeship here. Sometimes there is no response at all, as there was no direct response on Marlon's part to Jimmy's need, although I think Marlon was aware of his need. It didn't stop Jimmy from learning much of what Marlon knew. There was more contact between Jimmy and Dennis, particularly when they were off on the location of *Giant* and able to communicate at close quarters. So, instead of a close apprenticeship with open teaching and learning, there is a covert apprenticeship, with learning by observation, and by getting as close to the admired one as possible. Creation that comes from it seems like mere emulation before it finds its own style, but that's true in any art. Writers and painters have always influenced each other. The style of a painter is very strongly affected by the person to whom he has been apprenticed or by the school to which he has belonged until he begins to find its application to his own creative needs, and it becomes stamped with his personality as he alters it and makes it his own.

Mike: There wasn't anyone before Marlon Brando for him to emulate, was there?

Stern: The animals, children, and God. Marlon is a true original.

Mike: The last thing you did with Marlon professionally was to write the screenplay of *The Ugly American*?

Stern: Yes. I had met Marlon and George Englund when we had all independently become interested in doing a film about the United Nations. George, with his incredible ability to persuade, had secured the cooperation of Paramount and of the Secretary-General of the United Nations. Paramount was financing the research trip and the development of a screenplay. The United Nations was to cooperate, for the first time to my knowledge, with a private, profit-making organization to the extent that they informed all their resident representatives in all countries of our impending trip and requested them to expedite introductions for us, so that we could go into the field and observe life at the village level and United Nations projects at the grass roots. It was an exhilarating and extraordinary experience. Marlon's fame as an actor was enormous. It was at its first peak. When we arrived at Manila, it looked as if it had snowed during the night. Whiteness everywhere! The white shirts of five thousand people who had spent the night waiting for Brando! It took sixteen motorcycle police to get us through the crowd to our hotel. We would make secret trips to the boondocks, sometimes at six in the morning, to avoid the mobs. We'd be driving along a dirt road in a jeep and a kid would sit up on his water buffalo and scream, "Hey, Kowalski," or "Viva, Zapata!" Marlon's genuine curiosity about people and his marvelous good humor and sympathy endeared him to everybody he met and made him a superb ambassador. That trip paid off for us when we attempted *The Ugly American*. We had been there.

Mike: Why do you think *The Ugly American* was not a success?

Stern: There may have been a number of reasons, but I am sure of two. One was that it cost a great deal of money to make. We used Thailand for the location, and the physical production was enormously expensive for such a thought-heavy subject. The other reason was that it was ahead of its time. We wrote a fictional story based on things we had observed about the United States' chronic inability to judge the aspirations of other nations. It was a prediction of disaster in Southeast Asia that nobody wanted to hear. Now Vietnam has happened. One finds little joy in having been able to predict such a thing.

Mike: Have your less successful films made it difficult to get other writing assignments?

Stern: After *The Ugly American* it took a long time. When you're out of a job, you realize how few things you are equipped to do. You start thinking about waiting on tables again. The face of the industry had changed during the period I was in my office writing *The Ugly American.* I had done two versions, with *The Outsider* sandwiched in between. Television had become more important, so the studios were making fewer pictures. But other writers were getting picture jobs, and I wasn't. I decided I would try to get some television work. I think motion-picture writers tend to have a rather lofty attitude toward the tube, and I was spoiled because I had been part of the golden era of live television in New York in the fifties when I had worked for Fred Coe. I got an agent who told me I would have to be prepared to tell two original story outlines whenever I went on a TV interview. I lasted for one. I walked into the office of two *children* whom I took to be assistants just beginning! It turned out they were the producers of the show! They asked me to be seated. Their eyes were as restless as the eyes of people at a class reunion who are dying to escape into the night! I tried to tell my stories, but I knew they weren't really interested. They didn't know who I was and had not seen the films I had written. They had only heard about *Rebel Without a Cause.* I got through the first story, and they said it had already been done! I got through the second, and they said that was about to be done! It interested me that I had spent a week dreaming up other people's stories, but I suppose it happens. The interview took a lot out of me. I felt like Willy Loman in *Death of a Salesman* as I closed my briefcase and tottered down the hall. I came home and went to bed. The phone rang. It was one of my dearest freinds, Joanne Woodward. I must have sounded terminal. She asked me what had happened and I told her. She said that coincidentally she had been thinking about the depressing state of her own career; she had not had the kind of role she could really get her teeth in since *Three Faces of Eve.* So she had decided, by God, to produce her own film! Her agent, John Foreman, who is now Paul Newman's partner, had read a review in *Life* magazine of a book called *A Jest of God* by a Canadian author named Margaret Laurence and had shown it to Joanne. (This later became *Rachel, Rachel.*) She had been excited enough to take an option on the book and called me to see if I would be interested in doing the screenplay. I read it and despaired. It had enormous problems because it was almost entirely an internal story, about a woman arriving at a certain point in her life having settled for a kind of protected isolation and who realized that if she didn't force herself to change, she would die without ever having lived. But, I agreed to try. It was on the most tentative basis. I had no faith that I could do it. I made myself nonexclusive for the first eight weeks. If I was able to become involved and discover a way to solve the screenplay, then I would become exclusive.

Mike: Were you and Joanne the only two people connected with the project at this point?

Stern: Yes. There was no director. Film financing people to whom Joanne had shown the book had little enthusiasm for it. They didn't think it was picture material in any sense. We had our own doubts! I did a series of notes, and Paul and Joanne and I went off for a weekend together to Palm Springs, where we were going to discuss my notes and really dig into the material. It was a very successful weekend. The neighbors, I'm sure, wouldn't agree, because the decibel reading of our arguments was horrifying. But we all knew each other so well we knew we weren't discussing personalities. We were discussing a third thing, which was the film. The screech of our brains as they tried to get on the same track, shift to the same point of view, always sounded terrible. That noise was characteristic from our first meeting right on through the cutting.

Mike: At what point did Paul decide to take on the job of director?

Stern: I really can't say there was any precise moment. Over a long period he became affected by the character of Rachel herself. By Rachel's ability to take a tiny step in a new direction. By her willingness to trade what had been comfortable, even though it had been a living death, for something unknown and without any guarantees whatever. Paul referred to it as "showing your ass." He said change was impossible unless you were able to "show your ass." I think it was the fact that Rachel was willing to show hers, that Paul was willing to show his, because directing was a tremendous challenge for him. He was untried. He had made an enormous reputation as a superstar and thought that if he directed, people would be lying in wait hoping he wouldn't come through. But mainly, he was willing to face his own fear. He knew he would be challenged every moment. Paul seeks out those situations which frighten him most. Even acting for Paul is not playing. Joanne is much more of a player. Any task for Paul is a gunfight at high noon. Directing was like that. No shadow out there to hide in. One of the results was that he directed the entire film in bare feet. Paul's apprehension shows in the amount of liquid produced through the palms of his hands and the soles of his feet. He had had experiences as an actor where his shoes filled with water to the point where you could see the line of salt all the way around the outside of the leather!

Mike: *Rachel, Rachel* seems to have been an ideal working situation in that the star, the director, and the writer were the best of friends and respected each other's talents completely.

Stern: Yes. Ideal! It never happens. Friends working on something they love and believe in and getting results and remaining friends. We thought from the beginning it would turn out to be a home movie at best, if it ever got to the screen at all. We couldn't imagine anyone being interested. Paul said, "Who cares about a thirty-five-year-old virgin?" And that became the advertising slogan of the picture. *We* cared, but would anyone else?

Mike: So all the time you were writing the script you were tailoring it for Joanne?

Stern: Yes. The first story conferences were funny. Joanne would sweep down the stairway in the character of a female executive and sit the way Cheryl Crawford * would and speak with that kind of earnest intelligence she admires so much in Cheryl and that Eva Le Gallienne has, too. It would make me laugh; then she would laugh. She'd say, "Oh, God, this isn't what I want to do. All I want is for someone to

---

* The highly successful Broadway producer who is known for being able to hold her own among the tough boys in the theater.

tell me where to stand, and I'll start acting. I'm no good at story conferences." The first real script issue that came up was the position in which a lady masturbates. I had a theory ladies do it on their backs. Paul argued for tummies. It became a hair-raising, three-way discussion that went on till two in the morning! Joanne wisely disappeared and shut the door. Paul lurched after her with his bedtime scotch, and I lurched toward my car. I said I could not proceed unless I had just one voice to relate to, that it would be impossible for me to deal with both of them, unless they had come to an agreement of their own. The next day I was sitting brooding over my typewriter, and there was a crash against my front door! This great hobnailed boot came in, followed by Paul in the complete uniform of a Nazi SS colonel! He stood there a moment glaring at me, then said, "I just wanted you to know who's boss!" and turned on his heel and marched out. So it was Paul and I, eyeball to eyeball, from then on. Joanne was spared the story conferences, and Rachel started on her back and ended on her tummy.

Mike: Estelle Parsons, Joanne's costar in the film, once told me your script was so detailed that the main thing Paul had to do as the director was to follow the script precisely.

Stern: I appreciate all the nice things Estelle said about my writing in your book on Tennessee Williams, but that is certainly not the case at all. It was absolutely true that my script was followed almost to the letter, but that's because it was born under both my eyes and Paul's. Paul never presumed to tell me how to write it, but he has qualities that are perfect complements to mine, and he considers I have qualities that are perfect complements to his. I tend to be very emotional in my writing, what he calls "baroque." He is much leaner in his disciplines than I. He's much tougher on himself than I am, and he demands more of himself, while I need to be prodded. He has an extraordinary instinct for the one revealing moment in the life of a character on the screen. I may write the same emotion three different times, but he will only do it once. So my baroqueness and his Spartan eye combine very well. If I feel a situation deeply, and if the needs of the characters within a scene are very powerful, I am not able to write about it directly. The dialogue may be ambiguous, but the intention carries. It's what Paul calls peripheral writing and what Zinnemann calls writing in grunts. My dialogue is very often deceptively oblique, but Paul understood every intention so that he was able to direct scenes exactly as I had envisioned them on the page, and I was able to trust him. Paul is also a modest man about the precise nature of his talents and a creator who is wise enough to recognize that filmmaking is a collaboration. He does not hold himself up as an *auteur* filmmaker any more than Zinnemann does. I think he realizes there is a certain amount of phoniness in that claim anyway. He has respect for everyone who has a skill to bring to a film. Primarily for the writer.

He insisted I be there with him from casting through the entire production, and even let me stay on through the editing. I was still writing dialogue when we were working on the final cut. On a couple of occasions I would be on the set with my face hanging over him like a Halloween moon, full of dire portents and witches' curses as I watched scenes taking shape which seemed askew from what my intention had been. I would race up to Paul or just stand there glaring until my glare turned him around. Then I would fill him up with my frustration. He would turn from me having received whatever I'd poured on him, sometimes reeling from the effect of it, and continue directing with the appearance of total calm! He had the ability to store the pressure and tension I handed him the way a camel stores water. He could turn from my assaults without passing his own frustration on to the actors. What they and the crew saw was a graceful, sympathetic, encouraging presence. But I figured my complaints and suggestions were fair dinkum because he had never restrained himself with me about the script. We had total honesty with each other, sometimes with great personal abuse and personal suffering, which is the license of very good friends, but it was always creative and usually constructive. I would suggest from time to time that perhaps he wanted me to return to California and let him alone, but he would always insist that I stay, until one point in the cutting when he said, "Get off my back." He had the ability to absorb whatever I handed out and turn it to good use on the set, if it had merit.

Mike: Paul had the good sense to let each person make his own artistic contribution.

Stern: Yes. For instance, when Bob Gundlach and Dick Merrell, who were the set designer and the set decorator, were creating Rachel's apartment in the gymnasium in Danbury, Connecticut, that we were using for a sound stage, they requested that Paul not come to the set until they had completed it. Even though it would have helped Paul to see the set he was going to be shooting in, he continued to rehearse on chalk marks in a church rather than ruin their surprise. When Dede Allen, who edited *The Hustler, Bonnie and Clyde,* and *Little Big Man* was given the film to cut, he stayed away. He said that I had had my jollies turning the book into a screenplay, he had had his jollies turning the screenplay into a film, and Dede should have her jollies turning the film into the shape of a motion picture. From time to time during the cutting she would call him, and he would go over and see what she had done and sometimes reserve comment until she had done more. Then, and only then, would he involve himself fully in the editing. He had a very clear vision of what he wanted, but he realized what an enormously creative person Dede is. He didn't want to block her talent in any way by giving her any instructions until she had used up her own creative imagination. We kept looking at cut after cut when the film was in the can. It seemed it could never get right. Then one day it was there! We were in the projection room, and I looked over at Paul, and he was crying. So was I, because he and Dede had somehow brought Joanne's performance into proper focus. It just clicked into shape suddenly. And we saw what magic it was. Joanne has the capacity to be invisible to everything but the camera and Paul's eye on the set. Even though I was four feet away from her most of the time, I could not see what she was doing. Paul could see it, and so could the lens. I think she is the ultimate screen actress, because she can communicate with that piece of apparatus in a way that is totally confidential. The lens eavesdrops on her and sees things no one else can.

As happens with all movies the time came when *Rachel, Rachel* had to be released. Joanne and Paul were on location in Indianapolis making the film *Winning.* They had an early showing of our movie there. Paul screened it for the racetrack drivers and called me up, very bewildered, to say they had all cried. They had come up and shaken his hand and told him what a beautiful, moving film it was. He said he tended to believe they only did it because he and Joanne were there. He asked me to have a screening in Hollywood. He wanted to know if people would cry if he wasn't in the audience. They did. Then he was worried because the Hollywood audience were friends of mine and perhaps they cried because *I* was there! So then we had a kind of gala premiere at the Plaza in New York. As we got into the limousine to go to the theater, Joanne all gowned and beautiful, we three all looked at each other and said, "Well, now we have to show it to strangers!" It was something we didn't want to let go of, because it was so personal. The fact that strangers identified with it and liked it was a great surprise to us and a tremendous affirmation of the private faith we had, and it fortified what I had always believed: The more specific, the more personal a story is, the greater universality it will have, and that to try to design a project for popular acceptance is one sure way not to get it. The experience of conception is a personal and private one. The experience of viewing a film is equally personal and private. A film is like a secret whispered from a pair of lips into a waiting ear.

Mike: Another actor who has recently become a director is Dennis Hopper. You wrote and he directed *The Last Movie*. How did that collaboration come about?

Stern: First, let's get the credit straight: The idea was his; the story was ours; the screenplay was mine before he chose to wing it on the set. Dennis called me having just come back from acting in a movie in Durango, Mexico, called *The Sons of Katie Elder,* which Henry Hathaway directed. He had a notion that he was very excited about, but he didn't know how to put it down on paper and needed some help. I said I would be glad to spend an afternoon showing him the screenplay form. He came to my house and told me the idea he had which he wanted to call *The Last Movie*. It had to do with façades and realities. He had a double concept. One had to do with a stuntman who stayed behind after a movie company left a location in a foreign country. The other premise had to do with what would happen to villagers when a particularly violent Western movie was shot in their midst and how they would relate to the movie sets that were left behind. He was fascinated by the idea of a Western façade superimposed on the buildings of a live adobe village and left standing there when the movie company departed, as had happened when the Hathaway company left its location near Durango. It provided Dennis with a very rich fabric with which to weave a story that would say something about America, about films, about reality, about dreams, about the effect of films on us, and about violence. He had some strong ideas about many of the characters and some of the events, but it became evident to us that he did not have a cause-and-effect story which would move along with increasing tension, arrive at a climax, and resolve itself one way or another. I went to my typewriter. Dennis stood behind me and described some of his ideas on how the film might open. I told him some of mine and said, "Watch me type." I wrote, "Fade In" and continued for two pages. He was entranced by the process of seeing his thoughts go through another brain, accumulate the thoughts in that brain, and come out on a page as screenwriting. It was more than a demonstration of form and more than he had bargained for.

He asked me to write the screenplay. We worked out a deal where we would be co-owners in the script and in the resulting film. The first step was to write an expanded treatment, a ninety-page narrative of the story with most of the scenes dialogued. We met every day and hammered out the story line together. Then I would go off and write it alone, sometimes a few pages, once an entire act. It was Dennis' feeling when I finished the ninety-page treatment that it was enough to be called a screenplay. He thought he didn't need a real shooting script beyond that. He intended to work as Fellini does: use the situations and the needs of the characters as a basis for improvisation. At that time Dennis was not known as a director since he had never directed anything. So we got nowhere. A few producers were fascinated by the treatment, but they were not attracted to the idea of an unknown director. Dennis' passion at those meetings and his conviction about the way he would direct were overwhelming and incomprehensible to most of the people we saw. There were quiet offers to buy the story, but I couldn't move without Dennis, and Dennis wouldn't move unless he could direct. I understood that completely since it was his conception in the first place. Once or twice we came close to getting a production, but those promises misfired, and I simply forgot about the project. Then a film came along called *Easy Rider,* and Dennis Hopper was suddenly the vogue. The opportunity arose again to make *The Last Movie.*

I had been convinced from the beginning a more orthodox screenplay was necessary because I thought it would be impossible to break down a ninety-page treatment into a shooting schedule. Besides, I had other ideas for the expansion of certain scenes. I believe a director should go in prepared with as clear a map as possible before he sets sail, or he cannot recognize the possibilities in the accidents that come his way. Dennis never quite agreed but finally became convinced enough to suggest we meet and work on the screenplay. He came to London where I was spending the winter. We had some extremely fruitful days, and I wrote a proper shooting script in a very short time. Unfortunately, when they went down to Peru to make the film, I was writing another script and couldn't go. He shot forty hours of film! The rough assemblage ran six hours! He neglected to film certain key scenes, and he let many of the improvisations get heavily self-indulgent. So, while the film had real brilliance in it, it never really made sense.

Mike: What was your most recent project?

Stern: An original called *Summer Wishes, Winter Dreams.* Joanne Woodward is in it, and Martin Balsam, and Sylvia Sidney, and my friends Dori Brenner and Ron Rickards. Jack Brodsky produced for Ray Stark. Gilbert Gates directed, and it's lovely.

Mike: In a recent interview, Stewart, you said you have a love-hate attitude toward writing. Why?

Stern: Well, I love people telling me they like my work, but I hate the process of writing. Writing becomes more and more difficult for me. I really don't know how to write! I seem unable to learn from one experience to the next because each story has demands which seem unlike any other. Of course, that's its fascination, too. You are being constantly taken off guard. The only thing that all my projects have in common is stark terror that starts the day I accept an assignment and doesn't let go until the day I write "Fade Out." Paul Newman gave me a brass bed once. The fittings are loose with age and rattle like teeth in an ancient skull. When I'm on an assignment, my heart wakes me in the morning because every beat of it is caught up by all these loose springs. When I was beginning *Rachel, Rachel,* I was so worried about not doing a good job that I literally didn't come out of my room for three days. I couldn't get out of bed. I was frozen with a terrible paralysis. The idea of sitting at a desk facing that ream of canary bond seemed impossible to me. I thought, "Stewart, you just have to write something. Let's start by putting down exactly what's happening now and forget *Rachel.* Just write about you. What is this? What's going on here? At least you'll have your pen in your hand." What was going on was another day was beginning in which I didn't want to haul myself out of bed. I wanted that day to begin and end without me in it! I heard my heart, and I thought, "What's a simile for that heart? It sounds to me like a garbage can lid rolling down a hill. Get up and write that." I got up and I wrote, "Fade In—Stewart's Bedroom. Stewart is lying in bed hearing his heart clattering as loudly as a garbage can lid rolling down a hill. Stewart's Inner Voice: 'Don't let it be day.' The Inner Voice argues: 'Get up.' 'I can't get up.' 'Get up!' 'I'm having a heart attack!' 'You've had heart attacks, you've had cancer every day since you were six years old. Now get up!'" Then from somewhere I heard this rather silly voice singing a nursery rhyme, "Lazy Mary, will you get up, will you get up, will you get up? Lazy Mary, will you get up, or you'll be late for school?" Suddenly I realized I was not writing about myself. I was writing about Rachel trying to get herself up and into the day. So I just crossed off "Stewart's Room" and wrote "Rachel's Room," crossed off "Stewart's Inner Voice" and wrote "Rachel's Inner Voice." I realized the song I had heard was Rachel's mother. I thought, "Why would she be singing a nursery rhyme to a woman of thirty-five?" I then realized Rachel was remembering that same voice singing that same song when she was a child being gotten up to go to school as a student. So the whole opening of the film came out of those three days of paralysis and the clashing of Paul's brass bed!

Mike: You've also been quoted as saying that writing is a process of asking questions, not giving answers.

Stern: It has to do with why we write. Or why *I* write. I think there are so many different people inside us, so many different aspects of ourselves, so many things unresolved! The question is how to resolve them, how to effect a harmony, how to give feet to Tennessee Williams' footless birds that can never land on anything because they have nothing to hold on with. My creative life is long periods of storm and siege, when everything seems in pieces, interrupted by short periods of calm during which everything has been put to rest and organized. There really is no answer until you come to the end of it. You may not even know what the answer is for a very long time, until people who see the film start telling you. It's like feeling along a wall in the dark looking for a hidden door. You keep pushing against the wall and suddenly you're in a dark corridor. You have to push your way along the corridor until another door yields. It's a constant search for daylight. Actually I think dark is not a bad image, because what you write in the dark is seen in the dark. I have long been aware of people's inability to reveal themselves to each other, of the barriers that stand in the way, the walls that words are, the fear people have at being recognized, of revealing the most sensitive parts of their own souls out of fear they will be misunderstood or injured. And also the feeling all of us share of being unique in our suffering, that we have

problems no one else has, that we have shame no one else has, that we
have committed sins no one else has. The first time I was really aware
of that was when the preview cards on my first film, *Teresa,* came in.
There was one, unsigned, which said, "I felt you spied on me. Thanks
for telling me what I have to do." I realized when I got that card that
maybe one of the functions of the screenwriter was to break down the
private walls which stand between all the people who are watching the
film. Each one of those people is locked inside his own skin. Many
think they are alone, that no one else can understand. So if some
understanding comes off the screen, it must be confirmation that they
aren't alone. And if there are many people attracted to that same film,
it must mean there are many people, even in that theater, who feel the
same way.

Mike: Your career began when the method of making films was still
under the factorylike approach of the major studios. Now, in the
middle of your career, you are functioning in the severe transition
Hollywood is undergoing. A large part of your career lies ahead in a
new and different Hollywood. How do you think the screenwriter will
fit into this new Hollywood?

Stern: It's very interesting, because as more and more people become
directors and call themselves *auteurs,* one wonders what the definition
of a script will be and, therefore, the definition of a screenwriter. My
own conviction is that the wise director, if he isn't a screenwriter
himself, will always value the importance of good writing and will
work closely with the writer he respects and give him his due credit.
With the advent of *auteur* directors who cannot write or think that
writers are unnecessary, I just don't know! The only defense is to
become a director yourself and be better than they are. It's so childish,
this greed for credit. We're all in this together. We need each other.
The grown-ups admit it. The children don't.

October 24, 1970

The Director

WILLIAM A. WELLMAN

Mike: You were born in Brookline, Massachusetts, Mr. Wellman?

Wellman: February 29, 1896. Leap year. So I'm seventeen years old! Been married five times, been in a war, made a hundred pictures, and I'm a very smart guy for a seventeen-year-old! Every four years on my birthday we give a party, and you have to dress according to my age. This has been going on for a long time. The widows of my friends are increasing. My friends have included baseball players, football players, athletes, boxers, some few actors, and a lot of my flying buddies. Reggie Sinclair, who was in the Lafayette Flying Corps with me, flew in from Colorado Springs last time. These are the damnedest parties you ever saw in your life, because it is always the same group minus the ones that aren't alive as the years pass. I always had a lot of athletes for friends. I like sports. I play golf now, but I used to box. When I was just a kid, I was making money playing hockey. I was good and could have gone to any college, but I wanted to be a flier. Flying was in its infancy then. I wanted to go to France and fly in the war over there. So I joined the Norton-Harges Ambulance Corps in order to get to Paris. Once in Paris I joined the French Foreign Legion. They in turn put me under the French Air Corps, which in turn put me, being an American, in the Lafayette Flying Corps, which was an outgrowth of the Lafayette Escadrille. There were sixty-six of these escadrilles along the fighting front, but only one of them was the famous Lafayette Escadrille. A lot of crazy kids in America heard about that flying group and wanted to get into it, so William K. Vanderbilt formed one like it which American volunteers could belong to called the Lafayette Flying Corps. I think there were about two hundred fourteen of us in it at one time. That was before America was in World War I. We were made the rank of second-class soldier in the French Foreign Legion and got three and a half cents a day. That was rugged. They kick the hell out of you, until you get your wings.

When you get to the front, if you have a little luck, they make you a sergeant, and you're a big guy from then on. If you had a leave and went to Paris, you couldn't pay for anything. But as soon as America came into the war and American soldiers were in Paris and getting more pay than French officers got, things really changed.

Mike: I understand you fellows learned to fly without an instructor!

Wellman: You have an instructor on the ground, but you learn to fly alone, by the seat of your pants! I had a little bad luck, but I got through it all right with a broken back, some false teeth, a plate in the roof of my mouth, and some occasional strange noises in my skull! The last six months of the war the American Air Corps invited me to join them. I was sent down to Rockwell Field in San Diego as an instructor in aerial combat. I used to fly the only Spad in America up to Los Angeles and land in Doug Fairbanks, Sr.'s, polo field and spend the weekend with him. That's when I got to know some of the picture people. I had met Fairbanks before the war. He was in a show in Boston called *Hawthorn of the USA* and used to come and watch me play hockey at the Boston Arena on Sundays. He asked someone to have me skate over and meet him, and I did. He invited me to come backstage sometime. I didn't know what backstage meant, but I found out. We became great pals. He sent me a cable once during the war. That war, publicity-wise, was just as it is today. I was lucky as a chase pilot, and you'd have thought I'd won the war! In the cable Doug said when the war was all over, he had a job for me. So that's the way I got started in Hollywood.

I acted in two pictures in 1919. I did *The Knickerbocker Buckaroo* with Douglas. It was directed by Albert Parker. Then I played an English sublieutenant with a white wig. I looked like a fairy! My big scene was to wade out in the surf in Santa Monica and rescue the leading lady from a boat and carry her to shore. On the way in I tried to make a date with her, we stepped into a hole, and she couldn't swim. I got her to shore and placed her very carefully at the director's feet. Then suddenly I remembered she was his wife! So I was fired, but they had to pay me my two-week guarantee. No guy ever made more money just stepping into a hole! I saw myself on the screen in these two pictures, and it was really pretty frightful. My long face looked like the face you see when you look in a funny mirror at an amusement park. So I quit acting. I went to Doug and told him how I felt, and he asked me, "Well, what do you want to be?" I pointed to the director, Al Parker, and asked how much money he made. When Doug told me, I said, "That's what I want to be!" It was all purely financial from the beginning. Doug told me I would have to start low, and I did. He got me a job as a messenger boy at the old Goldwyn Studios in Culver City. Coming down from an officer and a "hero" in the Air Corps to a messenger boy is being downgraded a little. Plus the fact I was married to a girl who was a star at the same studio, Helene Chadwick. The boss of the mailroom was very fond of me. He was a merry old soul with a very perverted sense of humor. He used to make me deliver all her fan mail to her dressing room every morning. It was a trifle embarrassing to her and to me, but her mother enjoyed it immensely. Because of her mother's powerful influence, I was eventually thrown out of the house anyway!

Mike: Will you tell the story about General John J. Pershing visiting the studio?

Wellman: Well, while I was a messenger boy, Abraham Lehr, the vice-president of the Goldwyn Studios, put an order out for all the grips, carpenters, electricians, and so on to report at noon, that he wanted to talk to us. He told us there was a big general coming to the lot the next day, and he wanted us all to wear our old uniforms. He said, "Of course, I know you will all be there. If there is anybody that won't, will you please raise your hand?" So I raised my hand. He said, "But I want you especially, because I want you in that French uniform. It will make a nice effect." I said, "There is no seat left in the pants." He said, "You take it to wardrobe, and they'll fix it up." I thought for a couple of minutes if I wanted to tell him to go to hell or if I wanted to keep that big money I was making. I was broke, so I wore the uniform the next day. We all lined up along the main drag of the studio. Way down at the end were all the stars. The Geraldine Farrars, the Lou Tellegens, the Pauline Fredericks, the Mabel Normands, the Tom Moores, the Barbara Castletons. The Goldwyn stars of that day. The general wanted to get down there, down where the fun was. He wasn't interested in inspecting a lineful of poor goddamn ex-soldiers and sailors. Anyway, the siren sounded, the gates opened, and the general's car rolled up, and when he got out, it was Pershing! He started down the line, shaking hands. He shook my hand. Then he shook the hands of the next two guys. Then he turned back to me and said, "Hey, where have I seen you before?" I said, "General, I better not tell you here." He snapped his fingers and said,

"Oh, that's it!" He came back and talked to me and said, "How're you doing?" I said, "Not too well." He said, "Well, what can I do for you?" I said, "Just take me aside under that big fig tree over there and talk to me alone a few minutes and make me look important in this hotbed of fakery." Which he did, while they all waited. The next morning Mr. Lehr sent for me. I went into his office, and he took me in and introduced me to God, Mr. Samuel Goldwyn, who told me in perfect English I was the kind of young man he wanted on the lot. So Pershing made me an assistant director! You meet the nicest guys in the strangest places!

Mike: And from there you went on to be a director?

Wellman: No! I was demoted after a while to the property department. I was the assistant property man for some Will Rogers pictures, *Just Call Me Jim* and *Jubilo,* and met the greatest guy I think I've ever known. Then I worked back into an assistant director and soon they gave me a chance to direct. I made a picture at MGM in 1926 called *The Boob* with a guy named George K. Arthur, an English comic. The girl was Lucille LeSueur who became Joan Crawford. They took one look at the picture and threw me right out of the studio. No one has been fired quicker and more enthusiastically than I was. So I started out as an assistant again with a director named Bernie Durning who was then making big melodramas at the old Fox Studio on the corner of Western and Sunset Boulevard. *Eleventh Hour* was one of them. Bernie was a big handsome Irishman, six feet seven, who was married to little Shirley Mason. He became my great pal. I was with him till he finally made me a director. Got me my chance. I started to direct Dustin Farnum in films like *The Twins of Suffering Creek.* Then I was promoted and became Buck Jones' director. One of the films with him was *Cupid's Fireman.* John Ford was directing the Tom Mix pictures. Then Harry Cohn, an independent producer, became interested in me. He hired me for a feature picture which I made in three and a half days and nights. B. P. Schulberg saw it, and they started bidding for me. Schulberg won by twenty-five bucks. He offered me two hundred and fifty dollars a week. Cohn only offered me two hundred and twenty-five. I went with Schulberg, but never did a picture for him, although he paid me all the time. He was busy manipulating to take Clara Bow, the big star then, along with him to Paramount, where they were getting rid of Jesse Lasky. When Schulberg was made head of the studio in 1926, he brought me in, too. The first picture I made was . . . I can't remember the name. Thank God I can't!

Mike: *The Cat's Pajamas?*

Wellman: You would! With Betty Bronson. The New York office didn't like it; but Schulberg fought for me, and I was given another picture. I made it with Florence Vidor, Lowell Sherman and Clive Brook. It was called *You Never Know Women.* It won the artistic award that year, 1926, and it got me *Wings* to direct. *Wings* was the first air picture. We went down to San Antonio, Texas, for nine months to make it. It made stars out of Gary Cooper, Buddy Rogers, and Richard Arlen. Clara Bow was the female star. It was the first Academy Award winning picture. The Academy Awards began that year, 1927. After that I made Gary Cooper's first starring vehicle, *Legion of the Condemned* (1928). It was another flying picture costarring Fay Wray.

Mike: What were some of your other films about flying?

Wellman: I think *Island in the Sky* in 1953 is the best one I ever made. *The High and the Mighty* (1954) has made the most money for me. There was a fantastic dogfight in *Men with Wings* (1938) with Ray Milland and Fred MacMurray. *Gallant Journey* was a film I thought would be wonderful, but it was awful!

Mike: Although you've made mostly action films, you have been a director with wide variety.

Wellman: That's true. I've done comedies, dramas, war films, Westerns, musicals. Just about anything imaginable. I wrote and directed the first film of *A Star Is Born* in 1937 with Freddy March and Janet Gaynor. She got an Oscar for it. So did I. I made several pictures with Clark Gable, like *The Call of the Wild* in 1935 costarring Loretta Young from the classic Jack London story, and *Across the Wide Missouri* in 1951. They are Westerns of a sort.

Mike: Which was your favorite war drama you did?

Wellman: *The Story of G.I. Joe* in 1945 was a most wonderful story of the GI written by Ernie Pyle. Ernie came up here to the house, and we sat right here and worked on the screenplay. At first I hadn't wanted to do that picture because I had never done a picture about the infantry. I was a flier who had been shot at by the French infantry during World War I. I just loved the infantry! Motion pictures usually had made war too glamorous with gorgeous nurses in hospitals and romantic furloughs in exciting places. Well, I never saw any of that. Of all the many hospitals I was in I never even saw a good-looking French nurse. And I was young enough and looking for them all the time! I never saw any of that camaraderie stuff either: Two guys getting friendly and they can't bring each other down and they wave good-bye and fly off! To hell with it! If I could get a guy in a tough spot, that was his tough luck. Anyway, I didn't have any experience of the infantry, but after getting to know Ernie Pyle, I decided to make the picture. He was a terrific man. About the second day he was here he said, "I hate to ask you this, Bill, but there are two personalities in the motion-picture business I'd like to meet." I didn't know Ernie well, but I knew he didn't want to meet any dames. He just wasn't that kind of a guy. I said, "OK. Who are they?" He said, "Bill [W. C.] Fields and Gene Fowler." Both of them were among my best friends. I got on the phone to Fowler and said, "Hey, come on down here. There's a guy that thinks you're a hell of a man." He said, "Who could that be?" I said, "Ernie Pyle." He said, "I'll be down in five minutes." He only lived a couple of blocks away, and he came down. That meeting started a great friendship. Then Ernie asked me to call Fields, and I told him I couldn't; but Gene could. Although I was a very good friend of Bill Fields, he was mad at me because I had gone on the wagon. He wouldn't have anything to do with me. That was when he was getting ready to die. He would insult me when I would go to his house. At home he used to lean on one of those boards like they use on the sets to keep the girls from wrinkling their dresses. Poor guy. He wouldn't let me in the house. He said, "Get out of here. You're a traitor. When you start drinking, you can come back again." He really wasn't kidding. I hate to tell you how many times I had been loaded with Bill Fields! He was one of the funniest guys the world ever made. Gene Fowler took Ernie to meet Fields, and I didn't see Ernie for three days. When he came back, he was still walking about a foot off the floor. I would have loved to have had a recording of the conversation those three guys must have had. They didn't have any dames. Just the three of them went in and drank and talked and had fun. Must have been one of the most wonderful times you can imagine. So when my wife, Dottie, and I had this little dinner party for Gene, his wife, and Ernie, Ernie was still pretty well done! I had to carry him out of the house. When he went out the door, he looked up at Dottie and said, "Dottie, good-bye. And I really mean good-bye."

He went up to San Francisco and shipped out to the Pacific and got killed by a sniper.

Mike: Then he never saw the picture?

Wellman: No. Never saw one foot of it. Never knew anything about it. But his story was so true and honest and so much of himself! The GI's all loved him. He was their God. It's odd that most of the people I know think the film *Battleground,* which I directed in 1949, was a better picture. I don't agree with them. *Battleground* was a bigger picture, but *The Story of G.I. Joe* stands alone because of its honesty. They wanted me to use Gary Cooper to play the platoon leader. Cooper was a very good friend of mine, but I didn't want Cooper. I had it in my contract that I wouldn't make the picture unless the actor I wanted to play the part played it. I looked and I looked. And finally I saw a guy walking down Sunset Boulevard. My assistant was with me. We were out for lunch. I said, "That looks like the guy!" I went up to him and said, "Hey, you an actor?" He said, "What's it to you?" I said, "Well, I'm a director. My name is Bill Wellman." He said, "I know who you are. I've played in two pictures. I've supported a dog in two pictures." I said, "Will you come down to the studio? I'd like to take a test of you." He said, "It's for *G.I. Joe.* Christ! Everyone in Hollywood is going to play that." I said, "No, I really want to test you. Come on down and try." So I selected the scene in the script where the officer is exhausted and he is writing the letters to the mothers of the kids who have been killed. It's a beautiful scene. I did it against a wagon wheel. I could have used that test in the picture! Every once in a while someone will give you a performance where you just can't say anything it is so beautiful. This guy testing was named Robert Mitchum. He got the part and played opposite Burgess Meredith's portrayal of Ernie Pyle.

In *The Light That Failed* (1939) Ronald Colman did one scene that left everyone speechless. He and I didn't get along at all, but when it was all over, he said, "Mr. Wellman, what did you think of it?" I said, "I don't know. I didn't see it; but I heard it, and it sounds beautiful." You know, with that wonderful voice of his. I printed that one take. I'm the kind of director that works awfully fast. Not because I try to save money, but because I think fast. I told one producer, "Look, I can't change my way. I make mistakes, but I make them fast and cheap. If you want them slow and expensive, don't hire me." I used to print the camera rehearsal. Fooled a lot of actors that way! But sometimes they did the scene better for a rehearsal. I knew enough about making pictures to know what was good. If an actor would complain that he didn't say the right words in a take, I'd say, "To hell with it, you can say them now," and I'd change the angle of the camera setup and keep going. That was my way of getting spontaneity out of a scene, by fooling the actors! Behind that camera I'm the best damn actor in Hollywood. They all said, "He's a tough son of a bitch, but he always knows what he wants." Hell! I didn't always know what I wanted! I'd bluff them. I had one little guy I always used in my films named George Chandler. He was president of the Screen Actors Guild for a while and is my best friend. He was in thirty-seven of my films, from that dumb-faced messenger boy in *A Star Is Born* right on. We had an understanding on my sets so that if I got stuck, I had a little cue I'd give him, and he'd do something distracting like sneeze or make a big fool of himself. Then I would let go at him. I'd get so goddamn mad I'd say, "OK, we'll rest for ten minutes." Then I'd go in my little bungalow and work like hell and try to straighten the scene out. Later on, if I didn't have George on a picture, I'd have a cameraman like Bill Clothier or Archy Stout and we'd have an understanding to get into some loud argument when I wanted to stall for time. We never had a real argument. It was just a chance to keep up this great reputation I had. Hell, I used to get so screwed up I didn't know where I was. And I worked harder than any director in this business.

Mike: Your nickname of Wild Bill is just a put-on?

Wellman: No, I used to be pretty wild! I always had great troops with me. We played, and we worked; but the minute the bell rang on a sound stage for silence you could hear a pin drop on my set. But when I yelled, "Cut. Print," I'm telling you all hell broke loose. We had wild troops. That's why Ronald Colman didn't like working with me. It offended his dignity. He thought everything should be so reserved and proper. Hell, you'd go screwy in this town if you kept driving yourself all the time. You'd end up in the hippie house.

Mike: The pictures you did with John Wayne must have had wild troops, too.

Wellman: Sure. Duke, of course, is a fantastic guy. He's the biggest star this business has ever had excluding no one! You can look at him in old movies on television and see him at the age of twenty-one, then you can see him in *True Grit* [1969] at age sixty-seven. Nothing can stop this guy. He's got that wonderful walk. He's got that way of talking. And he knows the business. But he has an inclination to try and direct. He and I had a contractual understanding he wouldn't try to direct on my pictures. Once or twice he tried to break it, and I told him in front of everybody, "Look, you come back here and do my job, and I'll get out there and do yours, and you're going to look just as absurd behind the camera as I look in front." And he'd lay off it. Later he did direct a picture of his own. That *Alamo* thing. Acted in it, too. Too many jobs. It's tough enough just to direct a picture. I used to produce and direct a lot of them, *Beau Geste, The Light That Failed*, but I cut that out and settled for picking my producer. I'd get a guy who was afraid of me, so I could handle him.

Mike: You always picked your own story also.

Wellman: Yeah, and I picked some bum ones, too. I bet you can't find a director that's made any lousier pictures than I have. And not from an overacting standpoint. I just picked the wrong stories. But every once in a while you get a story like *Public Enemy* (1931)! Zanuck was head of Warner Brothers when I did that one. I've made more pictures for Zanuck than any director, and I've never called him anything but Mr. Zanuck, or nothing. I don't know of many people I admire more than him. Not now when he is in New York, but when he was working out here. This guy worked! He'd work all night long. He was the greatest producer to get an idea quickly. To get a director and a writer together and all enthused and knock it out fast. You go to him and there's none of this, "I'll let you know in a few days." You got an answer, even if it wasn't the answer you wanted. He and David Selznick didn't have to call up anybody in New York, who in turn asked whoever to hell he's married to, or living with, what they thought of it. Anyway, the story *Public Enemy* was brought to me by a couple of druggists from Chicago. They had never written a thing, but they ran a drugstore in a neighborhood where all the tough guys operated. They said to me, "Will you please read this? We think it is good." It was called *Beer and Blood*. I read it and went nuts about it and went to Zanuck, who was also at Warner Brothers then. He had just made two fine gangster films, *Little Caesar* and *Doorway to Heaven*. They were very successful, and he thought he would screw it all up by doing another. I had to beg him to read it, but after he did, he went nuts too. He said, "Give me one reason why you think I should let you do it." I said, "Because I'll make it the toughest goddamn one of them all." He said, "OK. You can do it." Where do you get a producer like that today? We started shooting. Eddie Woods was the lead, and James Cagney was in a secondary role. I did a couple of days' work, and I said to myself, "Wait a minute! This is all wrong." I called Zanuck from the set and said, "We got the wrong guy in the wrong part. We got to put this crazy guy Cagney in the lead part." Zanuck said, "I haven't seen any of the rushes." I said, "Well, you better." He saw them and called me back and said, "Make the switch." And I shot the first two days over. The film made James Cagney a star.

Mike: It's the film with the famous scene in which he pushes the grapefruit in the face of his girlfriend.

Wellman: Yeah, in Mae Clarke's face. That came from my own experience. I had trouble with a gal I was married to. Now I'm not going to hit a girl. That's like hitting your mother. What good does it do you? But I was so annoyed with her I tried to think of a way I could do something that I wouldn't be put in jail for, and that was it. I put it right in the picture instead of doing it to her. I thought, "This is too good to spoil it." So Cagney did it in the picture, and he did it beautifully! Cagney's a wonderful guy!

Mike: Have you had favorite actors and actresses?

Wellman: Every director has his opinion. I've used a lot of them from Richard Barthelmess to Tab Hunter, and the best actor I've had the pleasure of using is Hank Fonda. His performance in *The Ox-Bow Incident* is one of the best I've seen in my life. He looked dirty and tired and played the hell out of that character. We got along beautifully. Unfortunately, I only made one picture with him. I had bought the story from Harold Hurley when he was thrown out at Paramount and was broke. I said, "I'll give you five hundred dollars more than you paid for that." He said, "You got yourself a deal." I gave him sixty-five hundred bucks and thought, "Oh, God, this is going to be great." I loved the story written by Walter Van Tilburg Clark. I went to David Selznick, and I couldn't sell it to him. I went to every studio I'd made money for, and they all thought I was nuts. At first I didn't go to Zanuck at Twentieth Century-Fox because two years before, we had had a heavy argument. We weren't even speaking. Finally I called up Zanuck's secretary, a lady he had had for years and whom I knew well. When I said, "This is Bill Wellman," she said, "HELLO!! What do you want, crazy man?" I said, "I want to talk to your boss." She said, "Are you nuts?" I said, "No. Just ask him if he will speak with me." She said, "OK. Are you ready to be embarrassed?" I said, "Yeah." So she buzzed Zanuck and said, "Bill Wellman wants you on the phone." Zanuck said, "Put him on." We got connected and Zanuck said, "What do you want?" I said, "I got something I think you'll be interested in." He said, "You have? When do you want to come over?" I said, "I'll come over right now." He said, "OK." So I went right over with the story and told it to him. He said, "Let me read it, and I'll let you know soon." This is a busy guy. He works all the time. But he read the story that night and the next day called and said, "Come on over here. You've got yourself a deal." I went over and he said, "Bill, it'll never make a dime, but it's the kind of picture I'd like to have you make. I think it will do the studio good and me some good. It's a prestige picture, and if you do a good job, it will do you a lot of good too. It's yours, but you have to do two more pictures for me sight unseen." I said, "OK. What are they?" He said, "*Buffalo Bill* and *Thunder Birds*." I did the first with Joel McCrea, Linda Darnell, and Maureen O'Hara. *Thunder Birds* was an airplane picture with Preston Foster and Gene Tierney.

Mike: You had already made *Roxie Hart* with Ginger Rogers at Fox?

Wellman: Yes.

Mike: Didn't you make several pictures starring Barbara Stanwyck?

Wellman: The best picture I did with Barbara Stanwyck was *The Great Man's Lady* in 1942. She had to grow into an old lady, and it was one of the best performances ever given by anybody. She was sensational. We also did *So Big* together in 1932. This is a great gal and a great actress. There'll never be another Stanwyck, believe me.

Mike: Was she your favorite actress?

Wellman: One of the very special ones. Another was Carole Lombard. She was the only really beautiful woman who was also a comedienne. Most women who are funny are not so pretty, but she was exquisite. We were close friends. She loved my kids and my wife, Dottie. We went out together. That was the one time I knew Clark Gable well because they were married. When I finished directing her in *Nothing Sacred* in 1937 for David Selznick, she signed a contract with him for two pictures a year for five years. Her career tragically ended in 1942 when she went away on the war bond selling tour and was killed in a plane crash. That was one of the great tragedies with which I felt somewhat involved. Another tragedy was in 1948 when I was on location filming *Yellow Sky* which was written by Lamar Trotti. He had also written *The Ox-Bow Incident* screenplay for me. We were contracted by Zanuck to do a series of films together. He was a very quiet little Southern guy. One of the top Hollywood writers. Near the end of *Yellow Sky* he had a heart attack and literally died in my arms.

Mike: Why did you decide to retire after you directed *Lafayette Escadrille* in 1960?

Wellman: The story was too close to me, and it nearly broke my tough old heart when they wouldn't let me make it the way it had really happened. The screenplay was adapted from a true story I wrote about World War I called *C'est la Guerre*. That was the expression during the war. Everything was *C'est la guerre*. If anything unfortunate happened, a guy got killed, it was *C'est la guerre*. Every bloody thing in life was *C'est la guerre*. "It's the war!" This story was a tragedy. The story of a pal of mine whom I had gone to school with and was on probation with. We joined the war together, flew together. Then he got kicked out of the service because a second lieutenant hit him with his riding crop, and he hauled off and knocked him right on his ass. They put him in the can, but we got him out that night. We broke in and let everybody in the jail out! The story had a tragic ending, but by the time Warner Brothers got through with it, it had to have a happy ending, or they said it wouldn't sell. The happy ending destroyed the whole thing, and I got out of the business because of it. It ended up having nothing to do with the Lafayette Escadrille, because of those smart alecks in New York. . . . Oh, boy, don't talk to me about producers! I'm not very popular with the producers, nor they with me. However, I liked David Selznick. He and his brother, Myron, went through a period when they were both broke and flat and I was so-called big at Paramount. So I got David his first job as a producer. I dared Schulberg to hire a guy named Selznick because I knew he was a brilliant boy. In a year and a half he was running the studio! You couldn't ask for a better producer. I made two pictures not *for* David, but *with* David. In my estimation he was the greatest because he had taste. I wish they had somebody like that around today. Outside of David there's only been one other producer ever allowed in my home, and that was a mistake! So you know what I think of producers! As far as the actors are concerned, the stars, I haven't been too fortunate with them. I've made pictures with most of them, but I don't think I'd win any popularity awards. An actor is a peculiar sort of a guy. He's not like you or me. I'm not downgrading them particularly, but they are a different breed. They look in the mirrors all the time. They have to. They have to see what they look like and say lines to themselves. They look at their faces to see which is the best side to be photographed. You know, one of two things has to happen: You've got to fall in love with that guy you're looking at, or you've got to hate the son of a bitch!

Mike: How do you spend your time nowadays?

Wellman: My son, Bill, Jr., was accurate when he wrote of me, "He is very happy enjoying his seven children and eleven grandchildren, doing some writing, playing golf, hunting garden ants, trapping gophers, clobbering moles, directing the gardeners, swimming twenty to forty laps per day, watching sports on television and once in a while drinking a little beer."

March 11, 1970

The Producer

PANDRO S. BERMAN

Mike: I believe you began your career in 1923, Pandro.

Berman: That's right. I left high school in New York City and came out to Hollywood.

Mike: And immediately went to work at RKO Radio Pictures?

Berman: It was called FBO at that time, Film Booking Offices of America. The studio had been built on Gower Street by a company called Robertson-Cole, which was owned for the largest part by a group of English bankers. The FBO people bought the studio and reorganized it. My father, who was a distribution man and sold film on the East Coast, formed the FBO with several other men. My first job at the studio was with a two-reel outfit which made a series called *The Telephone Girl.* The screenplays were based on H. C. Witwer material and were mostly written by Darryl Zanuck. Some of the performers were Alberta Vaughn, George O'Hara, and Kit Guard. I was about what could be called the third assistant director to Mal St. Clair. I also worked as a script clerk, an easy job compared with today, because there was no dialogue to keep track of. The notes you made were merely penciled scribblings of whether the actor wore his hat when he came in the house from the outside. That is, seeing that one scene matched the other as to wardrobe, props, and movements.

Mike: Did you have in mind becoming a director someday?

Berman: No. I never had any such intention. I wanted to be a producer from the beginning. But first, I worked my way up to being a first assistant director. After a while the man then running the studio, Bernie Fineman, suggested I move into the cutting room. I didn't like the idea too much, because I had worked myself up from about twenty-five dollars a week to fifty. Going into the cutting room meant going back to twenty-five dollars a week. However, it turned out to be one of the best things I ever did. It was a job in which I learned a great deal about the business. Since there were no unions yet, it was not difficult after only six months for me to get a chance to cut a film and become a full cutter. Needless to say, I didn't know very much about cutting. I don't think I did much for my first picture. The director, Wesley Ruggles, was very kind. He came in and recut the film himself!

Mike: Directors like to do that anyway, don't they?

Berman: Not quite to that degree. He actually cut the film with his own hands. Most directors prefer to sit in the projection room and talk about how a film should be cut. The experience was very valuable, and after a couple of pictures, I began to know my job. Then I did a lot of cutting on Westerns. We were making Tom Tyler Westerns, Fred Thompson Westerns, and Westerns with a dog. The next step in my career was that I was offered a job by Harry Cohn in 1927 to go to Columbia Pictures to run the cutting department for him. I took that job and worked six months of a one-year contract until I was dismissed.

Mike: Why were you let go?

Berman: It happened that Harry Cohn left for a long trip to Europe, just after he hired me, and his brother, Jack, came out to run the studio. I was fired because of my ignorance of the techniques of running an office! I didn't have a secretary, and I used to write letters in longhand to the New York office with instructions about editing and cutting or cuts that were done by the censor board. One day Jack called me to his office and said, "Let me see a copy of that letter you sent to New York." And I said, "I haven't got a copy." He threw me out!

Mike: So, you went back to work at FBO?

Berman: Yes, but by that time it had become RKO. This was during the administration of William Le Baron. The company had been sold to RCA. In the short time I was at Columbia sound had come in. Frank Capra had directed one of the first Columbia sound pictures, *Power of the Press,* in 1928, during which I learned a lot about what had to be done in setting up the cutting department for sound. As a result of that experience, William Le Baron was glad to get me back at RKO, and he made me head of their cutting department. I was in the job almost two years before I talked Bill into making me his editorial assistant. I was put in charge of the editing of the pictures made for him. He made some of the best early sound films such as *Rio Rita* and *Cimarron.*

Mike: Didn't Le Baron make you a producer?

Berman: Yes. Sometime in 1930 there was a picture about to start which nobody really wanted to do. The producer assigned to it walked off. About a week before it was to begin shooting, Bill said to me, "Well, I think now I can let you produce a picture." I guess he couldn't get anyone else to do it. It was called *The Gay Diplomat* and starred a man named Ivan Lebedeff. We had a pretty mediocre picture when I got through with it. We took it out to preview one night and weren't too pleased with the results. But within the next couple of days, we got hundreds of preview cards raving about it! Raving about Ivan Lebedeff, this great new star who had appeared on the horizon! It took us quite a while before we learned they were all sent in by Ivan Lebedeff himself! He had managed to get into the stock room and take a couple of hundred preview cards!

Mike: Did Le Baron give you other pictures to produce?

Berman: I did two more for him, *Way Back Home* with a radio actor named Seth Parker, and *Men of Chance* with Ricardo Cortez. Just about that time Bill Le Baron left the company and David Selznick came in. None of the pictures I had made were much good, and David had been instructed by the New York office which hired him to clean out everybody in the studio! He did clean out a lot of people, but when he came to me, he was very considerate. He said he had been told that he should throw me out because I was only working there on account of the fact my father had been one of the organizers of the company. My father had died in 1925. This was about 1931. David said he would like to give me a chance to keep a job, but that he wasn't going to let me produce. He suggested I go back and do for him what I had been doing for Bill Le Baron before I produced: work as his editorial assistant, which I did. After about nine months he had a problem with a film he wanted to make starring Constance Bennett called *What Price Hollywood* (1932). He called me in one day and said, "I want to turn this over to you. You go ahead and work on putting the film together, and, if it looks any good, we'll let you make it." I consider *What Price Hollywood* the first picture I made that was really good. George Cukor directed from a screenplay by Gene Fowler. It was a very bright, touching, and funny movie which was subsequently remade by Selznick in 1937 as *A Star Is Born* and became a sensational success a second time. It was also a success a third time when Judy Garland and James Mason made it.

Mike: Did George Cukor begin his career at RKO?

Berman: No. He had begun at Paramount. But he came to RKO and did *A Bill of Divorcement* for Selznick.

Mike: Didn't Paramount, Columbia, and RKO work closely together at this time in trading stars and directors?

Berman: If so, I wasn't aware of it. It was a pretty independent operation at RKO. Perhaps in the selling of films to the theaters there was some level of cooperation. Maybe Paramount ran RKO pictures in its theaters or vice versa. RKO had a pretty good theater chain of its own in those days.

Mike: How did you come about making the early Fred Astaire-Ginger Rogers musicals?

Berman: They began about 1933, shortly after David Selznick left and Merian C. Cooper came in to run the studio. I made nine of them. *The Gay Divorcee* was the first, *Roberta* was the second, and *Top Hat* the third. Actually the first Astaire-Rogers appearance at RKO had been in *Flying Down to Rio* in which they were billed as a dance act. Dolores del Rio and Gene Raymond had the leads. After that RKO was eager to find something for Astaire and Rogers, so I got *The Gay Divorcee* and *Roberta* from the New York and London stages.

Mike: Were you responsible for teaming Fred Astaire and Ginger Rogers?

Berman: I teamed them as stars. In *Flying Down to Rio* they had not been given much to do except dance. In forming a team with Ginger Rogers, it was a tug-of-war with Fred Astaire. He had just completed a long engagement with his sister, Adele, as costar on the New York stage. When Adele married, he suddenly found his career upended, but he wasn't too happy to consider forming another team with somebody else. He wanted to be an individual. It was a bit of a struggle to get him to make *The Gay Divorcee*, although he had already worked with Ginger. He reluctantly agreed to go ahead. After each of the nine pictures I made with them, he said he wouldn't do another one. The pictures were very successful, and Fred had a piece of them. I gave him ten percent of the profits.

Mike: Stars were taking a percentage in those days?

Berman: They weren't, *he* was! He was about the first man in Hollywood I ever heard of getting it. I gave it to him and to the musician Irving Berlin. RKO was in a kind of shaky position. They didn't have a lot of capital and were glad to get people to do something for a percentage rather than a salary. None of the other studios would entertain such an idea because they were in a position to spend the money and keep the profits.

Mike: Was RKO building a stable of stars at that time?

Berman: To a certain degree. Katharine Hepburn was being built up, along with Astaire and Rogers. But it was a modest stable, not comparable to the star stables of MGM, Paramount, or Warner Brothers. There wasn't enough money.

Mike: Was your picture *Morning Glory* (1933) the first film to gain prominence for Katharine Hepburn?

Berman: I'd like to believe that, since I made it and it got her the Academy Award, but actually she was a success in her very first film, *A Bill of Divorcement*. David Selznick had put her under contract from the Broadway stage, and that's how I got her for her second film role in *Morning Glory*. I remember the night Katharine Hepburn, George Cukor, and I attended the preview of a picture we made together called *Sylvia Scarlet* (1936). That picture was actually responsible for the emergence of Cary Grant as a comedy star. He was wonderful in it. The picture itself was completely wrong for audiences. They didn't know what it was all about. The preview was in Huntington Park and was such a disaster I think there were about twelve or fourteen people left in the theater when it ended! We went up to George Cukor's house and sat around and moaned and groaned, not knowing what to do about the situation. And I'll never forget this, because George will never let me forget it: He says that he and Katharine said to me, "Now don't you worry, because we're going to make up to you for this. We're going to make another picture for you free!" George says I replied quite seriously, "Oh, my God, no! Anything but that!"

Mike: The film which brought Bette Davis into the limelight was also one you made, *Of Human Bondage,* in 1934.

Berman: Yes. Bette was nominated for the Academy Award, but it went to Claudette Colbert for *It Happened One Night.* It's always been my opinion that Bette's performance in *Of Human Bondage* helped her get the award the following year for *Dangerous,* which she made at Warner Brothers Studios.

Mike: Did you usually get along well with your stars and directors?

Berman: I think so, but from time to time it is the job of a producer to be tough with the members of a shooting company in order to get the thing done. Schedules and budgets have to be met. When I was producing *Gunga Din* in 1939, the company had some scenes to do on location in the mountains at Lone Pine. George Stevens was directing for me and using a big cast and crew. George was supposed to stay on location only ten days, but he overstayed, and overstayed, and kept shooting. About thirty days from the time he started, I went up there on a Saturday night determined to tell him he was coming in the next week, finished or not! If he didn't, we would just yank the props from under him. I arrived on the location set. I looked up and saw George high on a roof making a battle scene with Douglas Fairbanks, Jr., Victor McLaglen, and Cary Grant who were jumping over bodies and around the roof. I waved to George. He saw me and waved back. I said to the assistant director, "What time do you finish?" He said, "In about forty-five minutes." I said, "All right, I'll sit around and wait." Time passed. The company broke. People began to disappear, and I waited for George, and George didn't show up. I got hold of the assistant and said, "Where's George? Is he over at the hotel? Where's he going to be?" The assistant said, "Oh, he told me to tell you he was very sorry, but he had a date back in town. He's left already. He's on his way back into Hollywood." I thought, "What do I do now? It's Saturday night, and I have to get this message across." I went over to the Lone Pine Hotel and stayed there Saturday night and Sunday night because I knew I'd never find George in town. At about six o'clock Monday morning, he was back, and I was there on the set waiting for him. I got the message across! Of course he already knew what the message was. That's why he had avoided me by leaving. He figured I'd go back to town and forget about it for another week or so. But I stayed there! He finished location the next few days and came up with a fine picture. He was a slow director in those days. I don't know how he works now.

Mike: In 1934 you became head of production at RKO.

Berman: Well, the first time I took it I never was officially supposed to be the head. Merian Cooper was running it, and I worked for him. One day he called me into his office and said, "I'm going away. I'm not going to give you any telephone number or address. You're in charge. You make the decisions until you hear from me." He disappeared, and I didn't hear from him for months! Nobody else did. It turned out he had been stricken with some sort of attack. It might have been his heart. I don't know. But he went off to a mountaintop in Honolulu to take care of himself. It was a very smart thing to do, because he is a healthy gentleman today. When he came back to the studio, I went back to what I like doing best: producing my own pictures! So that was the first time I had the studio in my lap. Later, when the company changed hands, as it did almost every year, a fellow I liked very much became president, Leo Spitz. He asked me if I would take the job of studio head, which I reluctantly did. I never liked being an executive. I held the job for a while until Leo Spitz quit and George Schaefer took over. Then things began to happen which I didn't like, and I resigned. Schaefer wanted me to stay and produce pictures for him, but I quit the company completely in 1939 after seventeen years of working for about seventeen different administrations.

Mike: At RKO you had made some of the best films ever produced. I especially admire *The Hunchback of Notre Dame* (1940), *Mary of Scotland* (1936), *Winterset* (1936), *Room Service* (1938), and *Stage Door* (1937). With that reputation any studio in town would have been happy to have you come with them when you left RKO!

Berman: In April, 1940, I made a deal with Louis B. Mayer and became a producer at MGM. I had always had that in back of my mind, because Louis had been after me for many years. He was a very farsighted man. He was the kind of man who would call you up and say, "I want you to go to work for me." Once I said to him, "I'd certainly like to do that, Mr. Mayer, but unfortunately I just signed a five-year contract with this company." He said, "I didn't say when, did I? I want you to go to work when you're through there." Not many men were thinking that far in advance in those days, and I doubt if they are now.

Mike: Did you take any stars or story material with you to MGM?

Berman: Nothing. I remembered a couple of properties I had fooled around with at RKO and I got MGM to buy one of them for me. That was *Ivanhoe*. The concept of *Ivanhoe* for the motion pictures had actually started at Paramount. I bought whatever old screenplay Paramount had and took it to RKO. Later I was able to bring it to MGM, where we created a completely new script and filmed it with Robert Taylor and Elizabeth Taylor starring.

Mike: Weren't you responsible for Katharine Hepburn's moving to MGM?

Berman: No. I did more films with her at RKO than I ever did at MGM. At MGM I made three of her films, *Sea of Grass, Dragon Seed,* and *Undercurrent.*

Mike: Do you credit yourself for the discovery of any talent or for developing actors and actresses by giving them their first breaks?

Berman: I have done some of that, but I don't think I'm the best at it by any means. In 1944 I gave Elizabeth Taylor, perhaps, her first break in *National Velvet.* We've already mentioned Katharine Hepburn, Bette Davis, Fred Astaire, and Ginger Rogers. David Niven had his first good part with me in *Bachelor Mother* (1939), and Leslie Howard was in *Of Human Bondage* (1934). I think there were other people who brought waves of great talent into the business. Hal Wallis was one of the leaders in doing that.

Mike: After *National Velvet* you made several pictures with Elizabeth Taylor.

Berman: Yes. I had her in *Father of the Bride, Father's Little Dividend, Ivanhoe, Cat on a Hot Tin Roof,* and *Butterfield 8,* the picture she wanted least to do of her whole career.

Mike: Why didn't she want to make *Butterfield 8*?

Berman: First of all, she was through with her MGM contract except for one film for which she was to get a hundred thousand dollars. She had already signed a contract with Twentieth Century-Fox for a million dollars to do *Cleopatra* and was anxious to go and make it. She was doing her best to get out of her MGM commitment, so she wouldn't have liked anything we wanted her to make. I don't know to this day if she really hated *Butterfield 8* or if it was just her ploy. In any case, it was a long story before we forced her to do it. We told her quite clearly that she would never, never make *Cleopatra* until she finished with us. What she said and what she did is beyond belief. How furious she was! She said to me, "You'll be sorry. You'll never get a picture out of this. I just won't act. You can make me do it, but you can't make me act in it." I said, "I'm not worried about that, because I'm quite sure out of respect for your co-actors, members of your guild, you'll get out there on the set and you'll do your job." She said, "I won't show up! I'll be late!" I said, "I'll take that chance." So we went to New York to make the picture. In one of the meetings I had with her and her agent before we started shooting, I said, "Now look, I'm going to tell you something. You're going to win the Academy Award with this picture!" She roared with laughter. So did her agent. They thought I was some kind of nut. They professed to think it was the worst script ever written. Anyhow, we made the picture, and she did give us a little trouble here and there. It was no more than she has given everybody on all her pictures: a little late once in a while. A little sick once in a while. Didn't like the clothes. Insisted on changing this and that. The main thing was that Eddie Fisher was in the picture, and they were married at the time. Eddie wasn't too happy with his part. He got a couple of his writers who had been writing TV shows for him, and he went to work with them to rewrite our script!

Mike: To build up his part!

Berman: And to make himself more important than the other male star, Laurence Harvey, and so on. One day Liz and Eddie called me to come down to their hotel rooms. They handed me this batch of papers and said, "Now, this is something we *would* like to do." I wouldn't even look at it. I walked over and dropped it in the wastebasket. She came flying out of that couch with her nails ready to scratch my eyes out! Spitting and hissing! I said, "I won't read it. I'm not interested in any rewrites. I have a writer on this picture whom I respect, and he has done a fine job. We're going to make the script we've got!" Needless to say, we made the script we had, and that didn't make things any more pleasant around the set.

Mike: After she got the Academy Award for her performance, didn't she change her attitude toward the picture and admit you had been right?

Berman: She didn't change her attitude at all! She still makes statements to the effect people just gave her the award because she was sick in bed in a London hospital near the point of death, and it was all done out of sympathy, that she didn't deserve the award. She's never changed her tune.

Mike: Didn't the two of you actually feel close since you had done so many films together?

Berman: I'm very fond of her. I've never been angry with her. But she was angry with me. I can tell you that!

Mike: Perhaps she knew you so well she thought she could afford to be angry with you.

Berman: Possibly that. I've heard stories from mutual friends and people who have worked with her that she kind of smiles about the *Butterfield 8* experience and is sort of sheepish about it.

Mike: As things turned out, you matched the right star with the right story, which is one of a producer's greatest tasks. Did you usually find, or select, your own story material for films?

Berman: That was my major function. You see, I was never what you would call a promoter or a man who could raise money to make pictures independently. I didn't consider myself a businessman, although I was pretty good at keeping the costs of my pictures down because I had a desire to. What I did more than anything else was to be a working producer under the shelter of a major studio. That meant my greatest contribution was to find the story material, develop it into a screenplay, get a director, cast it, and make the picture, usually using other studio personnel for all these jobs. To make a distinction between the producer I am describing and the producer of today, the producer of today is more of an agent, a packager, a promoter, or a financial man who will put things together and take them to a studio, a distribution company, or a bank and get financing. That method has had a very great effect in that the producer has abdicated his function as the creative man in the setup. He has gone to other business activities, leaving the director as the creative influence. Today in the industry the director is the boss. He is the one who decides what he is going to make, how it should be written and by whom, who is going to star and other key talent. Then he makes the picture having virtually no one over him. Whereas in my day, under the Louis B. Mayer system, which was not just Mayer but was prevalent throughout the whole industry, the producer had that function. Strangely enough, the long period in which the producer had these duties was the second phase in the industry, because originally it *was* the director who did all these things. If you go back far enough to the old boys like D. W. Griffith, you see that the director was the first creative influence in the making of motion pictures. They ran the show then, as now. It was only at a certain time when directors began to get extravagant that Mayer, or somebody, dug up the concept of putting a supervisor in charge who could hold the director down in terms of budget. Little by little that developed to where the producer became the important cog in the wheel. He made the decisions or approved of all decisions, both artistically and financially. Louis B. Mayer used to say, "Give me a screenplay that I like, and you've done your job as producer." He thought everything that was to be film footage should be on paper, and that was the movie. His filmmaking factory took over from there. He had a stable of actors, directors, and technicians. If you didn't use one, you'd use another. Sometimes you'd have one director on a picture for a while, and if he got sick, instead of calling the picture off for a week as they would do now if Mike Nichols took ill, they'd say, "Jack Conway isn't well. Let him rest. We'll put Harry Beaumont on it for a week, and he'll pick up where Jack left off." That's the way we made pictures. Of course, it's not the way it's done now.

Mike: Do you prefer the way it used to be done to the way it is done today?

Berman: I've produced over one hundred films, but I wouldn't want to be a producer the way films operate today. That is, I wouldn't like the job a producer has today, because as I say, he has become an agent. Of course from a director's point of view today is a much more satisfactory time. He's in control!

Mike: Is it desirable to good filmmaking that one man, the director, can say, "This is the way its going to be"?

Berman: It's absolutely nonsense, because there are only about three or four pictures a year that come out of a director having complete control which are commercially and artistically sensational. About ninety-seven percent of pictures made now are bad pictures and lose money! In the early days, before the competition of television, almost all pictures made money, and I think there were just as many outstanding pictures then as now. In fact, if you go around and talk to the public, you discover they think there were a lot more. The integrity of the screen has been damaged. The license that has been taken with the sex and skin flicks and so on has lost us a vast audience of people. In the end, the picture business is going to suffer very, very seriously. So there is no question in my mind which was the better system, but you won't find many directors who agree with me. Making a picture is not a one-man operation. It involves many talents from the wigmaker to the cameraman, and in back of them all stands the writer as the most important asset. I've always claimed, and I still claim more than ever, that I can get a good director, a good cameraman, a good crew, good actors, and a good production manager, but the only thing I can't get is a good writer. There just aren't enough good writers writing good stories. That's all! They are too scarce. The ones that are good enough, what do they need you for? They're like Tennessee Williams, you know. They don't need pictures. Therefore, the great shortage in the motion-picture business is the stories.

Mike: Speaking of Tennessee Williams, Pandro, do you remember when he was under contract to MGM in the early forties, before he gained success?

Berman: Oh, yes! I brought him out! I'll tell you how that happened. I had a dear friend who was my story editor over at RKO, Lilly Messinger. I later got her a job at MGM after I moved over there. In terms of Hollywood, Lilly Messinger discovered Tennessee Williams, who was an unknown boy. She brought him to me, and I put him to work. I remember the incident quite clearly. It was a very charming sort of thing. I had a pretty lousy book called *Marriage Is a Private Affair* (1944) which I wanted to get a screenplay out of for Lana Turner. So I gave it to this young boy. He said, "What shall I do?" I said, "Well, just see what you feel like doing. You know. If you want to write a treatment to see how you handle this book for the screen, you do that. Whatever you feel like. Eventually, we'll write a screenplay if you want to write it." He went away and came back in a week or two and handed me a bunch of pages. I read them, and they were beautifully written. But what he had done was, he had selected one scene about three-quarters of the way through the book and elaborated on that. It was a scene with a man and woman driving a car and talking. It went on for about thirty pages. Just conversation. Lovely conversation, but he hadn't dealt with the story in any way. He hadn't decided what characters he wanted to use or what story he wanted to tell. He had just sort of liked the idea of writing a long scene about them riding through the country at night, talking. So, I said, "Gee, this is lovely. I like it very much, but don't you think we'd be better off if first, before you got into these long dialogue scenes, we try to figure out together what story we're going to tell? What we want this to be about? Which characters in the book we are interested in using? Which ones we want to drop and so on?" He said, "I don't really think I could do that." And he didn't. He walked out!

Mike: He never wrote a full screenplay all the time he was under contract?

Berman: No. That was all he ever wrote. That one scene. I'm proud of myself for one thing. I remember I said to him, "Look, you don't have to write this. Maybe you'd like to write an original of your own." That's the only thing I did right. I said, "Maybe we'd rather make something of your own in place of this." At the time, I think he did have a little something of his own up his sleeve, but he wasn't about to divulge it to me or anybody else. I think it was *The Glass Menagerie*.

Mike: It's interesting that after Tennessee did become so successful on Broadway you were the man who produced two of his best plays for the movies.

Berman: Yes. I loved making *Cat on a Hot Tin Roof* and *Sweet Bird of Youth*. And I tried very hard to get his agent, Audrey Wood, to sell me *Night of the Iguana*. She promised to let me have first crack at it; then I never heard from her again.

Mike: Typical of Audrey Wood, I've noticed. Ironically, Tennessee *thinks* he "fired" her in 1971. Did you personally go after obtaining *Cat on a Hot Tin Roof*, or did the studio?

Berman: It was a very odd thing. I was in New York on my way home from Europe, and I saw the play. I went into the New York office of Nick Schenck, and I raved about it. Louis B. Mayer had already left the studio, and Dore Schary was running it. I don't remember exactly what Schenck said to me, but it was to the effect that Dore Schary had seen the play and liked it, and a deal might be made. So I came back to Hollywood and went to see Schary. He said, "Yes. I do like it, but you know, I've already picked out Sol Siegel to make it. I've got a package all set up. I'm going to do it with Grace Kelly, and I've got Josh Logan to direct it." I said, "Too bad, because I'm crazy about it." Six months went by, and Dore Schary called me and said, "Do you still like *Cat on a Hot Tin Roof*?" I said yes. He said, "Well, I guess Sol Siegel doesn't want to do it. Why don't you take it over?" I said, "Boy, will I take it over! I'm delighted!" He said, "I have a little bad news for you, though. Grace Kelly is going to get married, and we can't get her for the part." I said, "That's fine. I never wanted her." He said, "I wish you'd sit down and write a letter to Josh Logan and tell him that you can't get Grace Kelly and that you are going to do the picture instead of Siegel, and you'd like to get together with him." So I did. Wouldn't you know that in the reply from Josh he said he had lost interest! Here I was at last where I wanted to be in the first place. I had the property without Grace Kelly and without Josh Logan, and I had freedom. Then a strange thing happened. I formed a partnership with another producer, Larry Weingarten, about that time. Larry fell in love with *Cat* and asked me if he could produce it. Since we shared fifty-fifty in everything we did, and I was going to Paris to make *The Reluctant Debutante* with Rex Harrison and Kay Kendall, I said, "OK, Larry, you take it on." Larry got a credit on the picture. We got Elizabeth Taylor to star as Maggie in it through Mike Todd, and we got Paul Newman to play Brick and Burl Ives as Big Daddy. At first we thought of casting the role of Brick with a very talented television actor named William Schatner. For a brief while George Cukor was to direct the picture. Later Joe Mankiewicz was a possibility to direct. Finally, I hired Richard Brooks, who had written and directed *The Blackboard Jungle* for me. I knew Richard could do a good screenplay for *Cat,* as well as direct it. The picture worked out very well for everybody. It was a smash!

Mike: When you made a film of *Sweet Bird of Youth*, you used almost the entire Broadway cast in the roles they had created. Do you have strong feelings about casting Broadway actors in their original roles?

Berman: Yes. I have followed that approach since way back in 1936 when I made Maxwell Anderson's hit play *Winterset* into a movie and used the whole New York cast, Burgess Meredith, Margo, Eduardo Ciannelli, and so on. I liked doing that, although sometimes it was hard to get Hollywood to go along with it. The studios had their own stars under contract whom they had to put to work.

Mike: Are you in favor of doing remakes of old films?

Berman: Not as much as I once was. I especially used to be in favor of remaking silent films into talkies. At the present I don't advocate remaking any film, because things change too fast to know if old stories are still valid screen material. For instance, I had more assurance in 1952 when I took an old story like *The Prisoner of Zenda* and remade it. Although it had been a silent film in 1922 and a talkie in 1937 when David Selznick made it with Ronald Colman and Madeleine Carroll, I thought nothing of making it a third time with Stewart Granger and Deborah Kerr. I felt so confident it would be a hit again, and it was! Things have been changing so radically since about 1955 that I wouldn't dare remake any film since that date.

Mike: I believe that once a film has been done to near perfection like the original *Mutiny on the Bounty* with Clark Gable and Charles Laughton, it should be left alone. Classics like that should not be remade.

Berman: Yes. It's a crime to make those over. The only pictures I ever made over were pictures that had been forgotten after a period of time. Let's say there might have been a couple of films on *The Three Musketeers* before I made mine in 1948, but they were over with. Nobody who went to pictures today had seen them. I feel that the mood of the world has changed more in the last ten years than it changed in the last seventy-five years. Things that appeal to people today are so radically different from what appealed to them in the past. In the old days you used to be able to count on all the people inside a theater to register the same emotions.

Mike: Do you think the current leaders of Hollywood put out a product that is in tune with the public mood and demand?

Berman: I think they do in terms of not being hidebound to the past. What I think is unfortunate is that they are fumbling as they struggle to try to pinpoint the mood of the people. They can't find it!

Mike: Do you think movies are such an influence that they can set the mood of the people?

Berman: I think movies reflect the mood, not create it. If you could say films created a mood, we would have overcome war. We would have overcome the race problems. All the things that pictures have been preaching for forty years would have taken effect, and they haven't.

Mike: In the last two or three years there seems to be an intensity in the making of so-called message films. The makers of these films appear to want to be an influence on society almost more than to entertain.

Berman: Oh, I'm sure they want to be an influence. I'm sure we also wanted to in my day. When I made *Winterset*, I was trying to present a message. We always did that, but we never succeeded! We never changed anybody's mind. The radical right stayed radical right, and the radical left stayed radical left. The middle ground stayed out of it entirely.

Mike: So you think message or propaganda films don't really hold much weight?

Berman: I honestly think that. However, I don't limit it to films. I don't think propaganda itself holds much weight. Human beings are what they are, and you are only capable of feeling and reacting to situations depending on yourself. If you are a black man, you react one way. If you are white, you react another. If you are very poor and out of work, you are not going to feel the same as Henry Ford feels that day about things!

Mike: Do you agree, however, that films exert an influence on styles and taste?

Berman: Of course. Before, I was speaking of influence in terms of gut politics. I don't think films can make people Democrats or Republicans, fascists or antifascists. I certainly think they have a great influence on what women wear, what makeup is used, what furniture is used, what paintings and art are sold, and what music is sold. Things like that. Movies have had a vast influence on the whole world in these areas.

Mike: Needless to say, television has become the influence today. Never before has such constant entertainment been so easily available to the masses. The enormous amount of product needed to keep television sets active has cheapened the quality of what the public sees. Why haven't more of the top talent in motion pictures moved into television production? It would surely improve the quality of that number one mass communication medium.

Berman: Even though fewer films are made, perhaps picture people, such as myself, had rather make one film every two or three years in the manner in which we are accustomed to and knowledgeable about than be more active in television. I think films made for television are no better than the B pictures movie studios used to make. In 1967 I retired from MGM largely due to slowdown in production, but as an independent producer I have made two films since at Fox, *Justine* and *Move*. Any future film I might do depends on my getting a great story, that all-important ingredient! Meantime, I watch the changes taking place, happy sometimes, sad sometimes, but always aware of my good fortune at being a part of Hollywood during its most fruitful years.

October 15, 1970

Production Manager

JAMES PRATT

Pratt: I came to California from Colorado via New Mexico. When I was seventeen, I enrolled at USC to take journalism, but after one semester I dropped out because of family problems. I had to find a job. Through a friend who was a timekeeper at the old Metro studios I became a laborer on their work gang in 1923. The pick-and-ax gang! About four months later the Metro company merged with the Goldwyn company to form Metro-Goldwyn.* Almost all the people who had been working at Metro were taken along to the Goldwyn facilities in Culver City which had originally been built by Thomas Ince. But I left Metro to go to work as a laborer and grip at the United Studios, Inc., which is now the Paramount lot. I guess you could say I stopped being a laborer and became a technician in 1925, when United and First National jointly produced *The Lost World*, which was the first prehistoric adventure film. We had to animate these huge animals and Dinosauria creatures which we built for the picture. Some of the best trick cameramen in the business got their start on *The Lost World*. In fact, it was a training ground for people in various trades such as special effects and miniatures. Because of my work on the film MGM thought I must have had unusual knowledge in technical matters and hired me to work in their prop shop. The first *Ben Hur* was still being made, and I was assigned to work on the construction of miniature Roman galleys. We made hundreds of them about six feet long for the sea battle sequence filmed off Catalina Island. These were added scenes for the footage of the battle which had been shot with real ships in Italy. Another highly technical film of

* In 1924 Louis B. Mayer came in to make it Metro-Goldwyn-Mayer.

the day on which I worked was the World War I epic directed by King Vidor, *The Big Parade*.

Mike: What kind of salary were you making at that time?

Pratt: It was a low-paying business. Nobody got much money except the top creative people. When, in the late twenties, I was a timekeeper at MGM I got thirty dollars a week. There weren't any unions to speak of yet. They came in later in the Franklin Roosevelt era.

Mike: Before unions, anyone who wanted work at a studio in any capacity gathered outside the studio and hoped to get picked for a job, didn't they?

Pratt: Yes. If your job on a picture ended, you could make the rounds of other studios. There was a lot of moving about. When sound came in, I was out of work at MGM because they closed down long enough to build facilities to make talking pictures. I took odd jobs at any studio that offered work. My field centered on construction work. In 1930 I was hired to go on the long-lasting location filming of *The Big Trail,* one of John Wayne's first pictures. It was directed by Raoul Walsh and filmed in the seventy-mm process called Grandeur. We traveled all over hell's acre and back! Yuma, Arizona, Jackson Hole, Wyoming, Missoula, Montana, the Oxnard Sand Dunes, Sequoia National Park, and several San Fernando Valley sites. We had a big company with over a hundred wagons! It is significant that an outdoor picture of such large scale was made in sound at that day. It cost about two million dollars. If made under the same circumstances today, that picture would cost as much as any film ever produced. I don't count *Cleopatra* because that received all kinds of charges for many reasons.

Mike: What production company made *The Big Trail*?

Pratt: It was produced and released by William Fox. I worked at the William Fox studios until they got into financial difficulties during the Depression and Chase Manhattan Bank took them over. Then Darryl Zanuck and his group came in, and it became Twentieth Century-Fox in 1935. So I went over to Columbia Pictures and worked on crews doing various jobs. Eventually, I became Columbia's location construction man and worked on films all over the Western United States. One of the most popular spots to shoot was Tucson, Arizona. In the middle of a hot summer in 1939 I was in charge of the construction of the historic replica of old Tucson: Tucson as it was about the middle of the 1850's. It was built for a film called *Arizona.*

Today it is still used for features and television. That construction job was a very big project, and I consider it a turning point in my career since it established me as an organization man. Previously I had the status of a construction foreman.

Mike: Did you remain with Columbia during the World War II years?

Pratt: No. In 1942 I worked for Walt Disney on a film he made for the armed forces. After that I worked with the Signal Corps at their facilities at Astoria, Long Island, for a couple of years. The last year of the war I began working for International Pictures, a new company headed by William Goetz and Leo Spitz. We rented space at the Samuel Goldwyn Studios on Santa Monica Boulevard in Hollywood. My job was backlot coordinator. I worked with a tough, but talented, director in the person of Fritz Lang on the film *Woman in the Window*. I enjoyed working with him and never had any trouble because I leveled with him completely.

In the fall of 1945 International Pictures elevated me to a production manager. It was a big advancement for me because it put me in the executive end of the business. The first film on which I was production manager was *The Stranger*. The producer was Sam Spiegel, or S. P. Eagle, if you prefer. He had been going around town with the screenplay of *The Stranger* under his arm looking for a deal. Orson Welles was tied into it, and he may have been part of the problem. Anyway, International decided to make the picture with Welles starring and directing. At the same time he was doing a radio show, writing a newspaper column, and working on his version of a Broadway production of *Around the World in Eighty Days*. This was quite a long time before Mike Todd did that as a movie.

Mike: *The Stranger* also starred Loretta Young and Edward G. Robinson, didn't it?

Pratt: Yes. And we had a most talented cameraman in Russ Metty. We were a kind of enthusiastic group of young filmmakers who were, by God, going to make something out of this good script. I laid out a schedule and made up a budget. Orson and I got together and went over these items in full detail with complete honesty and no bull. It was very important to make Orson realize he had to stick to this budget and schedule. I reminded him that he had a pretty bad press and that film backers were reluctant to trust him with their money. You see, Orson is a perfectionist and never knows quite when to quit. We convinced him a successful film must have discipline. Filming began and went along fine. Orson got pretty well what he wanted all the way through shooting. Spiegel has a great faculty of being at the right place at the right time and picking the right guys and getting them together, even though they shouldn't be together, and keeping them from each other's throats while they make a film. He did it with *Moulin Rouge, The African Queen, The Bridge on the River Kwai,* and others over the years.

Mike: Did Orson Welles and Edward G. Robinson work well together?

Pratt: Yes. Although Robinson was concerned with one minor problem. He believed one side of his face photographed better than the other. He came to me one day very worried and politely explained this belief. He said he felt that Orson as the director and one of the stars was favoring himself and failing to give him, Eddie, proper coverage. I spoke to Orson about the situation, and he corrected the matter quietly.

Mike: Was the picture finished on schedule?

Pratt: Yes. I think it was the first time Orson Welles had done that. He also finished forty thousand dollars under the budget! It was an extremely successful picture at the box office.

Mike: So you started off as a production manager with a winner! What are the tasks of a production manager?

Pratt: The production manager can be defined as the guy who translates all of the words, phrases, and ideas from script form into the practical and physical form of bolts, nuts, nails, cloth, equipment, labor, and so on. There's no way to separate this total process and break it down into who contributes what. Everyone on a film has to be a contributor on the creative team or the whole thing won't work right from the beginning. In doing all the things it takes to keep a production buttoned together, the so-called physical production fellow, such as myself, has to know the script as well as anyone. He has to be involved in the total process of filmmaking. The philosophy I have practiced is that my job is not to save money, but to oversee the intelligent expenditure of money. The desires and needs of the creators sometimes warrant a defense and an affirmative action on the part of the production manager, such as his going to the front office and fighting for more money for something that is reasonable and correct for the picture on the basis of its artistic content. I have done that often. Any attitude which places the creative group on one side and the physical group on another side is a lot of baloney. I am concerned nowadays with that attitude. Since the making of a motion picture involves many hands, there must always be an overlap between the creative and physical counterparts.

Mike: How do you basically distinguish one group from the other?

Pratt: To begin with, every written budget which is drawn up by the production manager for every film has what we call the above-the-line costs and the below-the-line costs. There is actually a heavy black line on the budget sheet which separates these two types of costs. The above-the-line costs are the producer's area of control and are concerned with story, direction, cast, and ornamentation, or mounting. This is your creative or artistic talent, which, once negotiated, becomes a fixed cost. Below-the-line costs are the production manager's area of operation. His concern is the physical planning and execution of the operation of making a film and cost control. He may not participate in story conferences or producer and director meetings unless the physical planning and costs are involved. He is largely responsible for the expenditure of vast sums, often many millions of dollars, on a single film. Below-the-line costs might vary if problems arise which interrupt the shooting schedule, such as bad weather, illnesses, and mishaps. Because artistry and industry meet at the hands of the production manager, to be judged as to quality and costs, it is necessary to have a high degree of empathy between the producer and the production manager.

Mike: In your career you have not only been the production manager on individual films but were from 1946 to 1967 the executive production manager of an entire studio!

Pratt: Yes. In the spring of 1946 we at International moved our operation to Universal Studios in Universal City to make a picture called *Temptation* starring Merle Oberon and George Brent. That summer Universal and International merged, and I was appointed general production manager for the new Universal-International Pictures company. The old Universal had many personnel who had grown up there since the studio opened its gates in 1915. It had always been under approximately the same management from the front office in New York. William Goetz and Leo Spitz instigated new policies. There had been a tremendous prosperity for Hollywood during the war years. Night and day about all people everywhere could do was go to the movies. Financially, that was truly one of the golden periods

of films. In the postwar period many things came along to beset the
industry. The "Consent Decree" broke up the ownership of movie
houses by the major studios. The loss of this protection of block
booking was the first problem, but the major change in the prolific
film industry was the competition of free television. Other competitive
elements were suburbia living, desert and mountain cabins, and even
window air conditioning! It used to be that in the summer the best
way to get cool was to go to an air-conditioned movie house.
Increasingly, families have their own air-conditioned place with one
or two television boxes around. So back in the late forties studios
began battening down the hatch for a new way to continue operation.
To merge with other studios was one solution. The Universal-International merger also involved the J. Arthur Rank Organisation in
England. It was an effort to improve Universal's product and,
releasewise, compare with the other majors. Therefore, in the first year
after merger we decided to make pictures which would be competitive
with any studio in town as to quality, talent, and story material.
Somehow it didn't work, and the studio took a big loss in 1947–48.
Mike: What were some of these films?
Pratt: *All My Sons, Another Part of the Forest, Time Out of Mind, The
Exile, The O'Flynns* and *Up in Central Park.* There were about a dozen
in all.
Mike: At the same time, didn't you sign on a lot of new talent as
contract players?
Pratt: Yes. We had an acting school and developed such people as
Rock Hudson, Piper Laurie, and Tony Curtis. We also made
multi-picture deals with some of the older well-established stars. In
fact, Universal began the whole profit-sharing trend when we
negotiated with James Stewart to make two films, *Harvey* and
Winchester 73. Stewart had done *Harvey* very successfully on the
Broadway stage, and he wanted to repeat it for the movies, so he
agreed to do *Winchester 73,* if Universal would make *Harvey* first. I
went to the studio bosses and said, "Look, fellows, we're making a lot
of pictures that are basically running from three to five hundred
thousand dollars each below the line. What would you say if I told
you we could make *Harvey* for about the same amount below the
line?" Actually we had already spent a lot of money above the line
since we had acquired the stage play for one million dollars! Stewart

had his choice of taking a salary or fifty percent of the net. He chose the percentage. We made *Harvey* in black and white for a below-the-line cost of about four hundred thousand dollars. The outcome generated enough cash flow so that Universal-International didn't get hurt much. Stewart had already been set to make *Winchester 73* for no salary, but for fifty percent of the net profits. When we went into production, our studio was humming as well as any in town. We made *Winchester 73* for about eight hundred and fifty thousand dollars' total budget! Nobody could be sure of its success. It was just another Western. But as it turned out, it became a classic almost comparable to *High Noon*. The break-even figure was just a little over two million dollars. It grossed something like four million! So everybody was very happy. Stewart's percentage deal paid off quite well.

Mike: Don't you think it is better to give a star a percentage of a film rather than a large salary?

Pratt: Yes, but the percentages should be smaller than they are. And when they take a salary, the salaries should be smaller. The whole thing has gotten out of hand. After a very successful film called *The Pink Panther*, Peter Sellers asked for and got seven hundred and fifty thousand dollars a picture. The average well-known leading man around Hollywood was getting four hundred thousand top. If Sellers could get seven fifty against fifty percent of the profits, actors like James Stewart, Cary Grant, and John Wayne figured to get at least as much. So the numbers game started. And when Elizabeth Taylor got one million dollars for *Cleopatra*, other big stars began asking that amount. This meant a great deal to their agents, taxmen, and other business associates because all of them work on a percentage basis. The higher the stars' salaries got, the more they got. That much salary against the tax structure meant mostly prestige. However, it was real money as far as the outlay of the studio was concerned. On top of the high salaries there were other demands such as staffing, crew, dressing rooms, expense accounts, and the chauffeur-driven limousine twenty-four hours a day!

Mike: In these days the average big star only makes one film about every year and a half, so they have to make each job count financially. The lack of their productivity has made costs higher in all areas. At the same time, there are the low-budget films without stars which make good profits. Other low-budget films make no profit. The various experiments in how to go about making a profitable film within our present economy seem endless. Where do you think the metamorphosis the industry is undergoing will lead it?

Pratt: The current situation in Hollywood, the fading away of the business as we have known it, is too complex to fully understand yet. After all my years in production, I must be qualified as an expert. I think the old captains of the business—Sam Goldwyn, Louis B. Mayer, the Warners, William Fox, Winnie Sheenan, Darryl Zanuck, Walt Disney, Hal Roach, Adolph Zukor, the Cohns, and others were, first and foremost, businessmen. They were often called pirates, but they made unquestioned contributions to the total process of filmmaking. A lot of people who maligned them couldn't carry their luggage. These men knew from witnessing the evolution of the business that the bringing together of the peculiar combination of people and things that it takes to make films is a manufacturing process. It is one of the most complicated manufacturing processes. These hardbitten, tough men have disappeared. In the last few years a new group came in which, with few exceptions, has little knowledge or understanding of the complexity of the whole thing. They think you hire top talent and send them out to make big pictures. True, but where is fiscal responsibility? The studio heads make the mistake of sending more money to people who should not be permitted loose with so much of it.

Mike: What began this line of thinking?

Pratt: *The Sound of Music* was the turning point. The huge amount of money it made, and is still making, hit with a tremendous impact. But before it was made, almost all Hollywood thought, "How the hell are you going to sell the cornball story of the Trapp family?" The critics almost universally crucified the picture. It was called old hat, and they wondered how anyone could dare to make a picture like this in the modern era. But somehow there was something in the picture that was visually exciting and that the empathy of millions of people worldwide met on. They said, "Yes! We like it!" So it did four hundred percent of normal business at the Wilshire Theater in Beverly Hills, and it also did four hundred percent of normal business in a theater in Osaka, Japan, or on a bedsheet in the jungle of Brazil. For one fleeting moment Zanuck and his men put this together. The phenomenal success of *The Sound of Music* surprised everyone, and so the desire to make a blockbuster became the order of the day. The new group of studio executives took over, and there was a whole new ball game all over town. Decisions were made about 1967 to go ahead with productions which, it was hoped, would emulate the success of *The Sound of Music*. The outcome had a predictability to anyone who had been around as long as I had and who wasn't looking at anything with a jaundiced or cynical eye, but was just watching the movements, machinations, ambitions, and ideas of men who make films. I believe it is true that if you give creative people their full head, artistic merit may result. But, always, there must be fiscal responsibility. No matter how good a film is, if it cost too much to make, then it may not return the money. Filmmaking has always required that you get the money back so that you can use it to make another film. There has always been a revolving credit from a bank, but more or less a production company lives from hand to mouth. At present nearly every studio in town has financial trouble because of tight money and letting costs get out of hand.

September 2, 1970

Associate Producer

HANK MOONJEAN

Mike: You are a perfect example, Hank, of a guy who came up through the ranks to become an associate producer. How did you get your start?

Moonjean: My career began at MGM in 1955 in a unique way. I had received two degrees in the department of cinema at the University of Southern California, where I studied film production and, as a minor, publicity. Then I had gone into the Korean War. The day I was discharged and came home to Los Angeles I wrote two letters to MGM: one to the head of publicity, Howard Strickling; the other to the studio production manager, Walter Strohm. Within two days I received a phone call from the production department saying they'd like me to come in for an interview that day! I went out to the studio, but my appointment was delayed many hours because there was a crisis on the production of *Ben Hur* in Rome and nobody seemed to have time to talk to me. Eventually, I met Mr. Strohm and his assistant, Joe Wood. They asked me about my background. Then Mr. Strohm said, "I see from your letter that you speak fluent Turkish!" I explained that I was of Armenian descent and that both my parents were born in Turkey and that, when I was a child, I spoke Turkish, Armenian, and English. Mr. Strohm said the timing was perfect because they were looking for someone who spoke Turkish since the studio had plans to make a film in Turkey based on the Leslie Blanch novel *The Wilder Shores of Love.* It was to be directed by George Cukor and star Ava Gardner. I was hired to be a sort of liaison between the studio and the Turkish location. My duties were vague, but I was very happy to be with the studio. I worked in a minor capacity with Mr. Cukor for two months doing research and just listening and observing to see what the problems would be. However, the picture was canceled. In its place, Cukor made another picture with Ava Gardner called *Bhowani Junction.* It had nothing to do with Turkey, but nevertheless, I was made the liaison between the studio in Culver City and the location filming in Pakistan. After this production, I was made a second assistant director. At MGM they had a pool of second assistants who were assigned, temporarily, to films in production on large sequences that required an additional assistant or two to help the full-time first assistant and second assistant who are a part of every production staff. I moved around on many films in that manner. The first film I worked as a full-time second assistant was *Kismet* which Vincente Minnelli directed. Several years later, after *Raintree County*, I was promoted to a first assistant director. After working on several excellent films terminating with *The Unsinkable Molly Brown*, I became a combination first assistant director and associate producer under such producers as Max Youngstein, Joe Pasternak, Lawrence Weingarten, and Pandro Berman. Outside of MGM, I've worked in that capacity for George Axelrod when he produced and directed his own screenplay *The Secret Life of an American Wife* and for Paul Newman and John Foreman on their production of *WUSA.* At present I am an associate producer to David Merrick with whom I did *Child's Play.*

Mike: Is it your ambition to work yourself up to being a full producer?

Moonjean: Actually, I want to be a director, but I thought it would be easier for me to become a producer first. I know more about producing than directing. That is, I don't think at this time I can direct highly specialized material such as musicals and comedies, although I could direct certain other material. As a producer I feel I can do any type of film. I have the knowledge of organization, finances, and preparation it requires. These are the areas I really shine in. Also, in today's market I think there is a greater need for producers than directors. Directors seem to be far more plentiful.

Mike: At present you work most often as an associate producer. What are some of the duties of that position?

Moonjean: The associate producer is to the producer what an assistant director is to the director. He assists in putting all the parts together and helps the producer prepare the production for filming, as well as help prepare the final touches for the release of the film. He is involved with the screenwriter, the casting of actors, and is, in essence, the right arm of the producer. It is not as exciting a job as being an assistant director, because the assistant director is always right there on the set where the action is. The associate producer works from his office and is at his busiest in the planning of the film and at the end of the film in postproduction work like music, editing, and looping. The actual shooting of the film is where the fun is! But the associate producer is not involved on the set every day.

Mike: How do the duties of the associate producer differ from those of the production manager?

Moonjean: The production manager controls the operation of the physical aspects that keep a production working. The director controls the artistic aspects. The producer and his associate oversee all these aspects combined. The production manager is the associate producer's direct contact to the set. He is hired by the producer or the associate to fulfill all the duties that are required on the set for production reasons. Therefore, he is the producer's representative on the set. Rather than the producer or his associate going down on the set to make changes or give direct orders, the production manager is told by them what is to be done. An associate producer doesn't tamper with a set because, hopefully, he has a top production manager and a top assistant director, and it is their function to see that the set runs smoothly. The only person on a set that the associate producer would work directly with is the director. In most other cases production personnel are dealt with by the production manager.

Mike: If you are an associate producer under one man who is the director-producer, aren't your duties more demanding?

Moonjean: Yes. Under director-producers like Elia Kazan, William Wyler, and Billy Wilder, the associate producer actually functions as the producer because these men are spending most of their time directing. That's how I functioned with George Axelrod. Although I was, by title, associate producer, I was, in fact, the producer, so that George could concentrate on directing and other creative aspects. On that production I was also the assistant director, so I was sort of doing everything!

Mike: Don't some associate producers work for the same producer over and over?

Moonjean: A few. The one man who comes to mind is Paul Nathan, who has been Hal Wallis' associate producer for many years. His position, I should think, encompasses more duties and carries more authority than that of the average associate.

Mike: Who are some of the directors you have worked with?

Moonjean: I've worked with many, many directors, but the ones I have enjoyed the most are Stuart Rosenberg, George Axelrod, Richard Brooks, and Joshua Logan. I worked with George Axelrod nearly eight months, and there was never a dull moment! Lots of laughs every day. He was marvelous. I'm sorry the picture wasn't more of a success. Two of the pictures I did with Richard Brooks were *Cat on a Hot Tin Roof* and *Sweet Bird of Youth*. Both were Tennessee Williams plays for which Richard wrote the screenplays as well as directed. I also did *The Catered Affair* with him, which Gore Vidal wrote. Richard had a peculiar quirk about not letting scripts off his set. He actually would have everyone, stars and all, turn in their scripts at the end of each day's work. On *Sweet Bird of Youth* Ed Begley, who played Boss Finley, was always reluctant to give up his script. He said he needed it at night to study his role. I had to take it from him just the same, but he ended up getting the Academy Award for best supporting actor that year. I suspect more cast members had thermofaxed copies of their scripts. I guess I am also partial to Josh Logan because he gave me my first break as a first assistant director on *Tall Story*. He also gave Jane Fonda and Gary Lockwood their first breaks on that film. Even though I never worked with him again, he has been loyal in asking me to work on each film he directs, including *Paint Your Wagon*. Unfortunately, I have always been in the middle of doing another picture. With Stuart Rosenberg I've established an extremely gratifying work rapport, having done all his feature films to date. Our relationship began with *Cool Hand Luke*. I've truthfully never seen any director work so well with actors, and he has that knack of getting the most out of writers by stirring up their creative juices.

Mike: Your career began just as television was beginning to dominate Hollywood. That domination has resulted in the major studios changing from the giant film factories they were to more or less distributors and backers of motion pictures. What do you think of the New Hollywood this economic situation has caused?

Moonjean: I think what's happening to Hollywood should have happened twenty years ago. I never saw so much money squandered as in the major studios. It seemed to be spent, in many cases, for no rhyme or reason. Everything cost too much, and that is what has hurt the industry. In the operation of the large studios many of the top brass have been nothing but whores! These so-called talented people took advantage of their positions. Money was thrown away. Whenever they had an economy drive, they would get rid of an electrician or a security guard or cut down on janitors. If you total up all that money, it wouldn't amount to much. On the other hand, producers sat around who never produced, but yet got several thousand dollars a week salary! There were other studio personnel of the old regime, who were in the industry many years during the heyday of Hollywood, who never really functioned, yet drew large salaries. They would just become rich, tired old people. This was one reason studio overhead kept getting higher and higher. The end result of the breaking up of the studio complexes will be wonderful. They are getting rid of all the "woodwork."

Mike: Do you think higher union demands have been a major contribution to the economic upheaval of Hollywood?

Moonjean: No, as a production man, I don't think so. In minor areas the union demands may have been unfair, but not enough to be a real influence. Crews here deserve being well paid. I think the best crews come from Hollywood. They are the most fantastic you can have, including Europe and New York. I can say that because I've worked all over the world. Hollywood crews are more knowledgeable and harder-working. These excellent crews are not what makes a budget too high. The prohibitive costs of production come from the upper echelon. Fortunately, now, many of the top talents will forgo an exorbitant salary in favor of a percentage of whatever profit the film makes. If the picture is a hit, they make very good money. If it is a flop, the studio or other financial backer does not have to take all the consequences of a big loss.

Mike: But exorbitant salaries still exist.

Moonjean: Oh, yes. If you have a film budgeted at two million and get certain of the superstars, it becomes three million dollars. Basically because of this, I think, the agents and the actors have caused the current depression in Hollywood.

Mike: Do you think any of these high-salaried superstars justify their demands by being a box-office guarantee?

Moonjean: No. In today's film market the most important thing in the success of a product is the story. A good story has become hard to find. Let's face it. They are running out of material because television eats up so much of it. In Los Angeles there are over a dozen channels, and it takes a lot of story material to take up all that time.

Mike: As an associate producer do you have an agent?

Moonjean: Yes. I have enough status in the industry that I can find my own work, but my agent saves me the embarrassment of bickering over money and screen credit. At present, to the best of my knowledge, I happen to be the highest-paid person who works both as an associate producer and as a first assistant director. But that fact doesn't make a dent in any production's budget!

Mike: What actor have you worked with most often?

Moonjean: Paul Newman. I did *The Rack, Somebody Up There Likes Me, Until They Sail, Cat on a Hot Tin Roof, Sweet Bird of Youth, The Prize, Cool Hand Luke,* and *WUSA.* Paul is extremely professional. In all our work together he has never given me a problem. He always knows his part and is always on time. People on the set enjoy him. Crews like him. Of course, we never laugh at his jokes. The only one who laughs is Paul himself! And when you tell Paul a joke, you could be rolling on the floor with laughter and there's not a crack in his face! I've worked with Joanne Woodward also. She is equally as professional as Paul, and I think they make a marvelous couple. She is as devoted and interested in his career as he is in hers. They've made a happy combination of their careers and their private lives.

Mike: Haven't you worked a lot with Elizabeth Taylor?

Moonjean: More than anyone after Paul. Elizabeth is fantastic to work with. She's very exciting and lots and lots of fun. A good sport and very generous and loyal. She always would ask for me to work on her films. Since her early days at MGM, it has been common knowledge that Elizabeth Taylor does not like to get up in the morning. She always runs late but is honest in telling you that she will be late. We used to expect her in makeup at seven, and she wouldn't get there until eight. When I was a second assistant director, many times Elizabeth would not show up on schedule, and I would be sent to her house to get her. The servants knew me and would let me in. I'd go to her bedroom and wake her up. I've got to tell you, I've never in my life seen anyone as beautiful as Elizabeth Taylor when she gets up in the morning! No makeup, no hairdo, nothing! She'd say to me, "Why don't you put the coffee on?" I'd forget what I was up there for, and pretty soon the studio would have to send a car to get *me* so that I could get Elizabeth to come to work! When she got to the studio, she made up for all the time she lost. She always knew her dialogue, never caused any problems, and was anxious to do her day's work and get out. If she enjoyed her director and the part she was playing, she'd be much more excited. In many instances she was forced to do pictures in which it was an effort for her to perform. For instance, she didn't want to do *Butterfield 8*. She hated the script, hated her part, and made life miserable for the studio and for herself. However, she knew a lot of people's careers and livelihoods were at stake, and when all was said and done, she did the best she could. Consequently, she won the Academy Award.

After *Butterfield 8* Elizabeth and Eddie Fisher hired me to work for their own production company. I went to Italy with them while Elizabeth worked on *Cleopatra*. Their company had plans for two films: Charlie Chaplin was approached about directing Elizabeth in *Anna Karenina*. The other project was *The Gouffé Case*, for which we were pretty far along in negotiations and had talked with the great French director René Clement and with Alain Delon. When Elizabeth met Alain Delon, she said, "I don't think I want to play opposite him. He's prettier than I am!" No films were ever made because the company dissolved when Elizabeth and Eddie's marriage dissolved.

Mike: Is Elizabeth your favorite actress?

Moonjean: I love her, but I'm also crazy about Eleanor Parker, who I think is one of the best film actresses in the world. I worked with her on *Interrupted Melody*, but really got to be great friends when we did *The Seventh Sin*, which was a remake of the Garbo film *The Painted Veil*. Eleanor was the first person really to encourage me in my career. Because of her, I did some writing and sold two scripts to television. We have remained friends through the years, and I see her quite often.

Another gal I admire is Paulette Goddard. To me she is the most sexually exciting thing that has been on the screen. On all the pictures I do I get kidded by trying to get her parts in them. When we did *A Patch of Blue*, I suggested her for the part of the blind girl's mother, which Shelley Winters eventually played. Usually when producers see me they say, "We want you to do this picture, Hank, but there's no part for Paulette Goddard." Once I asked the cameraman Leon Shamroy if he had ever worked with her and if he didn't think she was one of the great beauties. He said, "Hell, if you think she was good-looking, you should have seen her mother!" Someday I'm going to get to work with Paulette.

One of the actresses I love the most is Debbie Reynolds. I was on what I consider her two best films, *The Catered Affair* and *The Unsinkable Molly Brown*. I also did *The Singing Nun* with her. As many films as she has made, I still don't think her talent has been used to its fullest potential. She works hardest of all the actresses I've ever worked with.

Mike: Do you have a favorite actor?

Moonjean: I was very fond of Montgomery Clift. When I worked on *Raintree County* and was living with my parents, I told my mother that whenever I got a phone call to write down the person's name and number, but not to talk much. Even though she had been in this country fifty years, she sounded like she just got off the boat. One day when I wasn't at home Monty called. Mother asked if there was any message. Monty said, "Yes. Tell him Montgomery Clift called." Mother said, "Spell it." Monty thought that was very funny. It took him about ten minutes to spell his name so that Mother got it correct. They turned out to be great friends. He used to call her once or twice a month from New York and always remembered her at Christmas.

Mike: Do you have a favorite story that happened on any of the films you've done?

Moonjean: Oh, yes! The funniest incident I ever witnessed was when we were making *Kismet* and doing the musical number "Strangers in

Paradise." That sequence had Ann Blyth and Vic Damone in it. The set was as beautiful as any paradise should be with flowers, a soft wind blowing, and this lovely song being played on the playback machine. We were setting up a long shot in which Vincente Minnelli wanted to use two peacocks: one in the background and one very close in the foreground. When the scene was to be shot, he wanted the peacocks to fan out their colorful tail feathers. Nobody seemed to know at the time that only male peacocks have that beautiful plumage and that they show it off only when they are sexually stimulated. So, when we were ready to shoot, the peacocks would not fan out their tails because there were no peahens on the stage. Minnelli said he would not make the scene until he got what he asked for. Everybody began getting nervous trying to make the peacocks cooperate. Time and money were being spent. Finally, the propman said he could wire the peacocks to the ground and wire their tails in a spread-out position. He nailed the poor peacock in the background to the sod on the stage floor and wired his tail. It worked fine! Then he did the same to the peacock in the foreground, but the camera could see the wire. He tried again and again to hide the wire; but each time the camera could see it, and Minnelli refused to change the angle of the camera. The propman came up with another extraordinary idea that saved the day. He got on his stomach under the peacock and stuck a finger up the peacock's rear end! The peacock fanned out his tail in all its glory! We shot the scene, and the propman pulled out his finger. The peacock closed his tail. For all the several takes the propman had to repeat the same procedure. Minnelli would say his usual line he says at the end of every take, "It's absolutely beautiful! Let's do it again!" One time Minnelli said that line when he was directing a film starring Frank Sinatra called *Some Came Running*. I didn't work on the picture, but the story is that Sinatra replied, "You can, but I won't be in it!"

Mike: Several people have told me Sinatra should exert more professional discipline at times.

Moonjean: I did one picture with Sinatra which costarred Gina Lollabrigida called *Never so Few*. One day we got word from the publicity department that the King of Belgium was coming to visit the set. Gina and Frank were tipped off that the press and television cameras would be there. The production department was quite worried about Gina's boobs showing too much in a very low-cut dress she was wearing. Someone kept throwing a shawl around her shoulders, and she kept removing it. She wanted her finer assets to show. There was a lot of tension, and it was very amusing. Finally, when he was presented to the king, Sinatra said, "Why, you're skinnier than I am, Charlie!" The king didn't remain on our set very long after that!

August 7, 1970

Assistant Director

RANDELL HENDERSON

Henderson: When I was a kid, my father who was an architect built me a little puppet theater. I made up shows and put them on for the neighborhood kids. The point is, since I was a kid, I've known what I wanted to do. Sometimes I think I've wanted it too much because I haven't been half as successful as I'd like to be. I'm in the business, but I'm still not doing exactly what I want to do. In college I thought I was very lucky. I heard other students saying, "I don't know what I want to major in. I don't know what I want to do." I always knew.

Mike: What college did you attend?

Henderson: Bard College of Columbia University. I majored in fine arts.

Mike: What happened when you finished?

Henderson: It was 1942, so I volunteered for the Army. I was sent to North Africa as a general replacement but was fortunate enough to be assigned to the Special Services Division of the Fifth Army. It was at that time I wrote and directed an all-soldier musical called *Egg in Your Beer*, a unique show in that the cast consisted of thirteen Purple Heart holders. It was the only soldier show to be produced overseas, then brought back to tour the States. It had a run of two and a half years.

Mike: Did this Army experience with show business help you in civilian life?

Henderson: I didn't have any trouble getting work as a stage manager in good summer stock companies and on Broadway.

Mike: Was that your goal?

Henderson: I wanted to be a full-fledged director and also to write. Being a stage manager is a monotonous job. You go to the theater every night and push the same buttons, give the same cues, and see the same faces. This is why I know so many actors get fed up with a long-run show. If it is a creative thing, it is bound to get mechanical. I mean, a star like Laurence Olivier is not going to do anything on Broadway for over a season, which is six or seven months.

Mike: Where did being a stage manager lead you?

Henderson: I became an assistant to the playwright George S. Kaufman. One flop after another, except for *Guys and Dolls*, which was the last show I did with him. Then I went to CBS Television as a stage manager, which led to being an associate director, then finally a director. I was on the CBS staff for ten years.

Mike: So it was television that brought you to Hollywood?

Henderson: Well, the bottom fell out of live television in New York around 1958–59. The so-called golden era was over. I was among the hundreds who moved to Hollywood, where there were better job opportunities in television and motion pictures. I was a member of the Radio and Television Directors' Guild which had merged with the Screen Directors' Guild shortly before I left New York.

Mike: Did you come to Hollywood with CBS?

Henderson: No. I was free-lancing, but I had an agent. My first show to direct out here was a segment of *Death Valley Days* starring Rhonda Fleming. And I did various soap operas.

Mike: Did your luck take a turn for the worse, or was it the condition within the industry that caused you to become an assistant director after having been a director?

Henderson: Around 1961 work became scarce in all phases of the industry. American companies began making more "runaway" motion pictures in Europe because it was a hell of a lot cheaper. And people who had always worked on feature films started working on television films. There were many more people than there were jobs. So, when I didn't get all the work I needed and wanted as a full director, I went to my guild and told them I was willing to take work as an assistant director. Ironically, they told me that, since I was on their books as a full director, I was not eligible to work as an assistant!

So I thought, "What kind of work can I do outside the industry to have some money coming in and still be available to take a directing job when another one comes along?" I went to a special school and got a license to sell real estate.

Mike: An awful lot of film people have done that from time to time. Some well known.

Henderson: It sustained me for three years until I had a call one day from my guild asking if I would consider working as an assistant director!

Mike: The guild's rulings on the matter had been changed?

Henderson: Well, times had changed, and I suppose the guild was meeting the requirements of the times. This was about 1965. There, rather unexpectedly, arose a shortage of assistant directors. They needed a second assistant director over at Paramount on *This Property Is Condemned* starring Natalie Wood and Robert Redford. I think that's the first time I met you, Mike, when you were an actor on that and also the dialogue coach. Since then, I've worked both as a first assistant and as a second assistant director. I like to keep working.

Mike: The first assistant is the guy who coordinates all the activity on a movie set. Keeps things moving at an efficient pace by doing countless chores. Where does his job begin?

Henderson: I'd say the first important thing a good assistant does is to break down a script. You're shooting out of sequence, out of continuity. You have to break the script down to the number of days it will take to shoot it, the number of actors it requires, the number of sets, exterior and interior. Usually, if you have exteriors, you try to knock them off first because if a day turns out to be bad weather, you can move inside to a cover set and shoot another scene. You don't have to hold up production waiting on good weather. Also, you try to knock off the actors as soon as possible because they are often getting paid by the day. It comes down almost like a budget job. You're thinking of money and cost of production all the time. That's right down to the extras, the people who are paid the least. But even extras are expensive if you have a hundred of them. *Hello, Dolly!* in one sequence had three thousand at twenty-nine dollars and fifteen cents a day! The unit manager, who is also called the production manager, and the first assistant get together and decide in what order the scenes will be shot. As no story is the same, no shooting schedule is the same. A chart of the shooting schedule is made on what we call a picture board. The names of every character are listed down the board. Across the top of the board each scene and the date it is to be shot are listed. By reading the board as you would a graph, you are able to tell who works in what, where, and when. The board is transferred in writing to a shooting schedule. This typewritten schedule is given to every department. I also like to give a copy to the principal actors.

Mike: Isn't the first assistant the closest man on a set to the director?

Henderson: Yes, and all directors work differently. And you may have a different director each job you have. The actors are also different each job. There is a lot of psychology involved in working with so many new people. It's not like going to a factory or office where you do the same thing and work with the same people day after day.

Mike: Doesn't a director often request the same assistant to work with him again?

Henderson: Oh, yes! Many directors have their regular assistants, and many first assistants have their own second assistants. I think the term "assistant director" is a misnomer. Although he is assisting the director, he is doing so many other things for the production. It sounds as if an assistant director is a person who helps the director direct, but that is not his function. Most assistants never become directors. Many men in the guild retire as first assistants. This is all they wanted to be.

Mike: Is the Directors' Guild of America as difficult as most film-industry unions to get into?

Henderson: Yes, but they have a training program now that they should have had years ago. They get young men from colleges all over the country. The studio pays them a living salary by the hour, and they get excellent training and experience actually working on a film.

Mike: Does your guild help you to find work?

Henderson: Every Thursday they send out an availability list of all guild members to every studio and producer who has signed a contract with the guild. That certainly helps.

Mike: Is nepotism very often involved in determining who gets work?

Henderson: They say it isn't. But certainly there are an awful lot of directors' sons and relatives who are first assistants. I've worked with good ones, and I've worked with bad ones. I worked with one very bad one last year. He just wasn't up to the job, but he was the son of a very famous director. An ambitious boy who had done some little television show, then got this job on a feature. And there is a big difference. The crew would come to me, and we would laugh about it. I finally got off the picture it was so ludicrous. With a bad first assistant the second assistant and the crew are made to look bad.

Mike: Do you obtain work very easily?

Henderson: The business at its best is seasonal and it's getting worse all the time. Say, the average busy season is from June through December. The current work situation is made more complex by the sincere efforts to bring more members of minority groups into film jobs, especially the blacks.

Mike: And one of our nation's more vigorous minority groups, Jews, are the majority group in the entertainment industry. So, when jobs are scarce, you probably are not on the top of anyone's list. But once you get hired, you become a hirer yourself in the selection of extras, don't you?

Henderson: Usually. We have in Hollywood several offices which handle most extras. Extras and stand-ins belong to the Screen Extras' Guild. Stand-ins are sometimes very important, especially to the cameraman. I'm a stickler on having good stand-ins. An assistant is busy enough without having to go around the set looking for the stand-ins. I had some on one film who were insulted when we yelled, "Second team!" which is the usual way to call stand-ins to come to camera. They said, "Look, you don't have to call us. We know when you need us."

Mike: Do you have anything to do with hiring of other actors?

Henderson: No, but we can perhaps get someone an interview with the casting director who screens day players and bit actors and brings the most likely prospects to the director to make the final choice. It is ultimately the director who casts actors. George Cukor went a step further on *Justine* and even selected every extra. Each day we'd have interviews of people who were to be used the next day. He'd been stung, I guess, by having people sent over at random. Very often Cukor will use a bit actor who does not say a line. A silent bit we call it, and it is usually done by an extra. In *Justine* there was a party scene, and ordinarily we would have used a lot of extras that day, but not a single one of these people was an extra. Of course, that's a little more expensive, but the director gets what he wants from the actors.

Mike: What is one of the more interesting films you've worked on?

Henderson: *Butch Cassidy and the Sundance Kid.* Almost the whole picture was shot on location. We were in Durango, Colorado, and St.

George, Utah. A typical day for me would be to get up at five thirty, have a quick breakfast, and start checking that all the equipment was on hand. I was the second assistant on that film. One of my duties was to see that Paul Newman and Robert Redford were dressed and in makeup and on the set on schedule. They were made up at the hotel; then we would go in cars to the location site which was usually a thirty- or forty-minute drive out to the middle of nowhere! Newman and Redford got along beautifully. There was no friction. These were two stars attacking a wonderful story. They had something going for them, and it comes across on the screen.

Mike: On an outdoor film like that did bad weather hamper your schedule?

Henderson: Not to any serious degree. But when I worked on *Zabriskie Point*, *good* weather set us behind schedule! We had shot just a portion of a sequence at the Hawthorne Airport in lousy winter weather. Then all of a sudden it cleared up! We had to sit there for three weeks waiting for the sun to go behind the clouds again! Uncontrollable factors like that put tremendous pressures on a production manager and an assistant.

Mike: And on a director, too.

Henderson: Yes. But the problems of a director and those of an assistant differ, although they are both always under a great deal of pressure. For instance, the director may worry about the overall quality of the scene being shot. Whereas, the assistant may have to worry about having only half an hour left of light to shoot and wind up that scene, so that he doesn't have to call those actors back the next day. That would cost money and also set the schedule behind a day. The assistant is forever concerned with keeping the shooting moving along to stay within the schedule and budget. If something doesn't go smooth, he is likely to be the first person asked, "What happened?" The responsibilities of an assistant are enormous.

Mike: I watched one of the best assistants in the business catch hell over and over again on an Otto Preminger fiasco. Often, if something went wrong, no matter who or what was to blame, Preminger would scream at him like a madman and foam at the mouth. Talk about pressure!

Henderson: Well, that isn't typical of directors.

Mike: I know, but Otto Preminger is probably the most unreasonable director in the world to work under. His Germanic attitude is old-hat.

We've been through two world wars and he's still acting like a World War I general. It just proves that some actors will do anything. Some will still work for him.

Henderson: Fortunately, most directors are a pleasure to work with. I especially liked George Roy Hill, who directed *Butch Cassidy*. And I thought George Cukor was just fine! He's the old school. He doesn't fool around with actors. I've seen some directors take an actor off in a corner and interpret for hours on end! Cukor will simply listen to a line reading, and if he doesn't like it, he will say, "This is the way I want you to say it," and he will read it for you. A lot of actors these days resent being given a line reading, but Cukor usually gets the reading he wants. On *Justine* one of the actors wanted to alter a line to fit his own interpretation. It was a simple little change, but Cukor said politely, "No, no! They spent a lot of money on these words!"—which is true and George Cukor was respecting the author. Many directors will let an actor climb all over a sentence.

Mike: I was a bit surprised to read some of the publicity for *Justine* comparing the star, Anouk Aimée, to Greta Garbo!

Henderson: Well, as I remember, Cukor came right out and said, "Garbo she ain't!" No one would know better than he, since he directed Garbo in *Camille*. Sophia Loren had been up for the lead in *Justine*, but she was pregnant. She would have been marvelous.

Mike: Have you enjoyed working with some stars more than others?

Henderson: I like working with any actor who is a real professional and concentrates on his contribution to the overall good of the company. One of the most important things to an assistant is that an actor be on a set on time and be prepared. I once worked on a television series with a "newcomer star." He was a guy who worried only about personal comfort and luxuries. He was never on the sound stage when we needed him. On the other hand, I recently did a television show guest starring Henry Fonda. He was always on the set in his chair and ready when the director needed him. This professional discipline is one thing many of the young actors have to learn. Many of them assume behavioral attitudes they think will get them treated like a star. Demanding attention, rather than gaining respect, which is the true mark of a professional.

Mike: How many assistant directors does a film generally have?

Henderson: There is always only one first assistant, but he can have several assistants under him. When we filmed the big parade sequence for *Hello, Dolly!*, they hired about a dozen second assistant directors who had to handle all these thousands of extras. That was one of the most exciting films I've ever worked on. I loved being in on it because it was the real old Hollywood and will probably never happen again. It was about the biggest call for extras ever in Hollywood!

Mike: Do you feel a creative outlet as an assistant director?

Henderson: No. One reason is that the amount of paper work an assistant must do on a picture is ridiculously enormous. Something should be done to remedy this load. Some of the studios are trying. MGM has cut its paper work in half. There are things like vouchers for extras. And every actor in a picture, whether he knows it or not, punches a time clock. Even the stars. On *Butch Cassidy* I used to have to make out a time card for Paul Newman and the rest of the cast every day. It listed their hours to arrive in the morning, what time they reported to wardrobe, to makeup, what time they appeared on the set, what time they went to lunch, what time they returned from lunch, what time they were dismissed for the day.

Mike: Couldn't an actual time clock be used by everyone?

Henderson: It used to be one way of doing it. In fact, there's a funny story about Harry Cohn in the old days at Columbia wanting his actors, even Rita Hayworth, to check in on a time clock he installed on each sound stage. He thought it would improve the efficiency of the studio. It was a wonderful idea, but maybe an actor wouldn't have a call until later in the day, and he would arrive on the set and punch his time card in the middle of a take and you'd hear the sound of the clock stamping the card! It would ruin the take! So that system was soon changed, and the responsibility was handed down to the assistant director.

Mike: What other paper work do you have?

Henderson: A production report is made out at the end of each day's shooting: how many scenes were shot and the minutes for each one; the number of camera setups; the film footage exposed; what time your first shot is in the morning. In other words, it is a log of the day's work kept mostly for the production office to check on the efficiency and economy of the company as a whole. Sometimes I think they are trying to turn assistant directors into bookkeepers! I don't see the need for most of this intricate paper work. However, one item is very necessary, and that is the call sheet. The call sheet is made up near the end of each day's shooting and gives the requirements for the next day's work. It lists all the actors, crew, and other workers who will be needed and what time they are to appear. It lists the equipment and props and food, if any, and all details pertinent to the day's work. I'd like to get out of the production end of films, although some of it can be exciting, like working on *Hello, Dolly!* and *Butch Cassidy.* But there are not too many pictures like that to go around, and I like to keep busy. I love the creative end of films. That's where I want to be. I like writing, and I'm writing a screenplay now which I think has a good chance of selling.

November 2, 1969

Director of Photography

JAMES WONG HOWE

Howe: I was born in China and came to America when I was five years old. We arrived in the summer of 1904 and settled in a small town called Pasco, Washington. It's a railroad division where my father had worked before going into business and saving enough money to return to China to get the rest of us. When he died in 1914, I left home because I didn't get along with my mother. Besides, I wanted to see the country. The rest of the family remained to take care of the business, which I didn't like. I liked athletics, baseball and boxing, something that was challenging. I was very competitive. When the Knights of Columbus or the Elks would have a smoker, they would always have us kids up to box. I was pretty good, very fast, and you can see from my face I never got busted up. One night I was boxing with a good friend of mine, an Irish boy named Willie Hogan. We weighed about eighty-five pounds. Fleaweights! In the excitement of the cheering crowd we fought harder. I hit Willie, and he went out! There was a promoter present named Charlie Yost from Portland, Oregon. He thought he could put more weight on me and make me a flyweight. So he trained me over a two-year period and got me to go to Portland. I boxed around the Northwest. It wasn't big-time. After a while I went down the coast to Astoria, Oregon, where my uncle lived. He packed salmon in a fish cannery. They always hired Oriental help. He got so much a case, furnished the labor, paid them, and fed them. I stayed with him about a year; then I drifted down to San Francisco for a while. I continued to Los Angeles in 1916, when I was seventeen. In Los Angeles I tried to get on as a boxer but never made it. I needed money, so I got a job as a busboy at the Beverly Hills Hotel. After about three months there I got into an argument with one of the Chinese cooks and got fired. My next job was as a delivery boy for a commercial photographer named Raymond Stagg. I rode around on a motorbike and carried the photos in a bag which read "Stagg Photos"!

Mike: Did working for this still photographer lead to your becoming a movie photographer?

Howe: No. That came about because one day I was in Chinatown when they were filming a Mack Sennett comedy. While I was watching, I noticed the guy cranking the camera and realized I knew him from Portland. He was Lynn Powers, a friend and a good lightweight. He had come down to box. In those days a few stars had stables of boxers the way they have stables of horses now. Out in Vernon a place called Jack Doyle's had four-round bouts every Friday night. This was during World War I and continued into Prohibition. In Los Angeles, you couldn't get a drink, but Doyle's had the longest bar in the country. Thirty-five bartenders! You had to walk through this bar to get to the arena. Lynn had fought there until he got busted up. Then some movie director took him in and got him a job as an assistant cameraman. Soon he became a cameraman. So, when I saw him, I went up and said, "Hey, hello, Lynn. What you doing?" He wore his cap backward and was cranking away. He said, "Jimmy! What are you doing down here?" I said, "I'm delivering pictures." He said, "You ought to get into this business. It's good. I crank these things and get seventy-five dollars a week. It's fun." I said, "How do I get in?" He said, "Go to a studio and find out who is in charge of the camera department and ask for a job as an assistant." I quit my delivery job and went out to the old Lasky Studio on the corner of Vine and Selma in Hollywood. That was in 1917. There were orange groves in what is now the heart of Hollywood. Vine Street wasn't even paved! It had rows of pepper trees which looked like beautiful weeping willows. I went in an office and inquired, and they told me to go in the back gate on Argyle Street where the laboratory was and see a man named Alvin Wycoff, who was in charge of the camera department. He was also the chief photographer for Cecil B. De Mille. They were just finishing a picture which I believe was *Joan of Arc* with Geraldine Farrar. I waited around a couple of hours and was about to leave when the gateman said, "There comes Mr. Wycoff now." I followed him into an office and introduced myself and said I was looking for a job as an assistant cameraman. He said, "Well, these cameras are very heavy to carry around. I don't know whether you can carry them." I said, "Don't worry about that. I may be slight, but I am very strong." He said, "I don't need an assistant. I just put a guy to work a few hours ago. But I can give you a job in the camera room, where we store the cameras and load the film. I want you to go down there and keep it clean. The boys throw these short pieces of film around, and they are very explosive and a fire hazard. When the time comes, I'll give you a job as an assistant cameraman."

Mike: These were the days before unions, of course!

Howe: Yes. You didn't have to worry about having a card to get in. It would be a lot different now. Mr. Wycoff said, "I can't pay you much money. Just ten dollars a week." I said, "When do I start?" He replied, "You're on salary now." I said, "Look, I'm all dressed up. I'm not going down there to be a janitor with these clothes on." He said, "No. I just want to show you the place and what to do. You come back tomorrow in work clothes." That's my introduction to a movie studio! I kept that camera room neat for about six months.

Meanwhile, De Mille had started another picture. They were shooting a scene with Gloria Swanson. She was in a cave, and a lion was to attack her while she was lying there. They had to have four or five cameras to shoot different angles and needed an extra assistant. I was sent to the set. My job was to hold the slate which identifies the scenes. Of course, I got a close-up all the time, by holding that slate! Mr. De Mille would see those close-ups of me with my Oriental face looking around curiously, and he was amused. He said to Mr. Wycoff, "I like that look. Keep him with us." So I became a third assistant cameraman with De Mille's unit!

I lived in a room in downtown Los Angeles, over the Third Street tunnel on Hill Street, for two and a half bucks a week, and took the streetcar to work for five cents a ride. Mr. De Mille used to come to work at ten in the morning and shoot until two or three in the afternoon before calling lunch. After lunch he would work until ten or eleven at night. After shooting I still had to work making up reports, cleaning cameras, and reloading the film. Many nights I'd miss the streetcar, which stopped running at midnight. Hollywood was like a little village. There were two hotels, the Christie Hotel and the Hollywood Hotel, which is gone now. I couldn't afford to stay in a hotel, and there was nowhere to sleep, so I would sleep on the set in Gloria Swanson's silk-sheeted bed! It was summertime, and the orange blossoms smelled great. It was heaven! The night watchman would come around and hear me snoring. He'd wake me up and say, "What are you doing here?" I'd say, "I missed the streetcar." He'd say, "OK. I'll wake you up before anybody comes to work." He'd wake me about six o'clock. I'd go across the street to a place run by Mother Harrin and eat breakfast. A cup of coffee and two doughnuts for ten cents. Then I would punch in at the studio about seven o'clock. I got a raise to fifteen dollars a week, which was great!

Mike: You learned photography mostly by watching the cameramen at work?

Howe: More or less. I thought, if I really wanted to be a photographer, I should buy a still camera and start by learning how to take regular pictures. I went down to Fifth and Main in L.A. where all the pawnshops still are and got a little five-by-seven view camera. I practiced by taking pictures of all the extras and bit players. They didn't have agents in those days. Every actor and actress would have to leave pictures with the casting office to get work. I got so I could make pretty good portraits, which I would enlarge to eight-by-ten prints and sell for fifty cents each. I made more money that way than I did as an assistant! I almost quit being an assistant to become a portrait photographer, but Mr. Wycoff advised me to keep doing both. He said, "A portrait is like a close-up in movies. It's a very important thing to learn. All the stars, especially the women, want good close-ups. If you can make them look beautiful, they will ask for you."

Finally they promoted me to run the second camera. That meant, after the chief cameraman got his camera set up, I would look through it and see what he had. Then I would set my camera close to his and try to duplicate his view, his angle. The negative made by my camera was sent to Europe and was called the foreign negative. They didn't have duplicating film, so they had to send a separate negative to Europe from which release prints were made. It saved money to pay duty on one negative instead of on many prints. To be a cameraman I had to learn to crank. I couldn't take my camera home to practice, so I bought one of those little old wooden coffee grinders. I turned it with a rhythm which I counted, "One and two and. . . ." Film had to go through a camera at one foot a second. One foot of film consisted of sixteen frames. Today it is twenty-four frames per 2 foot and a half, because of sound. As a second cameraman I began making twenty-five dollars a week! That, plus my still portrait work, at times earned me more than a first cameraman. I also used my still camera to make background pictures for the subtitles. For instance, for a subtitle like "As time went by . . ." I'd photograph a sand hourglass in the background. The directors liked my work, so they'd have me on their sets often.

One of the big stars at Famous Players-Lasky Studios was Mary Miles Minter, a beautiful young lady with blue eyes and long blond curls. I was on her set one day, and I asked if I could take a few pictures. She answered yes, that she would be pleased. I took three or four portraits, which I enlarged to eleven-by-fourteen prints and presented them to her. She said, "Oh, Jimmy, these are very nice. Could you make me look like this in a movie?" I said, "Why, yes!" Nothing happened until a couple of months later, when I was called into the office of Charles Eyton, who was a fight referee before becoming studio manager. He said, "You've been doing very well around here. I'm going to promote you to chief cameraman." I was really surprised. He said, "Mary Miles Minter wants you for her cameraman." I could have fallen through the cement floor! I said, "Oh, no. I've only been here five years. I'm not ready yet." He said, "Well, didn't you tell her you could make her look beautiful in the movies?" I told him about the stills I had made and that when she asked me if I could make her look like that in the movies, I had said yes. He said, "You've yessed yourself into being her chief cameraman. She's waiting to see you in her dressing room." I went to see her, and she had the stills on her dressing table. She said, "You know why I like these pictures, Jimmy? You made my eyes go dark!" We used orthochromatic film in those days causing blue to go white and red to go dark. It's the reverse today; blue goes black, and red goes light.

Well, Miss Minter's blue eyes went white on film. She said that sometimes her eyes photographed like glass and she looked as if she were blind. Now she was so pleased I would be able to photograph her eyes dark.

When I left her dressing room, I thought to myself, "How did I make her eyes go dark?" I racked my brain trying to remember. I walked back to the set where I had taken her pictures and studied the area. We didn't have the enclosed sound stages as we have today. We had stages with glass roofs with white muslin cloth under it. When we wanted to diffuse the sunlight, we'd pull the muslin closed. We also had artificial light, but we needed the daylight to help out because the film was slow. If we wanted to film for night, we had a black muslin we pulled over the glass. I looked around and saw a big piece of black velvet that had been used to make double exposures for a De Mille picture. I thought, "It must be that black velvet she was facing, causing her eyes to go dark. The eye is like a mirror, it reflects shades of light." So I got a little hand mirror and held it facing the black velvet. Sure enough, it was dark. I had a frame made five-by-six feet that I could move up and down and stretched a black velvet cloth over it. I cut a hole in the center and stuck my camera lens through. That was the way I made Miss Minter's close-ups! I kept the key light, the main light source, high up at a forty-five-degree angle so that it would not reflect in her eyes. The film was *Drums of Fate* in 1922. In Hollywood, the gossip was, "Do you know what Mary Miles Minter has done? She's imported herself an Oriental cameraman who photographs her while he hides behind black velvet, and he makes her blue eyes go dark!" Almost overnight I became a genius. Every blue-eyed actress wanted me to be her cameraman. I didn't have a contract with the studio, and suddenly I was being offered up to two hundred dollars a week by other studios. I went to Mr. Eyton and told him of these offers. He said, "Now, Jimmy, you're not going to leave us for a few dollars. We gave you your opportunity. We reared you. You're our boy. We'll give you a raise in time." He talked to me like a father and by the time he got through almost had me crying! He said, "I'll tell you what I'll do, Jimmy. I'll put you under a three-year contract. The first year I'll give you one hundred twenty-five a week, the second year one hundred fifty, and the third year one hundred and seventy-five! And with a contract you get paid if you're on a picture or not, but you can't work for anybody else unless we give you permission. How's that?" Well, to me that was something! I signed without even reading it!

They worked me every day. I did the first film Pola Negri made after she came over from Germany, *The Spanish Dancer*, directed by Herbert Brenon. He liked my work, and I became his cameraman. When the studio moved to new facilities on Marathon Street and became Paramount Pictures, Brenon went to United Artists to do a picture, and I went with him. From there I went to MGM for a while and then to Fox. Later I came back to Paramount and still later to Columbia. The only studios I didn't work for were Hal Roach and Universal. That's how I went through the silent film days. We had fun in those days. The cameramen all had to wear their visor caps backward to be able to look through the camera. And we all wore puttees, because our pants legs would get caught on the tripod. On location we would only have an assistant director, not the huge crew now required. If the director saw a house he wanted to shoot, the assistant would knock on the door. If nobody was home, we'd set up our cameras in the yard and start working. The assistant would keep a lookout for the owners. When he saw them coming, he gave a signal, and we quickly packed up and hopped over the fence and ran. That was another reason for wearing puttees. We could clear the picket fences and not get our cuffs caught.

Mike: While moving from one setup to another, you carried the camera on your shoulder?

Howe: Yes. Cameras weren't motorized then. They were Pathé cameras which weighed less than thirty pounds. I'll never forget the first time I mounted one on an airplane! It was for a scene in a picture with Richard Dix and Betty Compson called *The Woman with Four Faces*. Dix played a prisoner, and Betty Compson was his girlfriend. She made up like an old lady and went into the prison to see him. She kept telling him, "You must always look up above for help. Help will come from heaven, my son. Look above for help." So we had to photograph the prison from an old biplane. I sat behind the pilot. We were to use San Quentin Prison. They had gotten a permit for us to fly low over the grounds several times. It was one Sunday when the inmates were all playing baseball. The plane was to dive down and photograph everybody looking up. Then a rope ladder was to be dropped down, and one of them was to grab hold of it and be pulled out! Well, it was ridiculous. You can't do that. You'd yank his arms off. But movies in those days did anything for a thrill. I remember the pilot so well. He later became superintendent of the San Francisco airport. He dove down, and I was cranking away. We pulled up for another dive, and I noticed the guards pointing rifles at us! I thought they were making the scene look more real. So we dove down for another take, and I thought that was enough. The pilot asked if I didn't want one more to be sure we got it, and I said OK. We dove again. We didn't want the wings of the plane to be in the shot, so the pilot had to swoop down low then do what is called a side slip. When we got home, everybody came up to congratulate us! I said, "It's nothing. All in a day's work." Someone said, "You know what they were doing, Jimmy? They were shooting at you!" The permit was being sent by car and had not arrived at the prison before us!

Mike: Did you ever know D. W. Griffith?

Howe: No. He had his own cameraman named Billy Bitzer. The greatest! Many of the things they are doing today such as close-ups, dissolves, fade-ins, split screens, and moving shots were done by Griffith and Bitzer. When he made *Intolerance*, Griffith had the enormous set built on the corner of Sunset and Hillhurst. It stood there for years. I used to pass it going to work on the streetcar. He used as many as three and four thousand extras on that set! They had a dolly shot which they made by laying railroad track and putting a car on the track with scaffolding thirty feet high built on the car. They put two cameras on top of the scaffolding: one for long shots, and one for closer shots. Then several men pushed the car along the tracks! Today we have huge motorized cranes for shots like that. And we use helicopters. Griffith was a very inventive director and made many elaborate shots. There isn't much new today that he hadn't already tried.

Mike: Do you credit yourself for any camera firsts?

Howe: I made a fight picture, *Body and Soul* starring John Garfield, that required a lot of close shots of the fighting. It was difficult to follow the action with a big camera on a dolly, so I put on a pair of roller skates and used a hand-held camera while the man who was my grip pushed me around the ring. The resulting effect was very exciting. It brought the audience right into the ring. In movie theaters, the audiences would stand up and yell and root for the fighters! Well, I thought that was a first I had discovered, until just a few months ago when I looked in an old magazine and saw a picture of Sidney Franklin doing a shot for a silent film and he was on roller skates with a hand-held camera!

Mike: Nowadays the hand-held camera is used a great deal because of the light weight and economics of it, as well as other reasons. Do you have any objection to the results this has on the photographic quality of a picture?

Howe: There's no objection to whether a camera is hand-held, mounted, on a gyroscope, or however as long as you use the camera to record your scene in the most effective manner. To shoot just any scene with a hand-held camera doesn't have meaning. If it doesn't fit in, it is wrong. When I used the hand-held camera in *Body and Soul*, the unsteady effect was desirable. When a fighter would get a hard punch, I would even shake the camera a little, and the audience would get a jolt, too. Whenever I had to photograph an explosion, I'd mount the camera on a spring mattress, and when the explosion went off, we'd shake the mattress.

Mike: Have you had to do much trick photography?

Howe: Yes, but today there is a special effects and optical department for that. In the old days we did all the tricks with the camera. As late as 1937 I did a split-screen shot of Ronald Colman in *The Prisoner of Zenda* for David Selznick. Ronald had to play two parts, and in this scene he woke himself up, stood up and shook hands with himself all in full length!

Mike: When sound came in, did it present much of a problem to your work?

Howe: Cameras had to be put in soundproof booths like a walk-in refrigerator! They'd close us in there airtight because if you had any ventilation holes, the sound of the camera rolling would be heard. There would sometimes be two or three cameras in one booth. They were all photographing the same scene, and that made the job of lighting the scene very difficult. The cameraman, who directs the lighting of a scene, was always fighting with the microphone operators because we were forever getting shadows of the mikes! Yet the mikes had to be close to the actors to pick up their speech. These mikes were about a foot and a half long. At the beginning of sound they didn't even have booms. The mikes were hidden in flowerpots, behind lamps, and in chandeliers. You always knew actors were going to start talking when you saw them stop under a chandelier or beside a bouquet of flowers! But slowly the technique advanced so sound and camera could work better together. Smaller mikes were developed, lighting techniques improved, and finally the camera was able to come out of the soundproof booth and become flexible again. The director again had more latitude to tell his story because of more freedom in the use of his camera.

Mike: Do you find most directors know the workings of a camera quite well?

Howe: Unfortunately, a great percentage of directors do not understand the use of the various lenses and have to rely heavily on the cameraman. That's one of many reasons why the cameraman and the director are the two most responsible people on the set. Lighting and camera angles can determine mood and atmosphere. And the cameraman must photograph the actors, not how they look personally, but how they are supposed to look for that particular role, and especially for a particular shot. The cameraman has to know how to light an actor to make him look the way he should in a given scene. In this area the cameraman is a great aid to the director. The director is too busy with the actors to be expected to be very involved with the camera and its lighting. Very few directors know how to light a set. The only one I knew was Josef von Sternberg.

Mike: I'm sure he would have been the first person to have agreed with you. He took credit for everything. About a month before he died in 1969 I heard someone ask him what he thought of Lee Garmes as a cameraman. Garmes had won the Academy Award on the Von Sternberg film *Shanghai Express*. Von Sternberg replied, "No one ever worked with me without learning something!"

Howe: I started a film with him but didn't finish it because my contract expired. It wasn't renewed because of a previous disagreement over the use of some panchromatic film stock. The person in charge of the lab objected to my using it as it would mean he would have to make great changes in order to process the film, and he did not wish to do that. Ironically, every black-and-white film is photographed in panchromatic now!

Mike: You were one of the first cameramen to experiment in the use of it?

Howe: Yes. The first time I used it was in 1924 on the film *The Alaskan* starring Thomas Meighan. We had Canadian mounties in the picture with their brilliant red coats. The old-type film made red go dark, but we settled for that. However, up in Banff on location the scenery was so beautiful I was anxious to get it on film accurately. So I told my assistant to load up the camera with some panchromatic film. He did. I put on a light red filter to bring out the clouds, sky, and the snowcapped mountains. The scene followed an inside scene we had shot back at the studio with old-type film stock where the mounties get up and go out the door. On location we picked them up coming outside that same door. What happened was a big mistake! Because of the panchromatic film with the red filter, their red coats went white! We didn't know it until three days later, when they developed the film at the studio, and we got word blaming the wardrobe people for putting white coats on the actors. The poor wardrobe guy was going crazy. To this day nobody really knew what happened because I never mentioned it! When we retook the shot, I put back the old orthochromatic film and forgot the beautiful clouds.

Mike: So you had as many problems with color in black-and-white films as you did with it when color film itself was developed!

Howe: When color came in, it changed everything. The system of lighting had to be changed. We had to have arc lights because the light we used for black and white was not strong enough and was the wrong color temperature. Laboratories stayed busy developing better-quality film, cameras, sound equipment, and lights. Now Eastman has film so sensitive we can photograph a color movie the way we used to do a black-and-white movie.

Mike: I think that nearly all movies should be in color. Do you?

Howe: Yes. But sometimes a story benefits from black-and-white photography. I did a film called *The Molly McGuires* starring Sean Connery and Richard Harris. It's about coal mining in Pennsylvania in the early days. What a great subject to film in black and white! You have the black coal, the houses dirty from soot, and the dirty clothes and faces of the miners. The producer-director, Marty Ritt, wanted to film it in black and white. When this proposal came to the heads of the company, they said, "No. Later on, if we want to sell it to television, it has to be in color or they don't want it."

Mike: What are some of the outstanding experiences you've had while making a film, Jimmy?

Howe: Well, Mike, since you are a friend of Tennessee Williams, let's begin with *The Rose Tattoo*. It was produced by Hal Wallis, directed by Danny Mann, and starred Anna Magnani and Burt Lancaster. All fine people. Anna Magnani is an exciting and interesting personality besides being a great actress. She was brought over from Italy to play her first American film. She didn't speak or understand much English, so she had to have an interpreter. When we were in Key West, our Florida location, we were working next door to Tennessee Williams' house. It was getting late one afternoon, and I had a close-up to do of Anna. She has a small scar on her throat. That's why you nearly always see her photographed with a scarf or jewelry or something covering her throat. In this particular scene I had to photograph she was in mourning. Being the realistic actress that she is, she didn't want to wear any jewelry. I saw the scar and thought I would help cover it by throwing a little shadow over it. We were losing time because the sun was getting low, so I picked up an old broom and pulled out some straw to see if it would work, but I found it was too translucent. Anna was watching me all this time. I told my grip, my handyman, to get me something more solid. He said, "OK. You want a salad, eh?" I said, "Yeah, bring me a salad," just kidding around. While he was gone, I walked away to do something else. When we both came back to camera, Anna wasn't there. I thought she had gone to fix her makeup. After about ten or fifteen minutes Danny Mann came to me and said, "Jimmy, what did you do to Anna Magnani?" I said, "Why, nothing!" He said, "She's changing her clothes. She wants to quit the picture and go back to Italy. She's mad at you!" I said, "Mad at me? Why should she be mad at me? I didn't do anything." He said, "Well, you better go and see her." I went over to Tennessee's house which she used for her dressing room and knocked on the door. Someone said come in. I entered and saw Magnani changing her clothes. She looked at me like a tigress and said, "You no good! You no good, Jimmy!" I said, "Why do you say that?" She said, "You maka the joke with me. You know I come from Italy. I no speaka the English. I come to maka the great picture. I maka the pictures in Italy, but I wanta maka this great picture here. I worka hard. You know I not good-looking, but I gotta heart. I'm a good actress. You go ahead and maka joke with me!" I said, "Anna, what did I do to make a joke?" She said, "You say you gonna put a salad around my neck!" I said, "Anna, I told the man I wanted something more *solid,* and he joked with me and said 'salad.' We joke like that sometimes. Don't you joke like that in Italy?" She said, "I don't lika it you maka the joke." I said, "I'm sorry, Anna. I hope you're not really mad at me." She said, "I go back to

Italy. I don't lika you." So I walked away. We quit work for the day.

The next day I thought she would have forgotten about it. We arrived at work, and she wouldn't look at me. She got in front of the camera, and I was afraid to talk to her. I was in a hell of a position. Finally, I told Wallis, "Hal, you may have to bring another boy here to finish this picture. This can't go on. She's angry at me, and it's not going to help the picture." He said, "I'll talk to her. You stay on. Just humor her along and be as nice as you can to her." I said OK. I felt very bad about it. The next day we were walking down a path in opposite directions and we had to meet! I wasn't going to detour and go off another way. We almost bumped into each other; then she put out her arms, "Oh, Jimmy, you mad at me?" I said, "No, Anna, I'm not mad at you." She said, "Me no mad at you, too!" Then she put her arms around me and said, "Now we good friends. We maka the great picture." I said, "Anna we're going to make a very great picture. I'm so happy you're not mad at me."

She won the Academy Award for best actress! I won it for best photography! * When she made her next picture, she wanted me to be her cameraman, but I was already on one. They put Charlie Lang on hers. He's a very fine cameraman and photographed her very well. Charlie and I have different methods of working, but I don't think methods matter as long as the end product is good. I get Christmas cards from Anna still. She's a wonderful woman who really knows this business. I remember one comic scene in *The Rose Tattoo* where she is trying on hats. She said to the director, "Danny, I better not talka this line right away because the people will be laughing. If I talka the line now, they no hear me. I better maka the pause." She was so right. She knew her timing. I would love to do a film with her again.

Mike: Another great artist and unusual personality you worked with was Erich von Stroheim, who made the five-hour silent film *Greed*.

Howe: That was made before I worked with him, and the studio cut it down to two hours and ruined the picture. Von Stroheim always had battles with the executives, and that made it hard for him to find work as a director. Finally, in 1933 he had a story called *Walking Down Broadway* he directed at Fox. I was under contract there and was assigned to be his cameraman. I had heard stories he was difficult to work with, but I thought he was wonderful to work with and

---

* Mr. Howe won his second Academy Award for *Hud* in 1963.

extremely talented. He was very particular to detail. The film starred James Dunn, Boots Mallory, Zasu Pitts, and Terry Ray. One day Von Stroheim was directing Terry Ray, and he wanted a certain expression from him, something hysterical, and he couldn't get it. He worked for hours trying. Finally Von Stroheim called the propman over and said, "Do you have a very strong piece of thread about twelve feet long?" The prop man brought him a spool of thread and Von Stroheim took Terry Ray behind some scenery and said, "Take down your pants." Terry did, and Von Stroheim tied the string onto the end of his penis and brought the string down through his pants leg. Now he put Terry in front of the camera and said, "Action!" When he wanted the particular expression, he jerked the string!

Mike: That's a funny, if not typical, example of Von Stroheim's inventiveness!

Howe: I remember another scene that was in a penny dance hall. He said, "Jimmy, I'd like to have the camera dance with these people." I said, "How can I do that? It sounds impossible!" He said, "Look," and he picked up an ordinary standing lamp and waltzed around carrying it. He said, "All you have to do is build a little platform and mount your camera on top of this stand and the actors can dance with that!" We did, and it came out beautiful!

There was one scene where we had a big fire. It was in New York and in black and white. He said, "Jimmy, you know in New York how they always have streets torn up to work on them, and they have red danger lanterns hanging around so people won't walk into the holes? I'd like to hand paint all these lanterns red on the film strip and have everything else remain black and white. And when the fire truck comes, I want to tint its flashing light red and tint all the flames of the fire red!" I thought it was a great idea, but the studio turned it down because of cost. When the picture was finished and Von Stroheim was gone, they decided to remake the last three or four reels and hired Raoul Walsh to direct it. The picture was finally called *Hello, Sister*.

Mike: That's almost as bad a title change as when Fox changed the title of William Inge's play *A Loss of Roses* to *The Stripper*!

Howe: While I was working with Erich von Stroheim, he invited me for a visit to his home. It was a big mansion. I rang the bell, and he answered the door and told me to come in. The living room was empty! No furniture except a couch in front of the huge fireplace and stacks of newspapers. He said, "Jimmy, you see what they did to me?

I had to sell my furniture. This house is in hock, and I'm trying to save it. I sleep on this couch, and for heat, I burn the newspapers. They really blackballed me." I guess he was talking about some unfortunate experience before I knew him, but it showed how powerful the studios were.

Mike: Didn't Von Stroheim finally give up in Hollywood and go to Paris, where he worked as an actor until World War II broke out?

Howe: I know he was in America during the war, because I did a picture with him called *The North Star*. It was a Sam Goldwyn film starring Dana Andrews, Ann Harding, Anne Baxter, Farley Granger, Walter Huston, and Walter Brennan. Von Stroheim played a sadistic Nazi doctor. Lillian Hellman wrote it. It was a good film. We were friends with the Russians at the time they made it. Goldwyn wanted to make the Russians sympathetic and show how the poor peasants were fighting the war and getting massacred. It was a propaganda film, you could say. However, it didn't make any money because when it went into release, the whole relationship between America and Russia had changed!

Mike: Another unique film you photographed was *The Old Man and the Sea* starring Spencer Tracy in 1957.

Howe: That was made by Warner Brothers. Fred Zinnemann had started it in Cuba. They ran into problems there, so Warner's called them back and was going to shelve the picture. After a long delay, they began the picture over again with John Sturges directing. The Ernest Hemingway story is about a man alone in a rowboat in the ocean for three days and nights trying to catch a big fish. We needed a big marlin fish which weighed about fifteen hundred pounds. They chartered a fishing boat in Peru and spent a couple of months trying to land a big enough marlin. The biggest they could get was only nine hundred pounds. Finally, some man in a wealthy Peruvian fishing club caught one weighing about what we needed. The catch had been photographed on sixteen-mm film. The studio was able to make a deal to buy the film and we blew it up to thirty-five mm. It was used here and there throughout the picture.

Mike: Wasn't part of the picture made on location in Hawaii?

Howe: Yes. We shot off the Kona Coast. When you take a little rowboat out in the middle of the ocean, you can't control it for the close-ups and certain other shots. So we had a barge forty feet wide and seventy-five feet long which was secured to a towboat. Then we had outriggers about thirty feet long to which we anchored the rowboat with steel cables. We put a camera on the barge on a movable boom arm that we could swing out near the rowboat for our closer shots. Every morning at six o'clock for weeks and weeks we'd go out in the ocean! Spencer Tracy would be out there alone in that rowboat with the sun beating down on him, but being the actor and artist he was, he stuck it out. Nevertheless, he'd yell, "Get me out of here! This sun is getting too hot. Jimmy, how long you gonna take to get this shot? I'm getting seasick!" His complaining was more kidding than serious, but he did feel uncomfortable. After weeks in Kona, we came back to the studio and did some of the scenes using a big tank. That was a problem to match the authentic scenes we had taken in Hawaii, and we had to use an expensive mechanical fish.

Mike: Tracy was nominated for another Academy Award but didn't quite make it! But Dimitri Tiomkin got an Oscar for the score of the film.

Howe: I had made a couple of pictures with Spence before. One was *Power and the Glory*, one of the first talkies. William K. Howard directed it at Fox in 1933, and Colleen Moore costarred. Spence played a railroad laborer. I told him I didn't think he should wear makeup for the part. He said, "That's great! I don't want any makeup on this puss and look like a white-collar ad." That was the first time I photographed a leading man without makeup. Today very few of them wear makeup, unless they are playing a younger role. In fact, hardly any of the character actors use makeup now. Only the women, who always want to look their best!

Mike: Didn't you make several pictures with James Cagney?

Howe: Yes. I think *Yankee Doodle Dandy* made in 1942 was my favorite. I also photographed *City for Conquest* and *The Time of Your Life*. Jimmy is small in stature, but when he steps in front of the camera, he's bigger than life!

Mike: You've made pictures just about everywhere in the world. Which location would you say was the most primitive and difficult?

Howe: I suppose a film I did in 1932 with Wallace Beery called *Viva Villa!* Howard Hawks directed until he had some disagreement with the studio; then Jack Conway took over. The working conditions on that picture were very difficult because we were far into the interior of Mexico. The climate was hot and dusty! We had to haul in our water. Many people got sick. For living accommodations they had to bring out a train with a kitchen coach attached. The cook was Mexican, so we ate mostly Mexican dishes, which in this case were terrible. We were told not to go out nights because there were bandits! We had to sit in the train and play cards or chew the rag. In spite of all this, I enjoyed the finished picture, which was a rough and tough one about Pancho Villa and his bandit army rebelling against the government. There was lots of action. When we shot one battle scene between several hundred troops, the prop department issued blank bullets to the Mexican extras in order to get the sound and smoke effect. Some of these extras didn't like each other, and they put little pellets in the guns and really shot at each other! One day we had about fifty people hurt!

Mike: Jimmy, you've made over one hundred and fifty motion pictures, won two Oscars, and are still going at it! I'll bet you spend many quiet moments reminiscing back through the years, and remembering films like *The Thin Man, Algiers, They Made Me a Criminal, King's Row, Come Back, Little Sheba*, and *Picnic*.

Howe: When I think back to the silent days, I especially remember how much more fun we had. There were responsibilities, but not as great as today when costs of production keep everyone under pressure. Now I have the responsibility of a camera crew consisting of an operator, two assistant operators, a chief electrician and his assistants, my chief grip and his assistant! So, usually when you go out to make a scene, you have truckloads of equipment and carloads of personnel. In fact, the individual movie company producing one film in this country needs so many personnel and so much equipment that the economic burden resulted in more films being made in Europe as runaway production, as well as more films being made as inexpensive "outlaw" productions. Both runaway and outlaw films are able to function more or less free of the Hollywood unions. The most significant trend at the moment is the move away from the big studio complexes. Sound stages are not as necessary because sound equipment has become so advanced you can shoot anywhere and not worry about the outside noises. Sets inside a stage are also becoming obsolete because film is so sensitive you don't need the powerful artificial lighting systems. You can shoot inside or outside at the actual location nowadays, and it is much cheaper. There will always be the superfilms which have to utilize the huge studio facilities to a large degree, but they will be the exception. When I started in this business over fifty years ago, we did a lot of outside "street corner" shooting, and we carried our own lightweight equipment around. I've watched it come full cycle. Again, filmmaking can be done anywhere, and the small group that follows that camera around can call their own shots!

December 6, 1969

Art Director

PRESTON AMES

Ames: Let's put it this way: I never studied to go into motion pictures. Motion pictures was the result of an economic thing. But I was a student of art, music, and architecture for years. I went to school in San Francisco and went to the Mark Hopkins School of Fine Arts and studied painting and drawing. I went to the University of California, where I was in architecture for three years, and I went to Paris in 1927 for five weeks and stayed five years.

I am a graduate in architecture in France. I began my career there. I had to come home right in the middle of the Depression, and what do you do? So I worked for the fabulous amount of twenty dollars a week for Arthur Brown, Jr., who was one of San Francisco's great architects. After four and a half years that all fell apart. Then what do you do? Somebody said, "Why don't you try the motion-picture business? They're hiring all the architects in town." So I came down to Los Angeles, where I met Cedric Gibbons, who was probably the forerunner of all the great art directors in the business. He sort of set up a taste and style which films never had before. Beginning in 1936 I worked on the drawing board for him a couple of years, and then he put me onto a picture. I've been working ever since, and I've been thirty-five years in the industry.

Mike: So you began at MGM?

Ames: Yes. Most of my career has been there, but I've moved around a little bit. I did a couple of shows at Twentieth Century-Fox, and I just finished three consecutive pictures at Universal. But MGM is my home, and they've been very good to me. I've probably traveled with them a quarter of a million miles just to see the world and prepare new pictures.

Mike: Would you describe an art director as the architect of the set?

Ames: Very much so, and it's more than that. You have to get along with people. I've seen men with the greatest talent in the world who can't get along with people, and they don't have great careers. It's a compatibility thing. You have to have the patience of Job. You have to have the qualities of a cardinal. You almost have to be a CPA to keep up with the accounting these days. And you have to have strength in your convictions to be able to advise, to tell a director yes or no. You don't fight the director, you work with him, but you have to have the courage to express those things you feel are right or wrong. You have to know color, landscaping, marine architecture above and below the water. You have to be able to put on a piece of paper whatever strange things the script calls for. The best example of that probably is *The Fantastic Voyage* when somebody had to design a man's insides, so that they could photograph that and make it look as if you were traveling through your duodenum and your small intestine or whatever. This was great design! We like to be called designers. We don't like to be called "builders of sets." But to design something! I don't care if it's a cabbage patch or Versailles Palace, it still has to be designed to work for the camera, director, and actors so they feel at home in it. When they began the picture *The Lion in Winter* in England, Katharine Hepburn said, "I want to see your sets," and she was taken around by the art director and shown everything for a whole day. She was thrilled with the thought which had gone into it and that there was so much exposure for her, so much to surround the actors.

Mike: Would she have made suggestions if she thought there was something in which she wouldn't feel comfortable?

Ames: Might, yes. This is her privilege. Some actors like to feel they're going to tell you exactly what they want. I won't go into names; but they are very demanding, and it's contractual with them. They have the privilege of saying whatever they want about anything whether it's wardrobe, makeup, sets, or camera. But they are few and far between. The director is really the person who is head man. If it doesn't satisfy him, or the producer in certain instances, then it's your fault. If your set falls flat on its face, it means you haven't communicated enough with these two people to satisfy what they really had in mind at the onset. However, some producers and directors cannot express themselves too well. You sort of have to pick their minds and feed them words and say, "Is it or isn't it?"

Mike: Do you prefer a director to lean heavily on you so that you have a freer hand in your creation?

Ames: Well, you have two kinds of directors; you have a director who is perfectly happy to accept anything you give him because to him a set is just something he works in. But that's mostly on a small-budget picture where there isn't time to make changes, and it's one of the things where you do the best you can and away we go! Other directors are very demanding and require many, many changes. But that's all right because they're not too sure, and they have the time and the money to get what they feel is right. Time and money are two terribly important things in our operations, of course, to enable us to do what is right for a picture.

Mike: When you establish a good working relationship with a director, does he often request you on another picture?

Ames: Sometimes.

Mike: Who are some of the directors you have most respected?

Ames: The most challenging and the most difficult man in the world to work with is Vincente Minnelli. I've done a great many shows with him. He's an extremely demanding person, with knowledge, with taste. I did the two shows with him which got me these Oscars, *An American in Paris* and *Gigi*. Working with Minnelli has been a rewarding experience. I did *Airport* with George Seaton, who is a delightful, charming, eloquent gentleman of the old school who wrote the beautiful screenplay. The producer, Ross Hunter, was very demanding and wanted nothing but the very best, and he saw to it that we had the time and money to give him the best. You don't waste money, but you spend it so that it looks right on the screen.

Mike: What is the first thing you do after you've read the script?

Ames: Once you've absorbed what the script calls for, you have a round table of discussion with the producer, director, and whoever else might be involved. It might be the writer. If it's a musical, it's the composer and the choreographer. If it's some other kind of picture that needs technical people, you have them. You sit down, and you generally analyze how the film is going to be done. "Are we going to

do it at home?" "Are we going to do it abroad?" "Can we do it
economically?" "Do we have to spend a lot of money?" and so on.
You then get an approach to the how and the why of the picture.

Then, in my job, I sit down alone and do a breakdown, which
means I interpret each scene that is to be played in a certain area. If
the writer hasn't had diarrhea of the pencil, you can keep it down to a
fairly tight amount of sets. Sometimes you'll find you have a hundred
and fifty sets because the writer feels his story should move from one
set to another; but that is incidental, and they can be broken down to
perhaps fifty sets. Then these particular sets become a kind of format
for a lot of people, because they now know where things are to be
played. You discuss that a little bit. Then you sit down for two days to
two or three weeks and very carefully get a budget on each one of
these sets, and you total it and present it to management and say,
"Look, it's going to cost X number of dollars to do the sets for this
picture." There'll always be some argument pro or con. Sometimes
they'll say, "I'm sorry, you're spending too much." Sometimes, believe
it or not, they'll say, "You are not spending enough. This picture
requires more." Then, from that point on, you turn the problems of
the set over to the boys in the drafting room, who are able to take
your sketches and layouts and make a complete set of architectural
drawings.

These drawings are turned over to an experienced estimator, a set
estimator, who goes over every inch of this thing no matter what is
involved, whether it's paint, plumbing, landscaping, backing, you
name it. From him we get an accurate price. Now, if his price is
beyond the reach of our budget, then there is either something wrong
with the design or something wrong in the original conception of what
this thing should cost. And it's up to the art director to either say, "I
feel I've overdesigned it," and cut this design down, or if he feels this
is exactly what the producer and director wanted, he will then
approach them and say, "Gentlemen, I'm sorry. I made a boo-boo in
my estimate. I need X more dollars." They either say, "Yes, fine," or,
"Go back and figure it out again." The third phase of this monetary
thing is that, when the set goes into operation, which means it goes
into mill, plastic, painting and all the phases of construction, you then
have a cost rundown which comes in every week. You scrutinize this
cost rundown very carefully and make sure your money is properly
spent and that you are not going over budget. This didn't used to be

done as seriously as it is today when money is tight and the industry is really concerned about how much or how little they should spend, and rightfully so.

Mike: Don't you often reuse a set that has been in another picture?

Ames: Yes. For instance, in *Airport* we were very happy to find a lot of good standing sets at Universal that were suitable for small but important scenes where we could slip in and do our shooting and get out. On the other hand, I would build a rather important key set and realize out of that key set I might be able to create two or three more key sets by dressing, by lighting changes, by this and that little change.

Mike: The dressing of a set is the job of the set director, so he is one of your closest associates from the very beginning.

Ames: Right. We are a very important team. The decorator is only as good as the art director and vice versa. We are actually responsible for the completion of the set. It is our shoulders on which this burden lies, so that if anything goes wrong, we are the heavies, and if it's right, then that's fine. The costume designer will also confer with us several times. Particularly when you have a styled picture in which color, design, and everything else have to be coordinated.

Mike: Would you say your main goal in designing a set is to create the illusion the story calls for and in a manner so that the actors and camera crews have room to perform their work?

Ames: Yes. The cameraman is a guy we have to design for a great deal. Sometimes the art director will be working on a picture long before a lot of other people, including the cameraman, are engaged. So it is our problem to design the set, if it is tricky or complicated, so that the cameraman can light it. If you are so fortunate to know who the cameraman will be, that helps a great deal, because you might know his particular style of lighting. Never build a set which can't be lit. Never build a set which can't be moved about in such a way that the director doesn't have ease of operation. The most important thing today is that the set doesn't look like a set. It's got to look like the real McCoy. Your actor has to go into it and feel at home immediately. Otherwise it's just four walls and it's nothing. This is why half the filmmakers today want to go out on location and shoot the real thing. That's fine. In certain instances it's great, because you can do things and get things you couldn't afford to build, and they are of great beauty. I have run into this time and time again: A director will say,

"I have to shoot it all for real, or my actors will be very uncomfortable." I have proved to them that in certain incidences they are completely wrong because they'll get themselves into a little corner. The actors are frustrated. They can't move enough. The cameraman is dying because he can't light it. He can't move his camera. So you end up building a set!

Mike: Weather and climate must influence location filming tremendously.

Ames: I did a picture called *Quick Before It Melts* which was supposed to be in the Antarctic Circle. Obviously we weren't going down there! It was a comedy and a lot of fun and still needed the frozen wastes. We went to Nome, Alaska, and worked on the Bering Sea which is like eight or ten feet of solid ice out in the middle of nowhere! The temperature is far below zero and colder than building a dam! Obviously, you're not going to have an actor play a scene when he can barely even breathe. Consequently you set up the atmosphere with the actors or doubles the best as you can, and then you put the scene on a stage. What we did was take a stage which was a hundred and fifty by two hundred and fifty feet and create the Antarctic wastes with backing and the illusion of pack ice and with the inside and outside of these little huts that they built. That experience paid off when we were doing *Airport* in Minneapolis, where again the temperature was a problem and the wind made everything much colder. Everybody had said, "We have to do this outdoors, because you get the real breath and the real everything." Well, we got the real everything, all right! To the point where we suddenly realized to put important actors performing in an area where they would just freeze was wrong! So we designed our airport, our airplane, the whole thing and built it on the backlot of the studio so that we could work in comfort, even at night. The important thing in filming some scenes on location and others on a backlot set is that they match. You have to create on the backlot that which ties in with what has already been shot up in the freezing north. The same thing applies to a jungle picture. We did a thing called *Green Mansions*. The real jungle is one of the most difficult things in the world to photograph. There's no light. The insects are a problem you cannot believe. They'll eat you alive no matter what you do. You cannot put important people in that kind of position where they are liable to be bitten and develop welts, and sores, and dysentery, and all the horrors of it. When we did *Green Mansions*, we took the same stage in which we had filmed the Antarctic in *Quick Before It Melts* and built a real jungle. We grew live trees and flowers, orchids. We had artificial light going all the time. It was beautiful.

Mike: You had to work closely with special effects people?

Ames: Yes. In both films we needed "atmosphere" to indicate whether it was rain, fog, snow. These boys are past masters at creating this illusion. We had to go walking in the jungle in the fog and gradually have the fog turn into rain. The stage is a pretty holy thing when you need it for these types of controlled conditions. A picture which most people think was made on location is *An American in Paris*. But it was all done at the MGM studios in Hollywood. Gene Kelly had wanted the whole thing to be done in Paris, but we convinced him that this was another case calling for controlled conditions. You had special effects; you had day and night scenes; you had dialogue and choreography. To do it on the streets of Paris would have been suicide. It would have taken forever, and that much money was not available for this kind of thing. Today I still hear Gene say, "Sure, we shot the whole thing in Paris!" It's very rewarding to hear that! For the film *Gigi* in 1958, we did shoot some scenes in Paris. We used the old Palais de Glace, an old ice-skating rink which had been sort of modernized, and we put it back into its gay 1850 Victorian era to the shock and amazement of the management. That sort of thing paid off as it was a question of adapting yourself to an existing structure. But, again, when we got into the close intimate scenes in apartments, homes, and small areas, we did it on the stage.

Mike: Making a film in France must have been fun for you since you had lived there and speak the language.

Ames: I think like a Frenchman in the sense that I love the French and know them so well. And they respect me because they know I am a registered French architect. That requires tipping the hat. We arrived in Paris with a minimum American crew. We had an American cameraman, Joe Ruttenberg, a sweet, delightful guy who knew his business, but he was assigned a French crew that couldn't speak a word of English. The first time he got on the set, I stood very closely by to see how this setup would work for him. He wanted to have a particular size lamp spotlighting a particular size area, and he gave that word to the man who was going to interpret everything to the crew. There was a great deal of conversation, and Joe turned to me and said, "What are they talking about?" I said, "Well, Joe, I'll tell you one thing that they are saying is you really don't want that spot you are asking for at all, and they will put up what they know you really want." Joe said, "I don't believe a word of it!" I said, "Watch. This is what's going to happen." And sure enough they put two lamps in two places that meant absolutely nothing. He said, "What did they do that for?" And I said, "Joe, they don't think you know your business." He said, "Will you tell them please I do know my business, and I want the lamp exactly where I said?" Which I did, and they loved it. The next day, when they saw the rushes, they knew he was a master and always did exactly as he wanted. But communication was terribly important. The French work like Trojans. They are the hardest-working crews I have ever seen. None of this Latin *mañana* thing with them at all, but you have to prove to them that you know your business.

Mike: Hadn't *Lust for Life* also been shot largely on location in France in 1956, when Vincente Minnelli directed that?

Ames: Yes, we went to all the places where Vincent Van Gogh started. To Belgium where he worked in the coal mines. We actually opened up some of these areas and restored them back to the period when he lived there. We worked in Paris, in the fields outside Arles, and in Arles, where we had to reconstruct things which at that time would have been torn down or destroyed. We were always in the environment of this man to give the illusion of his inspiration as a painter. We planted a cornfield where we could have the crows come out! We restored bridges that he had painted. We were always in the light and atmosphere where he created his beautiful paintings. We even had to have two or three thousand paintings and drawings of Van Gogh. That was a tremendous problem, and we did it all kinds of ways. We had men who were masters at copying the technique of Van Gogh, so that we were able to show the paintings, drawings, and sketches in progress as the actor playing Van Gogh, Kirk Douglas, went through such scenes. And, of course, we learned much from these paintings as to how to design the sets and duplicate his surroundings.

Mike: Wasn't the approach to the film and the subject matter so artistic that the studio hesitated in making it?

Ames: The studio wasn't at all sure the public would accept this film because it didn't have many of the selling qualities they were used to. It didn't have any love life, no adventure, and so forth. The people who really sensed the quality and realized the potential of the film were the art museums. The film was really a beautiful rendition of a man's life and his paintings. It proved, if you have a beautiful story and it is beautifully told with a top cast, people will come to see it. A film doesn't have to have violence, discord, and sex to be accepted.

Mike: Did *Lust for Life* boost the sale of Van Gogh paintings and his popularity?

Ames: Sales, no, but the example again are the museums. When they had the Van Gogh exhibit at the museum here in Los Angeles, you couldn't get in for love or money. The people lined up like they were going to the circus. You could put the movie under the category of visual education, if you like. People suddenly realized here was a great artist. Of course, the thing so unbelievable about this man is that only one painting was sold while he was alive. One picture, bought by a little Russian girl who decided she liked the painting. His brother, too, realized this man was a great painter and kept him alive with food and paid for his paints.

I'd like to talk a little about the director who has a preconceived notion of his picture. This is a rarity. A man who will visualize the finished product long before it is even put on paper. This was always the case with Vincente Minnelli. Your sets had to conform to his preconceived notion. His whole photographic conception and his cutting and editing were there long before he started a picture. The man knew what he was after. He knew what he wanted to see on the screen. This made serious demands: more money; more time; more effort. Some people resented it. Some went along with it. But never did he ever let up with his one feeling of this was going to be the kind of picture he wanted it to be. And generally his films turned out to be beautiful.

Mike: To be an art director must require a great variety of knowledge on subjects past, present, and future since there are so many types of films made.

Ames: I feel there are about seven or eight areas of design that are very different from one another. There is the Western, which can be a pretty sophisticated show. *High Noon* was one of the most highly designed films from a point of view of suspense and everything else. Religious films like *The Greatest Story Ever Told* can be the most beautifully designed. Historical films require more research than others because you go from prehistory to present day, and you must know your periods of history and style in clothes, architecture, and furniture. A few years ago if you mentioned the name "Louie," the average man would think that was the bartender down the street. Now they will say which one do you mean? Thirteenth, fourteenth, fifteenth, or sixteenth or is it Louis Philippe? You have to know all about styles like these and be able to give the illusion of them. You don't copy the style. In motion-picture making, copy is rather a dirty word. In 1938 we did an expensive production called *Marie Antoinette* with Norma Shearer. A great many architects came to Metro to see our sets and congratulated Cedric Gibbons on his authentic reproduction of French Renaissance architecture, with particular emphasis on what he did with Versailles. Mr. Gibbons looked at these gentlemen and said, "If you will study very carefully what we did, you'll see we did everything except copy the architecture of Versailles, because if we had, photographically it would have been absolutely nothing. The molding and design are so delicate, so sensitive, they would never come across on the screen. So consequently, we had to redesign the entire thing so it would photograph properly!" That is what I mean by catching the spirit of what you are reproducing. In pictures of mystery and suspense you have fun with all kinds of effects, whether it's *Dr. Strangelove*, *The Cat and the Canary*, or *Great Expectations*. Then you have the very serious dramatic picture like *Heat of the Night*, *The Graduate*, and *Easy Rider*. You have to be in tune with this sort of moviemaking and be knowledgeable of that point of view. Then you have the big musicals. For a great many years at MGM we made some magnificent musicals which were highly successful in this country. You couldn't sell them to South America or Europe, however, because for one reason it is difficult to dub singing numbers into a foreign language. The story goes that any theater in South America that was screening one of these elaborate American musicals would have an old Tarzan picture in the back room. And if the audience didn't like the musical, the management would pull it right off and run the Tarzan film!

But along came a musical called *West Side Story*! That was the turning of the era. Something happened. There was a chemistry in that picture. It was beautifully designed and very stylized and was accepted everywhere with thunders of applause. From then on musical films have been more popular. The art director has all sorts of things to work with in these musicals. In *Mary Poppins* he worked with cartoons. In *The Brothers Grimm* there are puppets. And in *Kismet* there are all kinds of fanciful things to work out. And *Hello, Dolly!* was an art director's dream. It had, say, roughly a million-dollar set which was designed and spread out on the Twentieth Century-Fox lot. Musicals are especially highly stylized films for art directors. Each one seems to have its own uniqueness and are great films to work on.

Then there is the film of the future. A shining example is the picture *2001: A Space Odyssey*. In this case the art director was perhaps not the art director at all, but a man named Arthur C. Clarke who was instrumental in starting the picture. He had written a greal deal of science fiction and at the ripe old age of twenty-four or -five was hired by NATO to set up the entire program of outer space flight and behavior pattern. This man was a real present-day Jules Verne.

Mike: Did the advent of color films present particular problems to your job?

Ames: I must be honest and admit that to me there is nothing more beautiful than a well-photographed black-and-white picture. Sometimes you can get values in black and white that are marvelous. That is not easy to come by since the thing you are photographing has color but comes out black and white on the film. This means you still have to design and choose the colors you photograph. Black-and-white films have color control! In other words, you cannot put two colors together that, when photographed, will look like the same thing and have no contrast, no tone separation. We used to go into warm grays and cold grays deliberately so that we knew exactly how it would come out on the screen. Metro was about the only studio that used this technique. It was very successful and was studied very carefully by color consultants and coordinators who sat down and worked out this whole palette which we still use.

When color film came in, there were two schools of thought. I have held to one of them throughout. One was: Don't load your set and decor with color because it interferes with the action and story, it distracts. The other school was to put color everywhere you could think of. There was quite a hassle for a while, but the first school won out. Even today some cameramen say, "Why have you got so little color?" But when you see it on the screen, it's there. It is there in such a way that the actor, which is the most important thing, stands out. Now there will be times when accents of colors are required like in a psychedelic nightclub or an apartment which wants accent. The first phase of color was very difficult. We would paint an object with a specific color in mind, but with Technicolor's three-strip process, the color never came out just right. It wasn't anything that was a mystery. It was just the way the color film worked. We had to go to these highly experienced technical men and have them design a color that would actually photograph to look like the color we wanted on the screen. This was very tricky and complicated. Reds were difficult. Blues were an impossible situation. The palest blue would turn out to be a brilliant blue. Everything had to be brought down to the laboratory with color swatches, color schemes, color this and color that. The "lily," which was a card with a rainbow of colors on it, was the famous thing that was photographed right after a scene so the lab would have a faithful color reproduction of the colors that had been photographed in the scene because, even though you used the same type film, sometimes a reel of it might develop a lighter or darker shade. Things have changed now. We do have film that is about as faithful a color reproducer as you can ask for. Fidelity of color today is ninety-nine percent, and it is a joy because you paint something or put a fabric on something, and that exact color is what comes over on the screen. We no longer have to depend on the lab technicians to tell us the chemistry of the colors. But the art director, set decorator, and costume designer have to work closely together to coordinate the colors used in a picture.

Mike: Don't the colors an important star decides to wear in her wardrobe become a determining issue in what other colors are used in a film?

Ames: Sometimes. You don't want to have anything clashing. So if there is that problem, there is all the more reason for communication. I've seen it happen several times where a star has been shown sketches, materials, color, and everything, and when the actual dress appears, her reaction is, "I don't like the dress. I don't like the color or any part of it." Although she had approved it before. That means you have to convince her that it is really OK, but if she wins her point, you have to start all over again.

Mike: Have you ever designed a house or apartment or office for a film and have someone want to copy the design for their own home or office?

Ames: Sometimes the opposite will happen. A director will want to design a house for himself, and a show will come up where you will be able to design his idea, and he will be able to see how it really looks and study it. And if he likes it, that concept will go into his house. To me the most flattering thing that can happen is when a director or actor walks into a set I have designed and says, "This feels like home," or, "This looks the way I thought it would be." I did a picture called *Penelope* and designed a very nice Park Avenue apartment with a view of New York City. I love French architecture, and I introduced a few little feelings of the French, along with the modern. I went all out, with everything I possibly could. I spent money on things which I knew would never show on the screen because this was a set in which about a third of the picture played. It was a very important set, and there were a lot of rooms involved. There was an entrance hall, a hallway into a bedroom, a dressing room, a bath, a dining alcove, a terrace, a living room, a library, a kitchen, and all the *shmeer* that went with it. It created a feeling inside the actors, one of whom was Natalie Wood, that it would be nice to live in that apartment. Natalie loved it.

Mike: One of your more recent films to design sets for was *Lost Horizon*. Unfortunately nearly all the critics panned the film. As the reviews came out, it was as if each new criticism had to attack some other aspect of the film until they even said unkind things about your very elaborate sets.

Ames: Well, frankly, I thought I arrived at a good solution to our problem of what would the lamasery in Tibet look like. Everyone worked very hard at creating it. In fact, it was the hardest work I've ever done on any show! A physically difficult thing. I had a few minor differences of opinion with the producer, Ross Hunter, as to what was necessary to have the design look more mysterious and haunting. That is, I thought it should look more spiritual. Ross didn't, but his track record as a successful producer doesn't leave much room for arguments with him.

Mike: I think it is interesting that Ross Hunter is about the only producer who is usually presented to the public in the manner a director usually is. Newspaper ads and other publicity say, "Ross Hunter's *Lost Horizon*" or "Ross Hunter's *Airport*." That's a credit more often deserved by the director, who is the true filmmaker nowadays.

Ames: Well, Mike, there are certainly other producers who take that kind of credit, as you know. For instance, I have just finished a film called *The Don Is Dead* with Anthony Quinn. You can be pretty sure the film will be referred to as, "Hal Wallis' *The Don Is Dead*." Both Hunter and Wallis dominate their films and rightly so. They are men of good taste. In any film, I think one mind should dominate after having had a collection of many other talented minds at its disposal. Then the person with that dominating mind should get top credit. You see, all the other people automatically get credit within the prestige of names like Hal Wallis and Ross Hunter because everyone knows producers like that know who the best talent is and hire that talent.

Mike: Speaking of the "best talent," you have frequently done the sets for the Academy Awards presentations, right?

Ames: The Academy of Motion Picture Arts and Sciences is a very precious thing in my life. I joined it with the idea that I would contribute, and that is the only way I think you should join any organization. The academy gives you the opportunity of meeting all the important people in the industry and of seeing some films which are never seen by the public, unfortunately. I've worked with the Documentary Films awards and seen the most beautiful things. I'm presently working with the Foreign Films awards, and you see the best things from every country in the world. It is an education in itself, a particularly important education to the art director who has to know and learn what the rest of the world film industry is doing. The Academy Awards is the ultimate in recognizing the achievement of the best, and believe me, when you are presented with that seven-and-a-half-pound brass Oscar, you are a pretty proud chicken! I've designed a couple of shows for the academy.

At one time the photography for the telecast of the show was always criticized because it didn't look right. Nobody knew why it didn't look right. The first show I was asked to do happened to be the last one that was held at the Pantages Theater on Hollywood Boulevard. I conferred with a lot of my friends in television and asked them, "What is the most important thing about a camera for television?" And I was told that you have to get the camera close to the people. I said, "My God, the camera is as far away from the people as it can possibly be!" So we redesigned the whole show to allow the camera to get into the thick of the proceedings. So much so that the camera drives the live audience in the theater out of their cotton-picking minds. But many millions of people see a beautiful show on the tube because the show's director is not afraid to take the camera and put it on the stage and on platforms and move it around and get some fantastic camera performances. This takes a very talented director who has to work with twelve cameras. The cast has to be very aware of what is going on, since it is a live, no retake show. You have to have a crew that is extremely aware of the extraordinary changes between a live camera and commercials, and indoors and outdoors, and clips and frames and inserts! From that point of view, it is one of the most highly complicated but widely received shows in the world of television.

Mike: Another contribution you make is in giving your time to lecturing and speaking at universities and clubs about your broad knowledge and experience as an art director.

Ames: Well, I feel the least all of us in the industry can do is to guide young fellows and girls who want to get into the industry. Today the universities have some excellent schools of cinema. The Academy of Motion Picture Arts and Sciences is promoting and developing interest in film careers by actually engaging these students to work on professional productions, usually in observer capacity. Also, the individual producing companies have training programs in which young men are allowed the opportunity of working on pictures. These students are starved for information in all facets and fields of the industry. They want to know what the director does, what the writer does, how each individual on a production functions. They are always amazed how much time, patience and effort are put into making a motion picture. It has been a very rewarding experience to talk to these kids for two or three hours at a stretch and tell them what we do and help contribute to their knowledge of our business. I always end my talks by quoting from an art director named Alfred Junge. He summed up what I feel: "All that counts is an idea and the conception of the film as a whole, and the spirit and intelligence behind these. All the abundance of technical possibilities is there ready to be used by the creators. I believe in the evolution of films toward higher cultural and artistic standards in the future."

March 7, 1970

Set Decorator

ARTHUR KRAMS

Krams: My major training at an art school was at Parsons when it was still called the New York School of Fine and Applied Art. I went one and a half years in New York and one and a half years in Paris at their branch there. I began private work as an interior designer, first in New York and later in Chicago. However, motion-picture work was always my ambition. I wanted to go beyond just doing lovely apartments and lovely homes and contemporary things. I was quite thrilled with the thought of a much bigger palette of life to express. So I moved to Los Angeles where I soon became an assistant to the famous designer Adrian at his decorator shop on Sunset Strip. Adrian was head of costume design at Metro-Goldwyn-Mayer, and many of the glamorous celebrities of the time would come into his shop. I was quite thrilled and impressed, as a very provincial New Yorker would be, at meeting the idols of the screen actually in person! After Adrian married Janet Gaynor, he gave up his shop. At about the same time I went into business with a shop of my own. Through Adrian's kind efforts in strongly recommending me to Mary Pickford, I was engaged to redecorate her estate, Pickfair. Mary was very kind, and I met many other people who opened the doors of Hollywood to me. I got other important homes to do. Unfortunately World War II broke out at this time. People began to hold onto their money, because nobody knew what was going to happen.

During the war, Mary Pickford opened her estate to the USO every Wednesday. She provided food and soft drinks for the servicemen, and a Beverly Hills women's club provided attractive companionship for the boys to talk, dance, and swim with. There would be groups of from twenty to forty boys each week. I acted as Miss Pickford's host for the occasion.

Mike: When did you begin working at the studios?

Krams: In 1945 at Metro-Goldwyn-Mayer. It was fascinating to adapt my knowledge to an entirely new technique. During this training period I worked on sets for many films at once. My first complete film assignment was *Holiday in Mexico*. When I saw that film bearing my first screen credit, my name seemed to loom ten feet high to me!

Mike: Aren't set decorators one of the smallest group of workers in the industry?

Krams: Today they number about one hundred, of which approximately fewer than sixty-five are active. About seventy-five percent of those working are engaged in television filming, and the small remainder on feature pictures. That small remainder will grow smaller as film production decreases and our own movie producers keep expanding into so-called runaway production in Europe and other parts of the world. I bring out these facts to save young men who might aspire to become set decorators a lot of time and trouble. The union to which all set decorators belong protects its members strongly, and if additional ones are required, they usually draw them from the ranks of those with studio experience, like property men or set decorators now working in live television such as variety shows and specials.

Mike: Where does your role in the making of a movie begin?

Krams: Like everyone else's: with the reading of a screenplay. The script is like a Bible and is followed as the law whether it be a contemporary comedy or a drama, a Western, a musical, a period picture, or a larger-than-life spectacle. The only deviations possible are those called for by page changes that usually keep fluttering down throughout the shooting period or verbal requests from the producer or director. Usually the set decorators have conferences with the producers, directors, and art directors in the preshooting period to discuss the decorations of the sets in a general way: what is desired in the overall look of the picture. And more specifically, regarding certain sets in the picture where there may be a wide area of interpretation. The set decorator works more closely with the art director than with any other person. The art director approximates an architect. The decorator starts with a bare set, three walls and a floor, provided by the art director. Seldom is there a ceiling or partial ceiling since the set must be lighted from this area by the huge lamps on the high catwalks which surround the set. The fourth wall is open for the camera but later on may be mounted in place for reverse shooting. The actual decoration of this bare set is inspired by the characterization of the actors who are to perform in it. This information is, of course, gathered from the screenplay, which tells the action involved, the time, contemporary or period, the season of the year, whether it be day or night. These are some of the principal considerations.

Mike: Along with the colors you choose.

Krams: These days about ninety percent of films being shot are in color. There has to be a close working relationship with the wardrobe people to coordinate the costumes of the star so that the colors of the set and the colors she wears complement each other. We must set up a proper background for her wardrobe. It would be a dreadful thing, for instance, for a star in a blue gown to suddenly find herself sitting on a blue sofa. In laying out the set and the arrangement of furniture and props, we try to visualize the action of the scene or scenes involved so as to obtain overall efficiency. In cases of musicals we have to work very hard with the stars performing because many of them, such as Fred Astaire, will use the props to a great extent in his interpretation of a dance. So we have to watch the rehearsal and accommodate his requirements of the dance routine. I once had to do a set for a film in which Mr. Astaire starred. He is a great perfectionist and a very hard worker. One of his dances involved a ship's lounge. He was all over the place. He would pounce from the floor to a sofa, to another sofa, to a table, etc. In one particular part, he wanted to dance on a round table with what we call a very fast surface so that his agility would be increased. In another picture I did with Fred Astaire, *Easter Parade*, he made great use of a progression of different-sized drums in a toy shop. He utilized the sound of the drums along with the punctuation of his steps, ending up with a great big kick on a bass drum.

Mike: If it was your job to select these drums and place them where Fred Astaire asked them to be, didn't that overlap with the propman's job?

Krams: Yes. Decorating and props overlap with what we call a working prop, which is a prop that is handled by the actor. This then becomes the responsibility of the master property man on the company. When the selection of a prop is as special as it was on the Astaire picture, the propman will seek out the advice of the set decorator on what piece is to be used.

Mike: Is it true that in the property department certain props are reserved to be used only in class A productions?

Krams: No, there was no distinction between the properties that could be used. They were all in several different warehouses and could be used on any picture. However, one instance when a prop or a decorative piece cannot be used again is when it is a painting which had to be done of a principal actor as a story point. That painting is commissioned for the one specific picture and can never be used again.

Mike: I should think that oftentimes the star who played the character and sat for the painting would want to have it as a memento of the film.

Krams: That request has probably been made, but usually the painting is not done in the fashion a professional portrait would be done. It is geared for color as far as camera is concerned, or perhaps as far as wardrobe is concerned, it may be a period piece which the star would not care to own, as an interpretation of himself.

Mike: Have you ever used your own possessions to decorate a film?

Krams: Often. I've used smaller pieces or paintings of my own when I find they fit better than something I could find in the storehouse. There have been a few embarrassing experiences about such uses because every once in a while there are retakes on a picture long after the picture has been completed. One time I had used a number of my own small art objects in a picture called *The Barkleys of Broadway* after which I had gone on a vacation. I came home to think that my house had been burglarized of these objects because they were missing. I checked up and found they had to have a retake on the film, and it was necessary for the propman to find a way into my house and take these pieces back! Once I used the favorite painting I possess to a very fine effect. Three of the stars of the picture wanted to buy the painting; but it meant too much to me to sell, and I still have it.

Mike: Do you go into much research to get a set as authentic as possible?

Krams: A good deal of research. Not only in period pictures, but in any film when a special kind of decor is required by the action. I remember having to do a police station and going to the Hollywood station and finding out how the room looked where they booked prisoners and how they did it. I had to approximate the jail and the booking area and all the furnishings that were in that type of place.

Mike: A picture based on an historical event should be especially researched, I suppose.

Krams: That brings to mind a picture I worked on, *The Court Jester*,

with Danny Kaye, which was twelfth-century England. We had very
few props, furniture, lanterns, or anything of that period, so most of
these had to be designed and made at the studio. It became a costly
thing, but very worthwhile. I remember having to have a number of
heraldic banners for the picture, and I went through books on
heraldry but could not use the actual banners because of possible
legal repercussions. I had to mix up the motifs of various coats of
arms and have our drapery department make our own banners.

Mike: When photography on a film includes photographing miniature
sets, does that come under your jurisdiction?

Krams: That becomes a special effects piece of work, and I am in no
way involved.

Mike: Nowadays there are many independent prop rental and
decoration rental firms. Have you found it necessary to go outside the
studio to buy or rent certain objects or materials not available in
studio stock?

Krams: Sometimes, especially for drapery and upholstery materials.
And for certain art objects the writer may have indicated. I did a
picture called *Man with a Cloak* which was based on a period story by
Edgar Allan Poe. The story required a bust of Napoleon without a
hat. He had to be bareheaded, and I covered every nook and cranny
of Los Angeles and finally came up with one that was made of bisque
in an auction house. Had the owner of the place known of my frantic
search for this piece, he could have charged me almost any price, and
I would have been obliged to pay it.

Mike: Arthur, you won an Academy Award for *The Rose Tattoo*. Was
it one of your favorite films to work on?

Krams: Yes. One of the most rewarding in my career. I remember
having finished the interior of Serafina's home in the picture and
about to show it to the producer, Hal Wallis. I and several of my fine
associates stood in the background as Mr. Wallis came in with Anna
Magnani, who had recently arrived from Italy to play Serafina. She
spoke very little English, but when she was touring the set, she turned
to Mr. Wallis and asked, "Who is the decorator?" Mr. Wallis
beckoned for me to come over and presented me to her. She threw her
arms around me in an embrace, this most electrifying woman, and
thanked me profusely for portraying the way Serafina lived. Not the
way Anna Magnani lived, but Serafina. She thought I had caught the

essence of the character of Serafina in decorating her home. This was a thrill of great importance to me.

Mike: Your work has received eight nominations for Oscars. What are some of your favorites of these?

Krams: *The Merry Widow, Lili, To Catch a Thief, Summer and Smoke,* and *Career.*

Mike: *Summer and Smoke* was also produced by Hal Wallis. You have worked with him a lot?

Krams: Yes. Fifteen films. I have always felt that he was the most knowledgeable and able producer in the entire motion-picture industry. He understands everybody's contribution to a picture and is aware of his ability and tries to keep a coterie of the same talents around him in the production of his pictures, having great faith in them. He is a most versatile producer in that his pictures can be a drama such as *Summer and Smoke,* or a wonderful costume picture like *Anne of the Thousand Days,* or even an Elvis Presley show. Another Hal Wallis film I enjoyed working on was *The Rainmaker* with Katharine Hepburn and Burt Lancaster. Usually, and in this incident also, the crews found Miss Hepburn a delight to work with because she was interested in every phase of the film and had a very easy camaraderie with everyone. She insisted the sound stage be closed tightly to all visitors because in between costume changes Miss Hepburn liked to be very much herself and wear perhaps just some old Levi's and a man's shirt and no makeup. She liked her freedom that way and certainly did not want to be seen by reporters or any visiting groups at the time.

The picture I did starring Barbara Stanwyck also has fond memories for me. My work requires my crew and I to be in early if we are going to shoot in a new set that day. I might come in as early as seven o'clock for shooting to start about nine. One morning my crew and I came in before anyone else was on the stage. We began our work, and I suddenly heard footsteps overhead and looked up, and there was Miss Stanwyck running around on the high catwalk. I exclaimed, "Missy, what are you doing up there? What are you doing in here this early?" And she said, "Arthur, I just love the place. I love to be here. I love the work and can't get enough of it and the atmosphere."

Mike: Which directors have you most enjoyed working for?

Krams: I've worked with many of the great directors. Some of my favorites are Daniel Mann, Norman Taurog, George Cukor, Joseph Anthony, and Alfred Hitchcock.

Mike: With Hitchcock you did *To Catch a Thief*, didn't you?

Krams: That starred Grace Kelly and Cary Grant. I had to do a villa interior as Cary Grant's home on the French Riviera. Since he played a character with superb taste, I wanted to use some very fine paintings. It turned out I was able to use Cary Grant's own very valuable and wonderful collection of paintings from his own home in Beverly Hills. When I suggested this to him, he invited Grace Kelly and myself up one afternoon. We arrived there, and as Grace Kelly and Cary Grant and his wife and I were having cocktails, I sauntered around looking at all the collection of paintings, of which there were about a dozen. When I came back to the little group, Mrs. Grant turned to me and asked, "Which do you want?" I said, "I want all of them." We did manage to use all of them in the interior of the film's villa, giving Cary Grant a great sense of familiarity and ease as if the villa were really his own home.

Mike: Wasn't it while she was making *To Catch a Thief* on location on the Riviera that Grace Kelly met Prince Rainier?

Krams: Yes. Grace is a great lady. She was a delight to work with and thoroughly professional. We had a mutual respect for each other's ability in our own fields and therein started a friendship of many years which has included my having had the honor of being a guest at the palace in Monaco in 1958 after she became Princess Grace.

I found Alfred Hitchcock to be the most gentlemanly of all the directors I've ever worked for and a man of immense artistic taste and knowledge. He never raised his voice on a set. He spoke in very normal tones, sometimes subdued, and commanded a lot of respect and admiration from all people who worked on a set with him.

Mike: I take it you have worked with directors who *will* raise their voices in anger.

Krams: Many of them. Many who become a bit volatile and explode.

Mike: Have you ever worked with Otto Preminger, who has a reputation for that sort of behavior?

Krams: No, and, in fact, I don't think I would ever want to work with Otto Preminger.

Mike: I worked for him once, and it was the most uncivilized experience I ever had in my life, in or out of the movie profession! He behaved like a dictator who could make Hitler look tame. I remember he usually wore shirts with his monogram on them, "O. P." The first time I saw those initials I nicknamed him Old Pig. With some directors an outburst is a passing reaction, and he is apologetic afterward.

Krams: Most often.

Mike: Have you found stars very outspoken or loud in their temperament?

Krams: No. Only castigating themselves, sometimes, when they fluff a take.

Mike: Arthur, how do you like the fact that many films are made on actual location now anywhere in the world, as compared to the way they used to mostly all be made in a studio?

Krams: I find it a bit sad in that the realism sought by this type of filming has meant the loss of the glamor and romance that existed in the earlier days of filmmaking and the type of story that was used for that purpose. Pictures today seem to lack a story that can carry you away as a story in a book can.

February 27, 1970

Costume Design

EDITH HEAD

Head: I'm a native of Los Angeles and lived here all my life. After finishing at the University of California at Berkeley and getting an MA in French at Stanford, I began teaching school here.

Mike: While you were teaching by day you attended art schools at night, didn't you?

Head: Yes. Otis Art Institute and Chouinard Art School. I found out early I wasn't a very dedicated schoolteacher, and I liked designing. I think if you are unhappy at one job, you try to find another.

Mike: Did you attend art school with the idea of becoming a costume designer?

Head: No. Actually I had decided I was going to be a fabulous landscape and seascape painter. I was not majoring in costume design. All of a sudden I saw a notice in the newspaper saying that Paramount Pictures wanted costume designers to work on Cecil B. De Mille's epic *The Golden Bed*, with Irene Rich. It was 1924, and in those days the field was not flooded. There were opportunities in every branch, for every technician. So I borrowed a lot of costume sketches from all my friends. Never dreaming I would get a job, I went out and talked with Howard Greer, the head designer who was completely amazed because I had so many different kinds of styles. He said I was the most versatile designer he had ever seen! I got the job, and the next day I couldn't draw! Fortunately he was a man with a divine sense of humor and said, "If you have that much nerve, I'll teach you." That's a true story, but I don't advise anybody to try it nowadays.

Mike: You are now under contract here at Universal, aren't you?

Head: Yes, and isn't this the world's most beautiful suite of offices they have given me? And you see in the room, I have the world's greatest collection of miniature and antique sewing machines!

Mike: However, you were with Paramount most of your long career.

Head: Yes. Occasionally Paramount would let me do an outside film. I used to work with Barbara Stanwyck and Bette Davis a great deal. If certain Paramount stars were on loan-out to do a film, I would sometimes go with them.

Mike: Who were some of these stars?

Head: They go way, way back! There was Clara Bow, Carole Lombard, Marlene Dietrich, Gloria Swanson, the fabulous, fabulous Mae West, Rosalind Russell, Ginger Rogers, Zsa Zsa and Eva Gabor, wonderful Grace Kelly, Audrey Hepburn, Katharine Hepburn, Shirley MacLaine, Natalie Wood. I think I have probably dressed every star, male and female, dead and living!

Mike: Do some stars dress to conform to their image, to make themselves a more identifiable personality?

Head: In general, that's a mistaken idea. I think there was a legend that stars were extremely temperamental and demanded their egos be satisfied. The great stars—and I have worked with them—are so professional that they know if I dress them in a certain manner, it is not because I am trying to make them look like themselves. I am trying to translate them to the character they are playing in the film.

They know, even if it is something they don't personally like, that I am just helping them, and they go along with me. I must say that is one of the joys of working with stars because they are professional. All women are somewhat temperamental. There is temperament in any woman you dress, as well as in the stars. Actually the only lack of temperament is in the male stars. That is, as far as clothes are concerned.

Mike: There must be stars, however, like Mae West who project their own thing constantly, on the screen and off it.

Head: Mae West is different. She was the first great star I ever dressed. It was for a picture called *She Done Him Wrong*, which was based on her stage success *Diamond Lil*. It was Cary Grant's first film with her. Mae West came to me as an established star with a definite Mae West image: the hourglass figure, the feather boas, the diamonds, the great hats, the sex symbol. Even when I did *Myra Breckenridge* with her, I can say she was still the great Mae West and still a sex symbol. Mae West has never acted anything except the Mae West image, whereas an actress like Bette Davis or Audrey Hepburn or Grace Kelly varies according to the part. Grace Kelly played the richest and most glamorous girl in the world in *To Catch a Thief*; then she played a rather dowdy, middle-aged housewife in *The Country Girl* with Bing Crosby and won the Academy Award! So you have variety with practically every star. But Mae West, believe it or not, is and always will be Mae West. I think Gloria Swanson projects always an image of great elegance. She is one of the most elegant and beautifully dressed women in the world. I've never seen her at any hour of the day or night when she wasn't fantastically put together. I remember years ago, when she returned to the studio from her honeymoon in Europe, we all turned out to greet her. As she stepped from her leopard-lined limousine, then the Marquise de la Falaise de Coudray, everyone threw roses!

Mike: You designed her clothes in *Sunset Boulevard*?

Head: That was exciting. I based them on what she had worn in earlier days. I found it impossible to make her look like a has-been. Makeup had to do it.

Mike: She has an exotic glamor, as opposed to the natural glamor of a star like Loretta Young.

Head: I did many pictures with Loretta Young. She also was at Paramount the major part of her career. Clothes are her passion. She handles herself like an elegant model. In her first picture, *The Crusades*, she was only fourteen years old. I've had some actresses so young they had to have a schoolteacher with them. When I first worked with Elizabeth Taylor in *A Place in the Sun*, she was underage, so while we fit, she had her teacher there in the room.

Mike: You've said one of the toughest films you ever costumed was *Lady in the Dark* starring Ginger Rogers.

Head: That was a strange film, full of fantasies. It was taken from the Broadway play which had dream sequences and a fashion image. The magnitude of trying to project double images on the screen of fantasy and reality was a challenging problem. Ginger played a sophisticated woman who wore high-fashion clothes. In the musical number "Jenny Made Her Mind Up," I designed one of the most lavish dresses ever made in Hollywood: We made a mink skirt, split up the front and solidly lined in ruby glitter. Ginger's famous legs were encased in long sheer tights. Under a mink jacket was a blaze of the same ruby glitter. The mink alone cost fifteen thousand dollars. I still show this costume at fashion shows as a sample of the luxury that existed before the present era of budgets and economy.

Actually, the most difficult pictures I ever did were the great De Mille spectaculars. When you dress the actors for *The Ten Commandments*, you have done the biggest picture ever!

Mike: You don't consider yourself a fashion designer, but a studio costume designer.

Head: Exactly, because a fashion designer creates two or three lines of clothes a year. These are made according to their own desire of what they think is the look women should wear. It's their credo, their own projection. They do it to make money, of course, and to have fame. I make a costume for a specific actress for a specific picture. Whether it has fashion or not has nothing to do with it, but to help translate the star into the image she is projecting in this particular role. Occasionally I have done very successful fashion pictures, like with Audrey Hepburn in *Sabrina* and some with Grace Kelly that have had a great fashion impact on the world. It is even funny that the Dorothy Lamour sarong I designed became an image. Of course, it wasn't an authentic sarong, which covers one only below the waistline! My sarong was designed for a picture called *The Jungle Princess* in 1936. It was bright red with prints of white hibiscus. To find the right girl to fill it, Paramount conducted a nationwide beauty contest. One by one the state finalists were sent to my department. We'd dress each girl in the same sarong, tuck the same white blossom behind her ear, and slip the same shell bracelets on her arm. Then the pretty native would go over for her screen test. Among the candidates who arrived one day was Dorothy Lamour, a girl with dark hair twisted into a bun at the back of her head. She was wearing a sweater and skirt, high heels and a shoulder-strap bag. She was incredibly beautiful with clear, creamy magnolia skin, big blue eyes, and a big bosom. The minute she took off the sweater, half the "big bosom" came off with it! Falsies! She kicked off her shoes, pulled down her long, luxuriant hair and the red sarong was wrapped around her. Dorothy was younger than she admitted at the time, so we helped nature fill out the sarong to the proper proportions and used adhesive tape to hold it in place. From the least voluptuous of the contestants she became the very promise of voluptuousness and won the role! In time her figure lived up to that promise, and in the more than ten years of jungle and adventure pictures that followed Dottie was able to hold up her own sarong without any artificial means of support.

I started the whole Latin American feeling with Barbara Stanwyck in *The Lady Eve*, where she wore ponchos and all the Latin things which are now part of our fashion language. Even when Mae West did her first picture, *Vogue* magazine in Paris said, "Ah, the Mae West look!" In other words, if a designer does something for a fabulous star in a successful picture, the impact sometimes carries the fashion image into popularity.

Mike: Have you ever had a director project his taste into your costume design of his film?

Head: Directors have costume approval. One director who took that quite a bit further was Josef von Sternberg. When he was at Paramount directing Marlene Dietrich, he fashioned her completely. He was a Svengali. He had a great deal to say about sets, lighting, costumes, and even ran his own camera.

Mike: In that same era you dressed Jean Harlow.

Head: Yes, I did *The Saturday Night Kid* with her. I dressed her before she was a star. She was second lead and was glamorous and exciting. She stole scenes even then. I never dressed her after she became the celebrated platinum blonde.

Mike: You design your own clothes, don't you?

Head: I do all my own clothes and pick out all the fabrics. I think it is good to be your own guinea pig.

Mike: When a star has been especially pleased with a costume from a picture, does she ever want to have it for her own?

Head: They do. When they first wear it, they say, "Oh, I must have this!" But after they have worn it through a picture, it is pretty tired. Sometimes we make copies for them. Sometimes I do personal clothes for certain stars.

Mike: Don't you help some of the stars decide what to wear in public functions, such as the Academy Awards?

Head: I've been an adviser for the ladies appearing at the Academy Awards for about eighteen years. Actually what I do is explain the color of the set and try tactfully to arrange that they don't all wear the same color and look. But don't forget this is the one time of the year a star presents herself to the public as herself, not as a film character. And I have no right to say too much. I am more of a referee than a consultant!

Mike: Do you think people should dress more individually?

Head: I would urge them to. I think too many women have been sheep. I think they followed fashion blindly, the way a sheep follows its leader, without any relation to whether the garment was becoming to them. In the last few years, in getting away from that, we've gone overboard. This doing your own thing has gotten so bad that I almost wish we would go back to being sheep. I am hopeful we can have better dressed people without the conformity of either of these extremes. The huge change in male fashion really interests me. I am curious to see if men are going to turn out to be rams and follow the leader, the way girls have.

Mike: Speaking of male fashion, you have designed clothes for Bob Hope, Bing Crosby, Danny Kaye, Cary Grant—

Head: Fred Astaire, Steve McQueen, Paul Newman, and Robert Redford. I must say it is a sheer joy to work with men. There's something different between the psychology of a man and woman star. I can say to a female star, "This is a lovely dress. I'm going to make it in pale pink." And she'll say, "Lovely, but why can't I have pale blue?" I can say to a male like Cary Grant, "I'd like you to wear a blue sweater," and he'll say, "Fine." Yet each star is a personality. I remember when I first dressed Bette Davis. All of a sudden she rushed from the mirror, crossed the room, and threw herself on the floor.

Well, I wasn't sure she hated the dress that much, or she didn't feel well. I said, "What's the matter?" She said, "Don't you remember in the script it says I'm supposed to do that. I want to see if the dress works." Quite often when you dress a star for a sequence where you know there is going to be action, they want to go through the movements wearing their wardrobe. Mae West, when you fit her, does the entire scene, including dialogue! I must say it is absolutely fantastic, and if she is doing a number, she sings the whole song!

Mike: She must make a lot of her own suggestions about her wardrobe.

Head: I've worked with her so much I know exactly what she wants. I know her image. But the point is that most women take a long time to fit. Men say, "How soon can you get it off? Let's get the fitting over. I have to get to the golf course." But some women, like Marlene Dietrich, are tireless. She can stand for hours. She is the perfectionist of all time. On the other hand, Hedy Lamarr, during fittings for *Samson and Delilah* spent a great deal of time in a horizontal position. In the middle of a fitting she would say, "Edith, I must rest. When you have had children, you have backaches." And she would lie down as relaxed as a Persian cat and have something to eat sent up. She ate constantly! She had no temper, just an enviable ability to relax. Hedy knew what she looked like and didn't work at it.

Mike: Have you had actresses who don't enjoy a fitting session?

Head: A few women can't wait to get clothes off! Little Katharine Ross, for instance. She says right away, "Oh, it's fine. Come on, let's get it off." In other words, every star is a personality, and that helps to make my job the very exciting thing it is.

Mike: Are you much of an influence on them to keep their figures trim?

Head: Only if they ask me. And most of them do! I don't come right out and tell them to lose weight. I just fit the dress a little too tightly, so that when they put it on, they know they've gained weight. That's much more subtle.

Mike: Do you like the hippie look?

Head: I don't like it taken out of context on people who shouldn't wear it. I think the hippie look is for a certain type of, preferably, young people. I just don't happen to like older hippies!

Mike: Your creative talents go beyond costume designing. You have a regular column in certain newspapers, you often contribute articles to various magazines, and you have written a couple of books. In 1959 you wrote *The Dress Doctor* in collaboration with Jane Ardmore.

Head: I'm still getting royalties from that, and I am delighted because I give all of it through the American Indian Fund, which happens to be my pet charity. When I was very little, I used to live on the reservation a bit. The book itself is autobiographical and tells about the earlier stars with whom I worked. The second book called *Dressing for Success* is a "how to" book: how to dress to get a husband; how to dress to hold a husband; how to dress for all the things that happen in a woman's life.

Mike: I hear your home also carries out your artistic talents.

Head: Well, I can take no credit for that, because I am married to Wiard Ihnen, a very famous art director, decorator, and artist. A great painter. A Dutchman from Friesland. He is responsible for our house which is in that book on the Hollywood style of living. It is an old Mexican ranch house called Casa Ladera, and it is wonderful and beautiful. We enjoy having friends over for dinner. I am a little modest about my designing, but I admit I am a very good cook. It is a special hobby of mine.

Mike: Miss Head, you've won seven Academy Awards up to this date!

Head: Yes, and I've received thirty-one nominations.

Mike: That's remarkable!

Head: But it's not, because it covers a lifetime, and the group of costume designers is a smaller group.

Mike: Your Oscar-winning pictures are: *The Heiress* (1949), *All About Eve* (1950), *Samson and Delilah* (color, 1950), *A Place in the Sun* (1951), *Roman Holiday* (1953), *Sabrina* (1954), and *The Facts of Life* (1960). Can you say which is the favorite picture you have costumed?

Head: I have a definite favorite, but I didn't receive an Oscar for it. It's a picture directed by Alfred Hitchcock, with whom I adore working, called *To Catch a Thief*. In it Grace Kelly played a beautiful heiress. Beautiful clothes. Incidentally, Grace Kelly and Cary Grant are my favorite actress and actor.

Mike: Do you prefer to do a picture that requires contemporary dress rather than a period or historical picture?

Head: Oh, yes! Because you are designing. I think no matter how good a job you do with a period film, it is a reprise of something that has been designed before. It takes research. But when you are doing a modern dress film, you are on your own.

Mike: How did the change to color films affect your work?

Head: It's ten times much easier doing a film in color than it is in black and white. Even the simplest dress will carry because of the beauty of color. In a black-and-white film, you have to give much more attention to detail and line to compensate for the loss of color.

Mike: How would you compare the young stars of today with the older stars?

Head: There's a whole new crop of important young actresses. The difference between them and the actresses of the past is that none of these girls have what you call a trademark. In other words, Mae West is Mae West. She established something which was a definite person. The same for Joan Crawford and all of the really great stars. The thing today is not to be eccentric and unusual. Everybody is still to a degree an individual, but they do their own thing as a part of the look of now. I'm thinking of the girls like Jane Fonda, Katharine Ross, Jacqueline Bisset, Ali McGraw, and Joanna Shimkus. Those are among the finest of our young actresses, the young stars who are making a great impact. Naturally I am affected by the fashion point of view, and none of these stars are clotheshorses. They don't depend on the glamor image. They don't want a designer to say, "Now we are going to project a Katharine Ross look." They like to dress casually and want to be a part of the now scene. I would say nine out of ten young stars today deliberately do not project an image.

Mike: Is that because they feel an audience will identify more with the character they are portraying in a film instead of with the movie star they see on the screen?

Head: I don't think they would have even thought of that although it's a very bright idea. I think their whole point of view is that the star idea is old-fashioned. We are no longer in an age of superglamor. There used to be a star image in having an imported car, a Rolls-Royce and that sort of thing. Today they are not interested in the accouterments that made a star in the past. A great many stars always insisted on having their own designers. Some insisted on me; some on other designers. It was a sort of status symbol. You always had your own designer, your own hairdresser. These new girls couldn't care less. But there isn't one of them who doesn't have a glamor potential, or she wouldn't be a rising star.

Mike: Do you think the current trend possibly began with Joanne Woodward when she came to Hollywood via the New York method school of acting and rejected the glamor image in order to be her natural self? No pretensions or airs?

Head: No. I've worked with Joanne, and she is an exception. When we made the film *Winning* with her husband, Paul Newman, she played a girl who worked as a clerk in a car rental service. Her clothes were very simple. She likes to have a designer she knows along with her even if some of her wardrobe is store-bought. She likes to feel she has a professional to take the responsibility. She still has a slight hangover of conducting herself as a star, because she is a star. You see, these other girls are not really stars yet. I think that while Joanne has none of the clichés of stardom, she likes to have people around who she feels know how to interpret the character she has to portray.

Mike: Which of the new crop do you work with most often?

Head: I've done several pictures with Katharine Ross. She hates fittings. She's not interested in fashion per se. She wants to look right for the character she is playing. She's very intelligent. She has two of the largest sheep dogs in the world. They are as large as my sofa, and they come and lean on me and her while we fit. She's an enchanting person, very definite and determined not to be made into something she doesn't want to be. In other words, I say, "How about a ruffle?" She'll say, "I hate ruffles." She wants to look the way *she* wants to look. When we did *Butch Cassidy and the Sundance Kid*, which is full of ruffles, laces, and plumes, she said, "Fine, that's right for the period. I'll go along with it." But for a plain modern picture she doesn't want to dress in order to project a star image. Jane Fonda is the same way. I did *Barefoot in the Park* with her. She has her own concept of what she wants. The same thing with Jacqueline Bisset, who was in *Airport*. She isn't about to allow herself to be made into a fashion plate! All these girls personify what I call the new look. Ironically, it is an image, but it is the image of now.

Mike: Have you designed wardrobe for Candice Bergen?

Head: No, but I have met her and find her much more fashion-conscious than these other young girls, but in her own way.

Mike: You work fairly often with Liz Taylor, don't you?

Head: Yes. I did her clothes for the Academy Awards in 1971. And I did her costumes for a segment she and Richard Burton did on the *Lucy Show* with Lucille Ball. That was fantastic because they don't do much television! Liz is a perfect example of a star who likes to have a designer with her for all occasions. It's not that she's stuffy about it or considers it a status symbol. It's just that she is used to it. She has never in her life not had it! She grew up inside the glamor of the MGM factory. These other young ladies have grown up in an era when the studios do not spend a great deal of money for everything. Wardrobe people will go out and buy a dress or suit instead of having it tailor-made. It is another generation of thinking. It has nothing to do with age. It's just a part of the whole new look of motion pictures, and I hate it.

Mike: You prefer the glamorous approach to fashion and personality as exemplified, say, by Zsa Zsa Gabor?

Head: Oh! Zsa Zsa fits into no category whatsoever! She is a law unto herself! She is an institution. She represents femininity, love of diamonds, beauty, luxury, the Rolls-Royce. There is no question of her image. In fact, it even bears her name. I've heard people say, "You have so many diamonds you look Zsa Zsa!" Zsa Zsa herself has made a career of looking Zsa Zsa Gabor, and she's not dreaming of changing that. She's very shrewd and intelligent in spite of it all.

Mike: Do you think Natalie Wood has a particular image?

Head: Natalie is a very flexible young lady. She is a very beautiful girl both of face and figure who wears clothes beautifully and is very, very fashion-conscious. Like Liz Taylor, she was brought up to have anything she wanted. The most expensive clothes! I've done her clothes for years. She is in the status symbol class, but she can just as easily translate into the other class of the now look. If she has a picture where she wears blue jeans, she's not going to insist on having them made to order. But when the part calls for beautiful clothes, she likes wearing those beautiful clothes. She's one of the few actresses who has almost a double image! It depends on the picture in which she works.

Mike: The current young stars don't influence the public in fashion or style? They don't set the pace, so to speak?

Head: No. They aren't interested in it. They like to be amusing and gay and wear Indian headbands or serapes and ponchos and do whatever is the current fad. They like to go to funny little shops and buy amusing things. It's a completely new breed of young stars and a completely new language of fashion.

Mike: Do you think the lack of young stars with definite images has come about because the major studios are no longer in an economic position to operate as the gigantic machines which created and sustained their stable of stars?

Head: Partly. But don't forget a great many of the older stars were actually forced into a star image. The great stars of MGM, for instance, like Joan Crawford, Hedy Lamarr, Lana Turner, and Ava Gardner, were glamor queens, and glamor was the thing that made Hollywood so famous. Not only in women, but in men too, like Rudolph Valentino and Clark Gable. Now the studios are not building a star image. I don't think anybody, I know I haven't, is quite able to figure out what is happening or why it's happening, or what we're trying to achieve. But it is certainly antistar image, antiglamor, anti the whole fantasy of early Hollywood. Whether this is a temporary phase we are going through or is a permanent thing, I don't know. I cannot believe we are going on forever making pictures as we do now, and I cannot believe the star image is dead forever. I hope not.

March 10, 1970

Makeup

PERC WESTMORE

Westmore: I was born in Canterbury, Kent, England, in 1904. My mother, father, and six kids came to Canada and lived in Quebec, Toronto, and Winnipeg before moving to St. Louis. I've lived in most of the major cities in this country because my dad was what we call a floating cork. He was a wigmaker, and any place he could get five dollars more a week, he'd pick up the entire family and move. At age twelve I began working with Dad when we were living in Cleveland. We later worked in Pittsburgh awhile and from there headed to Los Angeles in 1920. We drove out in a 1919 Maxwell touring car! Every night we pitched a tent along the highway. We got as far as a little desert town outside Los Angeles called Hesperia when we burned off our fifth rear axle! We pitched our tent, and my dad, mother, and sister headed for Los Angeles to buy another axle. Dad left us five boys with one can of beans and a box of crackers, thinking he would return that evening. But it was the Fourth of July weekend, and everything was closed. Three days later he returned! The new axle was put in, and we drove on into Los Angeles and pitched our tent in a park in Pasadena. We had exactly four dollars and fifty cents to our name. Dad got a hotel room for one day so we could get a good bath. That afternoon my father and I went to a wholesale hair company and got jobs as wigmakers. My brother Mont got a job as a carpenter, Wally got one as a mechanic, Ern went to work for a sash and door works. Bud was too young to work. We were able to gather enough money to rent a little house our first week in town.

About four months later, Dad and I got better work in a wig shop called Maison Cesare. It was my job to get in early and wash out the basins and sweep the floor. Later in the day I made wigs. I had nothing to do with picture people, but one morning about six o'clock, while I'm cleaning up the place, there's a rap on the door. I see a guy with half a mustache who happened to be Adolphe Menjou. I opened the door, and he said, "What time does the wigmaker come in?" I said, "They don't open till nine o'clock. What can I do for you?" He said, "Well, you see here I accidentally shaved off half my mustache this morning. I'm playing Louis XIII in *The Three Musketeers* and I've got to be on the set at nine o'clock." I said, "Fine. Come on in the back." So I took a pattern of the right-hand side and made this little half mustache, trimmed it, dressed it, put it on him, and he went to the United Artists Studio. He walked up to Douglas Fairbanks, Sr., and said, "Look at this!" Fairbanks said, "Look at what?" He said, "Don't you see the difference? This is a false mustache." Fairbanks said, "You're kidding! Where did you have it made?" Menjou said, "Down at Cesare's place." Fairbanks said, "Oh, don't mention Cesare's name to me." It seemed Fairbank's wife, Mary Pickford, had at one time been having her hair done by Cesare, and he had, for some reason, gone into a temper tantrum and thrown her out of his salon. Menjou said, "This wasn't Cesare. It was some kid." Fairbanks said, "Let's get him out here. Stop the picture. I want all the mustaches and chin pieces remade." They had been shooting only three days. They called the salon and asked for me, but my father insisted he would go out and take care of the situation. He came back with patterns, and we made all the mustaches and beards for the show. That's how we got started at the studio. I worked on three Fairbanks pictures, then was hired at First National. I became the hairdresser for the Talmadge sisters, Norma, Constance, and Natalie, and for Billie Dove, Bessie Love, Elaine Hammerstein, Nita Naldi, Anna Q. Nilsson, and Corinne Griffith. I had to take care of several ladies every morning!

Mike: Weren't those the days when the hairstyle of a star would influence style all over the country?

Westmore: Yes. I had one head that I did about thirty-five years ago. That's Claudette Colbert. I cut her hair, and she's never changed it to this day! Other heads that I was responsible for are the Colleen Moore bob, the Mary Astor head, and the Jane Wyman head. Those heads are still being worn today.

Mike: How did you go from hairdressing into being a makeup artist?

Westmore: Through a picture called *The Lost World* in 1925 with Wallace Beery. We had to have an actor fitted out to play a gorilla. At that time there was only one recognized makeup artist in the industry. His name was Cecil Holland. He worked at Metro-Goldwyn-Mayer. I had to make this gorilla suit out of real hair to fit Bull Montana, who was a wrestler. The studio manager said to me they had to test the gorilla, so why didn't I make him up. The extent of my makeup in those days was making hairpieces and putting them on. So, not knowing anything about makeup, I got some plasterlin, and I painted Bull Montana's face with spirit gum. Not thinking the plasterlin had oil in it and wouldn't stick, I laid Bull Montana on a table and put the plasterlin all over his face and molded this gorilla face. I wouldn't let him sit up. Then it came to the point of having to put the hair on the face, so by breaking the eye of a small needle and using the needle like a stick I doubled each hair and pushed it into the plasterlin. I had all this hair sticking in his face when along came lunchtime. I still wouldn't let him sit up. I gave him a couple of malts through a straw. Finally, about three o'clock, I had to go to the bathroom. I said, "Don't move. Stay where you are." When I came back, Bull was sitting up, and this whole thing was in his lap!

I went to the production manager and said, "I'm sorry. I'm afraid I can't do it. You better get Cecil Holland over here." He said, "All right." I said, "I'll fix up a nice room for him next to my hairdressing room, and I'll help him and so forth." So Cecil arrived with his cases. I wanted to learn something about makeup, so I offered to clean his brushes and assist him. He said in his British accent, "No, no. That's not at all necessary, Perc. I'll take care of it." It got to where he'd lock the door on me. I used to peek through the keyhole so I could see something to learn. We finished the show, and he never showed me a thing. The last day of the picture Cecil was all packed up ready to leave, and I said, "Cecil, I want to shake your hand. I want to thank you for teaching me something." He said, "I didn't teach you a bloody thing." I said, "You did, Cecil. You never showed me one thing, but I am going to make makeup a profession. And everything that I develop I will expose within twenty-four hours. And in due time, we will have what is known as makeup artists." Years later, when Cecil became an old man, and these older fellows weren't getting work, I was head of the makeup department here at Warner's and had about thirty-five men on my staff. Jack Dawn was head of makeup at Metro. Between the two of us we decided to give these old fellows daywork. Rotate them, so that they could make a little money. Once I needed about four extra men for hair work for three or four days, and I called into the local union and said, "Give us four heads." In the group happened to be Cecil Holland, who showed up carrying a box with a strap over his shoulder like a hot dog man. I didn't want to send him to the set with that funny box. I had great respect for him and didn't want to embarrass him. So I said to my assistant, "Tell you what you do. We need a lot of mustaches and beards. Keep Cecil here in the department and put him in charge." When the engagement was over, Cecil came to me and said, "You know, Perc, I remember the time you told me you would expose every technique you developed." He was standing in the first big makeup department in Hollywood here on the Warner lot.

In the old days in this business, there was one company that developed all the film. The studios would complain about close-ups looking bad. Color of the lipstick looked wrong even though this was when all pictures were in black and white. So I sat down with the head of the studio, which was still First National, and I said, "I can tell you what the industry needs. I, as a hairdresser, see a player come in in the morning. One day she has on pink makeup and a bright red lipstick and blue eye shadow. Then another day she might come in with a different lip color and new makeup. What we need is a chart system and records on every player and what they wore and how they made up in each scene. Then, if we get that same player back in a future film, we can adhere to the way we know she has photographed before." With that idea they gave me a makeup department! The first in the whole industry. It was 1924, and I got a group of twelve character actors together who knew how to make up themselves from the basic stage makeup principles. I told them we were going to develop a profession known as the makeup artist. We got organized and even began training apprentices from among sketch artists, painters, and musicians. Anyone who had a touch of art in them. I trained all my brothers and brought them into the business. Wally just retired at Paramount after thirty-eight years! Bud is still head of the makeup department at Universal. Today a beginner has to have two years of college or accredited art; then he goes on the producers' roster and becomes an apprentice. The union allows one apprentice to every five journeymen. Over the years I've trained around sixty-five or seventy men in the profession.

Mike: Didn't you invent and enlarge upon makeup techniques as you worked with the stars?

Westmore: Yes. I remember one concept of makeup I originated on a show we made many years ago called *Stella Dallas*. It starred a silent film player named Belle Bennett. This was the days of the star with the full retinue: uniformed chauffeur, uniformed footman. While I would be dressing her hair, she would be surrounded by her cook, her business agent, her personal maid, and maybe a manicurist! The director and producer of the picture would look out the window every morning and see this great star drive up in her Rolls-Royce! Believe me, we all knew she couldn't act worth sour grapes! At that point I said to myself, "If that high-priced car and all that goes with it is what makes a star, I'll never drive anything but the cheapest car onto the lot." During that picture she had to age, which I would do through her makeup. At first I thought of hiring a friend of mine who was a good cartoonist to draw fine little lines on her face. Then, lying in bed one night, I conceived the idea of putting a base color on her face, then having her squint as I highlighted with a pencil all her natural lines and wrinkles. I got out of bed, went into the bathroom, and tried this on myself. I was about twenty-three at the time but looked in the mirror and saw a little old man standing there. Today this is known as the squint system for age makeup. I've gotten a lot of my techniques actually in my sleep! I've been able to retain them. I do things in the subconscious I wouldn't dare do in the conscious mind.

Mike: I suppose the major part of your work has been to make female stars look as beautiful as possible in a picture.

Westmore: Glamor is the word. At Warner's Ann Sheridan was known as the glamor girl. The way she got that title is: Every photographer in Hollywood was invited to take part in a glamor photo contest for a magazine that wanted a gal known as the Glamor Girl. I was invited to be in a group of makeup artists who selected one star to use as a model. I chose Ann Sheridan. Well, I knew exactly what was going to happen with everybody else: They would have the knees showing, and low cleavage to put across the sex appeal. I completely reversed that approach. I told my photographer I wanted a couch with a leopard skin on it, and I wanted to dress Annie in a long dress with a high neck made of monk's burlap and with a big rope tied around her waist. What I had going was the idea of leaving a lot to the viewer's imagination. I posed her on the couch in a position with her rump toward the camera, and that picture won the contest!

Mike: Have you had temperamental actresses who would not allow themselves to be made up not to look their best even though the part might require it?

Westmore: That's a question I've been asked a hundred times. I can say honestly and sincerely there might have been one or two players in the whole industry that I didn't get along with. There was one gal whose name I forget. She didn't go too far. She treated everybody like a servant, so I refused to let a hairdresser or makeup man touch her. I told her she was on her own.

Mike: Wasn't Bette Davis awfully temperamental?

Westmore: I did over sixty pictures with Bette Davis. Here was a gal, I don't care what the part, who would go along with the makeup I decided on. When she played Queen Elizabeth I in *Elizabeth and Essex* with Errol Flynn, I shaved her head halfway back! In history they didn't know if the old queen was a man or a woman. She had this peculiar hairline. Well, very few players would stand to have their hair shaved, plus shaving off their eyebrows. The first time we did it, Bette was a little reluctant, but she was always one to go all the way. I decided to give her a few drinks, and she said, "Well, let's go!" and before she knew it, she was shaved! Later on when she went back to work after having been out of pictures for four years with the osteomyelitis trouble, the first film she did was *The Virgin Queen* for

Fox. Again she had to be shaved! We went through the same procedure as before.

Mike: She requested you on the film?

Westmore: Oh, yes! I did every picture she did. I was known in Bette Davis' life by the nickname Charlie. It came from the character in the play *Strange Interlude* where the gal has all the lovers, and this one friend, Charlie, is always there. I went through many personal things with Bette. If I ever sent her a gift, it was always signed "Charlie." We both left Warner Brothers at the same time. I did one show with her at MGM, *The Catered Affair* in which she played Debbie Reynolds' mother. After that I said, "Bette, I'll never make you up again." Bette said sharply, "What do you mean? What's this all about?" I said, "Well, you and I are getting along in years. If you remember, in *Strange Interlude*, when Charlie gets old, he winds up marrying the lady! And that I never want to do!"

There is one thing I did with Bette's makeup which is very seldom done, and that is rouging the point of the chin. When I finished her makeup in the morning, if she was a good girl, I would just touch her chin with the rouge brush, and she would say, "Ah, I've been a good girl." So, when the Smothers Brothers TV show wanted Bette to play her characterization of Queen Elizabeth I, she said she wouldn't do it unless Perc Westmore made her up. It had been a lapse of about twelve years since I had worked on her. This was to be a one-shot deal for television, so naturally I wasn't going to shave her head again. I used what we refer to as a plastic cap which is glued down. I also glued down her eyebrows and drew others above them. For the finale on the show she had to appear as herself and be attractive. I had thirty minutes to make that change. We were really under pressure. Just as I finished, I picked up the brush and hit her on the chin. She looked up and said, "After twelve years, I'm still a good girl." She is one of the most intelligent gals I ever worked with. Many people have suggested to Bette to have her face lifted. Bette goes on record that is a thing she will never do. Why should she try to look like a kid? The public knows her age, and there are plenty of parts for her to play.

Mike: Do you think any actress should have her face lifted?

Westmore: In some cases I think it does a terrific thing mentally for the woman.

Mike: Have you had experience of a star rejecting your makeup ideas?

Westmore: Hardly ever, because when I do a makeup, I explain in detail what I am doing. Basically I use the camera the same as a scientist uses a microscope. With a head close-up on the screen you're getting a magnification from two hundred to four hundred times its normal size. We are able to analyze that face. If I do something wrong, such as the wrong shape of a brow for that particular face, it is going to show. That's the reason we make tests and sit down with the player and discuss the makeup problems.

A good example of that is when I did *The Blue Veil* with Jane Wyman. She played the role of a nurse from about twenty-six years old all the way to the age of seventy! The picture was shot in sequence. I explained to her everything I was doing each day. She is a stickler. She knows all about the camera and lighting. She can direct. She wants to know. When we were three days into the filming of the sequences in which she had to be seventy, I came down with a coronary. There were still three weeks filming. Jane Wyman finished her own makeup, and you couldn't tell where I left off and she started!

On every actor's makeup I explain why and how I do anything. For instance, when I worked with Paul Muni on films like *Juarez, Emile Zola,* and *Louis Pasteur,* he was interested in every detail. He was a stickler for authenticity. When he was preparing his role as a Mexican in *Border Town,* we went down to Olivera Street every day for a week and studied the faces of the young men. We would watch for certain boys and their clothes. If they were faded on the shoulder, elbows worn out, knees worn out—we can do this type of aging at the studio, but not with Muni—I would grab the boy and take him to a store and buy him two new suits to get that old one for Muni to wear in that film! He even hired Mexican servants in his house during the film! He had to hear the tones and accents of their voices. I remember, when he played Juarez, he went to the University of Mexico and got permission to take Juarez's hat, coat, and pocket watch out of the museum cases. He put the hat and coat on and held the watch to get the feel of these articles. A good salesman is a good actor. You have to believe in what you're doing. Muni was one man that I always respected because he was so concerned with the lives of the characters he played. Makeup had to be done to absolute perfection with Paul Muni. There was no just getting by.

Mike: You did many pictures with Humphrey Bogart, didn't you?

Westmore: From *Dead End* on! There was an unusual thing that happened to Humphrey Bogart when we had just got into shooting on *Casablanca*. He had a full head of hair, but on the third day he came into makeup, and I noticed a bald spot behind his left ear about the size of a quarter. I checked behind his right ear and saw a bald spot the size of a dime. I told him to sit in the makeup chair so that I could take his wig measurements. He wanted to know why. I said, "Bogie, you're going to lose your hair!" He said, "Aw, get away. You're kidding me." I said, "Get in the chair. We've got three days to get a wig ready!" I took the measurement, and we worked twenty-four hours a day to make the wig. On the third day, Bogie walked into my department with a pillow case with his hair in it. From the beginning I recognized his hair condition as a nervous condition. I knew his hair would eventually grow back, but we couldn't take a chance of holding up production. I fitted the wig on Bogie, and nobody on the set even knew it for at least a week. Jack Warner used to kid me that I had put something on his head to make him lose his hair so I would be the big man and show off my artistry. Ironically, in the picture there is a scene where Bogie goes to sleep in a barber chair as a Mexican cuts his hair. This means his hair had to be shaved during the scene all the way up the back and on the sides! In this case, I only used a toupee on top of his head and laid on false hair, as we lay on a beard, in the areas that had to be shaved off during the scene. The barber was actually shaving the false hair I had put on Bogie. That meant every day thereafter I had to put very short hair back on and make it a little longer each day so it would appear to be growing back out! Finally we got it to the length that he could again wear the wig I had made for him. About three weeks before we finished the picture, his real hair began growing out.

Humphrey Bogart had one quirk that very few people were aware of: He never could stand a tight collar. He always wore a loose or unbuttoned collar. The tie was always opened. Another thing is that if you looked very close into his eyes, they always appeared as though he were crying. I found this out when I had to take a death mask of him about a year before he passed away. We took these masks of all the contract stars so we could plan what makeup might be needed in advance of a picture. Especially if the star were out of town. When I took the cast, his eyes were closed. We take them with the eyes open now. That meant recarving his eyes to appear opened. I had to study about thirty still photographs of his eyes. It was the first time I recognized he always had that appearance of his eyes crying. Slightly moist, with a certain sadness, even though he played a tough guy.

Mike: Another very colorful male star at Warner's was Errol Flynn.

Westmore: I could fill your book with stories on him alone! Before Errol Flynn was brought to this country to play in *Captain Blood*, we had made extensive tests of George Brent, one of Warner's regular stars. The period called for shoulder-length hair. It seemed every wig we put on George made him come up looking a little feminine. In the projection room while viewing some of George's tests one day, Jack Warner said, "By the way, I just came back from England, and I saw a guy there doing a modeling show in a bathing suit. He's done a little acting. Let's get him over here and make a test of him." And with that Warner had them cable England, and we got Errol Flynn over here. After his very first test he was in! There was a saying from there on: "You're in like Flynn!" We never had many makeup problems with Flynn. But a funny thing happened between him and the makeup man we assigned to him. All makeup men carry a case they have their materials in. Errol Flynn had his man empty all the bottles and change the labels to things like "hair tonic," "skin freshener," "cleanser," and so on. But basically they were substitute names for scotch, gin, vodka, and bourbon! The makeup man would put vegetable dye in the whiskey to disguise it further!

Mike: Did Flynn share this portable bar with anyone on the set?

Westmore: He shared it with the makeup man, who eventually died from too much drinking! You know, Mike, with all the flamboyancy, gaiety, and laughter of Flynn, there was one time I actually saw him cry from his heart. He had a dog that he dearly loved. A schnauzer. Every time he went out on his yacht he would take the dog. One night he was returning from a trip to Catalina, and everyone was below drinking and eating. Errol called for the dog. Of course, in Catalina during the summer the flying fish fly. They jump on the boats. Evidently, the dog went for one of these flying fish and went overboard! Errol cried for three days after losing that dog.

Mike: Did your creative ability ever get expressed in ways other than makeup and hairstyling?

Westmore: Several times. Once was when I was working with Marion Davies on *Cain and Mabel*. Before the picture began, I had conceived an idea for a musical number which was a wedding procession. The whole stage was to be taken up with an enormous carved white pipe organ and a black background. As the camera dollied in, you noticed the carvings started to move. They came out of their positions and danced on the keys. The dancers would pull the stops on the organ keys, like for "violin," and the camera would pan up to the pipes which would open up and reveal girls playing the violin. By the end of the number all the stops were pulled, and you saw fifty girls playing different instruments. Then the bride and groom, Marion Davies and Clark Gable, walked down an aisle toward the organ. In the final shot the camera panned from the organ up to the sky, and there are the heads of fifty young boys singing! Well, I went to Marion's big bungalow, which had been brought all the way across town from the MGM lot, and told her my idea. She said, "I want W.R. to see all this." So when Mr. William Randolph Hearst came in about four o'clock that afternoon, he said, "I like it! Can we get Mr. Warner over here? And Busby Berkeley and Lloyd Bacon and the head of construction?" It was arranged. We showed all of them the idea, and Busby, who was the musical number director, said, "It's beautiful! I want to do it!" So Mr. Warner looked at Mr. Hearst and said, "But we don't have a stage tall enough for this." Mr. Hearst said, "What would it cost to raise one of the stages?" The construction boss replied, "Oh, between eighty and a hundred thousand dollars." Mr. Hearst said, "Mr. Warner, I will pay for half if you pay the other half." They raised the stage. It is stage seven on this lot today. While the number was being shot, I decided not to ever watch. The last day arrived, and Marion called me from the set and said, "Perc, come on down. We've just finished the whole number!" At the end of every picture we always had a cocktail party. I went down and Marion handed me a package. She said, "Here's a little something for you, Perc. I wanted to give you a Cadillac, but you know how wives are." I opened it, and it was a solid platinum wristwatch with numerals set in baguette diamonds! Then she handed me another package which was long and thin. She said, "Open it. It's from W.R." It was a beautiful alligator wallet with gold tips. Inside were five brand-new one-thousand-dollar bills! These things don't happen today in this business.

Mike: What picture required the most unusual or imaginative makeup?

Westmore: Probably *A Midsummer Night's Dream*. It was one of the films I most enjoyed creating the makeup for. It was Olivia de Havilland's first picture at Warner's. We had about five girls to test for the part, but before Olivia even tested, I said, "This is the girl!" I've been asked many times who in my opinion was the best proportioned beauty in a face, and I have always said Olivia de Havilland. The makeup for the picture was elaborate. James Cagney had to have the head of a donkey in one sequence. I cast a small donkey head that would fit over his own and be animated when he moved his own mouth. Mickey Rooney, who played Puck, had to wear a small mechanical box under his goatskin pants so that when he jumped up and down, his tail would move. The part of Oberon was played by Victor Jory. His chariot was to be pulled by palomino horses. I went to the director, Max Reinhardt, to discuss how these horses could be embellished with a look of fantasy. Reinhardt didn't speak English. He had a couple of German aides around to interpret for him. However, it turned out I was left alone in the office with him, and he said, "What we do?" In using broad gestures as I talked to him, I said, "Let me take big men, six foot six or bigger, and I will paint their whole bodies black. I will make big wings that go all the way from their wrists to their ankles, and we can put them on wires, and they can fly with the chariot!" Reinhardt looked at me and said, "Mr. Westmore, can you really do this?" I was shocked he could talk English. I said, "You speak English?" He said, "Yes. Don't tell anybody we talk together."

Mike: What makeup job presented the most problems?

Westmore: Mr. Warner loaned me to RKO for ten thousand dollars, to him, to create the makeup for Charles Laughton in *The Hunchback of Notre Dame*. Laughton was in England when I went to work on my preproduction makeup experiments. I had a death mask of Laughton's face. I made twelve copies of it and molded twelve different makeup ideas for the character on them. One idea was that one eye would be grotesquely deformed and low on the cheek. Laughton arrived and came in and looked at these heads. One, two, three. That quickly. "Oh, no, no, Perc! You see, it should look like the seashore, the eye. The water running in and running out." I had spent about two weeks, day and night, doing all this modeling and coloring, and he looked at it for three minutes! From then on I knew Mr. Laughton and I would be having conflicts. My assistant, Gordon Bau, who is now head of the department at Warner's and an excellent lab technician, and I began more experiments. We started to take casts. We would model molds and bake rubber masks in them for eight to ten hours. We'd take the rubber out of the mold and put it on Laughton's face. He'd say, "Oh, no, no, that's not it." We got to a point where we had cast an apple barrel full of molds before we settled on one. For the false eye itself, I built a little copper armature that fit over his nose and was attached to a copper lid I built over a glass eye. I ran a catgut from this copper lid and glued it to his upper lid, so that when he animated his real lid under the mask, the false eye on his cheek animated!

Then we got to the part of taking a cast for the hunchback. Now I knew I had Laughton where I wanted him. He was down on his hands and knees, and we started laying all the plaster on his back. During this procedure he looked up at me and said, "Perc, can I have a 7-Up?" I said, "Yes, Mr. Laughton." As I was talking to him, I was shaking a bottle of 7-Up. I said, "I don't know whether I should go around and kick you in the fanny or let you have it right in the puss for all the grief you've put me through!" He said, "No, no, no, Perc, no!" And with that I let him have the 7-Up in the face, and I sneaked around and gave him a little boot also.

When we got all the makeup assembled and made the tests and everything was OK, shooting began at the RKO ranch here in the valley on exterior scenes. Gordon Bau executed the makeup for the entire cast. After three or four days I got a call from the head of RKO, Pandro Berman, to run out and see Mr. Laughton, that he was unhappy. This was the exterior set of the cathedral of Notre Dame. When I arrived, Laughton said, "You know, Perc, I think we should start this all over again." There were fifteen hundred people working on the set, and he had refused to work for a day and a half! He said, "Let's sit down and discuss this." We walked over to the doors of the cathedral, opened them up, went into the hollow stage, and sat down. I said, "What's on your mind?" He said, "You know, I want you to go to Pandro Berman and tell him you don't like the look of the makeup and you want to start all over. Then we will get Von Sternberg to make some sketches. I had dinner with him last night, and he was telling me his impression of how I should look." I got up from my chair, opened the two huge cathedral doors and said, "Mr. Laughton, out there are fifteen hundred extras, some of them with hungry bellies. If you are the last actor living, I will never touch you again. Go out and play your part. I am not going to Pandro." I left. Later that afternoon Laughton came to Warner's to see me and said, "Oh, Perc, forgive me."

Mike: He certainly was a perfectionist, and it showed in the results.

Westmore: In the scene in which he was tied and whipped in the town square, then left there in pain and thirst, there is a big close-up of him begging for water. The pretty girl, played by Maureen O'Hara, goes to him. He looks up at her with a tortured face and repeats, "Water." Well, for this close-up, Laughton had his wardrobe man kneeling behind him twisting his foot to give him actual pain that would register in his face. The camera kept rolling as Laughton looked into it and said, "Water." He would look around at the wardrobe man and say, "A little harder, a little harder," then back at the camera and say, "Water, water."

Mike: All that would have been on film; then the film editor chose the proper part to be used. I think it was one of the best close-ups I've ever seen.

Westmore: Yes. But Laughton gave me an awful lot of trouble. He was out of town when the premiere took place. I went to it. Afterward I walked across the street to a Western Union office and sent him a telegram to New York: "I've just seen the picture. You might think you're the greatest actor living today. Tonight I've seen you lay an egg in a belfry."

Mike: Actually he was magnificent in the role!

Westmore: But I refused ever to work with him again. Years later he was cast in *The Blue Veil* with Jane Wyman to play a corset salesman. I was sitting in a makeup chair directing the test of Janie as an old lady. All of a sudden someone behind me put his hands around my throat. I knew by instinct it was Laughton. I said, "Turn loose, or you're going to be very unhappy." I jumped up from the chair so that the chair was kicked back against him. From then on we became very good friends. His wife, Elsa Lanchester, was a sweetheart. We've laughed about these things together. I've got to admit Charles was a pro. But I think the two greatest pros that I ever worked with were Bette Davis and Paul Muni.

Mike: One of the biggest Warner stars in the late forties and fifties was Doris Day. Did you work on any of her pictures?

Westmore: Yes. I remember the first morning the director, Mike Curtiz, brought her into the makeup department. He had taken her off a band stage the night before. Here's a little girl that arrives, and all I could see was a gum-chewing, overbleached blonde. She was doing one-night stands singing with the band. Obviously she was curling and bleaching her own hair, which was practically a wreck. She knew nothing about makeup. Warner wanted her tested. He used to pay me a big compliment by saying, "We hire talent, Westmore does the rest." I started in testing Miss Day with every color of hair, length of hair, different types of makeup. Even to a hard type with black hair. I'd say we spent around fifty thousand dollars on tests!

Those were the days when Doris Day was a very sweet little girl, a wonderful girl. But as she grew, she began to change. We had quite a conflict one time. We used to do all the hair coloring for all the contract players right here at the studio. If a player wanted to go somewhere else, I would have to know the name of the salon. When you are in production, you can't have one color one minute, then go in for a touch-up the next week and have the color of your hair change. The only reason we did the hair coloring at the studio was to keep it under control! She took it upon herself to go to some salon in Beverly Hills and have her hair done while we were in the middle of a picture. There was a detectable change in the color tone. She continued doing this for almost two months. Then I received an exorbitant bill, which I got into quite a discussion with Doris Day about. To the point of an argument. From that day until this, we have never talked. In fact, the makeup man who started with her on the television series she does nowadays wanted me to come along as a second man and take Doris Day over, because he had another picture he wanted to do. I said, "Just mention my name to Doris Day, and she'll shake her head."

Mike: Doris Day had only been at Warner's two or three years when you decided to retire in order to look after your salon and cosmetic business.

Westmore: Yes. In 1950 I left Warner's. I ran my salon, wrote a book for the woman at home to use as a guide to her makeup and hairstyling, worked with an optical firm, and did the Art Linkletter TV show *House Party*. I also did *Queen for a Day* and makeup for twenty-five hundred queens! I even opened my own makeup school, but somehow I was not happy doing any of these things. I spent twelve unhappy years. Finally, I went to a very good psychiatrist and found out what was wrong: I was missing the creative thing of this business. That is when I made up my mind to close my salon, disinterest myself with my cosmetic line, and get back into motion pictures full time. I went to work at Universal, where I created the makeup for *The Munsters* television series. Lew Wasserman, who had been Bette Davis' manager, was now head of Universal. He knew I had been doing some lecturing. He was organizing the now-popular tour of the studio, and he had me lecture the women tourists. I would do my makeup in the morning and two or three forty-minute lectures the rest of the day. There were promises of bigger things, but at the end of two years they gave me a tie for Christmas!

I packed up my things and left. I came back here to Warner's, my old home. In the last couple of years I have done two big pictures here: Kirk Douglas in *The Arrangement* and Kirk Douglas in *The Crooked Man*. Kirk is a pro. A lot of people say he is tough to get along with. When I first met him, he said, "Perc, I want you to remember I am a star!" I looked him in the eye and said, "Yes, Kirk. I am a star in my business, too. Not only a star, a patriot." I enjoyed working with Kirk. At the present time I am doing the Bill Cosby TV series. Speaking of pros, he is one. It's like the old days on the set. It's a good morning with everybody. No confusion. Bill does not allow anybody who is loudmouthed or arrogant on the set. He doesn't smoke cigarettes, but he gives the cigars hell! He doesn't drink. You hear no profanity from him. And at the end of every show, there is the traditional cocktail party given by our production manager, Marvin Miller.

Mike: It's been exactly fifty years since you became a wigmaker at age twelve in Cleveland, Perc. Your career has been the most successful among motion-picture makeup artists.

Westmore: Do you know what I say about that, Mike?

Mike: What?

Westmore: I say, "I'm just a lucky barber!" And there's one thing I'm sure of: I'll never retire from this business again.

NOTE: Perc Westmore died shortly after this interview in 1970.

November 5, 1969 and
June 1, 1970

Hairstyling

NELLIE MANLEY

Manley: I'm pure Midwestern. My grandparents built the first house in Afton Junction, Iowa. I was born in Omaha, Nebraska. My mother died when I was four, and my grandmother and two aunts raised me. I was such a little brat nobody really wanted me. I was always running away. To this day I run away from anything I don't like. I just get on the train or plane and take off!

When I got married, I wasn't of age. I had to stay in high school another year. My husband was a traveling salesman for the Palmolive Company. In whatever town he would be working, we would spend the weekend together. One morning I woke up, and he said, "Let's go to California!" I said, "You're crazy!" He said, "No. Let's go today!" I jokingly said, "Fine. Fine." He got up and dressed and went out for a while. When he came back, he said, "Are you packed? I've quit my job and we're going to California!" We had a little coupe and some camping equipment. We began driving down the highway. When we were crossing the wheatfields, he stopped and got out of the car and took all the advertising Palmolive had given him and threw it into the fields! I knew then we were really going.

As soon as we arrived in Los Angeles, I got a job as a hairdresser. I had had a little training. One day I was reading an article in the newspaper about Cecil B. De Mille, and I decided I'd like to work on motion pictures. The next day I rode the streetcar all the way from Hollywood to the De Mille Studio at 6600 Washington Boulevard in Culver City and applied for a job as a hairdresser. The man I happened to see was George Westmore, the father of the famous makeup family. He was the greatest in the business. He hired me, and I worked as one of his assistants for a few pictures which Samuel Goldwyn produced at the same studio. The De Mille Studio and Goldwyn Studio shared the same address. I stayed with Samuel Goldwyn's company when he moved into his new studio in Hollywood about 1931. I was usually assigned to work on pictures starring Vilma Banky. In fact, in 1926 the first picture I did by myself was with Vilma Banky and Ronald Colman called *The Winning of Barbara Worth.* Gary Cooper had the second male lead. Vilma didn't speak English very well. She was from Germany. Once Mr. Goldwyn had me travel with her to Canada to renew her visa. When she married another big Goldwyn star, Rod La Rocque, the studio held a very elaborate and highly publicized wedding. They went to France on their honeymoon, and Mr. Goldwyn sent me along to be the personal hairdresser to Vilma. When I returned from this trip, I went to work for Paramount, where I remained for thirty-one years. They closed the makeup and hairdressing department in 1967, as far as feature films were concerned.

Mike: You went to Paramount about the time sound was coming in.

Manley: Yes. Some of the female stars there at that time were Carole Lombard, Marlene Dietrich, Fay Wray, Claudette Colbert, Jean Arthur, Louise Brooks, Mary Brian, and Clara Bow. One day they all grouped in front of the dressing room building and declared they were not going to talk in films! I remember standing in the doorway and hearing them discussing it very thoroughly. It was about six in the evening, and they had just come in from their sets. There was only one actress who held to their vow. Louise Brooks. She never did a talking picture. In one of her pictures they got a double who they put on a couch with her back to the camera. The actor she was playing with had his face to the camera. The two of them carried on a conversation in that scene, but the rest of the picture was silent.

Mike: In one morning's work you did the hair for more than one star, I suppose.

Manley: Oh, yes! Paramount had one big hairdressing room with three double-mirrored tables. It would be nothing to have all the lady stars sitting at these mirrors at the same time. They reported to the hairdressers the first thing when they arrived at the studio for the day. We would wash their hair, then iron it dry. In later years we used pincurls. Still later rollers came in. Now we use hot rollers. Technique has been upgraded all along. Before their hair was combed out, they went to the makeup department. Then they came back to the hairdresser. If an actress was to be on the set at eight, we would usually have to start working on her at six thirty. If you were shooting on location and had to leave the studio at seven, the actress had to be in hairdressing at five thirty. There is always a hairdresser present right on the set, because hair must be constantly kept in place so that it matches in each take. That's a very trying and precise job. You are always on your feet working. On the set a star usually has a portable dressing room or a trailer just outside the stage door. The hairdresser always keeps her supplies near this spot so as to be ready at a moment's notice.

Mike: Don't most actresses prefer to use the same hairstylist all the time?

Manley: If possible. You become rather personally involved with one another. When an actress comes in so early in the morning, you are the first person she talks with that day. She may want to tell you her problems! She may have had a fight with her boyfriend, or her husband, or the kids might have been ill all night! They have to tell someone about it! You become quite a confidante. It's almost like being a wet nurse! You have to feel for them and be able to cope with their daily worries.

Mike: What actresses have you most enjoyed working with?

Manley: I think I've worked with all the big stars, both men and women, and I can say to you honestly that I haven't found any that I didn't like. There was a short time that I didn't like Loretta Young. I guess I just didn't understand her. She always brought her own hairdresser in with her. Two or three times, this hairdresser had to leave the show, and I was told to go down and do Loretta's hair. I guess my feelings were hurt that I had to pick up somebody else's work. Loretta and I finally became very good friends. I adore her now.

Mike: When you discovered the best style for a star's hair, would she keep that style to help create a recognizable image?

Manley: Usually. I remember one director always told the girls, "If you change your hairstyle all the time, the public just bats its eyes and says, 'Who's that?'" So most of them kept to a basic style. Carole Lombard never did change. They wore very simple hairdos, unless they were doing a period picture.

Mike: During preproduction does the star come to you to decide what style she will have for the film?

Manley: Yes. You talk it over. You've both read the script and know what kind of character she is playing and what the scenes call for. You also have to be sure the director, producer, and cameraman all agree that what you are planning is right. We used to spend days screen testing hairstyles. Now, hardly any tests are ever made. When Olivia de Havilland did *The Heiress,* we spent a week testing her hair! It had to be a very severe hairdo to help her look like an old maid. I used braids and still kept a smooth line around her face.

Mike: Cecil B. De Mille used to make lots of tests of hair, makeup, and wardrobe, didn't he?

Manley: More than any other director I ever worked with. I did all his pictures during my years at Paramount. For *Samson and Delilah* he picked out an Indian wig we had in stock for Victor Mature to wear. We called in an extra to model the wig. I put it on him, and it was too long in back, so I kept folding it back and forth until it was gathered up above his neck. Then I put a piece of leather strap around it and tied a knot. De Mille, who never could remember my name, said, "Girl, that's it! We'll open on his back so we just see his hair; then when he turns around, we see it is Samson!"

Mike: Did you do much research for period pictures?

Manley: Yes, but most of my hairstyles were invented right on the set. Another example from *Samson and Delilah* was Hedy Lamarr's hair. We tested it while Edith Head tested her costumes. Hedy's own hair was shoulder-length and quite beautiful. De Mille said, "Tie it back." So I tied it back behind her neck. De Mille told Hedy to shake her head to make the hair switch. She did, but nothing happened. He said, "There's not enough hair. I want it to switch like a horse's tail." I ran upstairs to get a handful of hair, all the time picturing the rear end of a horse! Back on the set, I tied a heavy cord around part of this hair so it would stand out from Hedy's head and the remainder of it would fall like a horse's tail. She shook her head again, and De Mille liked the result. We named it the horse's tail, but when the publicity department got hold of it, it became the ponytail. That style was popular for many years!

Mike: The picture was one of the most successful of the many De Mille epics, wasn't it?

Manley: Yes. It was a difficult and long film to make. After it was finished I went to Hawaii on a vacation. When I returned to the studio, I was told Mr. De Mille wanted to see me. I threw up my hands and said, "Oh, now what have I done?" I went to his office, and he talked excitedly about the picture. He had an envelope in his hand he kept flipping. He said, "When I give you this, I don't want you to tell anybody what it is!" I practically ran to the elevator where I could open it in privacy. It was a check!

Mike: What was it for?

Manley: He had made me one of the recipients of what is called the De Mille Bunny Award. He gave certain people who had worked on *Samson and Delilah*, and other of his films through the years, a percentage of the money he got from *Samson and Delilah*. He never told anyone the exact percentage they were getting, but just the other day I got another check in the mail! When I pass on, the money coming to me goes back into the fund from which it comes.

Mike: I never heard of a producer making such a nice gesture.

Manley: It surprised me, because De Mille never let on that he liked you at all. He was a man who yelled a lot, as if it were a part of his showmanship. Once on a big spectacle a battle scene was being filmed, and the press was invited to watch. De Mille decided one of the hundreds of extras in the camera foreground needed a different wig. We didn't have any more wigs on hand. He picked up the microphone and proceeded, for the benefit of the audience, to tell me he spent thousands of dollars on tests and wigs, and I had put them in a vault so that he could not get to them!

Mike: Did he have a habit of yelling at you in particular? Some directors, like Otto Preminger, pick out someone they can harass throughout the production.

Manley: It seemed I was oftentimes getting it from De Mille! When we filmed the first version of *The Buccaneers* with Fredric March there was a German girl named Franciska Gaal who played a powder monkey. Every time we got her made up to look dirty and messy, she would go off and take out a pocket mirror and fix herself up. I was in her dressing room on the set with her one day, and I heard De Mille bawling me out unmercifully over the loudspeaker about her looking too good. As I left the dressing room, De Mille was about to go in. Out of the corner of his mouth he said, "We have to stick together!" Bawling me out was his way of getting to the actress.

Mike: Good directors like De Mille always have in their mind's eye how they want an actress or actor to look.

Manley: Yes. I remember William Wyler had exactly in mind how he wanted Audrey Hepburn to look when he directed her the first time in *Roman Holiday*. I did the hair tests for Audrey which were made in New York. At that time we cut her hair so that she had a little boy look. The picture was made in Rome. In the beginning of the picture we put three falls of hair on her head so that, when the time came in the story for her to get her hair cut, it was the falls that were being cut. Nevertheless, publicity poured out that she was wearing an Italian haircut!

Mike: What actress did you create the widest variety of hairstyles for?

Manley: Marlene Dietrich. I have a copy of the book *The Films of Marlene Dietrich,* and it amazes me when I look at all those photographs and realize I did her hairstyle in every one of them! I think to myself, "I couldn't possibly have done that many heads of hair," but I did all of Marlene's pictures at Paramount, and we became good friends. Beginning with her first picture in this country, she was master of it all. I mean, she could do most everything for herself!

Mike: Much has been said that the director who brought her to America, Josef von Sternberg, created her image by the way he dressed and photographed her. Did he tell you how to do her hair also?

Manley: No. That is sort of a myth. He was a great director, but I did with him only what I did with every other director. I'd do Marlene's hair for a role, then ask him if he liked it or not, and he would say yes or no or tell me to try something else. However, he was always very careful about photography, and he was a master of lighting effects. If there was a shadow on Marlene's face, he would move the light or tell Marlene to move a bit. Any director would have done the same. But he built a reputation of being the big boss and telling everyone else how to do their work. He didn't actually design her clothes, do her makeup, plan her hairstyles, or anything like that. That reputation has been very wrong.

Mike: I read Von Sternberg's autobiography, *Fun in a Chinese Laundry,* and, if a man can write that entertainingly, he must have had respectful talent in many other directions.

Manley: He was very set in his desires and opinions about how his films should be made, but his self-assertion overpowered his talent.

Mike: I believe more people have attained success in Hollywood through self-assertion or a unique type of arrogance than they have on talent and artistic ability.

Manley: A few personalities who have been humble have made it to the top. Dietrich was very withdrawn about expressing her personal desires or demanding personal comfort and consideration. For instance, in the second picture I did with her, *Catherine the Great,* she had to wear wigs. If one hair was out of place, Von Sternberg would yell at me. There was a problem one day when Marlene had to wear a wig on top of which was the imperial Russian crown. At nine o'clock we had her on the set ready to start work, and she suddenly said to me, "Oh, it's killing me! There's something sticking right into my head!" I wanted to do something about it, but she wouldn't let me. She didn't want to hold up production or get Von Sternberg annoyed. I suffered with her all morning because every time I looked at her, she gave me a tortured look. Finally, they called lunch, and I immediately walked to her and began correcting the matter. Not unexpectedly, Von Sternberg saw what was going on and calmly said, "Why didn't you tell me?" Marlene and I both knew that if we had told him during shooting, he would have jumped all over both of us!

Mike: Did you work with Dietrich when she went to England to make a film for Alexander Korda called *Night Without Honor*?

Manley: Yes. I was the first hairdresser ever sent with a star to work on a film in Europe. Marlene had a bathtub scene in that picture. She worked in the tub a whole day. She had on panties and a bra, but every time she stood up they were so wet it didn't make much difference! After every take she would step out of the tub and a wardrobe girl would wrap a large towel around her. We finished for the day, and Marlene stepped out of the tub for the last time. She turned around to the girl who was holding the towel, and both her feet slipped out from under her on the soapsuds! It was the funniest sight I ever saw. The wardrobe girl quickly threw the towel over her.

I remember another Dietrich picture on which the great cameraman George Barnes worked. Dietrich's blond hair was naturally shiny, but he wanted it to shine more for this picture. We discussed it, and he said, "Why don't we put some gold on her hair?" So I got a little bag of gold dust from the paint shop, and if George couldn't get the light to shine on a certain part of her hair the way he wanted it to, I would sprinkle the area with gold dust! By the time we were finished working every night the gold had settled on her scalp, and I would have to wash her hair and put oil on it. The next morning I would wash the oil off and start all over again.

Mike: Sometimes photographers are as helpful as directors at inventing things like that, aren't they?

Manley: George Barnes was always very helpful, and he always wanted things done correctly. The first time I was given a piece of hair lace to use on an actress, I didn't know how to put it on! It was a new concoction made by Wally Westmore. After work that night, I had to go over to the Westmore salon on Sunset and practice putting the hair lace on until midnight! The next day I was able to use it correctly on the actress, so that George Barnes approved and OKed it.

Mike: Is everything attached to the hair considered hairdressing, or is some of it wardrobe?

Manley: Any work on the hair is done by the hairdresser, but the wardrobe department may furnish accessories such as ribbons, bows, or clips. I like using things like that. I do it a great deal currently with Susan St. James, whom I work on at Universal. In fact, I have my own collection of accessories which is easier than turning them into the wardrobe department every day.

Mike: I think one of the most unusual hairdos any actress ever had was Veronica Lake's long blond hair which hung over one eye.

Manley: There was a very charming hairdresser at Paramount named La Vaughn Speer who created the Veronica Lake hairdo. Veronica had beautiful silky blond hair which had to be rolled just so to get that wave to hit at a certain angle over her right eye. Many times I watched La Vaughn slave over getting that wave perfect for the camera. And when Veronica went on, I'm telling you, she looked pretty elegant! A natural blonde is the most difficult hair to manage because it is a finer grain and soft and slippery. It just slides out of your fingers! Madeleine Carroll had about the finest head of blond hair I can remember. She was one of the most beautiful and gentle girls I've ever known. Everyone adored working with her. Mr. Westmore referred to her as "his girl."

Mike: Later there was another very ladylike blonde at Paramount in the person of Grace Kelly!

Manley: Now you're talking about *my* girl! When Grace first came to Paramount, they wanted to change her completely. She was doing a film which Alfred Hitchcock was directing. He said, "I don't want any of that hair hanging down. Make it simple." So I just combed it back and made a knot, and that's how Princess Grace got her plain hairstyle which she still wears often. To this day she affectionately calls me Mother Knot!

Mike: Did you ever work with the first of the famous blondes, Jean Harlow?

Manley: Yes. Her natural hair was a pale light blond. She didn't dye her hair platinum blond until she was fairly well known. To do that she used a prebleach that at that time was so strong it burned the hair up! It made her hair so dry and brittle that it would just break off. The scalp wasn't affected very much. Later, when we researched Jean for the film Paramount made about her life, *Harlow* with Carroll Baker, we found some still photographs of her as an extra sitting in a café scene in an old Paramount picture. We were able to make Carroll Baker look amazingly like Jean Harlow. After Carroll finished making *Harlow,* the studio sent her to London on a publicity trip. I was sent with her. We traveled by ship. The passengers all got off when we arrived in England, but Carroll and I stayed aboard for a press luncheon with about two hundred reporters and photographers. In the middle of this affair, Carroll and I retired to her stateroom and transformed her into the character of Jean Harlow. This was a planned publicity stunt which took only a few minutes to do. She reappeared in the dining room and stood by a large column. A spotlight was thrown on her, and you never heard so much whistling and hollering in your life! She really looked marvelous. The photographers took hundreds of pictures!

Mike: Did Carroll Baker dye her hair to look like Harlow, or did she wear a wig?

Manley: We made Carroll's own blond hair more blond.

Mike: How do you feel about the use of hair coloring in everyday life?

Manley: I think it can be quite beautiful. Most women and many men are using it because, of course, it can make one look twenty years younger. There are so many good products available. Often it is very difficult to tell if a person is using coloring or not.

Mike: Did the advent of color motion pictures cause more actresses to start using hair coloring?

Manley: Oh, yes! Most girls wanted to highlight the natural color of their hair. Actually we didn't know at the beginning what colors to use. I was one of many who were fishing to find out what certain colors of hair would look like in the developed film because the film did not reproduce color exactly. Orange came through quite strong! Lucille Ball always had bright orange hair, but she colored it even more vividly, so that when she was photographed she looked like a hot potato! She burned up the whole screen, but she could afford to do it because she was playing comedy. Incidentally, the most elaborate hairdo I ever created was for Lucy in a picture she did with Bob Hope. She wore a tall white wig with a birdcage in it! And with a live bird in the cage!

Mike: Have you found that the color of an actress' hair has any effect on her personality or temperament?

Manley: Not at all. I think to a degree temperament is influenced by one's nationality. And nationality, may, in turn, have something to do with the color of one's hair. For instance, I'll never forget the vivacious antics of Paramount's Latin star Lupe Velez. She was always into everything and always playing jokes. She was so full of pep they called her the Mexican Spitfire. I worked on her films at the same period that I worked with Marlene Dietrich. Lupe had a long romance with Gary Cooper. One day she was very late in showing up for work. I was told to stand by her dressing room and grab her the minute she came in and get her ready. At twelve thirty she stuck her head around the door and said coyly, "Nellie, baby, I have a present for you." I said, "Please, come on and let's get dressed. They're waiting for you!" She came in with one hand behind her and repeated, "I have a present for you!" It was a hairbrush because I was always saying, "Lupe, if you don't behave, I'm going to take a hairbrush to you." As I was getting her dressed, I asked her why she was late. She said, "The son of a beetch, he went out and bought himself a car, so I go out this morning and buy myself a car!" The day before Gary Cooper had bought himself a Duesenberg.

Mike: Didn't Lupe Velez also have a romance with the cowboy star Tom Mix?

Manley: Yes. I remember when we were on location up at June Lake one time, she would telephone him at the end of each day's work. There was only one telephone at the June Lake Lodge, and everyone would stick his head over the balcony and listen to all the phone conversations! Lupe would say into the phone, "Oh, Tom, I love you!" Then she'd look up at the boys on the balcony and say, "Son of a beetch!" She was a cute, adorable, misbehaving child. She was working at MGM when she committed suicide with an overdose of sleeping pills.

Mike: Do you enjoy going on location for a film?

Manley: I don't mind it, but I prefer the studio. I recently was in

Albuquerque to do a television film. I also go to Las Vegas on location. But the most elaborate location I ever went on was when we went to the Russian River in Northern California to make *Frenchman's Creek* with Joan Fontaine and Arturo de Cordoba. It was directed by Mitchell Leisen, who had been an assistant to Cecil B. De Mille. The men had to wear long curly wigs like Louis XIV! We had almost two hundred of these wigs we had to take on location with great care. The problem of keeping them all groomed was made more difficult by the fact we ran into rainy weather!

Mike: Do actresses wear wigs very often in films nowadays?

Manley: Very often. Whether it is a period film or not.

Mike: Do you like the everyday use of wigs by women?

Manley: Yes. Many times I've been very surprised to discover a person was wearing a wig. Women are getting to where they know how to care for them and how to wear them properly. You can soak and wash them in hot water, shake them dry, and put them on! They look exceedingly well, and I like them. It's the women with long dirty hair that drive me crazy. I hate the long hair on men, unless it has a Western look. Not to be able to see a person's eyes, or even their nose sometimes, is ridiculous. I told one young actress, "You can buy hair in almost any store in town, but your eyes are your own. Why don't you show them so people can see how beautiful they are?" I think the older actresses are more conscious of what goes on the screen. Even some of the new directors of today are not so concerned with seeing the faces of the actresses. They seem to just want to get the picture in the can and get away. Especially in television.

Mike: When you are between shots on a film and you touch up someone's hair, are you ever allowed to touch up her makeup as well?

Manley: Oh, no. Before the days of the union Paramount used to have four girls who did only face makeup. When the union was organized, all the makeup artists were men, and all the hairstylists were women. I'm the last of the thirteen girls who started the hairdressers' guild. There are a few male hairstylists now. Sidney Guilaroff is the most well known. He does Liz Taylor's hair. He was at MGM many years.

Mike: How does a girl get into your guild?

Manley: The girls have to have at least two years' experience in a beauty shop. Then they have to pass our examination. For this examination the applicants are locked up in a room. Each of them has a number, and they work on the hair of a model with a matching number. When the styling is finished, all the models come into another room where judges study their hair without knowing which applicant has performed the work. On this basis, the person who has done the work either passes or does not pass. Recently, we had among our applicants three colored girls. A colored hairdresser was also brought in to be one of the judges. Only one of these three girls passed the examination. The other two, through some organization, are protesting the results as being unfair! The guild tries to keep up its standards solely on talent and ability. Nothing else. It takes time for a girl to come out of a shop and be able to cope with the working habits on a movie set. You are always working side by side with a lot of men. There is hardly ever any place to sit down. You have to carry your equipment everywhere you go. And the hours are especially long. Your work has to please the actress, the director, the producer, and the cameraman! It is a lot different from the working conditions in one's private booth at a beauty salon.

April 3, 1970

Special Visual Effects

ARNOLD "BUDDY" GILLESPIE

Gillespie: My introduction to the motion-picture business came about as a result of having been in World War I when I met a guy named Cullen Tate. We used to call him Hesi Tate. He had been an assistant to Cecil B. De Mille. After the war I went to Columbia University and studied advertising and journalism and to the Art Students' League and studied art. I came to California in 1922, and the first thing I did was go out to see Hesi at Paramount Studios. Jokingly one day I asked Hesi if there was any job in the movies. He said, "Are you a draftsman?" I said yes. They needed a man for about two weeks, and I got the job. The picture De Mille was directing was *Manslaughter* with Thomas Meighan and Leatrice Joy. Paul Irebe was the art director. We worked seven days a week, an average of sixteen hours a day. I only got paid twenty-five dollars a week, but to me it was like being paid for going to school. I got the training for the whole workings of the art department.

Mike: What did you think of De Mille?

Gillespie: He was the first well-known person I came into contact with. He was a little bit misunderstood by his crews. He used to go into violent rages at the end of a day's shooting. I think he did this simply to proclaim his authority. He was the skipper of the ship more than any person I have known, and I came to know him very, very well. He had the support of the front office and did anything he wished. He was the total show. Money was no problem. He was the king, and for that reason I consider it a real privilege to have started my career as a kind of slave number forty-seven of De Mille's. I stayed on to do another De Mille picture, *Adam's Rib*, so I was at Paramount a total of eight months. De Mille had a layoff before his next scheduled picture, but I was able to get a job at the old Goldwyn Studio in Culver City working under Cedric Gibbons and Horace Jackson as a draftsman at sixty-five dollars a week. Samuel Goldwyn had built the studio but had already left to go over to a new studio in Hollywood, where he still operates.

Mike: Louis B. Mayer took over the operation of the studio in Culver City at about that time?

Gillespie: In March, 1924, the studio became Metro-Goldwyn-Mayer. *Ben Hur* was being made at a budget of four hundred thousand dollars, but it eventually cost four million. Another chap and I had saved up a little money and decided to go to Europe for a year. We knew, if we ran out of money, we could probably go down to Rome and work on the *Ben Hur* production. That's what happened. We had hit Paris during Christmas, and our money went fast! I stayed in Rome nineteen months working on *Ben Hur*. When I returned to the home studios of MGM in California, I was given a job as a unit art director under Cedric Gibbons. He was my real boss from then until he died in 1960. Cedric was a wonderful guy. From 1925 until 1936 I accumulated some two hundred and two credits as an art director. In 1936 I was made head of the special effects department and have been there ever since.

Mike: What do you classify as special effects?

Gillespie: The three main categories I have been concerned with are miniatures, full-size mechanical effects, and rear projection process.

These overlap into optical effects, into mat painting, and occasionally into animation. Animation has to be used so that it is not recognized as stop-motion photography, be it drawings or three-dimensional objects. It is quite different from cartoon animation. We use it on effects like denoting tracer bullets in war films. On at least ninety-eight percent of the films ever released by MGM, or any studio I would say, the special effects department has had some routine chores such as fire in a fireplace, rain or snow outside a window, and simple visual effects like that. These routine effects are generally handled by the property department because they do not present any particular problems. The relationship between the art department and the special effects department at MGM is very close. At some studios it has not always been equally harmonious.

Mike: Who was responsible for special effects before such a department was created?

Gillespie: Oh, there were people who made special effects before it was even called special effects. This work was coordinated under the art director of a picture. I remember when I was the art director on *San Francisco* with Jeanette MacDonald, Clark Gable, and Spencer Tracy. I had a great deal to do with the full-size effect of the earthquakes. It was my job to figure out how to do it, but I had a lot of help. *San Francisco* was previewed in Santa Barbara where there had been an earthquake about a year before. The day after the preview the film was the talk of the town because the earthquake scenes were so realistic. A few days later we previewed the film in Hollywood at Grauman's Chinese Theater. A wonderful-looking, raw-boned, red-necked woman sat in front of my wife and me. When the first rumble of the quake started, she sat up in her seat, eyes glued to the screen. During the destruction, she squirmed around like a contortionist. When the quake was over, she took out her handkerchief and mopped her face and was just getting settled down when the second quake hit! She went through the whole performance again. Her reaction was a real compliment. Jimmy Basevi did the miniatures. The miniatures are intercut on the screen with the full-size sets in which the real actors perform. That's when the audience swears they saw a building falling on someone. In full size you film a small portion of a building falling with a stunt man, then intercut it with a longer shot of miniatures showing the whole building fall. You can rehearse a full-size effect up to the point of actually doing the stunt. Stunt men insist on this. If it is, for instance, an automobile race and a skid, they go through it in slow motion, step by step, so that it is well planned and rehearsed. In miniature work where we are going to burn and destroy a city or blow up an aircraft carrier, you can't rehearse anything more than your cue.

Mike: You worked with Clark Gable and Spencer Tracy on another film called *Test Pilot*. Did you have many models of airplanes in that?

Gillespie: You call them models! My British cohorts call them models, too, but we call them miniatures. A model is something you put over a fireplace. A miniature is a working model. We used a lot of miniatures in *Test Pilot*. We did a miniature crash of a YB-17, the big bomber before the B-17. They had made the full-size set of the crashed plane and filmed Gable and Tracy crawling out of the wreckage, before we shot the miniature of the plane actually crashing. That was a bad thing to do because when you have a crash of a miniature, you have to duplicate in full size the shape of and position of the miniature wreckage. That is, your miniature is all smashed up, and you have to match that in your full-size set. Since the full-size set was already shot, we rehearsed three solid days with five cameras before actually filming the crash of the miniature YB-17. In *Test Pilot* we also used a lot of process shots: stationary sets in the foreground while the scenery and action in the background are actually being projected from the rear onto a screen. Most of the close shots of the actors in the airplanes were done like this on a sound stage with simulated weather. Snowstorms when necessary. Clark Gable didn't mind going through a certain amount of physical discomfort to get a scene. Spence would squawk, but generally with his tongue in his cheek. He was a wonderful guy. He wrote the foreword to my book, *Little Ones Out of Big Ones*. Other stars at MGM like Robert Taylor and Robert Young would tolerate discomfort also. They weren't temperamental.

Mike: I'm sure both male and female stars go through discomfort to get certain scenes. In the old days some stars even did their own stunt work. Especially Douglas Fairbanks, Sr.

Gillespie: Actually, in special effects I work closer with stunt men than I do actors. Often the effects we do are of natural disasters like the snow avalanche scene in *Seven Brides for Seven Brothers*. And in *Green Fire* with Stewart Granger we did a rock avalanche. There is an explosion that creates the avalanche which crashes down the mountain into the river and changes the course of the river. These scenes were all done in miniature, but sometimes a stunt man is doubling for the actor in the close shots which are intercut with the shots of the miniature effect.

Mike: *Ben Hur* is probably one of the most famous pictures for stunt work ever made. You have the distinction of having worked on two versions of it.

Gillespie: Yes. The *Ben Hur* with Ramon Navarro and Francis X. Bushman was generally made in Italy in 1923, '24, and '25. The chariot race was the highlight of the film. We had built a complete Roman circus in Italy, but the weather was wrong there in January, and the company came back to Hollywood. The race was eventually filmed right here in Culver City. The second unit director who shot all the thrilling close-up scenes of the race was named Breezy Eason, B. Reeves Eason. On the last version of *Ben Hur* with Charlton Heston and Stephen Boyd filmed mostly in Italy, too, in 1959, the race scenes were staged by the great stunt man Yakima Canutt. The second unit director was Andrew Marton. Between the two of them, they did a finer job than was done on the first *Ben Hur.* A sequence of this kind is largely the thinking of the man who dreams up the stunts. Yak Canutt, who is a past master, also had his son inventing stunts for the race. From there all the stunt men and other people involved had to get together to figure how to carry out the ideas. It might take two or three days to work out a method to do a stunt and be ready to shoot it.

Mike: How was the elaborate sea battle filmed in *Ben Hur*?

Gillespie: In the first *Ben Hur* we used full-sized galleys and sank them with real people aboard over in Italy. Later we used some miniature ones for additional shots. In the second *Ben Hur* the entire sea battle was done with miniature galleys and using intercuts to close shots of the actors. I was given the Academy Award for my work on the second version of *Ben Hur*.

Mike: What other films have won you Academy Awards?

Gillespie: *Thirty Seconds over Tokyo* (1944), *Green Dolphin Street* (1942), and *Plymouth Adventure* (1952). I guess the most intricate miniatures I've done were Jimmy Doolittle's B-25 bombers taking off from the carrier *Hornet* in *Thirty Seconds over Tokyo*. We used a scale of one inch to the foot and built about four-fifths of the deck of the *Hornet*. It was about sixty feet long, which shows that miniatures are not necessarily little. They can be anything less than full size. This miniature of the *Hornet* was set in our three-hundred-foot-square water tank. A miniature that big in a tank that small had to be kept stationary. We devised a method to make it appear the ship was moving. We made the ship rise, pitch, and roll hydraulically as we moved water past the ship with pumps and wave machines. The miniature bombers were attached to piano wires and took off with an overhead trolley controlled with little synchronous motors.

Mike: Have you done miniatures of cities being bombed?

Gillespie: Yes, but in scenes like that a lot can be left up to the imagination of the audience. In *Mrs. Miniver* audiences thought they saw London being bombed, but they actually didn't. We used a distant view of London, a skyline view, done in miniature with searchlights sweeping the sky, the sound of air-raid sirens, and flashes of bombs exploding. This miniature had originally been built for *Waterloo Bridge* with Robert Taylor and Vivien Leigh. We made use of it in *Mrs. Miniver* when Greer Garson and Walter Pidgeon are going into the air-raid shelter. Once they are down in the shelter, you have the feeling of their being bombed because of the use of sound and the rattle and shake of the room with dust coming down from above. You never saw any bombs hitting close by.

Mike: What about the bombing of Hiroshima you did for *The Beginning or the End?*

Gillespie: We did an atom bomb in that, but I think I'll let you read my book to see how we accomplished that feat! When officials at the Pentagon saw that picture, they were disturbed that the Signal Corps had never shown them this film before. That was quite a compliment. Actually, there was no real photographic record of the atom bomb over Hiroshima. The tail gunner of the B-29 that dropped the bomb was able to get one snapshot of the big ball of fire. That was the only research we had of what an atom bomb looked like from a distance.

Mike: Destruction by fire must be a challenging effect for you.

Gillespie: The most obvious problem with full-size fires is their proximity to people. There are various ways to make an audience feel an actor is in a fire, surrounded by flames, when there is no real danger. If you put fire between the camera and the actor and fire behind the actor and photograph with a long-focal-length lens, it foreshortens the distance so that the actor appears to be closer to the flames. He may get a little warm, but not in danger! The oil well fires in *Boom Town* (1940) and in the 1960 remake of *Cimarron* were done with process shots. The film of actual fires was projected onto a background screen, and actors performed in front of the screen as it was rephotographed. Here again, you can put fire between the actor and the camera for extra effect.

Mike: I remember in the remake of *Mutiny on the Bounty* Marlon Brando has to go onto the burning ship deck, and a flaming yardarm falls and pins him to the deck!

Gillespie: For that we used a tied-down camera, real fire, and a double for Brando who walked along the deck to a designated point, then fell. After that shot, we took the double out, and with the steady, unmoved camera we photographed the exact same area from the exact same angle and had the flaming yardarm fall on the exact spot where the double had fallen. Now we had two pieces of film which were put together with correct timing and a bit of optical mating out of the figure to obtain the visual effect desired. By the way, I did the original *Mutiny on the Bounty*, too, in 1935.

Mike: What about the burning of Rome in *Quo Vadis*?

Gillespie: A miniature set that is to be set afire is actually built so that it won't burn! The city of Rome in *Quo Vadis* was built almost entirely of plaster. It covered an area nearly nine hundred square feet. In other words, we built it in our tank. Copper tubes with nozzles were distributed into every building so that fuel could be fed and controlled. We used pilot lights to start the fire. As soon as the director said cut, we turned off the fuel supply, then went in with hoses and fire extinguishers to put out anything that might still be burning. With a controlled fire of that kind you can make several takes. We seldom destroy what we seem to destroy. With some minor repair work and a little paint a miniature city or ship can be used in other films. If you have a miniature field or forest on fire, it actually has to burn up, but many cameras are catching the blaze from different angles. When you are literally going to destroy something like that, it is terribly important that everything has been well prepared and rehearsed so that you get it right the first time and don't have to go to the time and expense of remaking it.

Mike: Like having a train destroyed in a wreck!

Gillespie: Train wrecks are normally done in miniature. However, in *How the West Was Won*, we had a full-size train wreck and a real train was used! The wreck was prolonged by the use of several cameras photographing from different angles. A certain amount of predetermined speed was reached; then the cars were derailed at a precise spot. It was also planned in advance where the derailed cars would go.

Mike: It was the most exciting train wreck I ever saw in a movie! I thought the sequence where the river raft was caught in the rapids was well done, too.

Gillespie: Yes. The long shots of the raft were made on the Feather River with doubles on it and intercut with shots made of the raft on a sound stage with real actors on it. Debbie Reynolds, Agnes Moorehead, and others. This raft was hydraulically controlled to pitch, tilt, and whirl in a small water tank while a process background was projected onto a screen behind it.

Mike: *How the West Was Won* had different directors and actors for each long sequence, didn't it?

Gillespie: Yes. I worked mostly with Henry Hathaway, a capable and competent director who has been misunderstood by probably eighty percent of his crews. I say misunderstood, but he has been very well understood! He saw to that! He wasn't exactly disliked. I think in some instances it was fear and in some cases jealousy because he is a fine director and a great technician. Few directors are such good technicians. John Sturges and Victor Fleming were. They had a sense of the physical phases of picture making. All three of these directors were stubborn. I think most talented people are stubborn. They have to be to get their ideas carried out. Hathaway insisted in *How the West Was Won* that a certain sequence be done the way he wanted it done. He turned a deaf ear to all the pleading that he cut down on costs because he wanted the sequence to be a success. If it was a flop, he would have been responsible. On the other hand, by spending so much money he would have also been responsible for that if it had still been a flop. But he knew the subject matter so well and how to do it that he went ahead with all confidence. You have to admire a man like that who is willing to put himself out on a limb. Even though it wasn't his money, it would have been his neck!

Mike: What film do you think you did the most interesting effects for?

Gillespie: *Forbidden Planet* because we did outer-space scenes, approaches to landings on planets, and the robot called Robbie. I had felt that most robots in science fiction movies had been a man in an aluminum suit. They all looked about the same, and I decided we ought to find a different kind of robot. I happened to think of the beautiful shape of the potbellied stoves of my youth. So Robbie the

Robot was designed basically from an old potbellied coal-burning stove.

Mike: You can really let your imagination go to work on science-fiction films, or any film that doesn't deal with the world and reality as we know it.

Gillespie: Sure. A fantasy film like *The Wizard of Oz* enabled us to create many interesting effects. The first one was the tornado, inside which Dorothy, her dog, and her house are taken to the land of Oz. We built the inside of the tornado in miniature and photographed it. Then we shot Dorothy and the dog inside the house looking out the window at the tornado they were carried up into. We did this by projecting the tornado film onto a screen which was the background out the window. You could see objects flying past the window, like the woman on the bicycle who later became the Wicked Witch of the West.

Mike: I especially liked the scene at the castle of the Wicked Witch when she sends out her army of flying monkeys.

Gillespie: It was originally decided to do the flying monkeys in cartoon animation. I was a little against this because I thought you would be able to tell it was animation on the screen. After a number of tests and experiments, they gave up the idea of animation, and we did it with miniature monkeys we cast and supported with twenty-two hundred piano wires! The wires supported them on an overhead trolley and moved their wings up and down. It was an awful job to hide the wires. They had to be painted and lighted properly so that they blended into whatever the background might be.

Mike: What about when the Wicked Witch herself is flying on her broom?

Gillespie: There is a scene where she takes off from her castle and soars into the air to skywrite the warning to Dorothy, "Dorothy Beware," signed "WWW," Wicked Witch of the West. The smoke comes out of the back of her broom. We shot this by pointing the camera up at the bottom of a glass-bottom tank into which we had put about half an inch of milk. Then we mixed sheep dip with a little nigrosine dye and put it in a stylus, with which we wrote from above and backward. A tiny miniature of the Wicked Witch on her broom was attached to the end of the stylus. The mixture of sheep dip and nigrosine dye being released in milk gave a cloudy, expanding effect just the way smoke does in the sky.

Mike: What was one of the toughest jobs you ever had to do?

Gillespie: I'd say a film called *Comrade X* with Hedy Lamarr and Clark Gable. The story takes place in Russia during the early days of the war. We had to do a whole armored tank sequence where the leads escape the country by getting into the general's tank. Dozens of other tanks follow, thinking the general is leading them. They go cross-country, through streams and rivers, and other obstacles. This was all done in miniature. Miniature landscape and miniature mechanical tanks! You can pull miniature race cars from underneath with a hidden cable in a slot, but when you have tanks going over contours and around corners and so forth, you have a big problem. A cable on the inside would not want to do that. We solved the problem by developing a sheave type cogwheel where the cable would go through a double series of spokes that allowed the cable plenty of freedom so that we could control it.

Mike: What film did you find most enjoyable to work on?

Gillespie: We had an awful lot of fun on the Tarzan pictures we made with Johnny Weissmuller. Being a frustrated stunt man, I used to go through all Johnny's stunts before him to show him how the set we had designed was to be utilized. We had all kinds of springboards and vines set up. There were nets to take care of him if he missed a swing! For the doubles of Tarzan, Jane, and Boy we employed a trapeze act called the Flying Cardonas. We had several acres of a jungle-type setting out at Sherwood Lake. None of the Tarzan pictures we made ever went to Africa on location, although on later pictures and on private trips I spent a great deal of time in Africa. In my profession I've had the fortune to have been all over the world. I've traveled many thousands of miles for MGM alone.

Mike: You must have worked with almost every star ever under contract at MGM. Did you enjoy working with some more than others?

Gillespie: Tracy and Gable certainly. Betty Hutton, Bob Taylor and Bob Young, Joan Crawford. Wallace Beery, Katie Hepburn. Outside work I was never too close to the people in the acting profession. Jean Harlow was an exception. My wife and I got to know Jean and her mother quite well. They had a beautiful house out on Beverly Glen. Jean was an exhibitionist in that she knew she had a beautiful body and didn't mind showing it, as long as it was not in a vulgar way. Nor did I ever hear her converse in a vulgar fashion or tell a questionable joke. She was a sex symbol, and that was fine with her and fine with her mother. But she was a very decent young lady.

Mike: One of my favorite actors who was in dozens of MGM pictures was Lionel Barrymore.

Gillespie: Lionel was an example of a guy who loved to work. We used to work Saturday nights often because the MGM production manager, Joe Cohn, would say everybody could sleep Sunday. It never bothered Lionel. He enjoyed being here on the lot more than anyone I knew. In 1919, when I was a student at Columbia, Lionel and John Barrymore were in a Broadway play called *The Jest*. A fraternity brother of mine named Van Wyck and I went to a matinee. We bought standing room only because we couldn't afford a regular seat. There is a scene where John is making love to Lionel's wife in the play. He bends her over, and there is a lot of panting and gasping. Van Wyck thought this was very funny, and right in the middle of this dramatic scene he goes, "Haw, haw, haw!" John Barrymore stopped and looked! Years later, when John was on the MGM lot, I told him I was with the guy who did that and asked him if he remembered the incident. He said, "Do I remember? How can I ever forget it? It ruined the whole show!"

Mike: What do you think of the way MGM was managed over the years?

Gillespie: From the early days until the present there have been certain individuals at this studio who have stood out. We have had especially good executives. A good executive is a man who surrounds himself with the best talent he can get and then lets them do their job. Cedric Gibbons, the head of our art department, was such an executive. Gibbons' great forte was that he gave people responsibility. And it was best they came through! He wanted to know what was going on, but granted a tremendous amount of freedom to his men.

This same attitude applied to Louis B. Mayer. I grew to know Mayer quite well. His whole theory was to get the best talent available. He had the finest stable of actors of any studio. He had the finest writers because he knew that writing was the birthplace of any creative result. A bad director cannot really ruin a fine script, but a good director can help it. I've always thought a writer should be on a pay-as-you-succeed basis instead of getting the tremendous salaries they get. Then if his writing was good, he'd realize more; if it was not good, he'd realize less. At one time Mayer had eighty senior writers and forty junior writers employed at MGM on a steady salary. That's what L.B. thought of writers! Mayer's greatest asset was Irving Thalberg, who was the studio's executive producer. There's never been another executive equal to Thalberg in respect to taste, certain ideals, judgments, and the ability to make decisions rather quickly. He was only thirty-six when he died. Mayer's wonderful general manager of the studio was Eddie Mannix, a bruiser-bouncer type. He was a great guy. The present studio is going through a revolution along with the other studios. A new-type product is being made that is dictated to by economics and the desire to get a feeling of realism in many films. The new directors and producers believe they have to go out to the actual spots to shoot. That's fine. Some very interesting things have come up as a result of this technique.

Mike: Do you think the film industry has an open door to new talent?

Gillespie: It seems fewer and fewer feature films are being made, but television is an enormous industry. It's terribly competitive because of the good pay and the glamor involved, and it has already developed its own establishment. Still, there is room for new talent. I've lectured several times at UCLA and USC, and the chaps come to me and ask what courses they should take to prepare themselves for my field of the industry. There is no single answer, but it is important to study architecture and sketching. After that, I say one must have a general knowledge of many, many things and grab any possible experience he can. There is always something you might see somewhere that might be of value to you. To grab adventure where and when you can has been my scheme of living. Walk around the corner to see what is there! Always strive to add to your experience.

March 6, 1970

Director of Musical Numbers

BUSBY BERKELEY

Berkeley: I was born in Los Angeles in 1896 and at an early age went to New York, where I was brought up in the theater because my mother was an actress. She was associated with Nazimova for fourteen years. The theater has remained my first love. I was a performer on Broadway seven years, and I directed twenty-one opening nights before coming to Hollywood. My twenty-second Broadway opening will be the 1971 revival of *No, No, Nanette* with my old friend Ruby Keeler.

Mike: What brought you to Hollywood back in 1929?

Berkeley: Eddie Cantor was going to do a picture called *Whoopee* for Sam Goldwyn, and they wanted me to direct all the musical numbers. It was my first time to work with Cantor. I did three more pictures with him at Goldwyn: *The Kid from Spain, Balmy Days,* and *Roman Scandals.* I started showing sequences of close-ups of pretty girls with *Whoopee.* It had never been done before.

Mike: From the Goldwyn Studio you went over to Warner Brothers?

Berkeley: Yes. I was under contract at Warner's for eight or nine years. The first film I did there in 1933 was a milestone in musicals called *42nd Street.* Darryl Zanuck produced it. It started a new popularity for musicals. It starred Dick Powell, Ruby Keeler, and Warner Baxter. Ginger Rogers had a featured part. Most of the same cast was in *Gold Diggers of 1933.* There was an earthquake in Los Angeles when we were shooting that. At the time it hit I had fifty beautiful girls up thirty-five feet high on platforms. I shrieked and hollered to them not to jump. They would have killed themselves. I yelled, "Sit down! Sit down!" No one was hurt, but the walls of the stage were shaking.

Mike: What were some of your other musicals during the early thirties?

Berkeley: I did *Gold Diggers of 1935, The Singing Marine, Dames, Footlight Parade,* and *Fashion's Follies.*

Mike: Since these light and gay musicals were made during the Depression, were they designed to make audiences forget the bad times they were having?

Berkeley: They weren't geared for the Depression, but they certainly made people forget their troubles for a while.

Mike: Even though some of them had unhappy or downbeat endings?

Berkeley: People loved those musicals and flocked to see them. It's a matter of history that my pictures brought Warner Brothers out of the red and into the black during the thirties. It was all due to the musical numbers.

Mike: Did you prefer concentrating on the musical numbers, or to direct the entire picture?

Berkeley: I preferred to do a whole picture, of course. While I was under contract, I would, between my own pictures, direct the musical numbers on other directors' films. I didn't limit myself to musicals, however. I directed John Garfield's first starring picture, *They Made Me a Criminal,* with Claude Rains, May Robson, and the Dead End Kids.

Mike: You switched studios in the mid-thirties and went to Metro-Goldwyn-Mayer, didn't you?

Berkeley: Yes. I started working for Arthur Freed. I made all the musicals teaming Judy Garland and Mickey Rooney: *Babes in Arms, Babes on Broadway,* and *Strike Up the Band.* Judy was fifteen when we made *Babes in Arms.* She called me Uncle and always wanted me right there when the camera was photographing her. She would not do a scene unless I stood by the camera, and afterward she would ask me how she looked and if she had done all right. She and Mickey had great respect for each other's ability. I don't know any two kids who could be better than those two were. Over at Universal they teamed a couple of very talented kids, Donald O'Connor and Peggy Ryan. And they had Deanna Durbin. But nobody ever topped Judy and Mickey. When Judy grew up, I directed her in one of my favorite films, *For Me and My Gal.* It was Gene Kelly's first starring film after he came out from Broadway.

Mike: What other MGM musical stars did you work with?

Berkeley: I staged many numbers for Ann Miller. And I did all the musical numbers and water ballets for two of Esther Williams' biggest films. One was the life of Annette Kellerman called *Million Dollar Mermaid.* The other was *Easy to Love.* I did one film at Fox which I really enjoyed making. It was *The Gang's All Here* with Alice Faye, Carmen Miranda, Edward Everett Horton, and Charlotte Greenwood.

Mike: Did you pick the talent for your films?

Berkeley: The principal players were usually under contract to the studio, but I could ask for certain contract players for certain parts. In my early career, my show girls, who became famously known as the Berkeley Girls, were all personally chosen by me. I used the same girls in several films. Sam Goldwyn started his Goldwyn Girls about the same time.

Mike: And way back in silent film days there were the Mack Sennett Bathing Beauties! Were your Berkeley Girls trained dancers?

Berkeley: If they knew their left foot from their right and could do ballroom dancing, that was enough for me. But above all, they had to be beautiful. They had to have a lush quality, not just be pretty.

Mike: Sometimes you had as many as a hundred girls in one number. Did you use a megaphone to direct them?

Berkeley: No. I have a pretty loud voice, and it carried a long distance.

Mike: How long would you rehearse a number?

Berkeley: That depended on the number. Some numbers only took two or three days to rehearse and shoot. Others took a week or so.

Mike: Did you design the costumes for your musical numbers?

Berkeley: I'd tell the wardrobe people what I wanted. Then they'd draw designs, and I'd choose from them.

Mike: Reporters, movie buffs, and students call you the King of Camp. Did you make your films with a campy approach in mind?

Berkeley: No. I didn't even know the word existed. Maybe it didn't then. My idea was to do something that had never been seen before on the screen. My main purpose was to entertain the public, give them something that would excite them and that they would revel in. I realized the camera was the medium with which to do that. The camera was the audience, and that's why I made a great study of it and am noted for my camera work.

Mike: Why did you use only one camera to film what is known as your spectacular ensemble numbers?

Berkeley: Because I knew exactly what I wanted to shoot. I did my cutting with the camera. That is, the cutter had to put it together the way I shot it. I set every shot in every film I ever made. I got behind the camera and showed the operator exactly what I wanted.

Mike: What are some of the camera shots you invented?

Berkeley: I originated a camera shot I call the top shot. One day at Warner Brothers I climbed up over the rafters and looked down on one of my numbers and thought it looked pretty good. So I thought to myself, "I better bring the audience up here and let them see it." Sometimes the ceiling wasn't high enough, and we didn't have the wide-angle lens, so I'd cut a hole in the roof in order to get the camera farther back to take in an entire scene. There are five or six sound stages over at Warner's where I put holes in the roofs! I was watching the Jackie Gleason television show and they used a top shot on the June Taylor dancers. Jackie came out when it was over and asked the audience how they liked the top shot, and they all applauded. He said, "Well, I just want you to know we didn't introduce that. It was originated in Hollywood by Busby Berkeley, who for my book I consider the best musical-comedy director ever!" I sent him a wire saying, "You're the best in my book, too, Jack!"

Mike: What other shots did you think up?

Berkeley: One time I had a monorail built from the rafters, and from this monorail I hung down a trellis of steel to which the camera was attached so that it could move up and down. The trellis in turn could move along the monorail. This enabled the camera to go places an ordinary camera boom couldn't go. Another time I needed a dolly track built thirty feet in the air on which I could roll my camera back and forth. They said, "That's impossible." The minute they said that was when I loved it. I loved to show them it *could* be done. They'd say, "You want a dolly platform thirty feet high? Are you out of your mind? We can't do that!" I said, "You can't? You got lumber, haven't you? And you're all carpenters. So go ahead and build it." They did. When we were filming the Esther Williams picture *Easy to Love* down in Cypress Gardens, Florida, we needed to build a special swimming pool called an Esther Williams pool. The art director and I went all around the lake trying to find a spot to build the pool, but we couldn't find one. So I said to the art director, "How about building a pool right out in the lake?" He said, "You've blown your top again!" I said, "No, I haven't. Can you build one for me?" They built one about twenty feet off shore, and it's still there. You can't give a studio anything they can't build. One time I wanted a hydraulic lift to telescope out of the water and the different levels to turn in opposite directions. They went crazy, but they built it. That was for a number called "By a Waterfall" in *Footlight Parade*.

Mike: You must have spent a lot of time dreaming up these ideas.

Berkeley: I used to get up early in the morning and shave, then get into a warm tub of water before going to the studio. I'd lie back and soak for three-quarters of an hour and quietly think up many ideas. When I'd get to the studio and ask for a certain difficult setup, they had the saying, "Oh, you've been in that tub again!"

Mike: Did you select the music for your numbers?

Berkeley: Always. We did original scores. We didn't wait till a show was a hit on Broadway and then put it on the screen.

Mike: And you used real singing and dancing talent. Nowadays a big star who can't sing at all will be put in a musical and have the voice dubbed. What's wrong with using genuine all-round talent?

Berkeley: You tell the producers that. I've tried to tell them for fifteen years. But those boys higher up know everything. You can't tell them anything.

Mike: Your films were never dubbed, were they?

Berkeley: No. My pictures had musical stars. Occasionally I would use someone thought of as a straight actress. For instance, Dolores del Rio made two films for me in which she sang and did pretty good! She was a sweet girl and wonderful to work with. She's still the reigning star of Mexico.

Mike: Most people think of James Cagney as a dramatic actor also.

Berkeley: He did all those gangster films at Warner's for years. But he was originally a chorus boy in New York. I asked him to do the number called "Shanghai Lil" in my film *Footlight Parade*. He said, "Gee, I can't dance." I said, "What are you talking about? You forget I know all about you way back in New York when you used to dance!" He was great to work with.

Mike: Did you get along well with most actors?

Berkeley: When an actor knows all the tricks, and he knows you know all the tricks, you get along like cream and sugar. I got along wonderfully well with the stars. One interviewer one day asked me how was so-and-so to work with, and I said, "Wonderful!" He said, "Everybody is wonderful with you." I said, "Well, they were wonderful. I never had any trouble with them. No temperament, or anything like that. They were all wonderful to work with, and they worked wonderful with me. So they *were* wonderful!" I never had any favorites, and I always wanted people to have fun when they worked with me. I'd try to give them a reason to laugh. I had a terrific amount of patience. On one film I had a guy who was playing a doctor, and one day he had a line about a patient with a broken leg, "I think you ought to send him to an orthopedic surgeon." That guy stumbled over the word "orthopedic" take after take. He just couldn't say the word. I had the patience of Job. The crew began a pool of money on what take I would finally get him to say it. Another director might have given up and said, "To hell with it. Get me an actor who can say orthopedic." But not me. It took me damn near an hour, but I finally got him to do it right. Even seasoned professionals can get hung up on a line or a word; Jimmy Durante kept flubbing a word when he played the ringmaster in *Jumbo*. I forget the word, but it was something funny, and he would make it funnier by his comments after he flubbed.

Mike: Do you take credit for discovering any stars?

Berkeley: Lots of the biggest ones started as show girls in my chorus lines: Betty Grable, Jeanne Craine, Virginia Bruce, Veronica Lake, Carole Landis, Jane Wyman, and Lucille Ball.

Mike: Did you get along with producers?

Berkeley: No studio or producer ever engaged me to do a picture and wanted first to know what I was going to do for a certain number. No one ever asked any questions of me. They just put Busby Berkeley under contract to do the picture, and that was it. They never asked me how I was going to do anything. They knew better. I wouldn't have told them anyway!

March 1, 1970

Film Editor

FRED Y. SMITH

Smith: When I was six months old, my family moved from Chicago to Mountain View, California, where we lived on a small fruit ranch. The year was 1903. Dad commuted by train every day to San Francisco for his job as traffic manager for Western Meat Company and the Libby, McNeil and Libby Company. In 1912 there was an event which put the family on the move again: My twenty-one-year-old brother, Victor, was a sophomore at Stanford. He took a leave of absence and went down to North Island in San Diego to learn to fly at the Curtis School of Aviation. People would flock from miles around just to see an airplane in those days. Pilots made a lot of money giving flying exhibitions. Victor finished the school and rented a plane to make his first professional flight. The plane was shipped to our hometown in big crates, and he assembled it himself. Tickets were only ten cents, but many friends wouldn't buy them. They said they didn't want to pay to see a boy killed. Victor took off from a hayfield next to the railway station, circled our heads, then flew to Stanford and circled the campus. Lots of people were seeing an airplane for the first time! He flew out to Ravenswood, a suburb of Palo Alto, to land in another hayfield. The plane turned over when it hit the ground, and he was killed. It was such a shock to our family I wasn't even allowed to say the word "airplane" anymore. They wanted to get as far away from that location as possible. My father had become president of the Transportation Club in San Francisco and a good friend to Stanley Dollar of the steamship line. We moved to Hong Kong, and Dad opened an office for the steamship company. We lived in the Orient about three years, until Dad was transferred to the New York office. After four wonderful years of prep school at Hackley, I went to Stanford to study to be a maritime lawyer.

Mike: At this time you had no ambition to enter the film industry?

Smith: I knew nothing about it, although my mother was interested in theater and had even written some plays that were never produced, and at Stanford I belonged to the drama club and enjoyed acting. Unfortunately, I became ill at the end of my second year and was told I had incipient tuberculosis! To rest and recover, Mother, my younger brother, and I took a cruise on the *President Taft*. I never danced and smoked so much and got so little sleep in my life! By the time we got to Manila I knew I didn't have tuberculosis. I stayed in Manila two years working for the Dollar Line and while there got interested in the Manila Community Players. My family kept writing me to come back home. There also was a girl in the States with whom I was in love.

Mike: So you returned to California?

Smith: Yes. The idea of acting in the movies had struck my mind. I had a very good wardrobe, tails, tuxedoes, and so on. I got some bit parts, and I did extra work. In one year's time I made all of sixty dollars! Luckily, I had saved up quite a bit of money in the Philippines.

Mike: Wouldn't working as an extra keep you from getting better parts?

Smith: Nowadays they say, "Once an extra, always an extra," but back then an extra had the opportunity of even becoming a star. Many did.

However, my career took another route, because one day First National Studios had one of those efficiency experts from New York come out and interview people for various positions in the operation of a big studio. I got hired as a projectionist. The projection rooms and film cutting rooms at First National were all in the same area. I really wasn't interested in projection, but I was very interested in cutting. Sound was just coming in. They used the Warner Brothers-Vitaphone sound-on-disc system. I spent a lot of time in the cutting room learning from an editor named Hugh Bennett. I would splice film, make up cue sheets, wind film, or whatever. Finally, I convinced Hugh I was capable of editing film, so he let me start cutting short subjects. The first full picture I cut was *Sweet Mama* with Alice White. The second was *The Truth About Youth.* Hal Wallis produced it. He was just becoming a producer after having been in the publicity department. Then I did a film called *College Lovers.* Speaking of love, at about that time, 1929, I married Olga Jamison, a studio secretary. We're in our forty-third year!

Mike: Didn't Warner Brothers also marry First National in 1929?

Smith: Yes, Warner's brought their own editors with them, so the First National editors were eased out. They kept me on because I was just a beginner and didn't have enough credit to step out on my own. My main work became putting music on pictures in which the dialogue was still read by the audience. Soon a better job was offered me through an editor friend, Harold Young, if I would work at the Paramount Studios in Paris, France. My wife and I moved to Europe, and I edited a few French films for the American director Harry Lachman. When Lachman was sent to the Paramount Studios in London, he requested I come there and work on a comedy starring Gertrude Lawrence, *Aren't We All?* I had my first real encounter with star temperament. Miss Lawrence didn't like the way she photographed in one bedroom scene that ran about one hundred and fifty feet of film. I couldn't understand why. Maybe she thought her nose was a bit shiny or something simple like that. So the cameraman, Rudy Mate, retook the scene. I looked at it in my cutting room and didn't think it played as well as the scene we already had. So I left the old scene in the picture. We had a preview, and Gertrude Lawrence was there. Everyone thought the picture was wonderful, but Miss Lawrence was fit to be tied by the tail. She raised hell!

Mike: Irving Rapper, who directed her in *The Glass Menagerie,* told me she was very concerned with being photographed attractively in that, too.

Smith: This happens often with female stars. Some of them think just one side of their face is good and will only allow that side to be photographed. Soon after my experience with Gertrude Lawrence, Paramount closed down its London production activities, and I was out of a job. We hadn't saved anything up and had been living from hand to mouth. I was about to ask the United States consulate for passage home when a new film company, Gaumont-British, amalgamated with Gainsborough Pictures with facilities at Shepherd's Bush, London. They signed me to a contract, and I worked for them three years. I became quite an Anglophile and considered becoming a British citizen.

Mike: Didn't Gaumont-British make trilingual films?

Smith: Yes. Each picture had an English, French, and German version. They used the same story, costumes, and sets and worked around the clock on eight-hour shifts with three different casts, directors, and crews! Sometimes my editing job took me to France or Germany. In Berlin in 1934 I met the head of the great film company Ufa, Erich Pommer. He had been an editor and had designed and made up the first German cutting table. Pommer is the only producer I ever sat down with and made a suggestion for a cut who put the film on the table, executed the cut, and spliced the film himself. These specially designed cutting tables from Germany and France have become quite sophisticated and are in popular use all over the world. I think, however, the Movieola is still the best editing machine being used.

Mike: When did you leave Europe?

Smith: We returned to Hollywood in 1935, and I was out of work exactly one year. Again, my friend Harold Young, who was now an established director at Paramount, used his influence to get me a job at MGM on a picture called *Last of the Pagans.* That began my eighteen-year career with Metro-Goldwyn-Mayer. My first assignments included two of Judy Garland's early films, *Babes on Broadway* and *Little Nellie Kelly.* George Murphy played her father in the latter.

Mike: Those were directed by Busby Berkeley and Norman Taurog, respectively.

Smith: Yes. Busby was a man who knew each shot he wanted, so he would only photograph the angles which he wanted to see on the screen. He didn't cover a scene from any other angle. This technique is called camera cutting. It is an inexpensive and fast way of making a film. W. S. "Woody" Van Dyke was the master of this style. He was the most versatile director I ever worked with and was the most reliable one at MGM because he always brought a picture in on time and on budget. He had, for years, made a flock of cheap Westerns during which time he acquired the camera cutting technique he used so efficiently in making big pictures at MGM.

Mike: Camera cutting must minimize the editor's job!

Smith: About all you have to do is take what we call the slates off the beginning and end of each shot. There's only one bad thing about camera cutting: If you strictly camera cut, you're bound to make a mistake sometime, and you have no alternate shot to choose from. In *Rose Marie* Woody Van Dyke made a hell of a mistake. Blanche Sewell was the film editor, and she told me there was a shot where Jeanette MacDonald goes into a room wearing a shawl around her shoulders. When they picked her up in the next shot entering inside the room, she didn't have the shawl. The scene required an expensive retake.

Mike: I saw a similar mistake in *Sweet Bird of Youth.* Paul Newman walks into the bathroom with a towel over one shoulder, puts the towel on a rack, but when the camera cuts back to him coming out of the bathroom, the towel is still in the same position on his shoulder.

Smith: One of the worst mistakes I've seen was in *Bonnie and Clyde.* The gang was always in that gray hardtop sedan. One of the boys has stolen a black phaeton. In one scene they all jump into the hardtop sedan to flee the cops, but when the cops catch them, they are in the black phaeton! Most directors would retake something like that, but they got away with it. Being an editor, it hit me right in the nose.

Mike: Do some directors use the same editor constantly?

Smith: Sure. Especially when they know the editor will interpret the story the way they want it. For instance, Jack Murray edited most of John Ford's films. A producer will also use a favorite editor. Years ago at Fox they used to say that Zanuck would tell his editors, "To hell with how the director wants it put together. You know how I want it put together, and you do what I say." That's one reason directors, through their union, had it put in their contracts they would have "first cut" privileges. They were given two weeks to do it. A temperamental director would insist on an editor doing exactly what he said to. Then, after the director left the production, the producer might say, "Now we will go to work." Oftentimes, the editor would have to change the picture back the way the producer wanted it.

Mike: Do you think the director should have the last say as to artistic control?

Smith: Yes indeed! I don't have much respect for the taste of many producers. They're businessmen. However, if a certain producer is responsible for choosing the story, director, and actors and putting all this talent together, he is really the genius behind the whole thing. The producer chooses a particular director because he knows that director will give him what he wants. If the film is good or bad, the producer should have the credit or the blame.

Mike: The trend today is for a director to have a story and actors, then go to a producer who will raise money for the project, isn't it?

Smith: Yes. When a director is hired under those conditions, he should have full authority to carry out his ideas right down to how each foot of film is edited. I personally believe a picture usually comes out better than the script has read. This is due to the talents of the director. He's really captain of the ship, although there may be an admiral in an office somewhere! Sometimes the star owns part of the film. Stars like Kirk Douglas, Paul Newman, and Jerry Lewis who are "producer" actors. They instruct their editors to make certain choices, and you'd better do what they say!

Mike: After you have read a script, do you go over it with the director to discuss his approach and style?

Smith: If you've never worked with the director, the film editor should be called in before the script is "frozen" and sent to the mimeograph department. A talented editor might suggest something that could be a big saving. He thinks in a logical manner. I'm talking about a very experienced editor, not someone who hasn't had this background. There are not too many of us in the trade. There are a lot of cutters who can use a pair of scissors. Almost anybody can do that. Damn few editors have the creative ability to think out certain situations in a script and make them much more dramatic or effective. We're very conscious of the time element. A picture is usually made far too long because they are always going to condense it when it is edited. Therefore, when I come across a scene in a script that doesn't lend itself directly to the story, I suggest it not be shot. Sometimes that advice isn't taken, and we end up with "the face on the cutting room floor." The amount of money an editor can save in unnecessary film not being shot, can pay for the entire editorial service on a picture.

Mike: Are you often given a free hand in editing a picture the way you feel it should be edited?

Smith: I've always wanted that privilege given me. This is something that is very touchy with an editor. I say, "Please let me make the first cut. Respect my talent, experience, and knowledge enough to let me give you the translation I think you want." That doesn't mean I'm perfect. I make mistakes like anyone else.

Mike: If you have worked with a certain director often, aren't chances better that you will have the right to a first cut?

Smith: Yes, because you have become attuned with his wishes. I don't think any editor tries to impose his own wishes or personality over a film. Once I have given that first rough cut, I am apt to go along with the philosophy that the director should make his own final cut. Unfortunately, instances do occur where the director is not a technical man and becomes lost in the cutting room. Or he may not want to take the time to cut his own film because he is involved with so many other duties. Editing a picture normally takes twice as long as the filming of it. The director may want to get started on another picture right away.

Mike: But you prefer the director to stay with a film until it is in the cans?

Smith: Yes. He should remain in authority until then. The worst thing that can happen to an editor is being forced to become the go-between for the director and the producer, who by the time the production is finished may not even be speaking to each other. That makes the editor the fall guy. The producer tells him one thing; the director tells him another. It's very uncomfortable and embarrassing to be in that position, and I've been in it a number of times! Once on a Greer Garson picture called *That Forsyte Woman* there was a young English director whom I personally liked. He often came into my cutting room just to visit, not particularly to discuss the picture. I finished the first cut and told him we were going to run the picture at a certain time and date for the producer and an executive. It's customary for the producer to invite the director to these first screenings. I didn't realize this director and producer hated each other. Just prior to the screening the director was sitting in the projection room when the producer entered with the executive. The producer didn't say anything, but he was livid! Afterward he called me to his office and said, "What do you mean by inviting this director?" I said, "I didn't invite him. I merely told him what was going to happen, and he came of his own accord." I think the producer tried to have me fired at that time. This shows the viciousness of some temperamental people in positions of authority.

Mike: Most producers and directors are even-tempered, don't you find?

Smith: Yes, and a pleasure to work with. Norman Taurog is a director who could get anything out of me with a kind, complimentary word. People appreciate a nice word or a bit of flattery. It's the son of a gun for whom you can do nothing right or who has to be the big brass about everything that causes trouble on a production.

Mike: The big brass today, whether they behave like it or not, are the directors. They often write, produce, direct, and edit their films.

Smith: In the old days, the studio had a production line that "assembled" a picture from original story idea to exhibition. The product was under the banner of the studio and bore its mark.

Mike: Now films are more often under the banner of a great director. The main credit will read, "A Film by Federico Fellini" or whoever, because the director has been the creator of the whole product. Such a credit began as legitimate artistic credit, but a lot of second-rate talent has the power to demand it, too. They capitalize on the phrase by using it to con the public into accepting them as artists. It reminds me of the term "superstar" which was invented justifiably for top personalities such as Elizabeth Taylor. Now publicity agents use the term to ballyhoo the public into thinking any of their clients are superstars.

Smith: In the long run the public knows who the real superstars are. A talent of high quality or a dynamic personality is usually recognized as the outstanding thing it is.

Mike: Isn't there a saying among film editors that the best edited picture is one in which you don't notice the editing?

Smith: Yes. You are so absorbed in the telling of the story that you are hypnotized. There is a new kind of editing in the less expensive films today where they don't bother to match a damn thing and everything is done to shock the viewer. I maintain that is a lot of baloney and is only a fad. It is founded on novelty rather than logic. For instance, in *Easy Rider* they didn't use dissolves. They would flash to a few frames of the oncoming scene, then go back to the scene in progress. This was repeated until you were into the next scene. Seeing something like that for the first time is clever, but once is enough. It's not nearly as pleasant as a nice smooth dissolve. People pay their way into a theater to be entertained, but today we don't have as many films to entertain as we should have. At the present stage of the industry most films being made are message films attempting to put over some damn propaganda. Political or antireligious. There's all kinds of propaganda being preached. Right now the vogue is also sex. There is an attempt to change the mores of our times.

Mike: I agree that the screen seems to have turned, not for the betterment of mankind, but for the destruction of our civilization.

Smith: I remember my wife was reading aloud to me once a newspaper article on *Myra Breckinridge.* The news reporter was not able to print the filthy phrases that are spoken in the film. *Play It As It Lays* is another example. I think pictures of this sort are doing more harm to our country than good. I've thought for many, many years the people who are responsible for the bad conditions that exist today are to a large degree the motion-picture producers.

Mike: In the majority of situations I guess it is the morally and ethically corrupt personalities who can claw their way to the top in the so-called celluloid jungle. Once at the top, their personal outlook is automatically expressed within the product they put out.

Smith: Perhaps they are not consciously doing it. But they certainly have a lack of good taste. Their desire to make a fast buck has always been the foremost objective. There hasn't been much idealism anywhere in this industry. For instance, Ernst Lubitsch was a good director, but he had a somewhat pornographic mind. There was always some subtle manifestation of this in his pictures.

Mike: Do directors and producers who make message and propaganda films tend to hire editors whose philosophy, attitudes, and opinions parallel their own?

Smith: Not necessarily. I know a Democrat can work on a Republican's film. Or a conservative on a Communist's. However, on the extreme message pictures all the people involved are probably of one persuasion. The trend in message pictures and vulgarity is so strong today that there are scripts I would not work on because I don't believe in them. I'm as anti-Communist as a person can get.

Mike: Sometimes a propaganda film can be a film of great artistry, and the propaganda is therefore more effective. The film *Z* is a good example. So is *Sounder*, which pretended to be realistic, but was very theatrical.

Smith: I know *Z* had a little Commie propaganda which is given you like a sugar-coated pill, but I suggested it be nominated for the American Cinema Editors "Eddie" awards. It had a wonderful editing style.

Mike: Are you ever given bits of a film to edit that you know would not pass the censorship rating code?

Smith: Once you agree to take a job, if the people who pay your salary tell you to leave something in, you leave it in. I would try to follow the code as much as I could, and they would have to tell me to do otherwise. I have had arguments with producers when I have thought a piece of film was too vulgar. Many times they agree with me and tell me to cut it down or trim it all out.

Mike: Haven't many editors become directors?

Smith: Yes. Among the most well-known editor-directors today are Robert Wise, Mark Robson, and John Sturges. Oddly, they all three came from RKO. Years ago Paramount used to have a man named George Arthur as head of their editorial department. He gave many editors a chance to direct! Cyril Gardner, Hugh Bennett, Edward Dmytryk, and Alexander Hall, who directed Mae West. Al's assistant back in those days was Barbara McLean, who has just retired after many years as head of the editorial department at Twentieth Century-Fox. She was a very capable woman. She edited the Bette Davis film *All About Eve*. One of the best-known British directors who began as an editor is David Lean. That came about in a unique way: One of the jobs of an editor is to correct mistakes made in filming the picture. One day David went to the studio head and said he wanted to be a director so he could have the privilege of making his own mistakes! He walked out of the room a director!

Mike: That was a stroke of good fortune for all of us!

Smith: A few editors who have been given a chance to direct have come back to editing. They either didn't like it or weren't capable.

Mike: I suppose some were given a chance because they had the right contacts, rather than superior ability.

Smith: Oh, you don't know the intricacies of the family politics that go on in Hollywood! It scares the hell out of you when you realize sometimes that it isn't necessarily what you know, but who you know that counts: I guess nepotism exists in banking, oil, and every other business, but in motion pictures there seems to be a little bit more.

Mike: What is your opinion of the way old films are cut to show on television?

Smith: I agree with George Stevens who sued one of the networks for ruining a film he directed, *A Place in the Sun*. Television people have not employed creative, old-time, experienced editors. They get these youngsters for as little as possible. Probably under scale in some instances. All they think about is the time slot. To hell with the story. This is the thing so handicapping to TV. You've got the seconds to count. An editor cannot do his best with a story when he has to go by a stopwatch. Television really massacres some of our good product, not only to fit the time slot, but to fit the commercial breaks. I champion George Stevens' complaint against television, but at the same time, I must say that although he is an excellent director, he is one of the worst editors in the business. He has full control over his products and sees the picture to its final version. Unfortunately, he falls in love with his work. In his film *Giant* he had certain things going for himself that he just would not let go of, even after they had served their purpose. Many directors and producers are guilty of holding onto things too long. They go too sentimental. Over the point of effectiveness. Over the climax. When you do that, you tend to lose your audience that you have been trying to capture and control. In *Giant* there is a scene where the boy's body is returned from the war. The coffin is on a freight wagon on the train station platform. The camera makes a beautiful shot beginning close on the coffin. It dollies slowly back until the coffin is only a little bit of a thing in the distance. It was so powerful and pointed in its conception! Yet George Stevens dissolved the shot into a funeral being held for the kid. This is what I mean by a dramatic concept going beyond the point of climax. Stevens' point had already been sold and made in such a beautiful way.

Mike: How does a newcomer get into the film editing profession?

Smith: If you went, unknown, to a studio and asked for work, you

would be told to get in the union first. If you went to the union, you would be told to get a job first. It's the old thing of passing the buck.
Mike: Would a college education get your foot in the door?
Smith: I would give the young graduate priority over everyone else, but you have this nepotism to deal with. The editors' guild is a small one and a tight one. Many members are there because their fathers were there. However, excellent schooling can be had at UCLA, USC, Ohio State, Columbia, and other universities. It is unfortunate that many of the students, when they get out, think they know all there is to know. Just because they have been exposed to all these techniques they think they can not only do them, but they tell other people how much better they can do them. Human nature again!
Mike: If they are lucky enough to get into the union, do they have to begin as apprentices?
Smith: Yes. We have about eight classifications in our union, and you've got to be in one of those at least eight years before you can be a full-fledged film editor.
Mike: What are those classifications?
Smith: After an apprentice, there is the assistant editor. Then the various types of editors are: sound effects editor, music editor, trailer editor, TV editor, animation editor, film librarian, and full-fledged film editor. In the old days, the film editor did everything. In the current trend toward independent filmmaking, he is more or less a supervising editor and hires his own crew of specialty editors. I first did that on a film starring James Cagney, *The Gallant Hours*. We used the MGM facilities. I hired all my assistants and was paid almost three times the salary I had been paid when under contract to MGM!
Mike: That's great for you, but unfortunate for the producer who has to hire so many editors for one film, because the union says so.
Smith: I have mixed feelings about the union, and I've been a union man since the days you would get fired if the bosses knew you were a member. Thank God I was in England in 1933 when the studios busted the power of the IATSE! They say if the cameramen had stayed out one more day, the strike would have been won. The studios were victorious until the Wagner Act came in in 1938; then all of a sudden everyone became unionized. The studios were cunning enough to participate in the forming of the memberships of these unions and in placing company people in key positions. At MGM the head of the film library, Eddie Hannon, was sponsored by Louis B. Mayer's

troubleshooting labor executive, Eddie Mannix, and won the election as our union head. A few years later we found we had a business agent who was a crook. He stole a lot of money from us, and we discovered he had a penitentiary record! Eddie Hannon still wanted to retain this guy. That's when I ran for president of our union and was elected. We were called the Society of Motion Picture Film Editors. When World War II came and most of us were in the service, the ones remaining had a meeting and put us into the IATSE without our being asked about it.

Mike: I belong to three unions, and although I believe they should combine into just one, I think even then it would be a "necessary evil." There is so much hypocrisy in some unions that they become a sort of farce.

Smith: In my opinion unionism takes a talented man and puts him down in the middle strata. It takes the lazy, inefficient person and brings him up to the same level as the talented person. God never made any two people alike, from thumb prints on! We are all different, and we are always going to be different. Thank God! Wouldn't it be terrible if we were all the same?

June 4, 1970

Sound Recording

BERNARD FREERICKS

Freericks: Although I was born in Hot Springs, Virginia, I was brought up in New York, where I lived in the Bronx for twenty-five years or more. As a very young man I had various jobs until I went to work for the Freed-Eismann Company which manufactured electrical equipment, specializing in radios. This job broadened my knowledge of the various apparatus employed in the recording and reproduction of sound and in the sending and receiving of sound, so that I came to be considered somewhat of an expert in the field. It isn't my nature to speak up about my own achievements, but one thing I am rather proud of is the fact that I was the first person to put a radio into an automobile. Unfortunately, I was unable to get a patent on the idea. It wasn't really an invention, anyway, but merely a logical conclusion that I happened to arrive at before anyone else did.

In the early days of the Depression, Freed-Eismann folded up, and I started looking for another job. Just at that time Warner Brothers came out with the first sound picture, *The Jazz Singer*. I figured my background in sound equipment and technique would help land me a job in this new phase of the movie business, so I went to apply for a job at the New York office of Warner Brothers. They said that if I went out to Hollywood, they would probably hire me there. Since I had a wife and two children, I thought that big a risk was not wise, so I went to the office of another film company, Fox. They took me on. My first job was working on the Fox Movietone News shorts. Our biggest assignment that fall was to film the Yale-Army football game! In November I permanently moved to Hollywood when Fox sent me out to remodel the existing stages on their original lot at Sunset and Western so that sound films could be made: I had them pad the old stages with a kind of heavy felt such as you put under a rug. They got by with that until they built their new studio and sound stages at Fox Hills in Westwood.

Mike: What were the first types of sound systems in use in Hollywood?

Freericks: At the beginning there were three techniques: Vitaphone was the Western Electric phonograph disc that Warner Brothers used. That was really something to cut, to edit! They had to take the sound off a master record. This master record was made from the individual discs which had been recorded for each scene. I remember visiting Warner's one time when I was shown a huge machine made up of multiple turntables. There were about twelve of these discs on the turntables. When one disc was edited, or recorded, onto the master disc, another one would pick up right away on a given cue controlled by the cutter. It was very difficult and complicated and took a lot of skill to operate. RCA had a sound system based on a vibrating mirror. It was not quite as good as Vitaphone, but RKO and a lot of independents used it because the royalty RCA charged for the use of its equipment was less than what Western Electric charged. Fox started out with the Fox-Case technique of an aeolite which fit into the camera. However, they soon got rid of it and made a deal with

Western Electric. They also had RCA equipment for a brief time when making some of the quickie pictures.

Mike: What was the first sound picture made at Fox?

Freericks: The first one we made at Fox in Hollywood was only a two-reeler called *The Family Picnic* in 1929. They imported a stage director from New York named Harry Delf. He couldn't understand why when an actor went out on the right, he had to come back in from the left. He and the cameraman had arguments about that all the time. It was the first sound picture to be filmed exterior and with running shots in an automobile. The microphone weighed eighteen pounds and was hung on a special frame built over the car. Ray McKee played the father and Kathleen Key was the mother. They had two children in the cast. The family was shown getting up in the morning, making the sandwiches for the picnic, driving into the country, and so on. At the end of the picture, the car is being towed in while a phonograph record plays "At the End of a Perfect Day." When they got ready to edit it, they didn't know what to do. The single sound system we used had the sound and the picture on the same negative, and the sound was twenty-one or twenty-two frames ahead of the picture! Finally, they got the film editor to cut the sound track off with a razor blade and slide it up and down with the picture until it matched, then stick it back on again! They did that with several pictures.

Fox made quite a few of these two-reel talkies before they tried a feature-length one. The first sound feature was to be a part talkie called *Mother Knows Best*, but as they went along, they kept writing more dialogue, and when the film was finished, it was a hundred percent talkie. In those days they made at least fifty pictures a year. Most feature pictures took twelve to fifteen days to make.

Mike: Since sound was such a novelty in the beginning, didn't they use a lot of sound effects and noises to the point of overdoing it?

Freericks: Yes. Not a space or sprocket hole on the film was left without some sort of sound! If you were putting music or any other sound on the film, you had to do it at the same time you recorded the dialogue, because they didn't have rerecording as we do today. For instance, if you had an orchestra playing for a dance and the people dancing had dialogue, you picked up everything at the same time. Then they dreamed up this thing we call the double system which is still in use: sound on one piece of film and picture on another. With that technique, in a dance scene a separate sound track of the music is made which is played back over a speaker called the playback when the scene is filmed. You can turn it off and on so that it doesn't interfere with the dialogue. Then in editing they put in the whole music score behind the dialogue using the process known as rerecording. Any sound that is added to the exposed film is rerecorded sound.

Mike: With the advent of sound did Fox have any stars who couldn't make the transition from silents to talkies?

Freericks: The only one I can think of was Tom Mix, who had made lots of cowboy pictures for Fox. They made a sound test of him. He was a big, rugged man, but had a high-pitched voice. Fox didn't continue making films with him, but he did make sound pictures elsewhere.

Mike: I suppose sometimes it wasn't the quality or pitch of a voice, but the ability to act with one's voice which made the difference.

Freericks: I remember Victor McLagen was really worried when sound came in, and the studio was testing all their people to decide who to keep and who to let go! I talked to Victor for about an hour one day. There were almost tears in his eyes. He wondered what they would do with him with his English dialect. I kept saying to him, "That's the one thing that's going to put you over, because you're not the run-of-the-mill actor."

Mike: Yes. His speech was an asset, and he had a great career in sound films.

Freericks: One of the heads of production at Fox in the early sound era was Sol Wurtzel. He said that anybody could make a motion picture, that all you had to do was drive up in your truck or car and set up the cameras. He said, "We're going to do things differently!" So in 1930 they decided to make a picture called *Lone Star Ranger* at a very remote and almost inaccessible location. We mule-packed to the Rainbow Bridge in Utah! It was the first time I had been on a horse. We rode little Indian ponies. The first hour or so I said, "Gee! This is great!" Then we came down to a deep canyon, and my pony's head would protrude over the narrow ledge of the trail every time he went around a curve. I was afraid he was going to stumble over. Also, when a horse climbs onto something, he puts his two front legs up one at a time, then his hind legs jump up with a jolt! After another two hours, I was getting so sore that I was standing up in the stirrups or swinging one leg over the saddle horn. This went on for eight hours!

When we finally arrived at Rainbow Bridge, the guide beamed and said, "There she is! Isn't she beautiful!" All I could think of was my rear end. I said, "Is there a stream of water down there?" He said yes. I walked down, stripped off my clothes, and sat in the ice-cold water! We had planned to get all our filming done the next day and the third day ride back up. However, no one had checked to find out what kind of sun the canyon got. We discovered it lasted only a very short time in the deep canyon, so we had to stay there five days! Meantime, all the Indians in the area learned we had a doctor, and they came to our camp to be treated. The doctor would give them an aspirin or a pill or put a Band-Aid on them. Of course, as long as they stayed there, they were going to eat our food! The last night we spent at the bottom of the canyon we had nothing left to eat for dinner. The next day we rode back up to Rainbow Lodge on Navajo Mountain.

Mike: The fact that sound equipment is constantly changing and improving would affect the number of members on a sound crew, but what are the usual positions on your crew?

Freericks: The sound mixer has charge of everything that involves sound and a sound crew on a set. The crew under him ordinarily consists of the boom man, who holds and manipulates the microphone which is attached usually to a mechanical boom, the cableman, the playback operator, and the recorder, who works with the recording machine and tape. On location the recorder is supposed to be able to repair all the equipment and keep it running. He does his work inside a sound truck which is some distance away from the camera, so that he is not necessarily able to view the scene being shot. The mixer, on the other hand, is always right on the set where he can see the actors, talk to the director, and manage his crew as he sits at his panel controls. Of course, the more microphones being used, the more he has to mix the sounds coming over them at various times.

It used to be when the director, or his assistant, gave the order to roll, the recorder was the man who pushed a button which started the camera rolling and the sound equipment recording. And at the command "cut," he would stop it. Now things are getting more mechanized so that you don't have to have so many men. Very often, nowadays, on location there is no recorder. The mixer has at his disposal several recording machines, usually the small Nagra type, that are preloaded with magnetic tape. The mixer is not allowed to reload the machines, so when the tape on one machine is used up, the entire machine is mailed back to the studio, and the mixer begins with a fresh machine. Also, there are many television shows made on stages that do not hire recorders. In this case, the recording machine is loaded for the mixer every morning by a guy known as the dummy operator. At noontime the machine is checked again to see if it needs reloading or rethreading. With this system it is the mixer who starts the camera and other equipment going when the order to roll is given. There is another system at use at Columbia Pictures in which the recording machine is started by a radio pulse that comes from the camera when it is turned on by the cameraman.

Rerecording, which involves the looping or dubbing of dialogue after a film is shot and the insertion of sound effects and music, has one man in charge. He may have two or three or four others who handle different panels for different effects. The music mixer has a very specialized job in rerecording and he most often works separately in that responsibility. Most of the men working in rerecording today used to be production mixers, sound mixers on the set when a film is in production. I myself have done every type job there is in sound at one time or another.

Mike: What were some of the other early pictures on which you worked?

Freericks: *Girl of the Golden West*, *Frontier Marshal*, *Rainbow Trail*, *Pigskin Parade*, several *Cisco Kid* pictures, lots of *Charlie Chan* pictures, *Chicken-Wagon Family* with Jane Withers, and *The Country Doctor*, which was about the birth of the Dionne quintuplets. We went on a tough location for that one! We traveled by train to the little town of North Bay, Canada, which is on a lake, and arrived in a blizzard! It was fifteen degrees below zero! After we checked into the hotel, we had to go back to the railway station to unload our equipment, which was one of the roughest jobs I ever did. The weather made the entire production hard to take. The director, Henry King, made us a speech. He said, "Never leave the hotel without your rubber overshoes, your overcoat, and your gloves because if you get pneumonia, there's nothing you can do about it!" It was remarkable that we were allowed to use the quintuplets outside in that freezing weather. I remember one day the five baby carriages were lined up on the front porch of the house with the babies so bundled up that you could only see their noses. We had permission to work with the quints one hour a day, in the middle of the day.

Mike: Were you able to record actual sounds, like crying, made by the quints, or did you use stock sound effects?

Freericks: I guess you could say the quints did their own looping! However, most of the studios do have a sound effects library which contains recordings of almost every sound imaginable. During my career I have had the opportunity to make recordings of several unusual sounds which are kept in stock. Once we were up at Sedona making a film called *The Last Wagon*. The wind would come up every day in these tall pine trees. We were recording the film in stereo, so we were using three microphones. One of the three boom men kept saying, "You know we're going to loop it, so why pay so much attention to it?" He was right, and when they called lunch, I kept my sound crew about ten minutes to make a sound track of the wind in the pines. There were at least a half dozen kinds of wind. However, the best wind sound I ever recorded was during the filming of *Yellow Sky* which William Wellman directed with Gregory Peck, Anne Baxter, and Richard Widmark. We shot in Death Valley and up at Lone Pine, and I recorded especially good wind sounds at both places. Such sound effects are traded among the studios. Occasionally an effect is bought. Today every studio in town has what they call the *Yellow Sky* Wind.

In 1935 I was working on a film in Arizona and we got hit by a terrific thunderstorm. Everyone ran to cover, but I made the recorder stay to make a sound track of the elaborate thunder. That was done on the old optical film and was used in all the studios for a long time until magnetic tape came in.

Mike: It seems you have been on an awful lot of locations to make films!

Freericks: In my home I have a big wall map of the United States with dozens of pins stuck in it to denote the places I have been on location.

Mike: Actually any place the company shoots away from the studio is considered location shooting, isn't it? Even if it's in the same city?

Freericks: Yes. I remember one film where we kept running back and forth between the studio and location depending on the weather. It was in 1941 when we made *To the Shores of Tripoli* about the Marine Corps and its training program. Our location sites were at the old Marine barracks at Camp Pendleton, which is about a hundred miles south of Los Angeles. We were housed in a hotel outside San Diego, but, if the weather was foggy or bad, we would have to shoot back at the studio. Many times we would be shooting at the studio when the fog would clear up back in San Diego, and we would get in cars and rush down there. We used hundreds of marines in the picture and showed them in the actual process of their tough boot camp training. One day I happened to comment on all the dust the wind was blowing around, and a young marine standing near me said, "That ain't dust. It's shoe leather!" The Monday after Pearl Harbor was attacked we arrived in San Diego to start shooting, and they wouldn't let us. They were on the alert for the possibility that the Japanese might even attack the California coast. I asked a marine lieutenant, "What have they got for shore defenses?" He looked at me and started laughing and said, "You see those five-inch guns? That's all there is here!"

Mike: I suppose you've been on foreign locations all over the world, too!

Freericks: Yes. Especially in the past ten years when so many American films have been made abroad because of economic reasons as well as a desire to shoot a film in the actual locale of its story. Probably the most difficult of these locations for me and my crew was when we were over in Formosa shooting *The Sand Pebbles* with Steve McQueen. It was a tough picture to make because most of it was filmed on that little gunboat with no room to move. My boom man was constantly having to crawl on his hands and knees in order to get the microphone in a position near the actors. Actually I enjoy most locations, although working at a studio is easier for a sound mixer.

Mike: Which foreign location have you enjoyed most?

Freericks: It would be a tossup between *Cleopatra* in Italy and *The Sound of Music* in Austria. I worked on *Cleopatra* for eleven months. I had my boom man and my recorder with me. We took on quite a few of the Italians as technicians. At first that presented a slight problem. Every film the Italians make, regardless of what it is, is looped. The sound man sits out in a truck somewhere and doesn't care what goes on inside the stage. The electricians and grips are always visiting with one another, walking around, and talking. Their little motorscooters go around outside the stage as if it were a racetrack. We put a stop to all this noisemaking, and they didn't like it, until we showed them the first day's rushes that were sent back. Then they understood what we were trying to do, that we were saving all the sound we were shooting to use in the picture. From that time on, we just blew a whistle before each take and everybody was quiet. At the end of the week there would always be some little party for them. The director would get bottles of wine and Italian cookies. Everybody had a good time on the picture. In fact, *Cleopatra* was an easy picture for all of us to work on. There was never an early work call. It took Elizabeth Taylor several hours to put on her makeup, so we never had a call before ten in the morning, and we always finished by six at night. We never worked on Saturdays, which is usually done on locations, until toward the end of the film, when we went to the island of Ischia. All of *Cleopatra*, the exteriors and the interiors, was filmed abroad.

When Fox made *The Sound of Music*, we went to Switzerland, Austria, and Germany because the script called for it. But all the interiors, except for what we call our cover sets, were filmed at the studio in Hollywood. We had several cover sets in Salzburg, Austria, so when it was raining, we could still shoot something and not lose any time or money.

One picture we did that you'd think was shot on location, but wasn't, is *The Snows of Kilimanjaro*. It was taken from the Ernest Hemingway novel and starred Ava Gardner, Gregory Peck, and Susan Hayward in 1952. If it were made today, they'd go straight to Africa! It was the type of picture where they throw everything at the sound man! All sorts of technical noises which interfered with the dialogue. There was a big set with a painting of Mount Kilimanjaro which went two-thirds the way around the sound stage. Then they put in trees, brush, tents, and all sorts of things to make it look like Africa. The trees and foliage had to move, so we had wind machines and wires everywhere. There was also noise from the dozens of arc lights up above the set. All this considered, we knew they would have to loop almost everything in a sound studio later.

The picture opened in Hollywood at Grauman's Chinese Theater, and I went to see it for the first time. I thought they had done such a wonderful job of looping that I called the head of the sound department, Carl Faulkner, to tell him so. He said, "We didn't loop a thing!" I said, "Well, gee, it was great!" He said, "I know, and I'm going to find out why!" The thing one forgets is that in a large theater like the Chinese you have two or three thousand people who are moving around and creating their own noises. Also, their clothes absorb a lot of the sound frequencies such as that produced by wind. If the theater had been half empty, you would have heard all the unwanted noises. Of course, under any conditions, a professional sound man is more aware of foreign noises than the average moviegoer or television viewer. Most of the television pictures that are shot out of doors have a lot of noise on them. Sometimes, if they are too noisy, the producer will go to the expense to loop them. However, in the majority of these cases the average person isn't aware of these noises anyway because the quality of sound you get out of the speakers on a TV set isn't very good.

Mike: The quality of sound first of all depends on the quality of the microphone used in recording, doesn't it?

Freericks: Yes. We get improved microphones every couple of years. In the beginning, microphones weighed ten to fifteen pounds. Now they just weigh ounces, and the quality of sound they produce is far superior. That is, if you have an expensive one, because you can buy microphones for ten dollars or you can buy them for four or five hundred dollars. Most of the professional microphones used in the studios cost between two hundred fifty and three hundred dollars. For a number of years we've had what we call radio link microphones. They cost over a thousand dollars. You hang them, say, under an actor's shirt and place an antenna around his neck which is hooked down his leg. There is a radio transmitter strapped to his back. So you don't have to run a cable from the microphone. There is receiving equipment which is plugged into the mixer. Unfortunately, the sound quality is not all that good.

Mike: Just the same, aren't radio link microphones coming into wider use?

Freericks: Yes. Especially for location shooting because now they don't pick up the ignition noise of cars passing by and various other noises. But, they weren't always so good. For instance, when we made *The Robe*, the first film in stereo sound and in CinemaScope, in 1953, I had to use a radio link microphone in a couple of scenes. At times there was an overlap of radio wavelengths, and one time you could even hear the Department of Water and Power at the service center in Rancho Park across from the studio calling their trucks to go such and such a place.

Mike: Do some moviemakers in this country make films without sound, as the Italians do, then loop everything later?

Freericks: I guess so, with very low budget films. But the looping would be difficult unless the actors are willing to say the lines exactly as they are in the script. That takes away a lot of an actor's individuality. When an actor recites lines on the Broadway stage, he doesn't necessarily have to follow the script every word. Nor does he say a line with the same timing and inflection night after night. In filmmaking, in order to match one angle of a scene with another, it is essential always to be consistent in dialogue and movement.

Mike: If during a scene you hear over your earphones an actor make a flaw or be hard to understand or you hear some outside noise, is it your duty to tell the director you haven't had a good take?

Freericks: Yes. When we did *Cleopatra*, the director, Joe Mankiewicz, came to me and said, "If anything goes wrong with the sound, just yell 'cut.' I won't even ask any questions. I'm depending on you." With some other directors, if you yell "cut," they'll slit your throat! So you wait until the end of the scene, then you go up to the director and say that at such and such a place such and such a thing happened. He has to decide if he wants to take the scene over, cover it by cutting to another angle or actor, or loop it. Sometimes, if it's a low-budget film, they'll leave it the way it is! One of the advantages of working with a fine director like Mankiewicz is that you are able to get a really good sound job. *Cleopatra* didn't win an Academy Award for sound, but it got a nomination. When I did *The Sound of Music*, the director, Robert Wise, would not let me yell "cut" if anything went wrong, but he was easy to work with, and the sound for the picture did win an Academy Award.

Mike: Do you ever go directly to the actor or star and tell him when he has made a mistake?

Freericks: It depends on the director. Some directors don't want anyone to talk to their actors. Other directors say, "Go ahead and tell them," like Robert Altman on *M*A*S*H*.

Mike: How do the actors take your suggestions?

Freericks: They love it if you can point out something that can be improved upon. They want to be seen in their best light, too. Actually, actors' voices don't give any trouble unless they are mumblers such as Marlon Brando whom I had on *The Young Lions* or another "method actor" whom I had on the remake we did of *Stagecoach*. You couldn't understand him at all. I would go to him and ask him to speak up or tell him that if he wanted to speak low, to enunciate his words so they could be understood.

Mike: Certain performers are famous for their voices such as Cary

Grant, Katharine Hepburn, and Mae West. Can you, through your technical skill, emphasize this aspect of their personality for them?

Freericks: We used to try that years ago, before we had rerecording, but it always messed things up a little bit. Now, if there is something that needs to be emphasized or deemphasized, it is done in rerecording with what we call an equalizer. Of course, to save money and time we try to get the sound as correct as possible at the same time the scene is being filmed, so that we have a minimum of rerecording. It depends on what they are willing to let go. For instance, a lot of our work on *M*A*S*H* was done out at the Fox ranch in Malibu Canyon. Since it was a war picture, as long as an airplane came over which didn't drown out the dialogue, they paid no attention to it. *M*A*S*H* is a good example of how some films are being shot today. We had a script, but I don't think we used ten lines of dialogue from it! Nearly everything was ad lib.

Mike: That must have been a headache for the script supervisor who has to keep a record of every word that is spoken.

Freericks: Yes. I had to set up a separate tape recorder for him so that when one of these ad-lib scenes was finished he could play it over until he got the exact dialogue down on his script. Otherwise he would have been lost! The method of shooting gave the film editor a headache, too, but he turned out a great job.* We did take after take and cut after cut to fit in with the others. I went up to the director one day and said, "The film editor doesn't care much for this kind of stuff, all this overlapping, does he?" He replied, "That's his problem. I like it." That attitude just about sums up filmmaking today. One used to feel a part of a team or family when working at a studio. The only place you feel that now is maybe on a television series where the same crew works together for six or eight months. On most feature motion-picture productions today it is dog eat dog!

December 2, 1970

---

* Even so, *M*A*S*H* received the Academy Award for best screenplay (based on material from another medium) in 1970!

Music Composer and Conductor

JOHN GREEN

Green: Although my parents were born in New York City, our family was a Middle-European-oriented family of means. In the days of my childhood every well-educated young man or young lady played the piano. My parents were examples of that. They were very good musicians. I myself began studying the piano when I was five. I had the same teacher my mother had had.

Mike: You studied from childhood to be a musician?

Green: I've studied music all my life, but my father wanted me to go into the business world. My mother wanted me to do whatever I wanted, provided it was honest, decent, and that I did the best I could to achieve the best of which I was capable. If I had wanted to be a very good bootblack, she would have given me all her support!

Mike: You went into the music field against your father's wishes?

Green: Yes. I wanted to hate my father and may have been better off if I could have. But there were so many, many things about him I admired. He was a man of great erudition and large culture. He had a divine sense of humor. Was a great dialectician. He spoke fluent French and fluent German. He was didactic. Terribly opinionated. He knew a great deal about many things, but he thought he knew everything about everything! He didn't have any bigoted prejudice against the arts, because he was too much in love with them himself, but he used to say to me, "Son, you can be a pretty good banker, a pretty good lawyer, a pretty good merchant, a pretty good preacher, even a pretty good doctor and hold your head high in the community and be a respected citizen. But, son, there's no bum like a pretty good artist, and I think you're pretty good!" So he didn't think I could make it in the arts. He felt I had major gifts as an administrator and an organizer.

Mike: When it was time to go to college, why did you choose Harvard?

Green: I enjoyed school and studying. The acquisition of knowledge was a pleasure, and I got good marks. I wanted to go to Harvard because in those days places like Juilliard, the New England Conservatory, Curtis, and Peabody were very much ivory towers. They didn't have the liberal arts point of view which later became part of their *modus operandi* when people like Bill Schuman became president of Juilliard. Harvard had always had a fine music school.

Mike: But your father wanted you to prepare yourself as a business-man?

Green: My father said, "So you want to go to Harvard and take your degree in music? Well, that's fine! You do that, and you pay for it!" Well, I enjoyed being a rich man's son! I still say don't knock it if you handle it with grace. One of the things I was looking forward to at Harvard was its cosmopolitan quality. I loved the city of Boston and all that it meant culturally and socially. I looked forward to living in deluxe accommodations and all the rest of it. I was damned if I was going to give that up, so I went along with his desire that I be an economics major. I did well in that and at the same time took all the music courses I wanted to take. I was graduated at the age of nineteen, the youngest man in my class. That pleased my father, but I've since learned that's too young to get out of college. My whole life has been out of kilter because of it. I should have majored in music, or I should have gone to Curtis or Juilliard. I think my life would have been a better life. As it is, I'm a sort of third- or fourth-rate Renaissance man. At least, reporters sometimes write that about me! If Leonard Bernstein is a first-rate Renaissance man, which I think he is, then I've got to be a third- or fourth-rater.

Mike: Your first popular song was published your last year at Harvard. How did that come about?

Green: A classmate named Charles Henderson and I had founded the Harvard Goldcoast Orchestra, a college dance band. We made some demonstration records which another classmate played for Guy Lombardo, whose band was popular around Cleveland. This was before he went to Chicago and really exploded. He liked the arrangements I had done on the recordings, and I got a long-distance telephone call from him. In 1927 a phone call from Cleveland, Ohio, to Cambridge, Massachusetts, was a big thing! He asked me how I'd like to come to Cleveland my summer vacation and work as an arranger. I made a hundred and fifty bucks a week working with Guy and his Royal Canadians, which was a hell of a lot better than being a runner on Wall Street for fifteen dollars a week. The style of the band was already well formulated, and I made arrangements in that style. That summer Carmen Lombardo and I wrote the melody which was to become "Coquette." Gus Kahn, one of the greatest lyric writers of the century, wrote the words. The song is still being very kind to Gus' widow and to the whole Green family.

Mike: After your graduation you went to work on Wall Street?

Green: For six months. I finally couldn't take it and decided to tell my father where to head in. Which I did! The first job I had after leaving Wall Street was as Gertrude Lawrence's accompanist. She was doing nightclubs and recordings in addition to her regular acting career. In 1930 I went to work at the Astoria studio of Paramount Pictures as a rehearsal pianist. A picture called *The Big Pond* starring Maurice Chevalier and Claudette Colbert was being made. It was a semimusical, and Irving Kahal and Sammy Fain had been engaged to write the score. The orchestrator, Robert Russell Bennett, became ill. I went to Frank Tours, the head of the music department, and asked if I could fill the vacancy. That was a pretentious thing for me to do after only two months at the studio, but I got the job! The first thing handed me to orchestrate was a song called "You Brought a New Kind of Love to Me."

Mike: Apart from your work at the studio, didn't you and Eddie Heyman begin writing songs together?

Green: Yes. Gertrude Lawrence needed some special material. She commissioned Eddie and me to write four songs for her at a total fee of two hundred and fifty dollars. Three of the songs never caught on, but the fourth one was "Body and Soul," which I don't have to tell you about!

Mike: When did you become a conductor?

Green: That same year, 1931. One day while I was recording at the studio, the head of the music department for the Paramount theater chain, Boris Morros, was present. He thought I had a future as a conductor and invited me to come and spend part of my time as an apprentice house conductor at the Brooklyn Paramount Theater. That was the real beginning of my conducting career. Until 1933 I appeared as a conductor at the Brooklyn, Minneapolis, and New York City Paramount theaters.

Mike: You continued writing pop songs as well as more serious music?

Green: Yes. In 1931 I had been commissioned by Paul Whiteman to compose a piece for his series of concerts called Experiments in Modern American Music. Seven years before, Paul had premiered George Gershwin's *Rhapsody in Blue,* which had been a cannon shot heard around the world. By way of comparison, my work turned out to be a cap pistol! It was, however, a decent piece which premiered at Carnegie Hall with Paul conducting and myself at the piano. I played the piece again in the summer of 1933 with the New York Philharmonic at Lewisohn Stadium. A very bright young executive in that new business called radio was in the audience. I had never met him before. His name was William S. Paley. Mr. Paley had just been given the Columbia Broadcasting System by his dad to keep him out of trouble! Of course, what he did with CBS makes him one of the business geniuses of our time. The day after attending my concert, he apparently called his friend Eddie Duchin, who by coincidence was a dear friend of mine, and asked him if he knew a guy named Johnny Green. I ended up having lunch with Paley that day, and the outcome was the beginning of my very lucrative and happy big-time radio career.

Mike: Didn't you organize your own dance band for radio and supper clubs?

Green: My dance band was an outgrowth of my CBS work. Paley thought I should have one. Although I prospered from Bill Paley's guidance, I believe the band sidetracked my career as a serious composer-conductor.

Mike: With all the success you were enjoying in the world of music did your father finally give you his support?

Green: My father had definite beliefs that a large income was a faithful barometer of success. I was making an awful lot of money with the band, and my father had been ruined financially with the collapse of the real estate market in 1931. I was making several thousand dollars a week while he was trying to put the pieces back together. So I had his large admiration!

Mike: Having your band led to your being the bandleader on the Jack Benny radio show?

Green: Yes, but not on CBS. It was the fall of 1935 that I came to

Hollywood for the first time as part of Jack's show for Jell-O on NBC. Then I did *The Packard Hour* with Fred Astaire. During that period I fell in love with and married Betty Furness, after divorcing my first wife. Betty and I have one daughter, Barbara. In 1939 I went back to New York and reorganized my own band to do the *Philip Morris Show* for two years.

Mike: How did the writing of your first Broadway show come about?

Green: Peter Arno, the "smart New York set" character and cartoonist for the *New Yorker* magazine, decided to venture into theatrical producing in 1931 with a financial backing from John Hay Whitney, the multimillionaire who later became the U.S. ambassador to Great Britain. Eddie Heyman and I were hired to write the score. The show starred Clark and McCullough, a big comedy team of the time, and was called *Here Goes the Bride.* It should have been called *Here Goes the Show* because it played only six performances on Broadway. That was the first of three cast-iron manhole covers I wrote for the New York theater. The second was in 1940, when I gave up the dance band to write a show called *Hy-Ya, Gentlemen.* It starred the late, and in many ways quite great, Ella Logan. Max Baer, the ex-prizefighter, costarred. Max had just made a movie called *The Prizefighter and the Lady.* In one scene he had stood between three girls on each side of him with his arms around the two nearest girls. They had done the conventional step called the kicks, and everybody said he was a musical-comedy star! The theater is still suffering from that kind of syndrome. Rex Harrison is the best example of it today. Except that Rex is great! My third flop as composer of the whole score of a musical was two years later. It was *Beat the Band* and had the distinction of being George Abbott's first flop musical. It eeked out a miserable four-month existence at the 46th Street Theater. That was the last thing I did on Broadway before coming to Hollywood as a staff conductor-composer for MGM in November, 1942.

Mike: Didn't Arthur Freed bring you to Metro?

Green: Yes. What happened was: At the same time *Beat the Band* was being written, Richard Rodgers, who is more like a brother to me than a friend, knew I needed some help. He persuaded me to go into the pit to conduct the last show he wrote with Lorenz Hart, *By Jupiter.* It starred Ray Bolger. Into the Shubert Theater one night came Louis B. Mayer, Judy Garland, and Arthur Freed with his outstanding assistant, Roger Edens. I could see them sitting in the second row as I entered the orchestra pit to conduct the overture. At that time pit conducting in New York theater had reached its nadir, its lowest ebb. The great pit conductors had already come to the West Coast. Alfred Newman, Bobby Dolan. Not meaning to boast, I received reviews that were bloody sensational. It was just that they hadn't heard anything decent in the pit for so long that a mere neat and fine job was big news. The MGM group came backstage afterward, and Mr. Freed, whom I had met previously, said, "You've got to come to Metro!" I didn't want to go to Hollywood. I had already signed to be the music director of the new Richard Rodgers musical, *Oklahoma!*, and I was particularly happy about that because Dick had teamed up with Oscar Hammerstein, II, whom I adored. I was a New Yorker lock, stock, and barrel. I was not in love with Hollywood or even liked it very much. However, the contractual offer made by Metro got to a point that it was too good to turn down.

Mike: So you went to Hollywood and became a member of the Freed unit?

Green: No. I got to Metro expecting to be in his unit, but I found myself a general composer-conductor under the whiplash of the music department and its then head, Nathaniel Finston. I had Mr. Freed's ear whenever I wanted it, and he was kind and good to me; but I didn't do a day's work for him until a few years later.

Mike: At that time the three major producers at MGM making musicals were Arthur Freed, Jack Cummings, and Joe Pasternak!

Green: Yes. All three were musically knowledgeable and musically sensitive, making them qualified to produce musical pictures. We have had some producers in the industry who never should have been allowed near musicals. Happily, Jack Cummings decided to make me his executive assistant in charge of music! Which I was from 1943 until 1946.

Mike: Didn't Cummings do most of the Esther Williams "water musicals"?

Green: He did *Bathing Beauty*, *Neptune's Daughter*, *Texas Carnival*, and *Easy to Wed*. I married one of the MGM Glamazons who swam in these films, Bunny Waters. We're still married and have two daughters, Kathe and Kim. Jack might buzz me to come to his office and ask me about some story he had read in the *Saturday Evening Post* or another magazine. He'd say, "What do you think of that for an Esther Williams musical?" If we did such a project, I was with it from first story draft through final answer print. I was in on everything: blueprinting the music, selecting the director, casting the film, rehearsing, at which time I began functioning as the music director. During rehearsals I worked with the various talents in laying out the vocals, the choreography, and so on. Under my direction would come as much assistance in arranging and orchestrating as I felt I needed. I always had a great deal of trouble keeping myself from being a hog and doing too much. There are a few of us like André Previn and Nelson Riddle who do the whole *shmeer*. When time came to record, I would be on the podium conducting. During shooting I was in charge of those aspects of the photography of musical numbers which involved synchronization between performers and the prerecorded sound track. After shooting comes editorial time, which is primarily the duty of the producer and director. The music director is involved with editing only depending on how much prestige he has. With the Cummings unit I was always intimately working with Jack and his film editor. After that comes the post-scoring job. At that point I would be a composer-conductor-arranger.

Mike: You were to Jack Cummings what Roger Edens* was to Arthur Freed and Saul Chaplin was to Joe Pasternak?

Green: Over the years the three of us were the right-hand associates of those producers. The basic difference between Roger and Saul on the one hand and myself on the other is that neither of them conducts, orchestrates, or is a composer in the larger forms. I'm talking categorically, not qualitatively, when I say I have a kind of versatility neither of them pretends to have. They don't write scores for dramatic pictures or conduct symphony orchestras. They do make musical arrangements and sketches from which orchestrators develop. It's difficult for me to say gracefully that I do the whole thing, but I do! When Roger or Saul are on a picture as associate producer in charge of music, they must have a Johnny Green or a Conrad Salinger or a choral arranger. I've worked happily under both Roger and Saul. When I was general music director and executive in charge of music at MGM from 1949 to 1958, it was impossible for me to do all that administrative work and then still be a music director on a film and do all the work alone. I collaborated with Saul. We worked together at Metro on *High Society, Summer Stock,* and *An American in Paris.* The latter got me an Academy Award in 1951.

* Roger Edens died shortly after this interview with Mr. Green.

Mike: You had won another Oscar in 1948 for *Easter Parade*.

Green: *Easter Parade* was a combination of Arthur Freed, Judy Garland, Fred Astaire, Vincente Minnelli, and Irving Berlin at their best. And I don't think Roger Edens, Connie Salinger, or I did it any harm! A funny thing happened during one of the prerecording sessions: Arthur Freed is a coin jingler. He's always got a pocketful of silver and his hand in that pocket! As advanced as recording was then, it was primitive compared with today. One day I was conducting one of the big numbers when Arthur and Irving came onto the stage. The red light was on, meaning to be very quiet. Arthur took a stance fairly close to the mikes where Judy and Fred were singing away. All of a sudden he began jingling those silver coins! I didn't know what to do. He was the boss. Then he started whispering to Irving. When Irving looked like he was going to answer, Arthur went, "Shhhhhhhhhhhhh." This happened several times. When the recording was played back, you didn't hear the coins jingling or the whispering. All you could hear was Arthur going "Shhhhh" throughout the piece!

Mike: In 1961 you got another Oscar for *West Side Story*.

Green: Saul Chaplin was actually the associate producer to Robert Wise on that. I worked as music director under the general supervision of Saul. The Oscar was presented to four of us: Saul Chaplin, myself, Sid Ramin, and Irwin Kostal. The latter two had been Leonard Bernstein's orchestrators for the original Broadway production. Lenny had a great deal to say about what was going to happen to this valuable property in Hollywood. As much as he loves Saul Chaplin and me, he does not love Hollywood or motion-picture making, and he was going to make damned sure his score was not mucked up. He had Ramin and Kostal put on the picture as his policemen because they knew his brilliant score so well. The collaboration of the four of us worked out since there was tremendous mutual respect. We had a lot of fun!

Mike: Your latest Oscar was for *Oliver!*

Green: I spent most of 1967 and 1968 in London making *Oliver!* When I arrived in England, I laid it on the line to all my fine British colleagues. I said, "Fellows, I'm going to do this whole music job myself, and I'm going to be a man who needs a staff of very gifted musical assistants. That's what you people are going to be. You will get proper credit that we will work out somehow, but it's going to be a single John Green job. If it stinks, I'm going to take all the blame. If it's great, none of you will share the nomination or the award if there is one. I will not be taking credit for your work, because I'm going to arrange it, adapt it, orchestrate it, and do the choral arranging. On *Oliver!* I'm going to be Roger Edens, Saul Chaplin, John Green, Connie Salinger, and Bobby Tucker all rolled into one! Anyone who doesn't want to be around on that basis mustn't take the job." On the film credits you read, "Music supervised, arranged, and conducted by John Green." On the next card you read, "Orchestrations and choral arrangements by John Green." Then you saw, "Additional orchestration by Eric Rogers," and then on a half card you saw, "Associate music director, Eric Rogers."

Mike: So you walked up alone to accept your fifth Oscar for two years' work. Most of the performers in *Oliver!* were genuine musical performers, weren't they?

Green: Yes.

Mike: I'd rather see that than some big dramatic star making a noble effort at song and dance.

Green: The whole syndrome of nonmusical performers playing musical parts has come to be known as the Harrison Syndrome. Rex Harrison never sang a note in his life as a musical performer prior to his enormous success in *My Fair Lady*. The key word here is a very precise word called "musicality." Lerner and Loewe found out, when working with Rex and probing the question if he could do the part, that he was loaded with musicality. In just speaking a song, his musicality came across. The same happened for Robert Preston when he did *The Music Man*. Any number of performers in the history of the musical theater have not been technically great singers, but you like seeing them perform whether or not you like their voices. For instance, Ethel Merman has been a great singing performer regardless of the timbre of her voice. Gertrude Lawrence had a peculiar voice but was a great singing performer. And look at how much musical comedy was done by Irene Bordoni and George M. Cohan while no one would accuse them of having had great voices! A great voice isn't necessary, but musicality is very necessary. In films, classic examples of nonmusical performers playing musical roles are Deborah Kerr as Anna in *The King and I*, Natalie Wood as Maria in *West Side Story*, and Ava Gardner as Julie in *Showboat*. Their voices were dubbed, but they were able to look as though they had done the singing. Their bodies moved in terms of music. The eyes, head, arms, and hands moved in terms of musical impulses. The ability to have these things happen is a big part of musicality. Without musicality you wind up with klutzes on the musical stage and screen. I've seen about twenty live stage performances of *My Fair Lady*, and I've seen some people playing Professor Higgins who should have been shot when they arrived at the stage door!

Mike: The picking of the correct voice double for a star in a film is very important.

Green: Doubling a star's singing voice isn't only a question of matching sound and timbre. You must select a double who has the ability to form words like the star being dubbed. Let's say you have an actor from somewhere in the Midwest who pronounces the word "water" in that particular Midwestern way. When time comes for him to sing, his voice double has to sing the word with the same pronunciation. Marni Nixon is a genius at doubling this sort of thing. When she dubbed for Deborah Kerr in *The King and I*, she was able to get Deborah's specific British accent and sound just the way Deborah would sound if she were a singer!

Mike: Do you have objections to using nonmusical performers in musical roles?

Green: You bet your sweet life I do! I think it's one of the sicknesses of today's theater. One almost gets the feeling that producers make it their business to get before them a roster of every competent musical performer in the business, and having assembled that list, they throw it in the wastebasket and say, "Now, let's cast the picture." One reason for this is that today's musicals have more dramatic plots and styles which increase the need for real acting talent. That's the legitimate part of it. On the other hand, most actors are hambones. They say, "If Rex can do it, I can do it." And all that money! Plus the royalties from the cast album! That's the nasty part of it. The nonlegitimate part.

Mike: There is also the tragic part in that the training ground has disappeared.

Green: True. There's no place left in the entertainment business for young people to be lousy, learn from it, and survive it. They're nothing on Monday, and on Tuesday they're on television performing for twenty million people. There's no such thing any more as coming up through the road. So you don't have the places for the development of a Fred Astaire or a Judy Garland. Could there be a better actress than Judy was? She was a real honest to God musical-theater performer. Sang like an angel. A great showman. Hell of a dancer, and a heart-rending actress!

Mike: Do you think there are all-round performers of that caliber working today?

Green: A few. Julie Andrews is the best of the crop. She's got so much talent it's just not to be believed! I'd rather work with her than almost anybody I know. She doesn't seem to *me* to have that "everybody's nanny" effect. *I* think she is *very* sexy!

Mike: How would you judge the two nonmusical performers who recently had hits on Broadway, Lauren Bacall in *Applause* and Katharine Hepburn in *Coco*?

Green: From what little I saw of either show on the telecast of awards for Broadway shows, I had the feeling Lauren Bacall got away with it brilliantly by virtue of her musicality and that Katharine Hepburn got by with the skin of her teeth. Katie is an old friend of mine, and God knows she's a great actress; but my hunch is that I wouldn't want her singing a score of mine.

Mike: One of your more recent films was *They Shoot Horses, Don't They?* Since the story takes place in a marathon dance hall, there is one piece of music after another. Did you write any of the songs for the picture?

Green: Of the thirty-one songs in the film, seven are mine. However, they are songs I wrote back in the thirties when the story took place. The picture is actually a musical documentary of that period. For the first time I had associate producer credit on a film. People would say to me, "Hey, this is something new for you, isn't it?" I had a quiet reply, "No, getting credit for it is."

Mike: A very entertaining contemporary movie was *Butch Cassidy and the Sundance Kid.* It's not a musical, but in the middle of the picture there is a musical number sung by an off-camera singer, which has nothing to do with the plot of the film! It seemed to me this song was intentionally thrown in for the sole purpose of having an added category to qualify for the Academy Awards. It served as an extra item to commercialize on.

Green: Having a real hit song in a movie is the greatest exploitation you can have. And one of the greatest ways to make extra money! Of course, "Raindrops Keep Falling on My Head" is a blockbuster! There are few hits ever of that stature.

Mike: Do you think this trend of putting a song in a picture, even though the song is out of context with the story, is a desirable trend?

Green: It's more than a trend. It's already an establishment which has undermined the quality of what had begun to be an art form. The art of scoring dramatic motion pictures has taken the worst beating in the world in the last few years. Much of what we worked for from 1930 through 1967 is right down the drain. Too frequently the governing factor now is "Can we get a hit record!" Not what is best for the picture. Too frequently they say, "Let's get ourselves a hit LP and shoehorn it into the picture as the score!"

Mike: What do you think about theme songs? Aren't theme songs ones that are more legitimately connected with the overall film, which at the same time publicize the film?

Green: Yes. Theme songs go way back to the era of songs like "Diane" in the film *Seventh Heaven* and the song "Charmaine" in *What Price Glory?* From the point of view of sheer exploitation *title* songs, I wrote one of the first big ones for *I Cover the Waterfront,* which was not even in the picture! Alfred Newman had written the score of the film before the publicity department at United Artists got the idea of having Eddie Heyman and me write the song for the sole purpose of advertising the picture. In order to do that efficiently, our song had to bear the title of the picture. It became an enormous hit, and subsequent prints of the picture had the song added instrumentally in the front and back.

Mike: Musical films have nearly always had title songs, haven't they?

Green: Yes, but we've been talking about straight dramatic films. During the time between about 1935 and the mid-forties, the title theme song as a commercial entity almost disappeared from film scores. Instead you had the great scores of Franz Waxman, Miklos Rozsa, Herbert Stothart, Alex North, Roy Webb, Max Steiner, and Alfred Newman, who were among the best of the film composers oriented to European musical styles. This group represented a neo-Lisztian, neo-Tchaikovskian approach to dramatic music. A little later the film composing fraternity fell heavily under the influence of the French Impressionists. Scores with a sound reminiscent of Liszt, Tchaikovsky, Wagner, and Richard Strauss had a Ravel and Debussy influence superimposed on them. Then Aaron Copland emerged in the field of serious concert music as "the American sound" and became an influence on the texture of film music. Copland, himself, only wrote a few film scores. His principal ones were *The Red Pony* and *The Heiress.* Various quasi-symphonic pieces emerged from such scores as Alfred Newman's *Street Scene,* Waxman's *Fury,* Bernard Hermann's *All That Money Can Buy* and Max Steiner's *Gone with the Wind.* Steiner had a superb feeling for the integration of music with drama. His scores did what a score is supposed to do: enhance the emotional impact, help in the setting up of atmosphere and mood, heighten suspense, augment shock value, and sentimentalize.

Mike: How did the theme song begin to creep in again?

Green: It's hard to pinpoint it, but Dimitri Tiomkin had something to do with it when you consider *High Noon,* which was an outstanding use of the title song. That song was designed to step out of the picture, but it was still good dramatic technique within the framework of the film because it commented on the action in a Greek chorus sort of way. It came into being as a valid musical device. Nobody said, "Let's have a hit record and see if it will fit into the picture." That attitude is deplorable! About the time of *High Noon,* all the major studios began buying record companies. They already had music publishing companies. Naturally, the studios wanted to make their record companies a moneymaking business, but when the values and standards are subverted, and the money is sought from other than the dramatic venture of the film, the important element of movie music is prostituted! Legitimate film composers such as Franz Waxman and Elmer Bernstein were put in the position of being engaged to write a dramatic score and being ordered to use a theme by Sammy Cahn and Sammy Fain!

Mike: Aren't some serious film composers able to write popular songs and some popular songwriters able to write film scores?

Green: Oh, yes. I began as a pop songwriter. So did Victor Young. And many legitimate film composers have been able to write pop songs. For instance, Dimitri Tiomkin, who wrote "High Noon," also wrote "The High and the Mighty" and "Friendly Persuasion." The greatest example of a film composer who emerged as a very important songwriter is Hank Mancini with "Moon River," "The Days of Wine and Roses," and "Charade." Hank's whole method in film scoring is to get that theme first and the resulting song is a natural consequence.

Mike: Who are some of the more current film composers of whom you think highly?

Green: Elmer Bernstein is the old man of the new boys! This group includes Jerry Goldsmith, Lenny Rosenman, Lalo Schifrin, Michel Legrand, and John Williams, who did *The Reivers, Goodbye, Mr. Chips,* and *Fiddler on the Roof.* Then there is John Barry, whom I think of as the British version of our Quincy Jones. I don't know quite how to evaluate either of them. They are a law unto themselves and highly successful. One of the greatest commercial successes in the history of movie music is the Maurice Jarre score for *Dr. Zhivago.* The sound track album has sold nearly three million copies and is still selling!

Mike: I was disappointed that his score for *The Damned* sounded so much like his *Dr. Zhivago* score. Which of your scores do you feel has been the most popular?

Green: I've written many dramatic scores, but the one that seems to have taken its place among the highly respected scores is *Raintree County.* At the time I wrote it in 1957, the theme song craze was upon us. My approach for this two-hour-and-ten-minute score was the Wagnerian leitmotiv structure in which the characters, the locales and even thoughts had their own individual themes. That put me within the possibility of developing themes which could result in popular songs. The picture flopped in its initial run, and therefore the score was hurt; but it was nominated for an Academy Award. Nevertheless, I lost to four hundred extras whistling a forty-year-old march which is one of the scandals in the history of the music awards: It was a brilliant device in *The Bridge on the River Kwai* to have that British regiment whistle the old "Colonel Bogie March," but there was virtually no dramatic score to speak of in the film.

Mike: Will you name a couple of your favorite movie scores by your contemporaries?

Green: Right off I think of the one and only score Leonard Bernstein wrote, *On the Waterfront.* The imagination and creativity of that score make the approach of many regular film composers seem pedestrian! I also greatly admire the scores written by the British composer Sir William Walton for the Shakespeare films made by the now Baron Laurence Olivier, *Henry V, Hamlet,* and *Richard III.*

Mike: Are you a fan of Burt Bacharach?

Green: His popular songs are certainly outstanding, but I feel he still has to prove himself as a film composer.

Mike: Will you comment on some of the performers you've worked with as I mention their names?

Green: Yes.

Mike: Let's begin with Mario Lanza.

Green: I'm one of the people who thinks if Mario Lanza had not been genuinely mentally ill and a victim of stupid people around him, and if he could have been made a normal, mature human being, there's no doubt he would have been the next Caruso. Certainly the voice, the temperament, the musicality were all there. I conducted all the operatic stuff that Mario did in all his films prior to *The Great Caruso*. In that one I collaborated with Peter Herman Adler, whom I brought to Hollywood from the NBC Opera.

Mike: Deanna Durbin.

Green: In 1947 I was brought to Universal-International by William Goetz and Leo Spitz for the specific purpose of rescuing Deanna Durbin's career. On the contrary, I'd say I finished her off! Deanna was beyond help at that point. I loved working with her, but she was one of those rare instances of a fine performer who had at one time achieved enormous success and stardom, then later lost box-office appeal. It wasn't just her growing up. It was also an unfortunate reputation she had acquired. It's funny, but there are some people with whom unorthodox behavior becomes box-office enhancement. Elizabeth Taylor is the classic example. I'm fond of Liz and have known her well since she was a child, but I'm sure the life she has led is not the one most parents envision for their daughters. Yet her carrying-on and her several husbands have enhanced her career! With Deanna, I think her reputation worked against her. She got a reputation for being difficult to work with. However, when I was working with her she was fascinating. She was a good enough actress and still sang like an angel. We got her weight down and made two very bad pictures. The first was *Something in the Wind* for which I served the multiple tasks of being her psychiatrist, vocal coach, and music director of the film. I also wrote the score. Leo Robin did the lyrics. The second film was *Up in Central Park*. It was death to do that kind of picture in black and white, but the budget wouldn't permit doing it in color. Both pictures were disasters. The public just did not want Deanna Durbin at that time, although she was very good in them. The sound tracks of her voice were wonderful.

Mike: Fred Astaire.

Green: When you talk about Fred Astaire, you talk about heaven! What more can I say?

Mike: Bing Crosby.

Green: Bing was a joy to work with. A tremendous pro!

Mike: Judy Garland.

Green: I worked a great, great deal with Judy and never had one minute's trouble with her. We were very good friends. During her worst periods of falling apart she was never late even to a piano rehearsal in my office. I was witness to trouble with her, but never experienced any personally.

Mike: I think that powerful word "charisma" is used too often for too many people. I've only known a couple of people who could completely fulfill the definition of the word: Judy Garland and Tennessee Williams. When I met Judy for the first time in 1964 at the Playboy Club in London, I was overwhelmed by her personal electricity combined with a compassion for others. Later I expressed my feeling about her to my director friend Nick Ray. Nick grinned and said, "Everybody has that reaction when they meet Judy. To know her is to love her."

Another member of that tremendous musical stock company at MGM was Kathryn Grayson.

Green: Katie was a wonderful dame with a barrelhouse sense of humor. Not too good a musician. Lovely voice. Nice to look at. Big star in her day.

Mike: Jane Powell.

Green: Another total pro. Never the giant star that some of the others were, but it was always a pleasure to work with her because she came prepared, knew her words, and was a good musician. One of these "picture-style legitimate voices with a pretty face" that worked.

Mike: Howard Keel.

Green: A very special guy. Practically seven feet tall! A virile, manly, Western voice. Strange fellow. He used to have his voice teacher in at five in the morning when he had an eleven o'clock recording! A frightened guy, but in his way a very good performer.

Mike: Frank Sinatra.

Green: I ran the gambit with Sinatra from where pictures were concerned he wouldn't work without me to where I got dumped! The last picture I did with him was *High Society* with Bing Crosby and Grace Kelly. A fabulous picture. You always have the great pros with whom, if you are a pro yourself and enjoy their respect, you have no trouble. Then there are the frightened actors with a certain personality, charm, and voice who are scared to death. These are the ones you can have trouble with. Sinatra is a one-hundred-percent pro, but he is so mercurial even a great pro can have trouble with him; but it's worth it. It was a thrill to work with him even in the last part of our career together when we were not getting along too well.

Mike: Jack Benny.

Green: I go back thirty-five years with Jack. As I said, he brought me to Hollywood for the first time as his bandleader and a radio actor. I did all the dialects on his Jell-O show that weren't done by Rochester, Sammy Hearn, and Benny Rubin. Jack and I have been inseparable. I've done many concerts with him playing his violin.

Mike: What directors are more talented at making musicals?

Green: Directors with an empathy for musical problems are the most successful. Men like Vincente Minnelli, Charles Walters, and George Sidney who came to Hollywood from a musical background. Vincente had begun as a stage designer in New York, then became a director of musical theater. Chuck Walters was a singer and dancer on Broadway and a choreographer. I never made a musical with Charles Vidor, but I did a film called *Rhapsody* with him which starred Elizabeth Taylor, John Ericson, and Vittorio Gassman. It was about the lives of a great pianist and a great violinist and the young woman who functioned in both their lives. The picture was loaded with music, and Charles Vidor was one of the most musically sensitive men I've ever known. May he rest in beautiful peace. At one time he had wanted seriously to be an opera singer.

Mike: How about Robert Wise?

Green: Bob Wise is one of those basically dramatic picture makers that, when he tackled two major musicals which were tremendous hits on the stage, *West Side Story* and *The Sound of Music*, came up as a great maker of musical pictures. He had Saul Chaplin on both pictures. Bob Wise did a third musical, *Star*, that did not fare so well.

Mike: On *Oliver!* you worked with one of the world's greatest directors, Sir Carol Reed.

Green: I have nothing but respect and affection for Sir Carol, but, during the production of *Oliver!*, we ran into situations which were very tough on me as a musician, especially when you have a man of the gigantic achievements of Sir Carol combined with a sort of dogged stubbornness that is characteristic of him. He was indeed the director! But he had never had any contact with a musical and is physically somewhat hard of hearing! This presented certain difficulties for me and my colleague, Onna White, the choreographer. In fact, there were a few times at which Sir Carol and I were at each other's throats. However, when Sir Carol got up to receive his Academy Award, he was gracious enough to point out that *Oliver!* was his first musical and to say how much he owed to Onna, Lionel Bart, and me.

Mike: The film speaks for itself. I think it's among the best films ever made. It showed a vast amount of talent on everyone's part!

Green: One thing you cannot alter anywhere in the theater, especially in motion pictures: It is the director's picture, even when you have the giant producers like Selznick, Zanuck, and Goldwyn, because it is the director who is there on the set with those actors and that crew. If it gets to the point where there is that much contretemps between the producer and the director, the producer's one prerogative is to fire the director. Fortunate is the director who acts also as the producer!

Mike: The number one collaborator with the music director on the big dance musicals is the choreographer, isn't it?

Green: Yes. And vice versa. If you've got anything but the best kind of dovetailing, understanding, co-working, mutual enthusiasm going between these two people, you've got yourself a sick picture. I've worked with them all. Jerome Robbins is one of the greatest. When I speak of Onna White, I always feel peculiar because I couldn't for one moment deny my emotional prejudices in her favor. I am so devoted to her and love her as a great gal apart from her choreography talents. I've also worked a lot with Gene Kelly and Michael Kidd. The choreographer is really the one who decides how the movie is going to move. The wedding of the music to the dancing and the movements is a very special art. A choreographer can be great for the stage, but not so great for the camera. Also, it is possible to be a music director and not have a sense of choreography.

Mike: What do you think about movie scoring today as represented by films like *Midnight Cowboy, Easy Rider,* and *The Boys in the Band*?

Green: Many of your modern scores are composites of various elements of sound put together: Phonograph records, guitar strummings, echo chambers, electronic sounds, and singing. You even see a picture scored by the Jefferson Airplane! A performing group suddenly composing the score for a motion picture! Some of this stuff is so awful I don't understand it at all. Yet some of it is great. I think the total score of *Midnight Cowboy* is one of the best I ever heard. Frankly, I don't think I would have known where to begin with that kind of score, but John Barry surely knew what he was doing! On the other hand, I hear the score of *Easy Rider,* and I don't know what that is. It just annoyed me from the beginning of the picture to the end. What's the future of this? As for *Boys in the Band,* that entire picture is scored from the legally acquired rights to certain phonograph records, and it works! I was very impressed with that. But we are in a state of flux at this point. You have young, twenty-seven-year-old Mike Curb as head of all music for the new MGM setup. It's an enormous job. It includes the studio, the publishing houses, and the record company. Everything! He may be a brilliant boy. I don't know. But his initial attitude was that you score a picture with songs. Guys in New York write a good song, so it goes in the film, and maybe a hit record comes from it. That has nothing to do with the valid approach of engaging a composer to sit down and write the score so as to fit the specific picture.

Mike: Do you feel creating the music effects for, say, *Easy Rider* takes little talent?

Green: I do. Many years ago I said I thought one of the main reasons for the success in professional media of these manifest amateurs, people who can play two chords on a guitar and have voices like foghorns, is the new public's unwillingness to recognize something better than themselves. The comfort of not having to look at a Fred Astaire and recognize the fact God gave him something He didn't give them. They don't like thinking, "He does something I can't do, so I have to sit here and applaud him." Today on major television these people see and hear other people playing guitars and singing about as badly as they do. So they say to themselves, "Gee whiz! I love him. He's no better than I am." This is the golden day of the amateur! However, among all these negative aspects there are those islands of very significant and important talent. There are some very talented people in the field of rock and roll, but the emergence of excellence in the arts is a fraction of the emergence of mediocrity. I think this is a result of a total abdication of editorial responsibility and a catering to the lowest common denominator of the public.

March 17, 1970

Script Supervisor

CATALINA LAWRENCE

Lawrence: When I finished high school in 1933 during the Depression, there just weren't any jobs to be had. So I went to secretarial school and learned to be a stenographer in English and Spanish. My parents were from the Costa Brava of Spain. My two brothers were fairly well known soccer players around New York. They had a fan who was also from the Costa Brava. He was head of the Spanish-speaking film market at Paramount Pictures in their building on Broadway. Through him I got a job taking dictation and typing scripts for a writer who was working on Carlos Gardel pictures. Carlos Gardel was the biggest star in Argentina. He was what Bing Crosby or Frank Sinatra has been to North Americans. I did about four of his pictures. Then he went on a personal appearance tour to South America. The plane crashed in Colombia, and he was killed. I was supposed to have gone, but my brothers said I was too young. The fellow who took my place was burned and scarred up terribly.

Mike: You were still a secretary at this time?

Lawrence: Yes. We continued making Spanish-language films. I would type the scripts the same day the writer gave me the dictation. In those days we used to type a sequence and shoot that. You didn't get a whole script at once. I would type all night, if necessary, so next day I could go sit on the set and watch. I was fascinated by that. The script girl on these pictures was previously employed by Al Christie, who did comedies for Paramount. When he needed her back, I was promoted to script girl. I was just fifteen, and I must have goofed up a lot! But I had been such a movie fan all my life! I had stacks of scrapbooks of Joan Crawford. Buddy Rogers was my idol. Shortly

after I went to work at Paramount, he made a picture there, and I was
in seventh heaven!

Mike: You were working full time at age fifteen?

Lawrence: This was before it was against the law for a minor to work
that many hours. I used to work day and night. I would sleep at the
studio and think it was great! We'd sometimes work until three in the
morning and start out again at eight. The studio was way out in
Astoria, and I lived near Fort Hamilton in Brooklyn, Bay Ridge. It
took me an hour and fifteen minutes to get to work. So I would sleep
in the dressing rooms of stars like Sylvia Sidney, and I thought that
was great! Sometimes they would be sleeping at the studio, too!

Mike: What sort of salary did you make?

Lawrence: My job wasn't a steady job, and I only got paid eighteen
dollars a week. When I wasn't working at the studio, I would get a job
at a travel agency or anywhere. But I would always go back to the
studio. I worked on all types of films.

Mike: When did you move to Hollywood?

Lawrence: In 1940. There wasn't much work left in New York. I had
been doing those Robert Benchley shorts. You know, those humorous
lectures he did: *How to Make Out Your Income Tax, How to Go to a
Football Game,* etc. He talked me into going to Hollywood. So I came
out with a whole bunch of letters, but they didn't do me a darn bit of
good. Back in New York there had been no union, but in Hollywood
you had to belong to the guild. I couldn't get in the guild unless I had
a job. And I couldn't get a job unless I was in the guild! Finally
Robert Benchley, who was by now living at the Garden of Allah and
working on a picture at Columbia, introduced me to the script girl on
the picture. She was on the board of directors for the guild and helped
me become a member.

Mike: Then you found work as a script girl?

Lawrence: No. I had to take a job at the Hal Roach Studio as a
secretary for Le Roy Prinz. He was directing musical shorts there.
Working at the Hal Roach Studio was great. Everybody got along
fine. It had a family feeling about it. Actually, Mr. Roach was too
good to everybody. A few people took advantage of him. He was
different from the other producers. He really thought about the crew
and their well-being and good working conditions. He was the first
studio head to want to stop working on Saturdays. In the old days
everyone was worked to death by long hours. The guys used to carry

whiskey on them to keep going. There was a lot of drinking at work then. It isn't that way now.

Mike: When the Hal Roach Studio was taken over by the Army Air Corps during World War II to make training films, what happened to you?

Lawrence: I was out of a job! The very day I got laid off I was walking down Hollywood Boulevard and ran into a director I had worked for in New York on some Yiddish pictures. He needed a script girl on some "soundies" he was making. "Soundies" were three-minute films, with a brief story, featuring every band and singer of the day such as Stan Kenton, Louis Armstrong, Ben Bernie, Duke Ellington, and the Dorsey Brothers. Sam Coslow was producing these for James Roosevelt. They were a sort of pretelevision thing because the film would play on a small screen when you put coins into a jukebox. These special-type jukeboxes were placed in hotel lobbies, railway stations, and some cafés and bars. I worked on them for a couple of years; then I went over to RKO Radio Pictures to do some of the *Scattergood Baines* features. Guy Kibbee played Scattergood.

Mike: From then on you got steady work on features?

Lawrence: Yes. I did some independent features; then finally I became the regular script girl on the *Hopalong Cassidy* Western features. The producer, Pop Sherman, was a marvelous man. We worked as part of the Paramount Pictures operations at the studio across from their main lot, the California Studios. William Boyd, who played Hoppie, had been under contract to Paramount for years. He was a handsome leading man in some early Cecil B. De Mille pictures. Everyone thinks of him as having always been Hopalong Cassidy. He fit the role well, and with his particularly unique cowboy attire created an outstanding image. We'd make two Hoppies on location; then Pop Sherman would produce, with the same production unit, a bigger budget Western. He usually starred Richard Dix in these. We did one called *Buckskin Frontier* and another called *The Kansan.* They often used the same stock company of actors like Jane Wyatt, Albert Dekker, and Victor Jory.

Mike: Meanwhile, back at the ranch, we find our hero, Hopalong Cassidy, and the dirty ole cattle rustlers shooting it out on horseback!

Lawrence: That's about the way the plot formulas went! And they made Hoppie one of the biggest Saturday matinee idols. I loved working for that Hopalong Cassidy company with a passion. It was the greatest company ever! Then Pop Sherman sent me over to Republic Pictures. I cried when I felt he didn't want me anymore, but what he was doing was getting me situated in another position because he knew the Hoppies were going to fold soon.

Mike: Republic was always the mecca for cowboy actors, wasn't it?

Lawrence: Oh, yes! I went to work for a director named Joseph Kane, who had a reputation of not getting along too well with script clerks. Somebody thought I could get along with him, so Republic assigned me to his unit. We did all the Roy Rogers Westerns. We were on location a lot of the time, and at some beautiful places. I loved it. They were the typical cowboy pictures with lots of chases on horseback and some country-western singing thrown in.

Mike: Most of the Republic cowboy pictures had some extremely good stunt work in them.

Lawrence: We had terrific stunt men! They were endlessly getting shot off galloping horses, staging fistfights, doing various stunts with wagons, and many other difficult and dangerous pieces of action. I remember one day one of the best young stunt men we had, Yakima Canutt, was staging a trick with a wagon: The wagon comes unhitched from the horses and is wildly uncontrollable until it turns over right in front of the camera. At the climax of the stunt when Yak had to jump from the speeding wagon, everything happened so fast and furious that he ended up with a body roll near the chair where I was sitting. He had broken both ankles!

Mike: Did you work on any Gene Autry pictures?

Lawrence: No. He was the top cowboy star at Republic, but he had differences with the head of the studio, Herbert Yates. Yates brought in Roy Rogers as a threat. When Gene Autry went into the service for World War II, Roy Rogers caught on with the public and became the top cowboy star. Later Roy had trouble with Yates, too. Yates wanted to release his pictures to television, and Roy didn't want them released yet. So Roy left Republic. By that time I had already stopped working on his pictures and was working on John Wayne's.

Mike: Actually, John Wayne was the biggest star at Republic, wasn't he?

Lawrence: Yes. He only made about two pictures a year, and he didn't limit himself to Westerns. Duke Wayne became one of the best friends I've ever had in this town. We worked closely together on many films, and I enjoyed every minute of it. He was friendly with everybody on the set and well liked. He was a great one for going out with the boys. He was never a ladies' man. They loved him, but in all the years I've known him he was strictly a one-woman man. I never saw him do anything I would consider ungentlemanly. And I would know, because sometimes on location for his pictures I would be the only girl with a hundred twenty-five guys! Like up at Lone Pine or Bishop during the war. I was with Duke all the time. He had several cronies. Great guys like Ward Bond, Grant Withers, and Paul Fix.

Mike: On about all of Wayne's films he gained a feeling of security by surrounding himself with loyal friends, to whom he gave loyalty in return, didn't he?

Lawrence: Yes. There are many filmmakers who employ the same people over and over. It's only common sense to use a so-called stock company of proven people.

Mike: In 1959 on one of Wayne's pictures, *Horse Soldiers,* directed by John Ford, I was a member of the stock company and enjoyed it. We went on location near my home in Louisiana.

Lawrence: On the locations I went on up in Lone Pine, I got sick and tired of being the only girl with over a hundred guys and still never having a pass made! At night the guys would always play cards around the hotel. I would stack the cards, stack the chips, and go out and get the drinks for the fellows. They treated me just like I was a kid sister running around for them. So one day I asked a wrangler named Buddy Sherwood, "How come nobody ever makes a pass at me?" He said, "Well, they're afraid you'd hit them, and if you didn't, we would."

Mike: Didn't guys you met outside the company ask for dates?

Lawrence: Yes. Right outside Lone Pine was the unfortunate spot where the government confined Japanese-Americans during the war. There were a lot of military guards there, and I was their pinup girl. I was a friend to all these kids away from home. They used to send me Christmas cards. I remember another time at Bishop, which had an air base nearby, I accepted a date with an Army Air Corps major. Some sergeant had asked me for a date the same night, but I had turned him down. My date and I and Duke and the whole film company were in a restaurant having dinner when the sergeant came in and indicated I hadn't gone out with him because I preferred being with an officer. That had had nothing to do with it. I guess the fellows thought I was being insulted, and all of a sudden fists started flying. Tables were turned over, and everybody inside and outside was fighting! It was scary, so I took off!

Mike: Someone should have been photographing it to use in the picture! Anyway, you continued to work on John Wayne pictures, didn't you?

Lawrence: Many more. When Duke became his own producer at Republic in 1946, his first film was *The Angel and the Badman*. We made it in Arizona. Gail Russell costarred. Harry Carey, Sr., had a wonderful part in it. He was one of the movies' first cowboy actors. He told me he started making cowboy pictures on Staten Island in New York way back in the early twenties.

Mike: Were you the script girl on the sea adventure film which again teamed Wayne with Gail Russell, *The Wake of the Red Witch*?

Lawrence: No. Two of the best John Wayne films I worked on at Republic were *Dakota,* which costarred Vera Hruba Ralston, and *The Flame of Barbary Coast* with Ann Dvorak.

Mike: Were they done on location?

Lawrence: *Dakota* was shot more on location than the other was. The last big location I went on with Duke was in 1952 after he had formed his present production company, Batjac. We went to Hawaii to film *Big Jim McLain.* The women in it were Nancy Olson and Veda Ann Borg. It was a great location, as you can imagine!

Mike: Why was it your last?

Lawrence: My son was born, and I didn't want to leave my home anymore. Now that he is grown I sometimes will go on location. Not long ago I went to Argentina for three and a half months to work on an American film called *The Sandpit Generals.*

Mike: Your fluency in speaking Spanish must have been useful in your many duties there. Let's talk about the duties of a script girl.

Lawrence: You know, Mike, I use the term "script girl" and "script clerk," but nowadays they prefer to be called script supervisors.

Mike: I guess that is more fitting, since it is a profession for men also! Where does a script supervisor's job start?

Lawrence: As soon as I get a script, I read it through to see if I can catch any holes in the story. Usually, I catch a lot of them because from the time the writer wrote the first version of the script it has had so many drafts made of it that a story point can get lost. The writer usually isn't around, so I go to the producer, director, or story editor and report what loopholes I've found. During this phase I also time the script. I take it page by page and act it out using a stopwatch. Then I start my breakdown of the script by making a list of all the important props, when and where they are used, and by what actor. For instance, an exterior shot may be made of an actor going into a house carrying a briefcase. A week later we film an interior shot that picks him up as he comes inside the house. I have to be sure he is carrying that same briefcase and in the correct hand, and that his clothes are the same and worn the same, and that his makeup is the same. In other words, I have to see to it that everything matches what has already been filmed of that sequence. I do this by writing notes on my script when I do the first breakdown before filming. I make more notes as the scene is actually being shot in order to record exactly what is going on. These notes are part of what we call continuity notes.

Then I break the script down for wardrobe changes. The wardrobe department also makes its own wardrobe plot. But I take each sequence from beginning to end and determine when and if a character should be in another wardrobe. For instance, a character can go from his home, to his office, to a cocktail bar. If it is the same day he would be wearing the same clothes. However, in the exact same succession of scenes you may want to establish that it does not all happen in the same day, so you have the character change clothes to denote the time change. Wardrobe worn by the actors is very important to the story in denoting time continuity. Some script supervisors leave all this to the wardrobe people, but I always check every actor out. If my name is going to be on a picture, I want it to be good. I get held responsible if something doesn't match.

Mike: And if something has been omitted in a scene!

Lawrence: Yes. We are responsible in seeing that the picture can be put together. That it can be edited. That everything matches. That there are no mistakes in the dialogue and that the script is followed.

Mike: You are the director's right-hand man.

Lawrence: That's right. Our main job is to keep him straight and not let him forget anything. We keep a record of every take of each camera angle in order to know if all the various shots the director wants are completed and can be put together into a smooth reproduction on film of the printed script.

Mike: You have to know a lot about cutting and editing.

Lawrence: Yes. In fact you could say we are the link between the director on his set and the film editor in his lab.

Mike: Your prime concern is that the director has shot everything that he needs and that it all matches, right?

Lawrence: That word "match" is our magic word. We actually check everything the camera is photographing to be sure it matches in every take. Big details such as whether an actor's tie is tied or untied in a scene or if a coat is on or off. And small details like if a button on a shirt pocket is buttoned or unbuttoned. Actions and gestures are most important to watch. If an actor puts his hand to his face on a certain line in a certain take, then he must always use that same gesture on the same line in all the other takes. The same goes for the use of props and any movement like the lighting and puffing of cigarettes. An actor can change a line, and I never say anything if it makes sense, because sometimes you can't read a line the way it has been written. But the words have to be close enough to match just like anything else. You make a note of the variation in the line reading. You have to be prepared to give a quick and correct answer if the director asks you things like, "On what line did he put out the cigarette?"; "Did she have her coat on when she left the room?"; "Did he open the door with his left or right hand?" Of course, well-trained actors can usually keep account of these things themselves and remember to match what they did in a previous take, but a good script supervisor keeps notes of all these details and doesn't rely on her memory or anyone else's.

Mike: Aren't Polaroid cameras used to check that wardrobe and makeup match in given scenes?

Lawrence: Features use them a lot, but in television they don't, because it's too expensive.

Mike: Do you have anything to do with making the daily call sheet?

Lawrence: That's the job of the second assistant director and is supervised by the first assistant director. They only come to me when an actor is finished on a picture and ask if I know of any reason not to let the actor go. Sometimes I may say we need one more close-up, or a wild line on the sound track, or something simple like that.

Mike: Do you help in making the shooting schedule of a film?

Lawrence: No, but when the schedule comes out, I check it against the script to see that every scene is accounted for.

Mike: How long before a film goes into production do you have a script?

Lawrence: On features I get scripts two or three weeks in advance. But in television, if it's a three-day shooting schedule, you get a half day to break it down! One duty I should mention is that we keep a record of the number of takes a director makes of a scene. We time each take and write down how much film footage is used each take. We check off which take or takes the director wants to have printed. Before a director says to have a certain take printed, he will check with me, the cameraman, and other key people to be sure all went well in each department and that it was a good take.

Mike: Do you generally find the directors you work with to be compatible?

Lawrence: I personally have never had a problem with any director. They are anxious for any suggestion that can be helpful. One of the kindest and nicest men I ever worked for was Frank Borzage. He was most patient and tolerant on a Batjac picture he directed called *China Doll*. I had great respect for him. Another director whom I especially liked and respected was Mark Robson. I was his script supervisor in 1951 on a Sam Goldwyn picture called *I Want You,* starring Dana Andrews, Dorothy McGuire, and Farley Granger. It was enjoyable working on that picture because Dorothy McGuire is my favorite actress. She's one of the nicest ladies I ever met.

Mike: What has your recent work been?

Lawrence: I have regular work doing a television show for Family Films. It is televised every Sunday and is called *This Is the Life*. It is produced by the Lutheran Layman's League. The stories are concerned with people in difficulties who solve them through Christian counseling.

Mike: Doesn't that regular work interfere with your taking a feature film assignment?

Lawrence: Not really. Television work is hardly ever a year-round job. And I could take a leave of absence if an unusually attractive feature film offer came along. Like one that would take me to location in Spain! A lot of American films are made there. I am of Spanish heritage, and I would love to see Spain!

April 7, 1970

Casting

RUTH BURCH

Burch: My enthusiasm and interest in the entertainment industry began at a very young age in Spokane, Washington. I would bribe my grandmother to take me to the double feature shows on Saturday afternoons. I quickly got to know the faces of the motion-picture performers both silent and early talkie. Being an ardent fan was to help me in my future career as a casting director.

Mike: How did that career begin?

Burch: My late husband was a singer during the last days of vaudeville. We traveled around the country that way and wound up settling down in Hollywood. My first employment here was in 1932 as a secretary at the Hal Roach Studios. In a short while I became the personal secretary and assistant to Mr. Roach. He later made me the studio casting director.

Mike: Being a casting agent means you have to keep abreast of all the activities in the field of entertainment. You must be aware of all the new talent that appears on the horizon. That's full-time involvement, isn't it?

Burch: You spend your evenings as well as your days screening talent, either in your office or by going to the theater, movies, or by watching television. You have to know who the entertainers are and evaluate their ability and talent for potential use.

Mike: What is the process usually followed in casting a picture?

Burch: The first step of course is to read the script and know the qualifications of each character. You form in your mind an idea of what each character represents. Almost spontaneously you think of actresses or actors who would be the personification of each part. From there, according to the budget and the desires of the producer and director, you make up a list of talent you think would be most suited to interview. Many things must be considered besides the budget: You must know who is available, who the director likes as a talent and doesn't like, how closely the tastes and opinions of the director and producer parallel each other. You have to interview people you feel will be compatible and congenial to both the director and producer. When you submit actors, it is extremely important to know if their price comes within the budget allotted for talent. Therefore, it is essential to know the personalities of the agents with whom you have to deal. There now are over one hundred and fifty agents in this area. As you deal with them, you learn which type of talent they handle and which of them will cooperate with you in negotiating a price or will hold fast and adamant to a set price. Sometimes an agent will quote a price much too high, so it is important to know if this agent is interested in the part for his client or whether he is simply interested in the dollar sign. Frequently, an agent will say the billing is the most important. At other times it is the prestige of the part. But it is more common for an agent just to ask, "How much?" Some agents handle very important people, although they are very small agents. Sometimes there are large and powerful agents who handle large stables of important talent, as well as lesser talent that may be just starting. I have found in my experience that when an actor remains with the same agent a number of years, you suddenly begin to identify actor and agent as one entity. It is quite a shock to your thought association when the actor changes agents! He may go with an agent who insists on raising his price tremendously, or he may go with one who is willing to lower his price in order to get a prize role.

When I began my career, there were many big and powerful agents who handled writers, directors, and stars. It was customary at that time for an agent to make a package deal using these combined talents. Consequently, whatever lesser talent that might be suitable to use would be easily included in this package: The agent took advantage of the demand for his major talent as a bargaining wedge in placing lesser talent in the same production. However, a great change has occurred in the last few years. Agencies have become absorbed by agencies. Smaller ones have melded with larger ones, larger ones have absorbed larger ones, so that now it is really a conglomerate of agencies as we knew them. The few small agents who still exist claim they are being pushed out of the picture because the large agents attract the more important personalities and therefore have more power.

Mike: Do you interview talent whether you are casting a script or not?

Burch: Yes. For a number of years it has been my policy to interview actors on a certain day between certain hours. It is not necessary for them to have agents. Anyone is welcome if he drops in during those hours set aside for that purpose. Regular appointments are also made by agents for their clients to come in and see me. Also, new talent in town from New York or Chicago or anywhere will call and come in. All these people bring their résumés and pictures. I won't say it is an easy matter to determine what their qualifications are. But usually you can tell by talking with them and examining their résumés what the nature of their talent is, what their training and experience has been. If they are interesting, I ask them, if they are not going to be doing a showcase, would they come in and do a reading or a scene with someone. Of course, I can tell a great deal from that. It isn't a foolproof talent gauge, but out of hundreds of actors I have screened that way, I have cast a few dozen. Most casting is done from talent I have been more familiar with. People whom I have used before who prove dependable. Or people I have seen as performers on television, in films, or on local stages.

Mike: Do you receive mail from people in various parts of the country who want to break into show business?

Burch: Almost every day! They send pictures and ask advice. I answer as many as I can, but sometimes these letters are from cranks or kookie people, and you can't reply to those, as a whole series of meaningless correspondence ensues. But when anyone asks for an interview by mail or telephone, I never refuse to see him. Naturally most casting is done from seasoned, well-trained professionals. Oftentimes, New York actors with a theater background are more reliable choices. Lesser-trained personalities have been able to get by in films, but live theater demands a more disciplined and stringent devotion to the art of acting.

Mike: Does having the right connections play a big part in helping some people to get cast?

Burch: I have nearly always been able to cast the person I felt was most suitable for a part and have rarely had anyone forced upon me because he was a friend, relative, or the romantic interest of a director, producer or writer. That type of casting probably exists, but I would assume in less important roles. Directors sometimes have their favorites, but they are their favorites because they are able to deliver, and in this day of hurried production schedules, when directors don't have enough time to work as carefully and as intently as they used to with an actor, they are eager to take somebody that they know can not only deliver but can add something to a dimensionless part. I don't necessarily think they have little cliques they use over and over, but they do ask for certain actors who have proven reliable. I have found that it is possible to force a director to use an actor against his will, but it is usually disastrous. When a director is not happy with an actor, he is unable to get a good performance out of him. So I am highly in favor of having the director pleased. Not that he always gets his first choice, but at least he does not have to take an actor he does not like.

Mike: The role of sex in casting, or who sleeps with whom to get a part, seems to have always been a custom in Hollywood, hasn't it?

Burch: That is not within my immediate experience, but I understand that it does exist. A young actor friend once told me a television producer had laid the cards on the table to him and bluntly said, "You scratch my back and I'll scratch yours." If he was to get any work, the actor said he would have had to play that game. I should think there are many eager and ambitious actors and actresses who readily go along with this game, but it must be frustrating for a seriously trained actor to have to function in that kind of situation in order to ply his art. In all professions throughout history there probably has been the well-off, influential person who uses his position to get what he wants sexually. While, at the other end, there is the aspiring young beauty, male or female, who uses his beauty to get what he wants. This practice most likely flourishes easier in Hollywood where flesh peddling to the silver screen is profitable, and morals are much more relaxed. It is just unfortunate that many people, who want no part of it, are caught up in this practice and forced to cope with it. It has likely caused some people to become stars who really didn't have too much ability in acting and caused other struggling professionals to give up in disgust.

Mike: I have heard some people intimate there is a financial payoff occasionally in deals to obtain parts. That is, if a casting director will give someone a job, he will receive a percentage payoff, or he will get a gift, or in some other way benefit.

Burch: I have heard of gifts being received that are returned. However, it is traditional and ethical to accept Christmas gifts from agencies and actor friends. The space under my tree is always covered with gifts. I have many friends outside show business, also.

Mike: When the studios were at their peak, wasn't most of the casting done from contract players?

Burch: Yes. Every studio had a substantial list of good talent, which included not only actors, but directors, writers, producers, and technical people. They were organized and operated similar to any large factory with a more or less permanent staff of employees. Within each studio the workers generally had a "company" feeling. When I began at the Hal Roach Studio, it was a fascinating place. It was like one big happy family because most people involved were actually family or close friends of the Roach family. The mother and father of Mr. Roach lived on the studio premises! They had an apartment which was like a small house where they lived for a number of years. When Hal Roach was called into the Army during World War II, his mother and her sister remained on the studio lot although the Army Air Corps took over the property as a training film center. It was, of course, against the military regulations for any civilians to live on the premises; so Mr. Roach, who was then stationed at Wright Field, was notified by the Army it was absolutely imperative he get his mother to move. He had tried many times before to set her up in a more attractive and comfortable dwelling. He told the Army this and said, "If you can get her off, do it!" But Mrs. Roach could not be budged, and she lived there the entire time the Army had the studio! The wash hung from the line, the garden flourished, and nobody but she could pick any of the flowers.

Mike: No wonder Hal Roach had a keen sense for comedy! Did the fact that the studio made mostly comedies and had so many funny people around make the atmosphere at work more casual and gay?

Burch: Oh, yes! But there was one tragic event during my employment at the studio. That was the mystery death of Thelma Todd in December, 1935. She was found dead in her car which was in her closed garage with the motor running. Thelma had done all her Christmas shopping for her many friends on the lot and had wrapped and marked the gifts. About three days after she died, her maid delivered these gifts to us. When we opened the packages and saw the greetings in her own handwriting, it was a tremendous shock. Her own personal thought had gone into these gifts, and it was a sad Christmas for everyone on the lot.

Mike: Is it true Hal Roach gave the great director D. W. Griffith his last movie work?

Burch: That's an interesting story. Griffith had retired in 1933, but Mr. Roach was able to hire him in 1939 as his associate producer on a film called *One Million B.C.* Mr. Roach thought it would lend prestige to the film, as well as needed financial aid to Mr. Griffith. The film was written, directed, and produced by Hal Roach, but D. W. Griffith was present on story conferences, directed a couple of screen tests, and cast some of the parts. There was no dialogue in the film since it was set in Stone Age times. There was, however, a lot of grunting during fights and anger and screaming while being chased by dinosaurs! One of Mr. Griffith's jobs was to audition and interview pretty girls to play these cavewomen roles. The auditions consisted of the girls having to run around his office terrified and screaming. Mr. Griffith was sixty-five and innocent in spite of how all this sounded to us down the hall a ways! The pretty girl who ran and screamed the best was Carole Landis. She was put under contract by Mr. Roach and starred in the picture which was shot mostly on the desert near Las Vegas. D. W. Griffith quit the picture just before it began shooting, after having worked on the production more than two months. I think he did not like the story, because he requested his name not appear on the credits.

Mike: *One Million B.C.* was made as a serious film, but I suppose it comes over more as a slapstick or camp film nowadays! Actually, the first dramatic feature Hal Roach made which, I think, stands up well today as a very good film was *Of Mice and Men.*

Burch: Full artistic control of that picture was given to the director, Lewis Milestone. I attended the first sneak preview with Mr. Roach, and I never saw him so nervous! He was accustomed to receiving laughs with a comedy and was unable to judge the silent reaction of this audience. He was terrified for fear it would be a bomb until the preview cards came in and proved the audience had sat spellbound! Nevertheless, the picture was not nearly as successful as it should have been owing to the fact that not a sufficient publicity campaign or launching was given it by the distributor. It has been shown many, many times on television and is always very popular.

Mike: Was Hal Roach releasing through MGM at the time?

Burch: Yes. Another film that was given poor promotion was the first *Topper* picture. Later on someone entered the situation and said

Metro had intentionally sabotaged it. A lawyer was engaged to sort out all the figures, amounts, and other facts, after which he felt Mr. Roach had two million dollars coming to him from Metro! They sued Metro and finally settled for a tenth of that amount. The two other *Topper* pictures were released through United Artists.

Mike: When Hal Roach went into military service, didn't you move down the street, Washington Boulevard, to the David O. Selznick Studios?

Burch: I worked for Selznick five years as his casting director. One of the most interesting films I ever cast was his production of *Duel in the Sun.* He had intended to make a low-budget film in black and white, but this simple approach evolved into a star-filled Technicolor epic! My casting job was particularly difficult since the script came to me in sections as the concept changed. There was a basic story, but along the way, things were added or changed such as teasers, epilogues, and prologues. The film had, in all, seven directors and nine cameramen! Among the directors who contributed were William Dieterle, Josef von Sternberg, William Wellman, and King Vidor. Vidor received the major credit. The first sequence was filmed long after the basic part had been finished. It involved the portrayal of the mother and father of Jennifer Jones to establish who her parents had been. Casting of the father was a problem which was only solved after Mr. Selznick had rejected many actors I submitted to him. He felt quite strongly about the depiction of this part, although it was not a lengthy role, because it carried an impact. I turned my talent search to New York actors where we arrived at a decision on Sidney Blackmer. Getting Mr. Blackmer out to Hollywood was another delay. A January blizzard held him up, so that he barely arrived in time to begin his sequence of the film.

Mike: Selznick was known for having definite ideas about all phases of a production. Fortunately, he had very good taste to complement his dictatorial power.

Burch: An example of a special Selznick touch was the big barbecue scene at the ranch of Gregory Peck and Joseph Cotten's family in which Mr. Selznick used his favorite camera shot that he used on many films: It is a long and elaborate dolly shot. In *Duel in the Sun* this shot consisted of a crowd scene where the camera moved slowly from one group to another, or one person to another, while they delivered dialogue. It involved about twenty speaking actors! Nobody got the script for this scene until two days before it was to be shot! The night before the shooting, Mr. Selznick had all the people who were working on the film in technical capacities gather on the set to be informed of the nature of the scene, watch the camera rehearsal, and generally participate in the excitement. When he himself arrived, he was horrified to find the set was not nearly large enough to do what he intended. He said it must be made larger. It must have more scope. Certain department heads replied there was nothing more they could do, that the whole sound stage was being utilized to capacity. Selznick said, "The trouble with you people is you don't think big enough. You must do this by tomorrow morning!" The next morning, after many hours of "golden time," the set was ready to his satisfaction.

Mike: *Duel in the Sun* was the only super-Western with a huge cast I can remember where nearly all the actors had to ride horses. Even poor old Lionel Barrymore had to lead a posse at the climax!

Burch: There was a close shot of Barrymore on a mechanical horse, but for all the other shots of his character on a horse we had to use a double because he was very crippled with arthritis. I searched far and wide for an actor who looked like him and finally came upon Dick Lane.

Mike: The Los Angeles sports announcer on television who does the roller derbys and wrestling matches?

Burch: Yes. He was a good horseman. Another actor who had to ride in the film, Joseph Cotten, had no taste for horses. I think he was a little frightened of them, and it was repugnant to him all the time he was involved with the creatures.

Mike: Were there unusual casting problems when you cast *The Paradine Case* for Selznick?

Burch: A few. That was a good script, but the film did not turn out to be as successful as we had hoped. Alida Valli was brought from Europe to star with Gregory Peck. Selznick had seen her in many Italian films and knew she was very beautiful of face and figure. Otherwise, the deal to star her was made "sight unseen." When she arrived in Hollywood, it was apparent she had been living on Italian pasta! She had gained about twenty-five pounds! Also, her teeth were in bad condition. No one was allowed to see her until she had reduced and been to a very fine dentist. She was a most charming lady and a good actress who spoke English fairly well. Another foreign talent in the film was the French actor Louis Jourdan. He was already under contract to Selznick. As the part was originally written he was the farthest from my notion of being right for it, but Mr. Selznick had an engaging way of changing a script to make it fit any of his contract actors he wanted to put to use. So this script was changed, and Louis Jourdan made his American debut and became a very successful performer from then on.

Mike: Did you get this screenplay given to you a few pages at a time also, as you were shooting?

Burch: I'm afraid so! I knew a large section of the picture was to be in a courtroom, but the scenes were not completely written when I had to arrange for the actors to play the various legal types one sees in such a court scene. I had to be prepared that anyone or everyone might be required to say a line or two. So, I hired all actors and no extras! Fortunately, with Selznick we had a rather general budget.

Mike: You don't think much money was wasted by not having a strict budget?

Burch: No. The company was run in a way that enabled the departments to work well with each other. Everyone was made to feel part of the overall setup, even though Mr. Selznick could be a slavedriver! We used to get memos by the thousands of words! The only time I got a short one was once when I had made a goof. He sent me a note simply saying, "Don't let this happen again."

Mike: Selznick disbanded his company in 1948, about the time the film industry began feeling the squeeze from television. You yourself went into the casting of many of the up-and-coming TV series, right?

Burch: I went back to the Hal Roach Studio, which had been left in a very good state of repair by the Army. Mr. Roach and Hal, Jr., had converted their operations completely into television. They were also renting space to other television filmmakers. I was not employed by the Roaches but established my own offices at their facilities as an independent casting director. I made individual deals for each episode I cast. Some of the shows made at the lot which I cast were *The Life of Riley*, *The Gale Storm Show*, *Racket Squad*, and *The Screen Directors' Guild Playhouse*. At the height of my TV activities I was casting some fifteen or more series at three different studios. Later I cast the *Andy Griffith Show* and the *Danny Thomas Show*. More recently I cast Andy Griffith's series called *Headmaster*. I also do features occasionally, and industrial shows.

Mike: You have had strong ties in the legitimate theater on the West Coast, too.

Burch: Yes. For a number of years I was the associate producer, then the producer at the La Jolla Playhouse in La Jolla. My happy twenty years as associate producer at the Sombrero Playhouse in Phoenix only ended when the theater shut down a few seasons ago.

Mike: So it is possible that in one week's work you have had to cast a feature film, an industrial show, a television show, and a stage play.

Burch: Many times! I'm constantly reading scripts, interviewing talent, and making casting deals for producers. It is an around-the-clock duty that I love. Thank goodness I seem to be the type person who gains more energy and momentum the harder I work.

September 11, 1969

The Pioneer Movie Producer

HAL ROACH, SR.

Roach: I was born in 1892 in Elmira, New York, and left home when I was in my teens.

My first adventure as a very young man out to make his place in the world took me to Alaska in 1910 where I worked as a laborer for about one year.

After a brief stay in San Francisco I made my way to Los Angeles in 1912. I was a very good horseman, and I got work as a cowboy and stunt actor in the budding movie industry. Every day I would fall off horses for one dollar a fall! One of the other guys doing this type of work became a good buddy of mine, Harold Lloyd. He had a natural ability for acting, but I soon found out I didn't, so I became an assistant director. In those days an assistant director was about the whole crew. The work was hard, but exciting. I learned all there was to know and decided I wanted to make my own films. Owing to fortunate circumstances I got enough money to form my own company in 1914. It was called the Rolin Film Company.

Mike: Where was this company located?

Roach: We took over the old Bradbury home in Edendale which is now part of downtown Los Angeles. My first short films were released by Pathé. Much later on, I released through Metro-Goldwyn-Mayer and finally through United Artists.

Mike: Did you only make comedies in the beginning?

Roach: We made everything. Dramas, comedies, and serials. Mostly one-reelers. In the early 1920's, we made a very popular adventure series of pictures called *Rex, King of Wild Horses*. Every time we made one it would be one of the ten best pictures in release. This wild horse idea was all drama. I mean, there was no comedy in that. Harold Lloyd was my first big comedy attraction. Soon afterward I conceived the *Our Gang* series, then still later I created and developed the team of Laurel and Hardy.

Mike: The Harold Lloyd comedies were all directed by you?

Roach: Yes, and I made up the story ideas for all the pictures we made. We would rehearse and enlarge upon these ideas in the mornings. By the afternoons we would have invented some very funny things and would put them on film. These were one-reel off-the-cuff comedies. One successful series costarring Harold with Bebe Daniels was *Lonesome Luke*.

Mike: There was no written script necessary?

Roach: We made pictures for several years before we had scripts. By the time we built and moved to the Hal Roach Studios on Washington Boulevard in Culver City in 1919 I had a few writers under contract. We began using some part of a script. Ten years later, when sound came in, we were doing practically everything from a script.

Mike: Even with a written script you still had to invent some of the comic situations right there on the set, didn't you?

Roach: All the time. I'd say fifty percent of written comedy won't play. Things sound funny on paper, but when you get on the set, they may not be funny. Therefore, you have to spend a lot of time rehearsing to see what is funny and what isn't, what works and what doesn't. In rehearsal you discover new gags as the actors and director work together from a basic script.

Mike: Do you think they are making comedies today as funny as you used to make?

Roach: No. Comedy is not so good today because in making pictures for television you don't have enough time to do the rehearsing necessary. They put canned audience laughter on the sound track and hope that will stimulate the viewing audience into thinking something is really funny and laugh along with it!

Mike: The canned laughter has made television audiences develop a conditioned reflex to laugh. I also think television has developed a conditioned reflex on the viewers' opinions, thoughts, and behavior. Individual taste and logic become stymied. Even most comedy is geared by the comedians to influence and persuade people's thought, rather than merely be comedy for the sake of comedy. Comics don't really seem funny anymore.

Roach: There are just as many funny people today as there ever were, but now you can't make comedies the way Mack Sennett and I did because it would cost too much money.

Mike: Were you and Mack Sennett very good friends?

Roach: Yes, although we were supposed to be enemies because of our public relations people. Mack and I thought very much alike concerning comedy. My comedy was just as broad as his to start. Slapstick plus! But I think, let's say, my comedies passed Mack's in popularity when I ceased to be as broad as he was and did comedy a little straighter. Actually, our styles differed because our stars differed. These stars were more an influence than the stories or gags. If I had had some of the people that Mack had under contract, I would probably have done the same kind of comedy with those people that he did.

Mike: In fact, you did have Mabel Normand under contract for a while after she had been the biggest star with Mack Sennett.

Roach: Yes. Her popularity had declined because of all the publicity she got in connection with the mystery murder of William Desmond Taylor, a director who was a close friend of hers. Mack let her go. She and Richard Jones, who had been the top producer for Mack, came to me. We did a series of twelve two-reelers with Mabel, but she never regained the immense following she had enjoyed previously.

Mike: Why did Richard Jones leave Sennett when Mabel Normand left?

Roach: I don't know. Actually I was about to hire Irving Thalberg, who was leaving Universal, but when Jones became available, I took him in preference because he was a comedy man and Thalberg wasn't. Norma Shearer was also coming to work for me. She and Thalberg had not yet met. They both went to MGM, got married, and had marvelous careers. Thalberg and I were always good friends.

Mike: Did you get along with Louis B. Mayer?

Roach: Mayer and I were good friends, too. We got along well in business matters. For many years MGM distributed my pictures on a percentage basis through their parent company, Loew's Inc. There was a very close relationship between their lot and mine, which were also physically close in Culver City. Many times MGM used writers, directors, and performers whom they borrowed from me. I also borrowed talent from them. If some VIP was visiting MGM, I was usually invited there for lunch.

Mike: Was Louis B. Mayer in any way your boss since MGM released your films?

Roach: Not at all. The only person I answered to was Nicholas Schenck at Loew's in New York. The MGM studio out here had absolutely nothing to do with anything I produced. If they wanted to use any of my talent, they almost always called Schenck and asked him to ask me.

Mike: Were your *Our Gang* comedies released through MGM?

Roach: Nearly all of them. The early ones, however, were made before MGM came into existence.

Mike: For how many years did you make the *Our Gang* series?

Roach: About seventeen, from 1922 until 1938. We had about eight different groups of kids. Getting the first group put together was the toughest thing. We had to decide on exactly what would make up the gang members: what types, what ages, and how many. They were always at the age when kids grow rapidly, but it was easy to replace a child actor who outgrew his part. They sort of came along knocking at our door!

Mike: How did you put the original gang together?

Roach: We happened to have a colored boy working with Harold Lloyd at the time. He became Buckwheat. The little girl was our still cameraman's daughter. The good-looking kid was the brother of Harold Lloyd's future wife. That is, Mildred Davis' brother, Mickey Daniels, who had just done a feature at Universal. They were the nucleus of the first group. Joe Cobb, the fat kid, came later, as did Farina, Spanky, and Alfalfa. One very well-known gang member was Jackie Cooper.

Mike: Did the dog outgrow his part, too?

Roach: Oh, yes. It was a funny thing how we got the first dog. Universal was making a series called *Buster Brown*, based on the comic-strip character. In this cartoon the dog had a circle around one eye. We wanted a dog for the first *Our Gang* picture, and the best-trained animal was the same one Universal used. The circle had been put on with some chemical, and no one knew how to get it off. I said, "To hell with it. Leave it on." So we did. Over the years there were probably five dogs used in making the gang comedies. We had to put a ring around the eye of each new dog.

Mike: Your most successful comedy pictures were with Stan Laurel and Oliver Hardy. How did that team begin?

Roach: They came to my studio separately, and it was my idea to make a team of them. I had wanted a pair of funny guys and had tried teaming other contract players, but none was the right combination until I put Laurel and Hardy together. We made their first two-reel film, *45 Minutes from Hollywood*, in 1925. They were most competent comedians, very nice people to know, and got along well with each other, and modestly well with me! They saw little of each other outside the studio. In their private lives they did not mingle much socially. Stan Laurel was the more creative of the two. He was one of the best gagmen in the business. He was not very good on story construction but was great on inventing individual pieces of business. The two of them were my most enduring stars.

Mike: You also thought of the idea of teaming a pair of funny women to make a series of short comedies. The original team was Thelma Todd and Zasu Pitts. Where did you find them?

Roach: Thelma, like several other actresses and actors, had gone to Paramount's theater school. When Paramount let her go, I thought enough about Thelma to put her under contract. Zasu Pitts was a well-established comedienne. I teamed them, and we made many very successful comedies; but when Pitts became too expensive, I had to replace her with Patsy Kelly. The formula remained the same: Thelma Todd, the good-looking girl, was the straight man, and the not so good-looking other gal was the comedienne. Although Thelma was very funny herself.

Mike: Did you direct many of these short comedies?

Roach: Yes. There was never a time while the Hal Roach Studio was in existence that I wasn't supervising the whole movie lot. I directed many shorts and at least one or two of our feature pictures a year when we began making features. Wrote God knows how many! These things were done in order to keep my hand in them, see how they were doing, what was going on, what were the changes, and so on. I directed the studio's first talking film just to see what it was like. One of the stars, Edgar Kennedy, came across in it with a voice like a pansy! After a lot of voice training he learned to talk better in later pictures. The first time I ever sat in a projection room watching the daily film strips, a voice after each scene would say, "That's good." This kept happening until I got irritated and I jumped up, turned around to everybody in the room and asked, "Who the hell keeps saying, 'That's good'?" I was red-faced to learn it was my own voice on the sound track at the end of each take!

Mike: At the same time sound came to Hollywood, you brought something else new to the community, horse racing!

Roach: Being an Irishman, I have always been a lover of horses. One of my favorite sports was playing polo. I used to play a lot with my good friend Will Rogers at his polo grounds off Sunset. To reinstate legalized horse racing was an ambition of several Hollywood personalities. I was able to bring it about, in partnership with others, when I founded the Santa Anita Racetrack in 1934. It cost five thousand dollars to be a member of the club, and the cream of Hollywood belonged.

Mike: Did you ever make any comedies on the subject of horses?

Roach: No. Animals are funnier when they can be drawn. That is, drawn to look funny and given a funny voice.

Mike: How did the advent of Walt Disney and the animated cartoon effect your short "live actor" comedies?

Roach: Animated cartoons took over the business! It was impossible to compete with them, because they had an unlimited ability to fantasize. You can make drawing-board characters like Mickey Mouse, Betty Boop, Popeye, and Pluto do almost anything. You can have a cartoon dog run over by a car and do it as comedy! Imagine doing that with a real dog! Animated cartoons were so good and unique and so popular that I had to go into the making of full-length comedies. In about 1936 my studio began feeling its way into features to see what we could make that would be profitable. The only thing we had suitable was Laurel and Hardy. We started making full-length features with them, but that wasn't enough to keep the studio busy. We began to search for story material. One of my contract writers came across the Thorne Smith book *Topper* and brought it to me. I liked the idea of the invisible ghosts do-good couple and the comic situations that were potential to get them involved with. We made the first *Topper* in 1937 with Cary Grant and Constance Bennett playing the ghosts and Roland Young as Topper. Roland played Topper in two following films for me. All three pictures were very popular.

Mike: What other comedies did you make?

Roach: Of several we made, the two best were *Merrily We Live* with Connie Bennett and Brian Aherne, and *There Goes My Heart* with Fredric March and Virginia Bruce.

Mike: With the success of these full-length comedies you decided to make full-length dramas and adventure films, didn't you?

Roach: Yes. Most studios had their dashing leading man who was identified with hero parts. I signed a virile young man named Victor Mature to play those type parts for me. I directed him in three action pictures: *Captain Caution, Captain Fury*, and *One Million B.C.* As far as pure drama is concerned, the best film we made was *Of Mice and Men.* My studio production head, Milton Bren, conceived the idea of making that novel into a film, and he made the deal with the author, John Steinbeck, and engaged Lewis Milestone as director.

Mike: Your production activities expanded rapidly during this period. Also, in 1937 you became involved in a situation in Italy that was both extraordinary and controversial. Will you tell about that experience?

Roach: It centered on an idea of filming some of the Italian operas in their original setting. Italian national spirit was very high. Mostly because of the unification and guidance of Benito Mussolini, who was, I think, a good dictator as far as the Italian people were concerned. They adored him so much that at night he couldn't go out in public because all the people would do was to turn and look at him and yell, "Duce! Duce!" He couldn't go to the opera. He couldn't go to a football game. All he could do for entertainment was stay at home and look at movies. He looked at all the good American movies, and he looked at all the bad Italian movies, and he went nuts. He said, "Why, with the great literature of Italy, the great paintings, the great music, are we so behind in motion pictures?" And it made him eager for Italy to do something important in the motion-picture industry because he thought it, too, was an art. He wondered why it wasn't an art for the Italians, as well as for anybody else. I don't know why I was the person they got hold of and invited to Italy to discuss the deal. Anyway, I went to Rome, but I didn't want to make a deal, so I kept making it tougher. The tougher I made it, the more determined Mussolini became. I was to make four pictures for world distribution, ten pictures for European distribution, and forty pictures for Italian distribution. The Cinecitta Studio, a ten-million-dollar studio, was turned over to me, as well as eight million dollars in credit from the largest bank in Italy. I owned fifty percent of the company and the bank owned fifty percent. Young Vittorio Mussolini, the dictator's son, was to be my partner, and he had the right to buy twenty-five percent of the bank's fifty percent. He didn't get anything free. Benito Mussolini was getting nothing out of it except his desire to make good pictures in Italy. As our trademark we decided to use the head of a ram in the way MGM used the head of a lion. And we called the company RAM. I remember the time in *Il Duce*'s large office, which had no chairs, when he asked me what RAM meant. He spoke English just like you hear an Italian speaking in the movies. I thought he was going to be annoyed at my name having to come before his, but when I told him RAM meant Roach and Mussolini, he said, "Dat'sa good!"

The history is very interesting while I was in Italy. For instance, there was a problem from the beginning since the motion-picture industry is a Jewish business, and Italy was a Fascist country. But Mussolini was not anti-Semitic. That's the first thing I asked him. I said, "Any sanctions against Jews? If so, no deal." And he assured me not and gave me all the dope. The government gave me all their records on how many Italian Jews there were and how many Jews had come into Italy since they had been coming out of other countries and what their positions were and so on. There was no Jewish problem in Italy until it was created by Hitler.

Even so, Vittorio Mussolini's visit to Hollywood was much discussed in film circles. He sailed to America with me on the same ship. Since he was from a Fascist country and there were so many refugees here, some with Communist leanings, who had fled Germany, there was a movement to ignore him. I gave a large party for him. Some Jewish people who were in the motion-picture business called other people and asked them not to come. But because they asked them not to come, they came as protest. I mean, people like David O. Selznick and Louis B. Mayer, these people all came.

My studio was taken over by the Army Air Corps. They had a

top-secret operation which consisted mainly in the use of an enormous relief map of the Japanese mainland and islands. This map covered the entire floors of my two largest sound stages and was made in amazing detail and perfect scale to show all railway routes, highways, harbors, rivers, dams, bridges, and everything. In the ceilings of the sound stages were rigged cranes, cables, and other devices so that a movie camera or a still camera could move over any section of "Japan" and photograph bombing routes for pilots and navigators to study.

Mike: You were in no way connected to the operation of your studio for military purposes during the war?

Roach: No. After the war I returned to Hollywood and started making the "streamlined comedies" again, with United Artists putting them with a longer feature to make up a double bill. However, United Artists came out with about ten bad pictures which nobody wanted. They couldn't sell them to the exhibitors; therefore, they couldn't sell my comedies. United Artists went through a very bad period, and when they flopped, Metro-Goldwyn-Mayer gave me a contract to make these streamliners. I had made the deal with Metro that I would finance the pictures myself. When we were ready to go into production, we found out we didn't have the money to finance them. A large amount of money had disappeared. I don't want to say how, but not very legally. So that's when we went into television production. My son, Hal, Jr., was producer of most of our television series. We made *My Little Margie*, *The Screen Directors' Playhouse*, *Telephone Hour*, *The Stu Erwin Show*, *Racket Squad*, and a raft of others.

Mike: You never made any more feature films?

Roach: Yes. We made a few low-budget films, but it was the television productions which were the most lucrative.

Mike: In 1959 the Hal Roach Studio got involved in a stock merger with outside interests which terminated in the studio's being closed through bankruptcy! Do you mind commenting on that personally tragic event?

Roach: I only care to say that as a result of that stock manipulation, a man named Gueterma served time in a penitentiary. However, the last I heard he was walking around free.

Mike: You and your family lost the studio and all the property connected with it?

Roach: Yes. The buildings and real estate on Washington Boulevard were auctioned off in 1962. I now maintain offices in New York City and make frequent business trips there.

Mike: It's ironic to realize the man whose films gave, and still give, the world so much laughter and happiness was dealt such an unhappy blow by some unscrupulous wheeler dealer.

September 16, 1969

The Pioneer Television Producer

ALBERT McCLEERY

Mike: I know, because of our close friendship, Al, that you have one of the most colorful backgrounds of anybody in Hollywood. You have devoted yourself to community theater, Broadway theater, motion pictures, radio, and television. And you have functioned as a writer, teacher, director, producer, and promoter. How did a boy from Lawrence, Kansas, get into such an energetic career?

McCleery: I guess I've been in the habit of being on the move since I was a youth and attended thirty-six different schools in nine different states. This included my college education at Texas Christian University and Northwestern University's School of Speech and Theater Arts. After that I attended the Pasadena Playhouse's School of Theater. In 1931 I founded the first arena theater in the Midwest, the Georgian Little Theater in Evanston, Illinois.

Mike: And that began your professional career which took you to Broadway as an assistant stage manager for Katharine Cornell and Guthrie McClintic, then a staff writer for *Stage* magazine, radio dramatist for Ethel Barrymore, novelist, and finally screenwriter at Columbia Studios until the outbreak of World War II. You served five years active duty in the U.S. Army Signal Corps, which I know would make a book within itself. But it is your experiences after the war as a leader in the developing television industry which make you an authority on the early history of that entertainment medium.

McCleery: Well, immediately after the war I was director of dramatic activities at Fordham University. My television career began in 1949 when I joined NBC's TV Programming Department as a staff director.

Mike: You rose to a senior executive producer-director rather quickly and were responsible for such regular programs as *Cameo Theatre, Hallmark Hall of Fame,* and *NBC Matinee Theatre.* These shows were during the era which saw the most rapid expansion of television into the American home and was therefore a time of enormous influence on the motion-picture business. I would like to ask you to discuss the impact of television on the Hollywood movie industry.

McCleery: Until 1950 one could speak of Hollywood and movies as being the same thing. But since 1950 television has been the temperature of this town. By all the laws of economics this should be a ghost town. Except for television Hollywood is dead and doesn't know it. If you get your charts out and look at runaway movie production, you'll realize that the money that sits in the Bank of America is all exported out of Hollywood. For every movie that is filmed in Hollywood, you've got five, six, or seven that are totally financed out of this area. They're just not doing them here, and there isn't any reason why they should be doing them here.

Mike: You're saying that moviemaking doesn't need a physical center any longer?

McCleery: Yes.

Mike: Because the ease of traveling anywhere in the world to shoot a script at the actual location of the story and the technical advances, facilities, and know-how in so many other countries make it more economic and interesting to spread out?

McCleery: Yes. The whole incestuous kind of economics that grew up around the rise of the great Hollywood studios is basically unsound today. It was created to perpetuate family dynasties, entourages, and natural camaraderie of people who are out to make a fast buck and have done it together since they were twenty years old. So economically, this town is unfeasible. Even as early as the excursion of outsiders like Joseph P. Kennedy into this area in about 1928, and later Howard Hughes, these outsiders have never really succeeded. This town had a way of just economically absorbing people, regardless of the constant discipline that the banks would try to exert as they made their multimillion-dollar loans.

Mike: You mean money was unwisely spent or large sums were unaccounted for?

McCleery: It's no secret that the skimming on motion picture production makes Las Vegas look like a sissy. I mean the Mafia could come here any day, and the most respectable studio could give them some lessons on how to make a fast buck and hide it from God, the IRS, and your own family. These are things you can say, but you can't prove. Even the Department of Justice has tried to prove it. The Internal Revenue Service has tried. But there isn't any doubt about it, that when you start to look at the budget for a picture, it becomes absurd. It becomes absurd, because having created these monsters of real estate in the middle of a growing community where they had no place being, they were able to hide this enormous skim-off. The skim-off has become "legitimate" now.

Mike: The accepted custom to expect since you can't fight it.

McCleery: In other words, you add thirty-three and a third percent to each day's operation of a motion picture which goes to *something!* You don't know where it goes! It is true now that when an independent producer comes to make a picture, he's a fool if he does it under the banner of one of the major studios. He's much better off if he just goes out and rents the space and disciplines his own production. This seems to be the current trend.

Mike: What indication was there back in the fifties that television would replace films?

McCleery: Rumor has it, and I don't see any reason not to believe it, that about 1947 the head of NBC, General David Sarnoff, made overtures to the Hollywood studios, which were still coasting on the prosperity of their war years, to come in and take an active and aggressive part in the development of television entertainment. The success of an NBC series called *Fireside Theatre*, which was on film, proved that you could make more money on the second, third, and fourth runs of a show than you could on the first. The fact that you could take these cans of film and resell them over and over again obviously convinced the hierarchy at NBC that some kind of wedding with the film industry would be a wise project.

Mike: To the mutual benefit of both industries from the start.

McCleery: Stories that were current at NBC as early as 1949 were that General Sarnoff literally got rebuffed by Hollywood studios. And

General Sarnoff is not a man who is used to being rebuffed. But, I mean, he got the polite treatment and a nice lunch and told they just weren't interested in that common stuff! Strangely enough, by that time, these movie tycoons had gotten "arty." They had begun to believe their own publications and ballyhoo that they were a true art form, and this bastard little box that people were putting in their living rooms was beneath them.

Mike: I remember the attitude in those days was that major stars would never go on television.

McCleery: Little did they know that major stars *would* do it and would *need* to do it. Anyway, there was no merger between the networks and the film studios. It is interesting to speculate what would have happened if the movie studios had really moved in and taken over television in the early days. Now NBC, CBS, and ABC are in the advantageous position of being buyers, and Warner's, Fox, MGM, Columbia, and other studios must go hat in hand to sell their products.

Mike: Isn't Universal in a stronger position?

McCleery: Universal, the extraordinary octopus of our time, is no longer in the true sense of the word a film studio. It is more a television studio. Universal today is the product of an "if you can't beat them, join them" technique, and they are owned body and soul by television-minded people. Let's face it, the old MCA agency with their very sensitive barometer of talent realized what was in the winds, and they shifted over from the world's largest talent agency to the world's most active television film studios. By going into television production themselves, you might say that MCA admitted that as agents they couldn't sell MGM, Paramount, and the others on the idea. It's as if MCA said, "Well, you stupid jerks, if I can't persuade you to do it, I'll do it myself." So they did, in sheer exasperation at the major studios' inability to recognize the handwriting on the wall. And now filmmaking as we know it is in its twilight age. There are new feelings, new temperatures, new pulses coming into existence. We won't recognize our own town in ten years. The remnants will be here. Such and such a lot might still be operating, but the basic wedding between films and television is fast going on right now, twenty years later than it should have. It is an economic wedding, shotgunned by the Bank of America, Chase Manhattan National Bank, the Eady

Plan in Great Britain, and coproduction deals between countries on both sides of the iron curtain. The green sheets of money are the covers for this wedding!

Mike: But don't you think many of the way-out films being made now would be considered unsuitable for television viewing?

McCleery: Well, I would say that the rise of the young producers and directors who are going so far to the left politically, socially, and in their exploitation of sex and deviation is a strange contradiction to my comments. You are right in wondering how they are going to put those products on television. But I'm telling you, they're going to be on television! In ten more years the family unit will be sophisticated enough to take *The Killing of Sister George* with considerable aplomb! No one would have believed it ten years ago that today a performer would turn around on the middle of an American screen and say, "Fuck you!" The point of it is that times are always changing. The children of today's school dropouts and shoulder-length-haired boys will not be shockable ten years from now. And the great concern for the preservation of the purity of minds between the hours of six in the morning and nine at night will have disappeared. People will say what artistically they choose to say any hour of the day or night.

Mike: What were some of the first important television programs to originate from Hollywood?

McCleery: The first dramatic show to originate here after the networks linked from coast to coast was to be produced by a man sent out from New York. He arrived, checked into a hotel, had a date at ten o'clock to meet an associate for breakfast at the Brown Derby across the street. He jaywalked across the street, got arrested, had an argument with the cops, they threw him in the back of the car, took him to the station, and it took until two o'clock in the afternoon to get him out of the station because he had gotten very difficult. He took the six o'clock plane back to New York and refused to do the show! That happened to be very fortunate for me because I inherited the post and moved the first dramatic show out here, *The Hallmark Hall of Fame*, in 1951. It was an hour show, and I must say the difference between doing an hour show here and an hour show on the East Coast was the difference between night and day. The crews here were younger, more cooperative, far better disciplined, and far more inventive. They had a tradition of being helpful to the directors and producers that the crews in New York just didn't have. The crews in

New York looked on producers as class enemies. Anything that the producer or director asked which was a little bit different from yesterday's request was immediately suspect.

Mike: The television crews in New York evolved from the legitimate theater, didn't they?

McCleery: Mostly. And their rules were designed to thwart the Shubert Brothers. Their attitude is "Screw the Shuberts, if possible." They have the famous expression, "Well, it's not in the book." The irony is nobody has ever seen that book! But they can always refer to it because they make it up as they go. And it's a fantastic thing. For instance, in New York a director is not allowed to touch anything. He cannot even pick up a cigarette lighter when he is showing an actor how to use it. He cannot touch that cigarette lighter! The actor, of course, may, but the director may not. On the West Coast there seems to be an unwritten rule that the director may, if necessary, do anything any crew member does, as long as a union man is standing by.

Mike: As long as the director is not eliminating someone's job.

McCleery: That's right. He could take a paintbrush and say, "No. The strokes should go this way." In New York there would be a work stoppage that would last three hours as punishment for daring to show one of their members anything physically. So to come out here and find the cooperation and spirit of these younger stage hands was an extraordinary thing. Almost from the day I came here, the word went back to New York from me and others that this was the place to operate. To begin with you had seventeen thousand actors to draw from. Casting calls were incredibly rich, although you did have a lack of the terrifically trained talent that you have in New York, people who were vocally trained, readable, and have great know-how in handling themselves under theatrical pressures. The film actors were often frightened, inexperienced, not easy to handle, and not very verbal. And honestly, many rather distinguished members of the Screen Actors' Guild did not know how to study a part.

Mike: They probably depended on coming on the set and shooting it until they got it right.

McCleery: For a director of a live TV show to say, "Look, you're supposed to know your lines and come in here and do them," was a shock to their system. That wasn't the way they had worked for many, many years. The ones who had never had any theatrical experience whatsoever were amazingly stiff at first. But regardless of these drawbacks, the wealth of talent in Hollywood was still impressive.

Mike: So the success of *Hallmark Hall of Fame* encouraged NBC to move other shows out here?

McCleery: Yes. *The Comedy Hour*, for instance, and other variety shows. CBS followed very fast on the trail. It didn't take long for intelligent actors in New York to know their days were numbered, and they began to move out here. They had had five years of great prosperity in New York in the era of the live half hour and hour shows such as *Danger, Kraft Theatre, Studio One, Robert Montgomery Presents*, and so on. At one time more actors were working in New York City than had ever worked in the whole history of the American theater. It was an incredibly lush time. From 1948 to 1955 was a golden time for actors in New York. The momentum continued out here.

Mike: Even though television has a much larger audience than movies and has replaced the movies as the number one mass medium, most people think of working in a movie as being the ultimate attainment.

McCleery: The cycle of a young person moving through development, exposure, discovery, and major opportunity in television and then moving into feature films is entirely a result of the economics of the day. It isn't logical or reasonable, but that is what exists. A Grace Kelly does forty parts on television, and then she gets her first break in films and is an "overnight success." Well, she was an overnight success for many months in New York in television. Everybody in television knew that this was a very lovely woman and a very lovely actress and was glad to get her services. You paid her the highest price that your budget allowed, or you weren't able to get her.

Mike: Television certainly opened the door to motion-picture careers for a lot of talented people.

McCleery: Television brought new blood to movies. You see, the motion-picture industry had become tradition-bound in one generation. If you weren't a son, a son-in-law, a nephew, or some other close relation of a movie mogul of the early days, chances were you would never be able to get into movies. Television was a wide-open door. Mostly because it was a new industry and the volume of production was so great. The turnover for parts was tremendous. In a three-year period as producer for the *NBC Matinee Theatre* I employed four thousand actors and bought over six hundred scripts. Many of the substantial thirty-five- to forty-year-old actors of today got their start on that program and other contemporary programs like *Playhouse 90* at CBS.

Mike: Do you think the gigantic task the television industry has in keeping the television tube fed has lowered the quality of entertainment? Does more *quantity* demanded mean less *quality* supplied?

McCleery: Again it's dependent on economics, commercialism, and people out to make a quick buck. The industry is full of people whose only creative ability is creating deals. Just because some actor, writer, director, or producer makes a huge salary doesn't mean his talent deserves it. Television is a vast business. One must realize that because of the widespread usage of television and its momentous coverage and programming it has in twenty years' time made more hours of entertainment than the world has known in the history of Western man. More than the theater, motion pictures, vaudeville, the circus, and all other media combined! We speak of ancient Rome as having "bread and circuses." The Roman populace sat in their arenas and watched the day-long circuses and combats and games, as they nibbled on the bread they brought with them. We associate these Roman circuses with the decline of the Roman Empire. There is an interesting parallel between Rome at its peak and ourselves. Just stop and think about the enormous amount of mediocre spectator entertainment that is being thrown at the massive television public today by the capitalist system in which the industry operates, while at the same time we are creating a bread-and-welfare state for ourselves. It's rather frightening if you delve into it. Are we sure television has not become the Roman circuses of our empire days?

October 2, 1969